THE SACRED BOOKS AND EARLY LITERATURE OF THE EAST

ANCIENT ARABIA
THE HANGED POEMS
THE KORAN

(VOL. 5)

Contents: The Last Semitic Conquerors; The Sudden Blossoming of their Literature; The Genius of Arabic Literature; The Hanged Poems; The Koran.

Charles F. Horne

ISBN 0-7661-0003-0

THE SACRED BOOKS AND EARLY LITERATURE OF THE EAST

VOLUME V

ANCIENT ARABIA

THE HANGED POEMS
THE KORAN

In Translations by

Captain F. E. JOHNSON, R.A., and GEORGE SALE, Esq., with Revisions and Explanatory Essay by SHEIK FAIZ-ULLAH-BHAI, Head Master of the Schools of Anjuman-i-Islam.

With a Brief Bibliography by

CHARLES C. TORREY, D.D.,
Professor of Semitic Languages at Yale University.

With an Historical Survey and Descriptions by
PROF. CHARLES F. HORNE, PH.D.

PARKE, AUSTIN, AND LIPSCOMB, INC.
NEW YORK   LONDON

" Let there be light."—GENESIS I, 3.

———

" There never was a false god, nor was there ever really a false religion, unless you call a child a false man."—MAX MÜLLER.

THE LATEST SUCCESSOR OF MOHAMMED.

The Grand Sheik or Sheriff of Mecca who in 1916 announced the Arabic Independence of Turkey.

CONTENTS OF VOLUME V

ANCIENT ARABIA

ILLUSTRATIONS IN VOLUME V

SACRED BOOKS AND EARLY LITERATURE

OF

ARABIA

INTRODUCTION

THE LAST SEMITIC CONQUERORS: THE SUDDEN BLOSSOMING OF ARABIC LITERATURE

THE Arabs are one of the most ancient races known to history. Historical records, which are perhaps earth's earliest, have been recently rediscovered among the ruins of Babylon and the other cities of the Euphrates valley; and these refer frequently to Arab invasions of the fertile valley and to Arab conquests over its fairest regions. The cultured classes of many an ancient Babylonian city were thus of the Arabian race, springing from the intermarriage of the fierce desert conquerors with the defeated valley folk. Yet in their own homeland the Arabs were among the last of Asiatic peoples to develop a written literature. We come down almost to the time of Mohammed, that is, to the sixth century after Christ, before we find among them any written books.

That the Arabs were thus slow in creating written literature was due to their peculiar mode of life. The art of words was highly honored among the most ancient Arab tribes. But to these dwellers amid the desert silence, the art was one of spoken, not of written, words, an art of polished and sarcastic oratory or of passionately chanted verse. The Arab prided himself upon three virtues: his generosity to those whom he accepted as his friends, his skill in the arts of war — that is, his handling of his horse and weapons — and, lastly, his mastery of his language. When a new poet of unusual merit appeared in any tribe, a festival of rejoicing was held; and the other tribes sent envoys to congratulate the fortunate folk, upon the honor and happiness that the gods had sent them.

That a people who so valued the arts of speech should have studied them for thousands of years without developing them into written forms is one of the striking oddities of literary history. Yet the causes of this oddity are obvious. The greater part of the vast Arabian peninsula is so barren that its people must keep ever on the move to find enough green food for the animals upon which they depend for their own existence. Hence they have no place for the storing of books, the preservation of libraries. True, there are in Arabia some fertile spots, in oases or along the southern coast, where Arab cities have grown up; but even the Arabs of these cities journey often and far into the desert. Its blank and burning sunshine is their true home; and in its vast solitudes a man's own memory is, even to-day, the best treasure-house for his books.

Hence Arabic literature in the written form, the only form in which it can be permanently preserved, does not begin until the sixth century of our own era, the century just before Mohammed. During this period there were several of the tribal poets so valued, that the idea was formed of honoring them by hanging copies of their best poems in the chief religious shrine of Arabia, the building called the Kaaba at Mecca. So the Arabic literature which we know to-day begins with these " hanged " poems, and they form the opening of the present volume.

THE SEVEN HANGED POETS

There were seven of these celebrated poems, each by a different poet. Unfortunately the seven poems are no longer preserved in the Kaaba — if, indeed, they ever did literally " hang " there — and the Arabs themselves are not entirely agreed as to either the names or the poems of these, their earliest writers. But the most noted among them are fully agreed on and highly treasured. Among them all, the poet probably earliest in date is Imru-ul-Quais, often spelled in our letters, which differ widely from Arabic forms, Amrulkais.

He was a prince, who by his passionate devotion to affairs of
love so angered his father, the sheik, or king, of the tribe,
that Imru-ul-Quais was banished to the solitary life of a shepherd. He thus escaped the destruction which came upon all
his people in a bitter tribal war; and he was left a tribeless
wanderer. He came finally, about the year 530, to the court
of the great Greek-Roman emperor Justinian, at Constantinople; and there the poet-wanderer was much honored.
Tradition says he was put to death by torture for winning the
love of a princess of Justinian's family. Mohammed declared Imru-ul-Quais to be the greatest of the Arab poets; and
the poet-prince is said to have been the first to reduce to a
regular-measured rhythm the wild individual chanting of the
earlier desert-singers.

A poet among the seven who is even more noteworthy is
Antar, or Antarah; for he was afterward made the hero of
the most celebrated of Arab romances. Antar was the son of
a negro slave-woman and was brought up as a slave in the
household of his Arab father. Such, however, was his
strength and courage that he rose to be the chief hero of his
tribe. He was also its chief poet, singing sometimes of its
warfare, sometimes of his love for its princess, Ibla or Ablah.
Ablah at first ridiculed the advances of the young slave but
afterward clung to him through all his career of glory and misfortune. The tales which later generations wove around
Antar are like those which the English built upon King
Arthur's life, or the Spaniards on the Cid. He has become
the national hero of his race.

If we pause for yet another of the "hanged" poets, it must
be for Zuhair, who is credited with beginning the philosophical and religious writings of his nation. Zuhair was among
the latest of the "hanged" poets and so nearly contemporary
with Mohammed that the two are said to have met. Zuhair
was then an aged and revered sage, a hundred years old; and
Mohammed, just beginning his prophetic mission, prayed God
to protect him from the witty tongue of the poet. That is, in
Arab phrase, he sought help against Zuhair's *djinn* or spirit;
for the early Arabs believed their poets to be genuinely

inspired; and as most of the poems were epigrams, brief, biting, and sarcastic, the inspiration was attributed to the evil spirits, the *djinns* or *genii* who were supposed to possess the earth equally with man.

Zuhair in his verses was less satiric than most of his brother poets. He strove to express deep thoughts in simple words, to be clear and by his clear phrases to teach his people high and noble ideas. He was a man of rank and wealth, the foremost of a family noted for their poetic skill and religious earnestness. In brief, Zuhair is the gentleman philosopher among Arab poets.

THE EARLY RELIGION OF THE ARABS

Since Arabic written literature begins only with the "hanged poems" and since none of these is of strictly religious type, we can only resort to tradition and to later writers for our knowledge of the religious ideas of the Arabians before the days of Mohammed. They themselves refer to those early times as constituting their "state of ignorance." Yet some among them had accepted the Jewish faith, some were Christians, and some believers in other foreign religions. From their own fathers, the Arabs inherited the very definite idea of a single, universal God, whom they called "Allah Taala," meaning The Most High God. A formula or prayer of those days which has come down to us says: "I dedicate myself, O Allah Taala, to thy service. Thou hast no companion, except such companions as thou art absolutely master of, and of all that is theirs."

Around this supreme god they assumed that there were many lesser deities, whom they referred to in a group as the Ilahat, or goddesses. To these Ilahat they showed more outward care and consideration than to the chief god. For, as they often said, lesser creatures needed the help of Allah Taala, but He needed nothing. Best known, or at least most worshiped, among the Ilahat were three goddesses, Allat, al Uzza, and Manah. These seem to have been specific stone idols, though Manah was probably an uncarved, natural boulder, and al Uzza may have been a tree. The shrines of these gods were many, chief among them being the Kaaba at Mecca, a celebrated and ancient stone building which contained 360 idols. These furnished subjects for worship on each day of the year, though some of them were more honored than the rest. Chief of the Kaaba deities were a black stone, probably a meteor, and an agate statue of a rain-god, Hobal, brought from some foreign land and trusted for divination.

Divination, however, was chiefly practised by means of the stars. So far did this go that many Arabs looked upon the stars as being gods themselves. Special stars had special worshipers. Indeed, Abu Cabsha, a worshiper of the star Sirius, set himself up as a prophet and tried to convert all the Arabs to a belief in his star. This fanatical preacher may have been an ancestor of Mohammed, or at least the Arabs found a similarity between the two; for when the latter began his fiery preaching he was promptly nicknamed by his calmly satiric countrymen, " the son of Abu Cabsha."

THE KORAN

It was to this world of thinkers, dreamers, fighters, a nation of orators rather than writers, that Mohammed came, to contribute to its literature his remarkable Koran. The first Sura or chapter of this was given to the world in the year 598 A.D., when the great religious reformer was forty years of age.

The religious aspect of the Koran may best be kept for discussion in the immediate introduction to the Koran in the present volume; but as a piece of Arabic literature the work is declared by all Arabs to be the chief triumph and culmination of their language. Repeatedly during Mohammed's lifetime, when skeptics doubted his divine power, both he and his followers responded by pointing to the Koran and challenging the language-loving Arabs to produce anything equaling or even approaching it in literary value.

To call the Koran a book is in a way misleading. It was composed as was the earlier Arab literature; each chant, or Sura, was announced separately, inspired by a particular occasion and recited to the prophet's followers. Often a Sura consisted of only a single stanza, brought forth by the necessity of the moment. Some of these Suras were not written down at all, but were preserved, according to Arab custom, in the memories of their hearers. Not until after the prophet's death were his many Suras gathered from every source and combined into the written volume which we call the Koran.

Mohammed always declared that these sayings were not his own but were revealed to him by an outside power. In taking this stand, however, he was making no new claim; he was but following the custom of his people with all their poets. Only instead of attributing his inspiration, as he himself had attributed the verses of Zuhair, to an evil genius, Mohammed claimed for his words a holier source. He declared they came from the Archangel Gabriel, who brought each Sura straight from God himself, as the divine source of all creation.

Readers who reject the idea of Mohammed's divine perfection will naturally reject also the Arab idea of the divine perfection of the Koran. Viewing it from a merely human standpoint they will find it an interesting collection of fiery human speeches, bold and impassioned appeals to a passionate people. Its music and literary grace are of course lost to us in translation; but its precepts are often high in thought and striking in expression, and its Arabic versions of old Hebraic tales of Noah and Abraham and Moses give it a permanent interest for both Jews and Christians. The Holy Book of the Arabs indicates that their nation stood at least as high as other Asiatic races of their day in both intellectual and moral development. The Arabs of Mohammed's era could think logically, live bravely, and meditate with pure nobility.

In the generations that followed immediately after Mohammed's death the Arabs were too busy fighting to give much time to literature. Under the stimulus of Mohammed's fiery teaching, their natural fierceness of temper was strengthened by an utterly reckless confidence in themselves and their cause. Sure of their armies' victory, and sure that each individual who fell would awaken instantly in Paradise, they defeated all their neighbors. Then, summoning each vanquished nation to their standards, inspiring each in turn with their own mad confidence, they carried their arms and their faith over all southwestern Asia and northern Africa. This was the work of the Koran. Within a single century after Mohammed's death, the broad belt of earth extending from India to Spain, including both Babylonia and Egypt, the lands of the most ancient civilization — all this was firmly Mohammedan. And through much of this region the peoples were speaking Arabic. It became almost a world-language. For a time, the Koran was taught more widely, and won more converts, than the Christian Gospels.

THE GENIUS OF ARABIC LITERATURE

(AN INTRODUCTION BY SHEIK FAIZ-ULLAH-BHAI)

" Poetry is the record of the Arabs."
— OLD ARABIC PROVERB.

THE GENIUS OF ARABIC LITERATURE

AMONGST the ancient nations, as history shows, there are few who have so large a treasure of sublime poetry and so abundant a stock of useful literature to boast of as the old nation of Arabia. The Arabs have always been remarkable for the great pride they have taken in the excellence of their language, the perfection of their literature, the sublimity of their poetry, the purity of their race, and the integrity of their moral character. Pure justice, free from bias or prejudice, fully admits that they have reason to feel this pride, and accords them a very high place among the civilized and literary nations of the Ancient World. These facts are well borne out by evidence derived from the history of the progress of literature, especially during the fourth, fifth and sixth centuries of the Christian era.

During the period alluded to, the literary genius was almost entirely monopolized by the Aryans, represented then by the Indians and the Persians in the East, and by the Romans in the West. The Indian literature was, however, confined only to a limited number of Shastris and Brahmins, and was inaccessible to the other castes, or the numerically much stronger public. The Persians had long cultivated and enriched their literature with a good deal of learning, borrowed from the Greeks and the Indians. Among the Semitics, the Syrians possessed a Hebrew literature of a superior character, which was not, however, cultivated to a very vast extent, and was confined only to a few Rabbis. These *litterateurs,* moreover, had risen to their greatest height and were now only hanging on the verge of decline, and were more or less giving way to the Romans, who, at the time we speak of, held their own against all the nations of the world, both in the political as well as in the literary realm.

Their literary supremacy was, however, the result of a long

working of the schools, established by Cicero, Virgil, and Livy, on the lines of the learning they had inherited from that defunct Grecian world which had long given way to the sway of the triumphant Roman arms. The Roman poetry, oratory, and rhetoric were merely offshoots engrafted on those of Homer, Demosthenes, and Aristotle. Much credit is certainly due to the Romans for the great improvement they made on the teachings of their mother-school, which elevated them to a high pitch of literary fame, and placed them at the top of the category of the civilized and refined nations of the time. But their achievements, though very noble and excellent in themselves, were merely parasitic, and had little originality to boast of.

About this time we find a new nation rushing upon the scene, and steadily progressing with long strides to the front of the literary world, neither by means of any learning borrowed from other nations, nor by any set examples to guide them, but solely by dint of the growth of their own natural faculties. This was the Arabian nation, which, living obscurely in a solitary peninsula, was cut off from the chief seats of learning and debarred by its own seclusion from all the advantages of a close contact with the civilized nations of the day, who regarded it merely as a degraded and barbarous nation. Notwithstanding its starting with such local and social disadvantages, this nation, which was destined by God to rise to great importance later on, and to succeed the Romans in presiding over the destinies of a great part of the world, bravely stemming the tide of adverse circumstances, deserves all praise for the high state of culture, civilization, and advancement which its people attained by means of self-development of those superior literary faculties with which it had pleased God to endow them.

Although the Arabic language was as old as any of the noble languages of the world, yet its literary fame was kept by God in store for a later generation. The history of its literature, properly speaking, dates only from as early as the beginning of the sixth century. Yet, within so short a period of time, extending indeed over not more than two centuries, the Arabs succeeded in carrying their literature to such an elevated pitch as earned them an immortal name among the most refined nations of the literary world.

Their progress was marvelously rapid in every department of literature — poetry, oratory, rhetoric, politics, history, moral and mental philosophy. The greater part of their early literature, however, consisted of poetry, which was the principal and almost the only record the ancient Arabs possessed, and it is said with perfect truth that "Poetry is the record of the Arabs." Poetry was the record of their usages, their customs, their habits, their ways of living, their wars, their virtues, their vices, their domestic affairs, their social advancement, their mercantile dealings, their creeds and beliefs, their sentiments, their moral progress, and in short all that would interest both a historian and a moralist.

The Arab minds were cast by nature in poetical moulds of the best type, and their speeches even were mostly poetical, or such as could readily be converted into rhythmical numbers. They had at that time no rules of grammar or versification to guide them; and yet their verses were scrupulously accurate and hardly ever went wrong. They had neither any fixed criterion of rhetoric, nor any canons of criticism; yet their idioms, expressions, images, similes, and metaphors were as accurate, as clear, as lucid, and as perspicuous as any of the subsequently established schools of the Post-Islamic times. One of the distinctive features of the primitive literature of the Arabs was that it possessed the real and rare beauty of being a faithful representation of nature, inasmuch as their images were derived directly from nature, and their composition was merely a real expression of their real feelings and a true reflection of their mental workings. False fame, vainglory, flattery, and empty praise were motives not known to those early Arabs, who led a simple and innocent life in the lap of nature, invested with all its concomitant virtues — bravery, courage, gallantry, truthfulness, innocent and sincere love, fidelity, generosity, liberality, charity, hospitality, and a hatred of cruelty and oppression. With the Arabs of those times poetry was a gift of nature, commonly bestowed on all alike, whether old or young, man or woman, rich or poor, high or low, noble or mean, townsman or peasant, who used it as a tangible expression of their emotions, a ready vehicle of what they thought and felt and a lasting record of their views, made more impressive and more perspicuous by illustrative similes, apt images, and suitable metaphors, such as were readily supplied by natural objects and scenes of daily observance.

Thus we see the common topics of their poetry to be domestic life, wars, heroic deeds, martial triumphs, travels, camels, horses, weapons, chase, love, reminiscences of old associations, hospitality, glory and genealogy of the tribe, panegyrics of noble personages and chiefs, records of their patriotic and virtuous deeds done for the good of their tribes, acknowledgment of their obligations, elegies, embodying posthumous recollections and commemorations of the virtues of deserving merits in proportion to their deserts. Precepts of sociology, political views, philosophical doctrines, maxims and proverbs were not lacking; but they were mere results of a direct observation of the objects of nature and of a deep contemplation of humanity in its simplest aspect.

Nor were the Arabs unconscious of the high poetical genius wherewith they were endowed by nature, of the great success of their literature, and of the rising fame and triumph of their literary talents. Poetry soon came to be recognized as a noble mental production, to be appreciated as a high accomplishment, and to be regarded as a qualification for exaltation of rank and esteem in society. Poets came forward to emulate and vie with one another to carry off the palm. This led to the establishment of a department of literary exhibition in the national fair of 'Okaz, which was held annually in Zu-l-Qa'dah, one of the four sacred months, in which war was forbidden to be waged. To it flocked merchants from Hejaz, Nejd, and other parts of Arabia. 'Okaz was the " Olympia of Arabia," where poets resorted and placed their poetic talents before the public for their judgment and award, which were always regarded as decisive and final.

The Arabic literature attained the zenith just at the time

when the faith of Islam made its appearance in Arabia, and the Koran marked the highest point to which the Arabic language and literature were destined to rise, after which, as the Arabs by the spread and the conquest of Islam came in contact with foreigners, they had reason to grow jealous of their noble language; and being afraid lest its purity might suffer from its contact with other languages, they were obliged to state the principles of grammar, to explain the laws of syntax, to discover the measures of prosody, to formulate the figures of rhetoric and composition, to define the criteria of lexicography, to determine the standards of phraseology, and to fix the canons of criticism, all founded on the basis of the universal principles that underlie the pure language of the pre-Islamic time. The simplicity of nature, however, was rapidly waning and giving place to artificial ornamentation, unnatural embellishment, and scholastic mannerism. Poets, orators, and writers then vied in indulging in poetic reveries, in giving full play to their imagination, in forming new sentiments, in inventing new metaphors and rare similes, in discovering the beauties of the pre-Islamic poetry, and in imitating by every artificial means in their power the flowing diction of that natural poetry the pathos and the effect of which, however, they strove to grasp with various but dubious success. They lay claim to no little credit, indeed, for the many improvements they made on the ancient style, diction, ideas and expressions, for the standard they fixed to regulate the imaginative work of poetry, for the canons of criticism they laid down, for the laws of language they enunciated, and for the many beautiful figures they invented. It was, however, mannerism, all in all, a noble imitation, but without the true spirit of real nature.

The progress of the Arabic literature may best be illustrated by comparing it to a gradual and grand ascent up a lofty mountain, richly clad in every variety of beautiful verdure, pleasant vegetation, particolored and fragrant flowers, verdant meadows, varied trees — all of wild growth; and rife with cooling avenues, refreshing arbors and stately alcoves, resounding with diverse songs of wild birds, whose varieties of notes, colors, and hues are objects of deep admiration and devotion to the votaries of nature. The summit was gained only at the appearance of the Koran, which occupied the proud position of a solitary eminence, beyond the reach of all aspirers, who fell short of it. A step further, and the declivity gradually led to a spacious plateau, abounding in fine valleys, laid out with beautiful gardens, charming flower-beds, gliding rills, well trimmed alleys, leveled turfs, and picturesque parks, all combined in beautiful harmony and resounding with the harmonious melodies of trained birds, while art spared nothing to make all as perfect as lay in her power.

It was thus at the time when Arabic literature stood at its highest position, that the celebrated Seven Poems, well known at the "Seven Hanged Poems," made their appearance. They stood at the summit of the eminence of Arabic literature, exulting with deserving pride at that enviable position and triumphing over the evergreen laurels, so nobly won by the superior elegance, eloquence, and purity of their language, their admirable images, and their vivid descriptions. They were universally admired by the public, who in order to testify their appreciation of their real beauties and the recognition of the obligation, which the Arabic language in no little measure owed to them, unanimously agreed to immortalize their fame by conferring on them the highest honor they could bestow — that of hanging them inside the Kaaba, the most sacred shrine of their worship, as a memorial to posterity, after they were inscribed in letters of gold on pieces of a fine white cloth of Egypt, whence they are also called " the Golden."

THE HANGED POEMS

*" They stand at the summit of the eminence of old Arabic
literature."*

— FAIZ-ULLAH-BHAI.

VOL. V.—2.

THE HANGED POEMS

THE POEM OF IMRU-UL-QUAIS [1]

Stop, oh my friends, let us pause to weep over the remembrance of my beloved.
Here was her abode on the edge of the sandy desert between Dakhool and Howmal.

The traces of her encampment are not wholly obliterated even now;
For when the South wind blows the sand over them the North wind sweeps it away.

The courtyards and enclosures of the old home have become desolate;
The dung of the wild deer lies there thick as the seeds of pepper.

On the morning of our separation it was as if I stood in the gardens of our tribe,
Amid the acacia-shrubs where my eyes were blinded with tears by the smart from the bursting pods of colocynth.

As I lament thus in the place made desolate, my friends stop their camels;
They cry to me "Do not die of grief; bear this sorrow patiently."

Nay, the cure of my sorrow must come from gushing tears.
Yet, is there any hope that this desolation can bring me solace?

[1] This is supposed to be the oldest of the "hanged" poems. Like the others it shifts abruptly from theme to theme, and is full of poetic comparisons. Indeed, its author is said to have started this fashion, winning for himself the name of "The creator of images."

So, before ever I met Unaizah, did I mourn for two others;
My fate had been the same with Ummul-Huwairith and her
neighbor Ummul-Rahab in Masal.

Fair were they also, diffusing the odor of musk as they moved,
Like the soft zephyr bringing with it the scent of the clove.

Thus the tears flowed down on my breast, remembering days
of love;
The tears wetted even my sword-belt, so tender was my love.

Behold how many pleasant days have I spent with fair
women;
Especially do I remember the day at the pool of Darat-i-
Juljul.[2]

On that day I killed my riding camel for food for the
maidens:
How merry was their dividing my camel's trappings to be carried on their camels.

It is a wonder, a riddle, that the camel being saddled was yet
unsaddled!
A wonder also was the slaughterer, so heedless of self in his
costly gift!

Then the maidens commenced throwing the camel's flesh into
the kettle;

[2] The poet in this and the following lines refers to an incident which
is thus told us: during his wooing of Unaizah he followed her and the
other maidens when they rode on camels to the pool Darat-i-Juljul. The
women bathed in the pool and he captured their clothes and would not
surrender these until each one came out of the water in turn and asked
for hers. They held back so long before they yielded to this, that afterward they complained of being faint with hunger. Thereon he lavishly
slew his camel so they could have it immediately for food. When they
had eaten, they would not leave him stranded in the desert, so divided
the trappings of his camel, each carrying home a part upon her beast,
while the carrying of the poet himself fell to Unaizah. She jestingly
protested that the howdah on her camel's back was too small for them
both.

The fat was woven with the lean like loose fringes of white twisted silk.

On that day I entered the howdah, the camel's howdah of Unaizah!
And she protested, saying, " Woe to you, you will force me to travel on foot."

She repulsed me, while the howdah was swaying with us;
She said, " You are galling my camel, Oh Imru-ul-Quais, so dismount."

Then I said, " Drive him on! Let his reins go loose, while you turn to me.
Think not of the camel and our weight on him. Let us be happy.

" Many a beautiful woman like you, Oh Unaizah, have I visited at night;
I have won her thought to me, even from her children have I won her."

There was another day when I walked with her behind the sandhills,
But she put aside my entreaties and swore an oath of virginity.

Oh, Unaizah, gently, put aside some of this coquetry.
If you have, indeed, made up your mind to cut off friendship with me, then do it kindly or gently.

Has anything deceived you about me, that your love is killing me,
And that verily as often as you order my heart, it will do what you order?

And if any one of my habits has caused you annoyance,
Then put away my heart from your heart, and it will be put away.

And your two eyes do not flow with tears, except to strike me
    with arrows in my broken heart.
Many a fair one, whose tent can not be sought by others, have
    I enjoyed playing with.

I passed by the sentries on watch near her, and a people desir-
    ous of killing me;
If they could conceal my murder, being unable to assail me
    openly.

I passed by these people at a time, when the Pleiades appeared
    in the heavens,
As the appearance of the gems in the spaces in the ornamented
    girdle, set with pearls and gems.

Then she said to me, " I swear by God; you have no excuse
    for your wild life;
I can not expect that your erring habits will ever be removed
    from your nature."

I went out with her; she walking, and drawing behind us,
    over our footmarks,
The skirts of an embroidered woolen garment, to erase the
    footprints.

Then when we had crossed the enclosure of the tribe,
The middle of the open plain, with its sandy undulations and
    sandhills, we sought.

I drew the tow side-locks of her head toward me; and sho
    leant toward me;
She was slender of waist, and full in the ankle.

Thin-waisted, white-skinned, slender of body,
Her breast shining polished like a mirror.

In complexion she is like the first egg of the ostrich — white,
    mixed with yellow.

Pure water, unsullied by the descent of many people in it, has
nourished her.

She turns away, and shows her smooth cheek, forbidding with
a glancing eye,
Like that of a wild animal, with young, in the desert of
Wajrah.

And she shows a neck like the neck of a white deer;
It is neither disproportionate when she raises it, nor unorna-
mented.

And a perfect head of hair which, when loosened, adorns her
back,
Black, very dark-colored, thick like a date-cluster on a heavily
laden date-tree.

Her curls creep upward to the top of her head;
And the plaits are lost in the twisted hair, and the hair falling
loose.

And she meets me with a slender waist, thin as the twisted
leathern nose-rein of a camel.
Her form is like the stem of a palm-tree bending over from the
weight of its fruit.

In the morning, when she wakes, the particles of musk are
lying over her bed.
She sleeps much in the morning; she does not need to gird her
waist with a working dress.

She gives with thin fingers, not thick, as if they were the
worms of the desert of Zabi,
In the evening she brightens the darkness, as if she were the
light-tower of a monk.

Toward one like her, the wise man gazes incessantly, lovingly.
She is well proportioned in height between the wearer of a
long dress and of a short frock.

The follies of men cease with youth, but my heart does not
cease to love you.
Many bitter counselors have warned me of the disaster of your
love, but I turned away from them.

Many a night has let down its curtains around me amid deep
grief,
It has whelmed me as a wave of the sea to try me with sorrow.

Then I said to the night, as slowly his huge bulk passed over
me,
As his breast, his loins, his buttocks weighed on me and then
passed afar,

" Oh long night, dawn will come, but will be no brighter without my love.
You are a wonder, with stars held up as by ropes of hemp to a
solid rock."

At other times, I have filled a leather water-bag of my people
and entered the desert,
And trod its empty wastes while the wolf howled like a gam-
bler whose family starves.

I said to the wolf, " You gather as little wealth, as little prosperity as I.
What either of us gains he gives away.   So do we remain
thin."

Early in the morning, while the birds were still nesting, I
mounted my steed.
Well-bred was he, long-bodied, outstripping the wild beasts in
speed,

Swift to attack, to flee, to turn, yet firm as a rock swept down
by the torrent,
Bay-colored, and so smooth the saddle slips from him, as the
rain from a smooth stone,

Thin but full of life, fire boils within him like the snorting of
    a boiling kettle;
He continues at full gallop when other horses are dragging
    their feet in the dust for weariness.

A boy would be blown from his back, and even the strong rider
    loses his garments.
Fast is my steed as a top when a child has spun it well.

He has the flanks of a buck, the legs of an ostrich, and the gal-
    lop of a wolf.
From behind, his thick tail hides the space between his thighs,
    and almost sweeps the ground.

When he stands before the house, his back looks like the huge
    grinding-stone there.
The blood of many leaders of herds is in him, thick as the
    juice of henna in combed white hair.

As I rode him we saw a flock of wild sheep, the ewes like
    maidens in long-trailing robes;
They turned for flight, but already he had passed the leaders
    before they could scatter.

He outran a bull and a cow and killed them both, and they
    were made ready for cooking;
Yet he did not even sweat so as to need washing.

We returned at evening, and the eye could scarcely realize his
    beauty
For, when gazing at one part, the eye was drawn away by the
    perfection of another part.

He stood all night with his saddle and bridle on him,
He stood all night while I gazed at him admiring, and did not
    rest in his stable.

But come, my friends, as we stand here mourning, do you see
    the lightning?

See its glittering, like the flash of two moving hands, amid the
thick gathering clouds.

Its glory shines like the lamps of a monk when he has dipped
their wicks thick in oil.
I sat down with my companions and watched the lightning
and the coming storm.

So wide-spread was the rain that its right end seemed over
Quatan,
Yet we could see its left end pouring down on Satar, and
beyond that over Yazbul.

So mighty was the storm that it hurled upon their faces the
huge kanahbul trees,
The spray of it drove the wild goats down from the hills of
Quanan.

In the gardens of Taimaa not a date-tree was left standing,
Nor a building, except those strengthened with heavy stones.

The mountain, at the first downpour of the rain, looked like a
giant of our people draped in a striped cloak.
The peak of Mujaimir in the flood and rush of débris looked
like a whirling spindle.

The clouds poured forth their gift on the desert of Ghabeet,
till it blossomed
As though a Yemani merchant were spreading out all the rich
clothes from his trunks,

As though the little birds of the valley of Jiwaa awakened in
the morning
And burst forth in song after a morning draught of old, pure,
spiced wine.

As though all the wild beasts had been covered with sand and
mud, like the onion's root-bulbs.
They were drowned and lost in the depths of the desert at
evening.

THE POEM OF ANTAR [1]

Have the poets left in the garment a place for a patch to be patched by me; and did you know the abode of your beloved after reflection? [2]

The vestige of the house, which did not speak, confounded thee, until it spoke by means of signs, like one deaf and dumb.

Verily, I kept my she-camel there long grumbling, with a yearning at the blackened stones, keeping and standing firm in their own places.

It is the abode of a friend, languishing in her glance, submissive in the embrace, pleasant of smile.

Oh house of 'Ablah situated at Jiwaa, talk with me about those who resided in you. Good morning to you, O house of 'Ablah, and be safe from ruin.

I halted my she-camel in that place; and it was as though she were a high palace; in order that I might perform the wont of the lingerer.

And 'Ablah takes up her abode at Jiwaa; while our people went to Hazan, then to Mutathallam.

She took up her abode in the land of my enemies; so it became difficult for me to seek you, O daughter of Mahzam.

I was enamored of her unawares, at a time when I was killing her people, desiring her in marriage; but by your father's life I swear, this was not the time for desiring. [3]

And verily you have occupied in my heart the place of the honored loved one, so do not think otherwise than this, that you are my beloved.

And how may be the visiting of her, while her people have

[1] This is the Antar, or Antarah, who became the most noted of Arab heroes of romance.

[2] That is, have the poets left any deficiency to be supplied? Have the poets of the former days left any poetry unsaid that the poets of the present day may say it?

[3] When there was war between the two tribes, there was little use his wishing to marry her.

taken up their residence in the spring at 'Unaizatain and our people at Ghailam?

I knew that you had intended departing, for, verily, your camels were bridled on a dark night.

Nothing caused me fear of her departure, except that the baggage camels of her people were eating the seeds of the Khimkhim tree throughout the country.[4]

Amongst them were two and forty milk-giving camels, black as the wing-feathers of black crows.

When she captivates you with a mouth possessing sharp, and white teeth, sweet as to its place of kissing, delicious of taste.

As if she sees with the two eyes of a young, grown up gazelle from the deer.

It was as though the musk bag of a merchant in his case of perfumes preceded her teeth toward you from her mouth.

Or as if it is an old wine-skin, from Azri'at, preserved long, such as the kings of Rome preserve;

Or her mouth is as an ungrazed meadow, whose herbage the rain has guaranteed, in which there is but little dung; and which is not marked with the feet of animals.

The first pure showers of every rain-cloud rained upon it, and left every puddle in it bright and round like a dirham;

Sprinkling and pouring; so that the water flows upon it every evening, and is not cut off from it.

The fly enjoyed yet alone, and so it did not cease humming, as is the act of the singing drunkard;

Humming, while he rubs one foreleg against the other, as the striking on the flint of one, bent on the flint, and cut off as to his palm.

She passes her evenings and her mornings on the surface of a well-stuffed couch, while I pass my nights on the back of a bridled black horse.

And my couch is a saddle upon a horse big-boned in the leg, big in his flanks, great of girth.

Would a Shadanian she-camel cause me to arrive at her

[4] He knew that her tribe would have to move on, as there was no forage left for their camels.

abode, who is cursed with an udder scanty of milk and cut off ?[5]

After traveling all night, she is lashing her sides with her tail, and is strutting proudly, and she breaks up the mounds of earth she passes over with her foot with its sole, treading hard.

As if I in the evening am breaking the mounds of earth by means of an ostrich, very small as to the distance between its two feet, and earless.[6]

The young ostriches flock toward him, as the herds of Yamanian camels flock to a barbarous, unintelligible speaker.

They follow the crest of his head, as though it was a howdah on a large litter, tented for them.

He is small headed, who returns constantly to look after his eggs at Zil-'Ushairah; he is like a slave, with a long fur cloak and without ears.

She drank of the water of Duhruzain and then turned away, being disgusted, from the pools of stagnant water.[7]

And she swerves away with her right side from the fear of one, whistling in the evening, a big, ugly-headed one;[8]

From the fear of a cat, led at her side, every time she turned toward him in anger, he met her with both claws and mouth.

She knelt down at the edge of the pool of Rada', and groaned as though she had knelt on a reed, broken, and emitting a cracking noise.

And the sweat on the back was as though it were oil or thick pitch, with which fire is lighted round the sides of a retort.

Her places of flexure were wetted with it and she lavishly poured of it, on a spreading forelock, short and well-bred.

The length of the journey left her a strong, well-built body, like a high palace, built with cement, and rising high; and feet like the supports of a firmly pitched tent.

[5] A she-camel, upon whom this operation has been performed, is swifter, stronger, and fatter than others.

[6] He compares the fleetness of the camel to that of an ostrich.

[7] Referring to the she-camel.

[8] The big, ugly-headed one is the whip with its heavy handle, or a cat.

And surely I recollected you, even when the lances were drinking my blood, and bright swords of Indian make were dripping with my blood.

I wished to kiss the swords, for verily they shone as bright as the flash of the foretooth of your smiling mouth.

If you lower your veil over yourself in front of me, of what use will it be? for, verily, I am expert in capturing the mailed horseman.

Praise me for the qualities which you know I possess, for, verily, when I am not ill-treated, I am gentle to associate with.

And if I am ill-treated, then, verily, my tyranny is severe, very bitter is the taste of it, as the taste of the colocynth.

And, verily, I have drunk wine after the midday heats have subsided, buying it with the bright stamped coin.

From a glass, yellow with the lines of the glass-cutter on it, which was accompanied by a white-stoppered bottle on the left-hand side.

And when I have drunk, verily, I am the squanderer of my property, and my honor is great, and is not sullied.[9]

And when I have become sober, I do not diminish in my generosity, and as you know, so are my qualities and my liberality.

And many a husband of a beautiful woman, I have left prostrate on the ground, with his shoulders hissing like the side of the mouth of one with a split lip.[10]

My two hands preceded him with a hasty blow, striking him before he could strike me; and with the drops of blood from a penetrating stroke, red like the color of Brazil wood.

Why did you not ask the horsemen, O daughter Malik! if you were ignorant, concerning what you did not know about my condition,

At a time when I never ceased to be in the saddle of a long striding, wounded, sturdy horse, against whom the warriors came in succession.

[9] That is, drunkenness makes him generous and not ill-tempered. The Arabs, before Mohammed, considered drinking with one's friends to show a generous disposition.

[10] That is, the blood was spurting and hissing from a wound in his shoulder.

At one time he is detached to charge the enemy with the lance, and at another he joins the large host with their bows tightly strung.

He who was present in the battle will inform you that verily I rush into battle, but I abstain at the time of taking the booty.

I see spoils, which, if I want I would win; but my bashfulness and my magnanimity hold me back from them.

And many a fully armed one, whom the warriors shunned fighting with, neither a hastener in flight, nor a surrenderer;

My hands were generous to him by a quick point with a straightened spear, strong in the joints;

Inflicting a wound wide of its two sides, the sound of the flow of blood from it leads at night the prowling wolves, burning with hunger.

I rent his vesture with a rigid spear, for the noble one is not forbidden to the spears.

Then I left him a prey for the wild beasts, who seize him, and gnaw the beauty of his fingers and wrist.

And many a long, closely woven coat of mail, I have split open the links of it, with a sword, off one defending his rights, and renowned for bravery.

Whose hands are ready with gambling arrows when it is winter, a tearer-down of the signs of the wine-sellers, and one reproached for his extravagance.[11]

When he saw that I had descended from my horse and was intending killing him, he showed his teeth, but without smiling.[12]

My meeting with him was when the day spread out, and he was as if his fingers and his head were dyed with indigo.[13]

I pierced him with my spear, and then I set upon him with my Indian sword pure of steel, and keen.

A warrior, so stately in size as if his clothes were on a high

[11] The richer Arabs gamble as to who shall kill his camel in the time of scarcity to distribute the flesh amongst the poor. The wine-sellers take down their signs when they have run out of liquor; the meaning of tearing down the signs being that he drinks up all their wine.

[12] The allusion is to the poet's killing Zamzam, father of Husain and Harim, who insulted him. See close of the poem.

[13] The dried blood was of an indigo color.

tree: soft leather shoes are worn by him and he is not twinned.

Oh, how wonderful is the beauty of the doe of the hunt, to whom is she lawful? To me she is unlawful; would to God that she was not unlawful.[14]

So, I sent my female slave, and said to her, " Go, find out news of her and inform me."

She said, " I saw carelessness on the part of the enemies, and that the doe is possible to him who is shooting."

And it was as though she looked toward me with the neck of a doe, a fawn of the gazelles, pure and with a white upper lip.

I am informed that 'Amru is unthankful for my kindness while ingratitude is a cause of evil to the soul of the giver.[15]

And, verily, I remember the advice of my uncle, in the battle, when the two lips quiver from off the white teeth of the mouth,

In the thick of the battle, of which the warriors do not complain of the rigors, except with an unintelligible noise.

When they (i.e., my people) defended themselves with me against the spears of the enemy, I did not refrain from them (i.e., the spears) through cowardice, but the place of my advance had become too strait.

When I heard the cry of Murrah rise, and saw the two sons of Rabi'ah in the thick dust,

While the tribe of Muhallam were struggling under their banners, and death was under the banners of the tribe of Mulhallam,

I made sure that at the time of their encounter there would be a blow, which would make the heads fly from the bodies, as the bird flies from off her young ones sitting close.

When I saw the people, while their mass advanced, excite one another to fight, I turned against them without being reproached for any want of bravery.

They were calling 'Antarah, while the spears were as though they were well-ropes in the breast of Adham.

---

[14] Here he again reverts to address his sweetheart. The Arabs may not marry with a woman of a tribe with whom they are at war.

[15] 'Amru, the 'Absian, who insulted the poet.

They were calling 'Antarah, while the swords were as though they were the flash of lightnings in a dark cloud.

They were calling 'Antarah, while the arrows were flying, as though they were a flight of locusts, hovering above watering places.

They were calling "O 'Antarah," while the coats of mail shone with close rings, shining as though they were the eyeballs of frogs floating in a wavy pond.

I did not cease charging them, (the enemy,) with the prominent part of his (horse's) throat and breast, until he became covered with a shirt of blood.

Then he turned on account of the falling of the spears on his breast, and complained to me with tears and whinnyings.

If he had known what conversation was, he would have complained with words, and verily he would have, had he known speech, talked with me.

And verily the speech of the horsemen, "Woe to you, 'Antarah, advance, and attack the enemy," cured my soul and removed its sickness.

While the horses sternly frowning were charging over the soft soil, being partly the long-bodied mares, and partly the long-bodied, well-bred horses.

My riding-camels are tractable, they go wherever I wish; while my intellect is my helper, and I drive it forward with a firm order.[16]

Verily, it lay beyond my power that I should visit you; so, know what you have known, and some of what you have not known.

The lances of the tribe of Bagheez intercepted you and the perpetrators of the war set aside those who did not perpetrate it.

And, verily, I turned the horse for the attack, while his neck was bleeding, until the horses began to shun me.

And verily I feared that I should die, while there has not yet been a turn for war against the two sons of Zamzam; [17]

[16] That is, I carry out my plans with sagacity and determination.

[17] I feared that I should die, before I had fought the two sons of Zamzam. 'Antarah killed their father during the war between the tribes

The two revilers of my honor, while I did not revile them, and the threateners of my blood, when I did not see them.

There is no wonder should they do so, for I left their father a prey for the wild beasts and every large old vulture.

of 'Abs and Fazárah, wherein the latter were defeated with great loss. Harim and Husain, the two sons of Zamzam, were killed shortly afterward.

THE POEM OF ZUHAIR [1]

" Does the blackened ruin, situated in the stony ground between Durraj and Mutathallam, which did not speak to me, when addressed, belong to the abode of Ummi Awfa ?

" And is it her dwelling at the two stony meadows, seeming as though they were the renewed tattoo marks in the sinews of the wrist ?

" The wild cows and the white deer are wandering about there, one herd behind the other, while their young are springing up from every lying-down place.

" I stood again near it, (the encampment of the tribe of Awfa,) after an absence of twenty years, and with some efforts, I know her abode again after thinking awhile.

" I recognized the three stones blackened by fire at the place where the kettle used to be placed at night, and the trench round the encampment, which had not burst, like the source of a pool.

" And when I recognized the encampment I said to its site, ' Now good morning, oh spot; may you be safe from dangers.'

" Look, oh my friend! do you see any women traveling on camels, going over the high ground above the stream of Jurthum ? [2]

" They have covered their howdahs with coverlets of high value, and with a thin screen, the fringes of which are red, resembling blood.

" And they inclined toward the valley of Soobán, ascending the center of it, and in their faces were the fascinating

[1] This poem begins, as do most Arab poems, with love longings, but soon drifts into praise of two peacemakers and the story of the feud between two tribes which preceded the peace. From this field the poem soon wanders to the philosophic maxims of the author. Zuhair is above all a philosopher.

[2] He fancies he sees the women again whom he saw twenty years previously, and he appeals to his companion to know if what he sees is real.

looks of a soft-bodied person brought up in easy circumstances.

" They arose early in the morning and got up at dawn, and they went straight to the valley of Rass as the hand goes unswervingly to the mouth, when eating.

" And amongst them is a place of amusement for the far-sighted one, and a pleasant sight for the eye of the looker who looks attentively.

" As if the pieces of dyed wool which they left in every place in which they halted, were the seeds of night-shade which have not been crushed.

" When they arrived at the water, the mass of which was blue from intense purity, they laid down their walking sticks, (*i.e.*, took their lodging there,) like the dweller who has pitched his tents.

" They kept the hill of Qanan and the rough ground about it on their hand; while there are many, dwelling in Qanan, the shedding of whose blood is lawful and unlawful.[3]

" They came out from the valley of Soobán, then they crossed it, riding in every Qainian howdah new and widened.

" Then I swear by the temple, round which walk the men who built it from the tribes of Quraish and Jurhum.[4]

" An oath, that you are verily two excellent chiefs, who are found worthy of honor in every condition, between ease and distress.[5]

" The two endeavorers from the tribe of Ghaiz bin Murrah strove in making peace after the connection between the tribes had become broken, on account of the shedding of blood.

" You repaired with peace the condition of the tribes of 'Abs and Zubyán, after they had fought with one another, and ground up the perfume of Manshim between them.[6]

[3] There are many enemies and many friends dwelling there.

[4] This refers to the temple at Mecca which was built by Ismail, son of Abraham, ancestor of the tribe of Quraish, who married a woman of Jurhum, an old tribe of Yaman, who were the keepers of the temple before Quraish.

[5] The theme changes here abruptly, to praise of two peacemakers.

[6] Some Arabs, making a league to be revenged against their enemies,

" And indeed you said, ' if we bring about peace perfectly by the spending of money and the conferring of benefits, and by good words, we shall be safe from the danger of the two tribes, destroying each other.'

" You occupied by reason of this the best of positions, and became far from the reproach of being undutiful and sinful.

" And you became great in the high nobility of Ma'add; may you be guided in the right way; and he who spends his treasure of glory will become great.

" The memory of the wounds is obliterated by the hundreds of camels, and he, who commenced paying off the blood money by instalments, was not guilty of it (*i.e.*, of making war).

" One tribe pays it to another tribe as an indemnity, while they who gave the indemnity did not shed blood sufficient for the filling of a cupping glass.

" Then there was being driven to them from the property you inherited, a booty of various sorts from young camels with slit ears.

" Now, convey from me to the tribe of Zubyán and their allies a message,—' verily you have sworn by every sort of oath to keep the peace.'

" Do not conceal from God what is in your breast that it may be hidden; whatever is concealed, God knows all about it.

" Either it will be put off and placed recorded in a book, and preserved there until the judgment day; or the punishment be hastened and so he will take revenge.

" And war is not but what you have learnt it to be, and what you have experienced, and what is said concerning it, is not a story based on suppositions.

" When you stir it up, you will stir it up as an accursed thing, and it will become greedy when you excite its greed and it will rage fiercely.

took oath with their hands plunged in a certain perfume, made by Manshim, as a sign of their coalition. They fought until they were slain to the last of them. Hence the proverb, " More unlucky than the perfume of Manshim."

"Then it will grind you as the grinding of the upper mill-stone against the lower, and it will conceive immediately after one birth and it will produce twins.[7]

"By my life I swear, how good a tribe it is upon whom Husain Bin Zamzam brought an injury by committing a crime which did not please them.[8]

"And he had concealed his hatred, and did not display it, and did not proceed to carry out his intention until he got a good opportunity.

"And he said, 'I will perform my object of avenging myself, and I will guard myself from my enemy with a thousand bridled horses behind me.'

"Then he attacked his victim from 'Abs, but did not cause fear to the people of the many houses, near which death had thrown down his baggage.[9]

"They allowed their animals to graze until when the interval between the hours of drinking was finished, they took them to the deep pool, which is divided by weapons and by shedding of blood.[10]

"They accomplished their object amongst themselves, then they led the animals back to the pasture of unwholesome indigestible grass.

"I have grown weary of the troubles of life; and he, who lives eighty years will, mayest thou have no father if thou doubt [11] grow weary.

"And I know what has happened to-day and yesterday,

[7] The misfortunes arising from war are double.

[8] Husain Bin Zamzam's father was killed during the war between the Beni Zubyán and the Beni 'Abs. When peace was concluded between the tribes, he made a vow secretly that he would kill one of the tribe of 'Abs out of the revenge for his father. This he did, but when the Beni 'Abs came to take revenge on him, Hárith Ibn 'Awf offered them one hundred camels as blood money or his own son to kill. The 'Absioms took the camels and spared his son. The poet is now praising them for their act.

[9] He killed no one while the peace was in force except the one person on whom he meant to take revenge.

[10] By the deep pool is meant war, and the meaning of the lines is that the tribes refrained from war for a certain time, after which they again had recourse to arms.

[11] A common term of imprecation.

before it, but verily, of the knowledge of what will happen to-morrow; I am ignorant.

"I see death is like the blundering of a blind camel;—him whom he meets he kills, and he whom he misses lives and will become old.

"And he who does not act with kindness in many affairs will be torn by teeth and trampled under foot.

"And he, who makes benevolent acts intervene before honor, increases his honor; and he, who does not avoid abuse, will be abused.

"He, who is possessed of plenty, and is miserly with his great wealth toward his people, will be dispensed with, and abused.

"He who keeps his word, will not be reviled; and he whose heart is guided to self-satisfying benevolence will not stammer.

"And he who dreads the causes of death, they will reach him, even if he ascends the tracts of the heavens with a ladder.

"And he, who shows kindness to one not deserving it, his praise will be a reproach against him, and he will repent of having shown kindness.

"And he who rebels against the butt ends of the spears, then verily he will have to obey the spear points joined to every long spear shaft.[12]

"And he who does not repulse with his weapons from his tank, will have it broken; and he who does not oppress the people will be oppressed.

"And he who travels should consider his friend an enemy; and he who does not respect himself will not be respected.

"And he, who is always seeking to bear the burdens of other people, and does not excuse himself from it, will one day by reason of his abasement, repent.

"And whatever of character there is in a man, even though he thinks it concealed from people, it is known.

[12] The wandering desert Arabs when they met used to present the butt ends of their spears toward one another if their intentions were peaceful, the points if they intended fighting.

" He, who does not cease asking people to carry him, and does not make himself independent of them even for one day of the time, will be regarded with disgust.

" Many silent ones you see, pleasing to you, but their excess in wisdom or deficiency will appear at the time of talking.

" The tongue of a man is one half, and the other half is his mind, and here is nothing besides these two, except the shape of the blood and the flesh.

" And verily, as to the folly of an old man there is no wisdom after it, but the young man after his folly may become wise.

" We asked of you, and you gave, and we returned to the asking and you returned to the giving, and he who increases the asking, will one day be disappointed."

THE KORAN

" Let none touch it but they who are clean."

—THE WARNING ALWAYS WRITTEN ON
THE COVER OF AN ARABIC KORAN.

*" The Koran is, unto them that believe, a sure guide and a
remedy; but unto those that believe not, it is a thickness of hearing in their ears, and it is a darkness which covereth them."*

—THE KORAN, CHAPTER XLI.

THE KORAN

(INTRODUCTION)

A FAMOUS Oriental critic once said that the best way to understand the Koran was to take the hint given by the Arabic writing, which reads from right to left, and so read the Koran backward, beginning with the last chapter. This suggestion is really worth following; for the Koran is not at all a book in our modern sense. It is not a complete discussion arranged in logical order. Each one of its Suras, or chapters, was proclaimed by Mohammed separately, as a chant or a prayer, a story or a warning, complete in itself, a single divine revelation.

These Suras were never combined by Mohammed into a book or even into a series. He recited them to his friends as occasion demanded. Sometimes the chants were not even written down, and were preserved just as Arab songs had been preserved for centuries before, by being treasured in the memories of wondering admirers. Only after the prophet's death, when his faith was spreading over half the world, did its leaders realize that trouble threatened from the variations appearing in the loosely memorized and repeated Suras. Some devotees treasured them in one phrasing, some in another. Fierce quarrels sprang up; a division into sects seemed probable. Then the leaders resolved that one authorized wording of the many Suras was needed; and they entrusted the task of gathering them to Zaid, one of Mohammed's comrades in Medina. This Zaid was therefore the editor and perhaps, to some extent of clarifying and reducing, the author of the Koran as we know it, and as every Mohammedan accepts it absolutely.

The gathering of the Suras was in itself no easy task. Zaid had often acted as Mohammed's scribe, and had preserved in a chest copies of most of the longer revelations. Some of

43

these he had written on scraps of sheepskin, some on palm-leaves; one at least Mohammed himself had traced on a flat bone. For other Suras, Zaid trusted his memory, others he collected from the lips of friends. There are in the Koran to-day several Suras which begin with two or three initial letters, apparently meaningless, which the Mohammedans themselves do not understand. These letters are regarded as a holy mystery; but there is at least a probability that they mark the initials of the men from whom Zaid received those Suras which he himself had not heard or known.

In grouping the Suras in order, Zaid performed one of the quaintest and most childlike pieces of mechanical book-making ever achieved by an editor. He did put first of all that celebrated Sura which had become the common prayer of the Mohammedans. But after that he merely arranged the Suras in the order of their length, putting the longest first. This leads us to the reason why the Koran may be best read backward. Zaid's arrangement is very confusing to one who would follow the chronology or development of Mohammed's life and doctrine. Moreover, each Sura can only be fully understood when regarded in its relation to the prophet's very adventurous life, his position of danger or of triumph at the moment of its revelation. Not only the tone of the speaker but even his doctrines changed much with his fortunes. A revelation proclaimed at one time was sometimes contradicted later. As a rule, the very short Suras at the end of the Koran were those first announced. They represent the early impassioned vehemence of the man, fighting for his faith, shouting out the eager, burning flame within him. As the chapters become longer they become calmer; they are the sympathetic addresses of a teacher instructing the followers who trust him. And the longest chapters of all are an almost mechanical welding together and smoothing off of the disjointed, passionate preachings of the earlier days. One would like to shift upon Zaid the responsibility for much of these longest chapters with their mixing of many themes. The editor may have thrown together much that the prophet proclaimed separately.

To the good Mohammedan, it must be remembered, the contradictions of doctrine in the Koran are not contradictions. Long before the Mohammedan scholar reads the sacred book itself he has been taught which of any two conflicting commands came first and was afterward replaced by the other. The first revelation he accepts as having been divinely ordered for the moment's use — to aid in the spreading of the faith. At first, for example, the Suras commanded the weak and persecuted Mohammed to deal peaceably with his enemies. Later, when he had power, he received the famed command to slay all who opposed his teachings. So again, if you would understand the growth of the prophet's doctrines, you had best read the Koran backward.

With these points in mind it is but natural that both Arabic and European scholars have made efforts to revise the Koran, to rearrange its Suras in chronological order. We have even had an English translation of this nature by Rodwell, in which the editor has placed the Suras as he thinks they were proclaimed. Unhappily, however, we have no positive guide as to their chronological order. Tradition tells us somewhat; the evidence of individual words and incidents and doctrines helps much. Yet no two editors, either Arabic or European, have ever wholly or even closely agreed as to the complete reordering of the Suras, or of the individual verses within them. Some of these verses have obviously lost their original context.

Moreover, even if scholars could agree, their reordered book would not be the Koran, the holy book of the Mohammedans. To the faithful, the book is so completely inspired of God, that even its confusion is accepted as an essential part of the whole, as having been ordained for some wise purpose. [1] They believe that the Koran has existed since

[1] Roughly speaking, the chronological arrangement of the Suras is somewhat as follows. The honor of being the earliest has been variously ascribed to the 74th, the 1st, and even the 68th. Generally, however, the 96th Sura, or at least its opening down through verse five, is regarded as the earliest revelation. After that, during the first four years of the prophet's preaching, followed Suras 74, 111, 106, 108, 104, 107, 102, 105, 92, 90, 94, 93, 97, 86, 91, 80, 68, and many others

the beginning of things, the perfect expression of God's law; and that in Mohammed's day the angel Gabriel brought the complete book forth from its eternal resting-place, and began revealing it to the prophet as each section fitted.

In literary style the Koran scarcely upholds this idea of its perfection. Its verses are arranged in a sort of chant, half way between poetry and prose. The lines do not at all follow the rather exact metrical rules which the Arab poets before Mohammed had established. Hence the Arabs of his day did not call it poetry. Yet the sentences have a vague rhythm of their own and they jingle with a constant rhyming, the combination bringing them much nearer in form to our idea of poetry than of prose. This haunting music is, of course, wholly lost in translation. Here is the Arabic of the first brief Sura, given, as nearly as Arabic words can be, in the English alphabet, so that the reader may catch the chanting hum of sound:

> Bismillá-hi'rah mání'rrahím.
> Al-hamdúlilláhi Rabbi' lálumín.
> Arrahmáni'rrahim;
> Maliki yomi-d-dín.
> Iyáka-Nábúdú, waiyáka nastáín.
> Ihdina'ssirát al mústakîm,
> Sirát alazina an niámta alaihim,
> Ghairi-'l-mághdhúbi alaihim waladhálína.

Before reading the Koran, since it is so obviously and completely interwoven with Mohammed's personal career, one should study quite fully not only his life but also the general conditions of life in the Arabia that he knew. Very briefly summarized these are as follows: The Arabs were then a race much like what they are to-day, proud and pas-

numbered above fifty. This period closes with the famous Sura number one; and the next years, leading up to the Hejira, open with 54, 37, 71, and others numbered above 10, and close with 7, 46, 6, and 13. To the final or Medina period belong Suras 2, 98, 64, 62, 8, 47, 3, 61, 57, 4, 65, 59, 33, 63, 24, 58, 22, 48, 66, 60, 110, 49, and 9. Sura 5 is usually regarded as the last of all, since it contains the solemn passage " This day have I perfected your religion for you," etc.

sionate, noble of thought but turning quickly to treachery, vehement fighters but scarcely persistent in battle. In religion they believed vaguely in a single god, but this idea was so overlaid with idol-worship that they seldom addressed or even considered the central Power. Large colonies of Jews pervaded the land, so that Mohammed had always Jews, and often Christians also, among his neighbors. The popular Arab worship centered around a black stone, which was deemed holy, and which was sheltered in the ancient building, the Kaaba, at Mecca. Pilgrimages were made to the Kaaba and religious rites enacted there; so that the Arab tribe, known as the Koreish, who occupied the rather barren town of Mecca, were much honored and acquired much wealth among their countrymen.

To this distinguished tribe of the Koreish did Mohammed belong. In his younger days he was not particularly noted among the men of his race. He fought and traded and tended camels and flocks as did the others. Probably he could not read nor write. He first came into prominence by marrying Khadija or Hadijah, a wealthy widow fifteen years older than himself. He was forty years of age when he announced himself to be inspired by visions, and to be a prophet of God. His wife Khadija promptly became his first and most devoted follower.

Mohammed's new religion was chiefly a vehement protest against the idolatry and immorality he saw around him. He accepted both Judaism and Christianity and drew from our Bible or from Jewish traditions most of the stories with which the Koran is filled. Only, he declared that he came as a new prophet to complete both of the older faiths. To him, Jesus was but one of the long line of God's prophets; and he, Mohammed, was also among these holy oracles, the last and most divinely guided of them all. He won converts slowly among his own people. As he preached against the idolatrous rites on which depended the whole prosperity of the city of Mecca, naturally the chief men of the tribe objected strenuously to his attack upon their fortunes. His bitterest enemies rose among these leaders of the Koreish.

Finally, after twelve years of quarrel, Mohammed had to flee from Mecca for his life. His few disciples fled with him, and the little band found refuge in a rival city, Medina, many of whose people had heard and accepted Mohammed's teaching. This flight from Mecca to Medina is called the "Hejira," and from it the Mohammedans date the beginning of their era. It occurred in the year 622 of our Christian chronology.

The Koreish were now so infuriated against Mohammed that they waged a war against Medina to destroy him. But the prophet's faction grew rapidly stronger. The Koreish began to fear him and sought a truce; and at length Mohammed practically conquered Mecca. He then very shrewdly declared that the city was still a holy place, pilgrimages must still be made there; the Kaaba was announced to be the sacred center of his religion, as it had been of the earlier idolatry. On these wealth-insuring terms the Koreish gladly accepted the new faith, and became eager supporters of their mighty kinsman. From commanding small bands of desperate men, Mohammed soon found himself leading eager, hopeful armies. He had visions of conquering the world; but he died in 632, before his followers burst forth from Arabia. The tremendous conquests of Mohammedanism were accomplished, in his name, by his immediate successors.

THE KORAN

CHAPTER I

ENTITLED, THE PREFACE, OR INTRODUCTION; [1] REVEALED AT MECCA

IN THE NAME OF THE MOST MERCIFUL GOD [2]

Praise be to God, the Lord of all creatures; the most merciful, the king of the day of judgment. Thee do we worship, and of thee do we beg assistance. Direct us in the right way, in the way of those to whom thou has been gracious; not of those against whom thou art incensed, nor of those who go astray.

CHAPTER II

ENTITLED, THE COW; [1a] REVEALED PARTLY AT MECCA, AND PARTLY AT MEDINA

IN THE NAME OF THE MOST MERCIFUL GOD

A. L. M. There is no doubt in this book; it is a direction to the pious, who believe in the mysteries of faith, who observe the appointed times of prayer, and distribute alms out of what we have bestowed on them; and who believe in that revelation, which hath been sent down unto thee, and that which hath been sent down unto the prophets, before

[1] In Arabic, *al Fatihat.* This chapter is a prayer, and held in great veneration by the Mohammedans, who give it several other honorable titles; as the chapter of " prayer," of " praise," or " thanksgiving," of " treasure," etc. They esteem it as the quintessence of the whole Koran, and often repeat it in their devotions, both public and private, as the Christians do the Lord's Prayer.

[2] This formula, called the Bismillah, is prefixed to all but one of the chapters of the Koran, and is used by the Arabs in opening most books.

[1a] This title was occasioned by the story of the " red heifer," mentioned in the chapter.

thee,[2] and have firm assurance in the life to come: these are directed by their Lord, and they shall prosper.

As for the unbelievers, it will be equal to them whether thou admonish them, or do not admonish them; they will not believe. God hath sealed up their hearts and their hearing; a dimness covereth their sight, and they shall suffer a grievous punishment. There are some who say, We believe in God and the last day, but are not really believers; they seek to deceive God, and those who do believe, but they deceive themselves only, and are not sensible thereof. There is an infirmity in their hearts, and God hath increased that infirmity; and they shall suffer a most painful punishment because they have disbelieved. When one saith unto them, Act not corruptly in the earth, they reply, Verily, we are men of integrity. Are not they themselves corrupt doers? but they are not sensible thereof. And when one saith unto them, Believe ye as others believe; they answer, Shall we believe as fools believe? Are not they themselves fools? but they know it not. When they meet those who believe, they say, We do believe: but when they retire privately to their devils, they say, we really hold with you, and only mock at those people: God shall mock at them, and continue them in their impiety; they shall wander in confusion. These are the men who have purchased error at the price of true direction: but their traffic hath not been gainful, neither have they been rightly directed. They are like unto one who kindleth a fire, and when it hath enlightened all around him, God taketh away their light and leaveth them in darkness, they shall not see; they are deaf, dumb, and blind, therefore will they not repent. Or like a stormy cloud from heaven, fraught with darkness, thunder, and lightning, they put their fingers in their ears, because of the noise of the thunder, for fear of

---

[2] The Mohammedans believe that God gave written revelations not only to Moses, Jesus, and Mohammed, but to several other prophets; though they acknowledge none of those which preceded the Koran to be now extant, except the Pentateuch of Moses, the Psalms of David, and the Gospel of Jesus; which yet they say were even before Mohammed's time altered and corrupted by the Jews and Christians; and therefore will not allow our present copies to be genuine.

death; God encompasseth the infidels: the lightning wanteth but little of taking away their sight; so often as it enlighteneth them, they walk therein, but when darkness cometh on them, they stand still; and if God so pleased, he would certainly deprive them of their hearing and their sight, for God is almighty.

O men of Mecca! serve your Lord who hath created you, and those who have been before you: peradventure ye will fear him; who hath spread the earth as a bed for you, and the heaven as a covering, and hath caused water to descend from heaven, and thereby produced fruits for your sustenance. Set not up therefore any equals unto God, against your own knowledge. If ye be in doubt concerning that revelation which we have sent down unto our servant, produce a chapter like unto it, and call upon your witnesses, besides God, if ye say truth. But if ye do it not, nor shall ever be able to do it, justly fear the fire whose fuel is men and stones, prepared for the unbelievers. But bear good tidings unto those who believe, and do good works, that they shall have gardens watered by rivers; so often as they eat of the fruit thereof for sustenance, they shall say, This is what we have formerly eaten of; and they shall be supplied with several sorts of fruit having a mutual resemblance to one another.[3] There shall they enjoy wives subject to no impurity, and there shall they continue forever. Moreover God will not be ashamed to propound in a parable a gnat, or even a more despicable thing:[4] for they who believe will know it to be the truth from their Lord; but the unbelievers will say, What meaneth God by this parable? he will thereby mislead many, and will direct many thereby: but he will not mislead any thereby, except the transgressors, who make void

[3] Some commentators approve of this sense, supposing the fruits of paradise, though of various tastes, are alike in color and outward appearance; but others think the meaning to be, that the inhabitants of that place will find there fruits of the same or the like kinds as they used to eat while on earth.

[4] This was revealed to take off an objection made to the Koran by the infidels, for condescending to speak of such insignificant insects as the spider, the pismire, the bee, etc.

the covenant of God after the establishing thereof, and cut in sunder that which God hath commanded to be joined, and act corruptly in the earth; they shall perish. How is it that ye believe not in God? Since ye were dead, and he gave you life; he will hereafter cause you to die, and will again restore you to life; then shall ye return unto him. It is he who hath created for you whatsoever is on earth, and then set his mind to the creation of heaven, and formed it into seven heavens; he knoweth all things. When thy Lord said unto the angels, I am going to place a substitute on earth, they said, Wilt thou place there one who will do evil therein, and shed blood? but we celebrate thy praise, and sanctify thee. God answered, Verily I know that which ye know not; and he taught Adam the names of all things, and then proposed them to the angels, and said, Declare unto me the names of these things if ye say truth. They answered, Praise be unto thee, we have no knowledge but what thou teachest us, for thou art knowing and wise. God said, O Adam, tell them their names. And when he had told them their names, God said, Did I not tell you that I know the secrets of heaven and earth, and know that which ye discover, and that which ye conceal? And when we said unto the angels, Worship Adam, they all worshiped him, except Eblis, who refused, and was puffed up with pride, and became of the number of unbelievers. And we said, O Adam, dwell thou and thy wife in the garden, and eat of the fruit thereof plentifully wherever ye will; but approach not this tree, lest ye become of the number of the transgressors. But Satan caused them to forfeit paradise, and turned them out of the state of happiness wherein they had been; whereupon we said, Get ye down, the one of you an enemy unto the other; and there shall be a dwelling-place for you on earth, and a provision for a season. And Adam learned words of prayer from his Lord, and God turned unto him, for he is easy to be reconciled and merciful. We said, Get ye all down from hence; hereafter shall there come unto you a direction from me, and whoever shall follow my direction, on them shall no fear come, neither shall they be grieved; but they who shall be unbelievers, and ac-

.cuse our signs of falsehood, they shall be the companions of hell fire, therein shall they remain for ever. O children of Israel, remember my favor wherewith I have favored you; and perform your covenant with me and I will perform my covenant with you; and revere me: and believe in the revelation which I have sent down, confirming that which is with you, and be not the first who believe not therein, neither exchange my signs for a small price; and fear me. Clothe not the truth with vanity, neither conceal the truth against your own knowledge; observe the stated times of prayer, and pay your legal alms, and bow down yourselves with those who bow down. Will ye command men to do justice, and forget your own souls? yet ye read the book of the law: do ye not therefore understand? Ask help with perseverance and prayer; this indeed is grievous, unless to the humble, who seriously think they shall meet their Lord, and that to him they shall return.

O children of Israel, remember my favor wherewith I have favored you, and that I have preferred you above all nations; dread the day wherein one soul shall not make satisfaction for another soul, neither shall any intercession be accepted from them, nor shall any compensation be received, neither shall they be helped. Remember when we delivered you from the people of Pharaoh, who grievously oppressed you, they slew your male children, and let your females live: therein was a great trial from your Lord. And when we divided the sea for you and delivered you, and drowned Pharaoh's people while ye looked on. And when we treated with Moses forty nights; then ye took the calf for your God, and did evil; yet afterward we forgave you, that peradventure ye might give thanks. And when we gave Moses the book of the law, and the distinction between good and evil, that peradventure ye might be directed. And when Moses said unto his people, O my people, verily ye have injured your own souls, by your taking the calf for your God; therefore be turned unto your Creator, and slay those among you who have been guilty of that crime; this will be better for you in the sight of your Creator: and thereupon he turned unto you, for he is easy to be reconciled, and merciful. And when ye said, O Moses, we will not believe thee, until we see God manifestly; therefore a punishment came upon you, while ye looked on; then we raised you to life after ye had been dead, that peradventure ye might give thanks.[5] And we caused clouds to overshadow you, and manna and quails to descend upon you, saying, Eat of the good things which we have given you for food: and they injured not us, but injured their own souls. And when we said, Enter into this city, and eat of the provisions thereof plentifully as ye will; and enter the gate worshiping, and say, Forgiveness! we will pardon you your sins, and give increase unto the welldoers. But the ungodly changed the expression into another, different from what had been spoken unto them; and we sent down upon the ungodly indignation from heaven, because they had transgressed. And when Moses asked drink for his people, we said, Strike the rock with thy rod; and there gushed thereout twelve fountains according to the number of the tribes, and all men knew their respective drinking-place. Eat and drink of the bounty of God, and commit not evil in the earth, acting unjustly. And when ye said, O Moses, we will by no means be satisfied with one kind of food; pray unto thy Lord, therefore for us, that he would produce for us of which the earth bringeth forth, herbs, and cucumbers, and garlic, and lentils, and onions; Moses answered, Will ye exchange that which is better for that which is worse? Get ye down into Egypt, for there shall ye find what ye desire: and they were smitten with vileness and misery, and drew on themselves indignation from God. This they suffered, because they believed not in the signs of God, and killed the prophets unjustly; this, because they rebelled and transgressed.

Surely those who believe, and those who Judaize, and

[5] The persons here meant are said to have been seventy men, who were made choice of by Moses, and heard the voice of God talking with him. But not being satisfied with that, they demanded to see God; whereupon they were all struck dead by lightning, and on Moses's intercession restored to life.

Christians, and Sabians,[6] whoever believeth in God, and the last day, and doth that which is right, they shall have their reward with their Lord; there shall come no fear on them, neither shall they be grieved. Call to mind also when we accepted your covenant, and lifted up the mountain of Sinai over you, saying, Receive the law which we have given you, with a resolution to keep it, and remember that which is contained therein, that ye may beware. After this ye again turned back, so that if it had not been for God's indulgence and mercy toward you, ye had certainly been destroyed.

Moreover ye know what befell those of your nation who transgressed on the Sabbath day,[7] We said unto them, Be ye

[6] From these words, which are repeated in the fifth chapter, several writers have wrongly concluded that the Mohammedans hold it to be the doctrine of their prophet that every man may be saved in his own religion, provided he be sincere and lead a good life. It is true, some of their doctors do agree this to be the purport of the words; but then they say the latitude hereby granted was soon revoked, for that this passage is abrogated by several others in the Koran, which expressly declare that none can be saved who is not of the Mohammedan faith, and particularly by those words of the third chapter, "Whoever followeth any other religion than Islam (*i.e.*, the Mohammedan) it shall not be accepted of him, and at the last day he shall be of those who perish." However, others are of opinion that this passage is not abrogated, but interpret it differently, taking the meaning of it to be that no man, whether he be a Jew, a Christian, or a Sabian, shall be excluded from salvation, provided he quit his erroneous religion and become a Moslem, which they say is intended by the following words, "Whoever believeth in God and the last day, and doth that which is right."

[7] The story to which this passage refers is as follows. In the days of David some Israelites dwelt at Ailah, or Elath, on the Red Sea, where on the night of the Sabbath the fish used to come in great numbers to the shore, and stay there all the Sabbath, to tempt them; but the night following they returned into the sea again. At length some of the inhabitants, neglecting God's command, caught fish on the Sabbath, and dressed and ate them; and afterward cut canals from the sea, for the fish to enter, with sluices, which they shut on the Sabbath, to prevent their return to the sea. The other part of the inhabitants, who strictly observed the Sabbath, used both persuasion and force to stop this impiety, but to no purpose, the offenders growing only more and more obstinate; whereupon David cursed the Sabbath-breakers, and God transformed them into apes. It is said that one going to see a friend of his that was among them, found him in the shape of an ape, moving his eyes about wildly; and asking him whether he was not such a one, the

changed into apes, driven away from the society of men. And we made them an example unto those who were contemporary with them, and unto those who came after them, and a warning to the pious. And when Moses said unto his people, Verily God commandeth you to sacrifice a cow; they answered, Dost thou make a jest of us? Moses said, God forbid that I should be one of the foolish. They said, Pray for us unto thy Lord, that he would show us what cow it is. Moses answered, He saith, She is neither an old cow, nor a young heifer, but of a middle age between both: do ye therefore that which ye are commanded. They said, Pray for us unto thy Lord, that he would show us what color she is of. Moses answered, He saith, She is a red cow, intensely red, her color rejoiceth the beholders. They said, Pray for us unto thy Lord, that he would further show us what cow it is, for several cows with us are like one another, and we, if God please, will be directed. Moses answered, He saith, She is a cow not broken to plow the earth, or water the field, a sound one; there is no blemish in her. They said, Now hast thou brought the truth. Then they sacrificed her; yet they wanted little of leaving it undone. And when ye slew a man, and contended among yourselves concerning him, God brought forth to light that which ye concealed. For we said, Strike the dead body with part of the sacrificed cow: so God raiseth the dead to life, and showeth you his signs, that peradventure ye may understand. Then were your hearts hardened after this, even as stones, or exceeding them in hardness: for from stones have rivers bursted forth, others have been rent in sunder, and water hath issued from them, and others have fallen down for fear of God. But God is not regardless of that which ye do. Do ye therefore desire that the Jews should believe you? yet a part of them heard the word of God, and then perverted it, after they had understood it, against their own conscience. And when they meet the true believers,

ape made a sign with his head that it was he; whereupon the friend said to him, "Did not I advise you to desist?" at which the ape wept. They add that these unhappy people remained three days in this condition, and were afterward destroyed by a wind which swept them all into the sea.

they say, We believe: but when they are privately assembled together, they say, Will ye acquaint them with what God hath revealed unto you, that they may dispute with you concerning it in the presence of your Lord? Do ye not therefore understand? Do not they know that God knoweth that which they conceal as well as that which they publish?

But there are illiterate men among them, who know not the book of the law, but only lying stories, although they think otherwise. And woe unto them who transcribe corruptly the book of the law with their hands, and then say, This is from God: that they may sell it for a small price. Therefore woe unto them because of that which their hands have written; and woe unto them for that which they have gained. They say, The fire of hell shall not touch us but for a certain number of days. Answer, Have ye received any promise from God to that purpose? for God will not act contrary to his promise: or do ye speak concerning God that which ye know not? Verily whoso doth evil, and are encompassed by his iniquity, they shall be the companions of hell fire, they shall remain therein forever: but they do believe and do good works, they shall be the companions of paradise, they shall continue therein forever. Remember also, when we accepted the covenant of the children of Israel, saying, Ye shall not worship any other except God, and ye shall show kindness to your parents and kindred, and to orphans, and to the poor, and speak that which is good unto men, and be constant at prayer, and give alms. Afterward ye turned back, except a few of you, and retired afar off. And when we accepted your covenant, saying, Ye shall not shed your brother's blood, nor dispossess one another of your habitations. Then ye confirmed it, and were witnesses thereto. Afterward ye were they who slew one another, and turned several of your brethren out of their houses, mutually assisting each other against them with injustice and enmity; but if they come captives unto you, ye redeem them: yet it is equally unlawful for you to dispossess them. Do ye therefore believe in part of the book of the law, and reject other parts thereof? But whoso among you doth this shall have no other reward than shame in this life, and on the day of resurrection they shall be sent to a most grievous punishment; for God is not regardless of that which ye do.

These are they who have purchased this present life at the price of that which is to come; wherefore their punishment shall not be mitigated, neither shall they be helped. We formerly delivered the book of the law unto Moses, and caused apostles to succeed him, and gave evident miracles to Jesus the son of Mary, and strengthened him with the holy spirit. Do ye therefore, wherever an apostle cometh unto you with that which your souls desire not, proudly reject him, and accuse some of imposture, and slay others? The Jews say, Our hearts are uncircumcised: but God hath cursed them with their infidelity, therefore few shall believe. And when a book came unto them from God, confirming the scriptures which were with them, although they had before prayed for assistance against those who believed not, yet when that came unto them which they knew to be from God, they would not believe therein: therefore the curse of God shall be on the infidels. For a vile price have they sold their souls, that they should not believe in that which God hath sent down; out of envy, because God sendeth down his favors to such of his servants as he pleaseth: therefore they brought on themselves indignation on indignation; and the unbelievers shall suffer an ignominious punishment. When one saith unto them, Believe in that which God hath sent down: they answer, We believe in that which hath been sent down unto us: and they reject what hath been revealed since, although it be the truth, confirming that which is with them. Say, Why therefore have ye slain the prophets of God in times past, if ye be true believers? Moses formerly came unto you with evident signs, but ye afterward took the calf for your god and did wickedly. And when we accepted your covenant, and lifted the mountain of Sinai over you, saying, Receive the law which we have given you, with a resolution to perform it, and hear; they said, We have heard, and have rebelled: and they were made to drink down the calf into their hearts for their unbelief. Say, A grievous thing hath your faith commanded you, if ye be true believers. Say, If the future mansion with God be prepared peculiarly for you, exclusive of the rest of mankind, wish for death, if ye say truth: but they will never wish for it, because of that which their hands have sent before them; God knoweth the wicked doers; and thou shalt surely find them of all men the most covetous of life, even more than the idolaters: one of them would desire his life to be prolonged a thousand years, but none shall reprieve himself from punishment, that his life may be prolonged: God seeth that which they do. Say, Whoever is an enemy to Gabriel [8] (for he hath caused the Koran to descend on thy heart, by the permission of God, confirming that which was before revealed, a direction, and good tidings to the faithful); whosoever is an enemy to God, or his angels, or his apostles, or to Gabriel, or Michael, verily God is an enemy to the unbelievers. And now we have sent down unto thee evident signs, and none will disbelieve them but the evil-doers. Whenever they make a covenant, will some of them reject it? yea, the greater part of them do not believe. And when there came unto them an apostle from God, confirming that scripture which was with them, some of those to whom the scriptures were given cast the book of God behind their backs, as if they knew it not: and they followed the device which the devils devised against the kingdom of Solomon; [9] and Solomon was not an unbe-

[8] The commentators say that the Jews asked what angel it was that brought the divine revelations to Mohammed; and being told that it was Gabriel, they replied that he was their enemy, and the messenger of wrath and punishment; but if it had been Michael, they would have believed on him, because that angel was their friend, and the messenger of peace and plenty. And on this occasion, they say, this passage was revealed.

[9] The devils having, by God's permission, tempted Solomon without success, they made use of a trick to blast his character. For they wrote several books of magic, and hid them under that prince's throne, and after his death told the chief men that if they wanted to know by what means Solomon had obtained his absolute power over men, genii, and the winds, they should dig under his throne; which having done, they found the aforesaid books, which contained impious superstitions. The better sort refused to learn the evil arts therein delivered, but the common people did; and the priests published this scandalous story of Solomon, which obtained credit among the Jews, till God, says the Moham-

liever; but the devils believed not, they taught men sorcery, and that which was sent down to the two angels at Babel, Harut and Marut: [10] yet those two taught no man until they had said, Verily we are a temptation, therefore be not an unbeliever. So men learned from those two a charm by which they might cause division between a man and his wife; but they hurt none thereby, unless by God's permission; and they learned that which would hurt them, and not profit them; and yet they knew that he who bought that art should have no part in the life to come, and woeful is the price for which they have sold their souls, if they knew it. But if they had believed and feared God, verily the reward they would have had from God would have been better, if they had known it.

O true believers, say not to our apostle, Raina; but say, Ondhorna,[11] and harken: the infidels shall suffer a grievous punishment. It is not the desire of the unbelievers, either among those unto whom the scriptures have been given, or

medans, cleared that King by the mouth of their prophet, declaring that Solomon was no idolater.

[10] Some say only that these were two magicians, or angels sent by God to teach men magic, and to tempt them. But others tell a longer fable; that the angels expressing their surprise at the wickedness of the sons of Adam, after prophets had been sent to them with divine commissions, God bid them choose two out of their own number to be sent down to be judges on earth. Whereupon they pitched upon Harut and Marut, who executed their office with integrity for some time, till Zohara, or the planet Venus, descended and appeared before them in the shape of a beautiful woman, bringing a complaint against her husband (though others say she was a real woman). As soon as they saw her, they fell in love with her, and endeavored to prevail on her to satisfy their desires; but she flew up again into heaven, whither the two angels also returned, but were not admitted. However, on the intercession of a certain pious man, they were allowed to choose whether they would be punished in this life, or in the other; whereupon they chose the former, and now suffer punishment accordingly in Babel, where they are to remain till the day of judgment. They add that if a man has a fancy to learn magic, he may go to them, and hear their voice, but can not see them.

[11] Those two Arabic words have both the same signification, viz., " Look on us "; and are a kind of salutation. Mohammed had a great aversion to the first, because the Jews frequently used it in derision, it being a word of reproach in their tongue. They alluded, it seems, to the Hebrew verb *ruá*, which signifies to " be bad or mischievous."

among the idolaters, that any good should be sent down unto you from your Lord: but God will appropriate his mercy unto whom he pleaseth; for God is exceeding beneficent. Whatever verse we shall abrogate, or cause thee to forget, we will bring a better than it, or one like unto it. Dost thou not know that God is almighty? Dost thou not know that unto God belongeth the kingdom of heaven and earth? neither have ye any protector or helper except God. Will ye require of your apostle according to that which was formerly required of Moses? but he that hath exchanged faith for infidelity hath already erred from the straight way. Many of those unto whom the scriptures have been given desire to render you again unbelievers, after ye have believed; out of envy from their souls, even after the truth is become manifest unto them; but forgive them and avoid them, till God shall send his command; for God is omnipotent.

Be constant in prayer, and give alms; and what good ye have sent before for your souls ye shall find it with God; surely God seeth that which ye do. They say, Verily none shall enter paradise, except they who are Jews or Christians: this is their wish. Say, Produce your proof of this, if ye speak truth. Nay, but he who resigneth himself to God, and doth that which is right, he shall have his reward with his Lord; there shall come no fear on them, neither shall they be grieved. The Jews say, The Christians are grounded on nothing; and the Christians say, the Jews are grounded on nothing: yet they both read the scriptures. So likewise say they who know not the scripture, according to their saying. But God shall judge between them on the day of the resurrection, concerning that about which they now disagree. Who is more unjust than he who prohibiteth the temples of God, that his name should be remembered therein, and who hasteth to destroy them? These men can not enter therein, but with fear: they shall have shame in this world, and in the next a grievous punishment. To God belongeth the east and the west; therefore, whithersoever ye turn yourselves to pray, there is the face of God; for God is omnipresent and omniscient. They say, God hath begotten children: God forbid!

To him belongeth whatever is in heaven, and on earth; all is possessed by him, the Creator of heaven and earth; and when he decreeth a thing, he only saith unto it, Be, and it is. And they who know not the scriptures say, Unless God speak unto us, or thou show us a sign, we will not believe. So said those before them, according to their saying: their hearts resemble each other. We have already shown manifest signs unto people who firmly believe; we have sent thee in truth, a bearer of good tidings, and a preacher; and thou shalt not be questioned concerning the companions of hell. But the Jews will not be pleased with thee, neither the Christians, until thou follow their religion; say, The direction of God is the true direction. And verily if thou follow their desires, after the knowledge which hath been given thee, thou shalt find no patron or protector against God. They to whom we have given the book of the Koran, and who read it with its true reading, they believe therein; and whoever believeth not therein, they shall perish.

O children of Israel, remember my favor wherewith I have favored you, and that I have preferred you before all nations; and dread the day wherein one soul shall not make satisfaction for another soul, neither shall any compensation be accepted from them, nor shall any intercession avail, neither shall they be helped. Remember when the Lord tried Abraham by certain words, which he fulfilled: God said, Verily I will constitute thee a model of religion unto mankind; he answered, And also of my posterity; God said, My covenant doth not comprehend the ungodly. And when we appointed the holy house of Mecca to be the place of resort for mankind, and a place of security; and said, Take the station of Abraham for a place of prayer; and we covenanted with Abraham and Ismael, that they should cleanse my house for those who should compass it, and those who should be devoutly assiduous there, and those who should bow down and worship. And when Abraham said, Lord, make this a territory of security, and bounteously bestow fruits on its inhabitants, such of them as believe in God and the last day; God answered, And whoever believeth not, I will bestow on him little, afterward I will drive him to the punishment of hell fire; an ill journey shall it be! And when Abraham and Ismael raised the foundations of the house, saying, Lord, accept it from us, for thou art he who heareth and knoweth: Lord, make us also resigned [12] unto thee, and of our posterity a people resigned unto thee, and show us our holy ceremonies, and be turned unto us, for thou art easy to be reconciled, and merciful: Lord, send them likewise an apostle from among them, who may declare thy signs unto them, and teach them the book of the Koran and wisdom, and may purify them; for thou art mighty and wise. Who will be averse to the religion of Abraham, but he whose mind is infatuated? Surely we have chosen him in this world, and in that which is to come he shall be one of the righteous. When his Lord said unto him, Resign thyself unto me; he answered, I have resigned myself unto the Lord of all creatures. And Abraham bequeathed this religion to his children, and Jacob did the same, saying, My children, verily God hath chosen this religion for you, therefore die not, unless ye also be resigned. Were ye present when Jacob was at the point of death? when he said to his sons, Whom will ye worship after me? They answered, We will worship thy God, and the God of thy father, Abraham, and Ismael, and Isaac, one God, and to him will we be resigned. That people are now passed away, they have what they have gained, and yet shall have what we gain; and ye shall not be questioned concerning that which they have done. They say, Become Jews or Christians that ye may be directed. Say, Nay, we follow the religion of Abraham the orthodox, who was no idolater. Say, We believe in God, and that which hath been sent down unto us, and that which hath been sent down unto Abraham, and Ismael, and Isaac, and Jacob, and the tribes, and that which was delivered unto Moses, and Jesus, and that which was delivered unto the prophets from their Lord: We make no distinction between any of them, and to God are we resigned. Now if they believe according to what ye believe, they are surely directed;

[12] The Arabic word is *Moslemuna*, in the singular *Moslem*, which the Mohammedans take as a title peculiar to themselves.

but if they turn back, they are in schism. God shall support thee against them, for he is the hearer, the wise. The baptism of God have we received, and who is better than God to baptize? him do we worship. Say, Will ye dispute with us concerning God, who is our Lord, and your Lord? we have our works, and ye have your works, and unto him are we sincerely devoted. Will ye say, Truly Abraham, and Ismael, and Isaac, and Jacob, and the tribes were Jews or Christians? Say, Are ye wiser, or God? And who is more unjust than he who hideth the testimony which he hath received from God? But God is not regardless of that which ye do. That people are passed away, they have what they have gained, and ye shall have what ye gain, nor shall ye be questioned concerning that which they have done.

The foolish men will say, What hath turned them from their *keblah*, toward which they formerly prayed?[13] Say, Unto God belongeth the east and the west: he directeth whom he pleaseth into the right way. Thus have we placed you, O Arabians, an intermediate nation, that ye may be witnesses against the rest of mankind, and that the apostle may be a witness against you. We appointed the *keblah* toward which thou didst formerly pray, only that we might know him who followeth the apostle, from him who turneth back on his heels; though this change seem a great matter, unless unto those whom God hath directed. But God will not render your faith of none effect; for God is gracious and merciful unto man. We have seen thee turn about thy face toward heaven with uncertainty, but we will cause thee to turn thyself toward a *keblah* that will please thee. Turn therefore

[13] At first, Mohammed and his followers observed no particular rite in turning their faces toward any certain place, or quarter of the world, when they prayed; it being declared to be perfectly indifferent. Afterward, when the prophet fled to Medina, he directed them to turn toward the temple of Jerusalem, which continued to be their *keblah* for six or seven months; but either finding the Jews too intractable, or despairing otherwise to gain the pagan Arabs, who could not forget their respect to the temple of Mecca, he ordered that prayers for the future should be toward the last. This change was made in the second year of the Hegira, and occasioned many to fall from him, taking offense at his inconstancy.

thy face toward the holy temple of Mecca; and wherever ye be, turn your faces toward that place. They to whom the scripture hath been given know this to be truth from their Lord. God is not regardless of that which ye do. Verily although thou shouldest show unto those to whom the scripture hath been given all kinds of signs, yet they will not follow thy *keblah*, neither shalt thou follow their *keblah*; nor will one part of them follow the *keblah* of the other. And if thou follow their desires, after the knowledge which hath been given thee, verily thou wilt become one of the ungodly. They to whom we have given the scripture know our apostle, even as they know their own children; but some of them hide the truth, against their own knowledge. Truth is from thy Lord, therefore thou shalt not doubt. Every sect hath a certain tract of heaven to which they turn themselves in prayer; but do ye strive to run after good things: wherever ye be, God will bring you all back at the resurrection, for God is almighty. And from what place soever thou comest forth, turn thy face toward the holy temple; for this is truth from thy Lord; neither is God regardless of that which ye do. From what place soever thou comest forth, turn thy face toward the holy temple; and wherever ye be, thitherward turn your faces, lest men have matter of dispute against you; but as for those among them who are unjust doers, fear them not, but fear me, that I may accomplish my grace upon you, and that ye may be directed. As we have sent unto you an apostle from among you, to rehearse our signs unto you, and to purify you, and to teach you the book of the Koran and wisdom, and to teach you that which ye knew not: therefore remember me, and I will remember you, and give thanks unto me, and be not unbelievers.

O true believers, beg assistance with patience and prayer, for God is with the patient. And say not of those who are slain in fight for the religion of God, that they are dead; yea, they are living: but ye do not understand. We will surely prove you by afflicting you in some measure with fear, and hunger, and decrease of wealth, and loss of lives, and scarcity of fruits: but bear good tidings unto the patient, who when a misfortune befalleth them, say, We are God's, and unto him shall we surely return. Upon them shall be blessings from their Lord and mercy, and they are the rightly directed. Moreover Safa and Merwah are two of the monuments of God: whoever therefore goeth on pilgrimage to the temple of Mecca or visiteth it, it shall be no crime in him if he compass them both.[14] And as for him who voluntarily performeth a good work, verily God is grateful and knowing. They who conceal any of the evident signs, or the direction which we have sent down, after what we have manifested unto men in the scripture, God shall curse them; and they who curse shall curse them. But as for those who repent and amend, and make known what they concealed, I will be turned unto them, for I am easy to be reconciled and merciful. Surely they who believe not, and die in their unbelief, upon them shall be the curse of God, and of the angels, and of all men; they shall remain under it forever, their punishment shall not be alleviated, neither shall they be regarded.

Your God is one God, there is no God but he, the most merciful. Now in the creation of heaven and earth, and the vicissitude of night and day, and in the ship which saileth in the sea, laden with what is profitable for mankind, and in the rain-water which God sendeth from heaven, quickening thereby the dead earth, and replenishing the same with all sorts of cattle, and in the change of winds, and the clouds that are compelled to do service between heaven and earth, are signs to people of understanding: yet some men take idols beside God, and love them as with the love due to God; but the true believers are more fervent in love toward God.

Oh that they who act unjustly did perceive, when they behold their punishment, that all power belongeth unto God, and that he is severe in punishing! When those who have been followed shall separate themselves from their followers, and shall see the punishment, and the cords of relation be-

---

[14] Safa and Merwa are two mountains near Mecca, whereon was anciently two idols, to which the pagan Arabs used to pay a superstitious veneration. Jallalo'ddin says this passage was revealed because the followers of Mohammed made a scruple of going round these mountains, as the idolaters did.

tween them shall be cut in sunder; the followers shall say, If we could return to life, we would separate ourselves from them, as they have now separated themselves from us. So God will show them their works; they shall sigh grievously, and shall not come forth from the fire of hell. O men, eat of that which is lawful and good on the earth; and tread not in the steps of the devil, for he is your open enemy. Verily he commandeth you evil and wickedness, and that ye should say that of God which ye know not. And when it is said unto them who believe not, Follow that which God hath sent down; they answer, Nay, but we will follow that which we found our fathers practise. What? though their fathers knew nothing, and were not rightly directed? The unbelievers are like unto one who crieth aloud to that which heareth not so much as his calling, or the sound of his voice. They are deaf, dumb, and blind, therefore they do not understand.

O true believers, eat of the good things which we have bestowed on you for food, and return thanks unto God, if ye serve him. Verily he hath forbidden you to eat that which dieth of itself, and blood, and swine's flesh, and that on which any other name but God's hath been invocated. But he who is forced by necessity, not lusting, nor returning to transgress, it shall be no crime in him if he eat of those things, for God is gracious and merciful.

Moreover they who conceal any part of the scripture which God hath sent down unto them, and sell it for a small price, they shall swallow into their bellies nothing but fire; God shall not speak unto them on the day of resurrection, neither shall he purify them, and they shall suffer a grievous punishment. These are they who have sold direction for error, and pardon for punishment: but how great will their suffering be in the fire! This they shall endure, because God sent down the book of the Koran with truth, and they who disagree concerning that book are certainly in a wide mistake.

It is not righteousness that ye turn your faces in prayer toward the east and the west, but righteousness is of him who believeth in God, and the last day, and the angels, and the scriptures, and the prophets; who giveth money for God's sake unto his kindred, and unto orphans, and the needy, and the stranger, and those who ask, and for redemption of captives; who is constant at prayer, and giveth alms; and of those who perform their covenant, when they have covenanted, and who behave themselves patiently in adversity, and hardships, and in time of violence: these are they who are true, and these are they who fear God.

O true believers, the law of retaliation is ordained you for the slain: the free shall die for the free, and the servant for the servant, and a woman for a woman: but he whom his brother shall forgive may be prosecuted, and obliged to make satisfaction according to what is just, and a fine shall be set on him with humanity. This is indulgence from your Lord, and mercy. And he who shall transgress after this, by killing the murderer, shall suffer a grievous punishment. And in this law of retaliation ye have life, O ye of understanding, that peradventure ye may fear.

It is ordained you, when any of you is at the point of death, if he leave any goods, that he bequeath a legacy to his parents, and kindred, according to what shall be reasonable. This is a duty incumbent on those who fear God. But he who shall change the legacy, after he hath heard it bequeathed by the dying person, surely the sin thereof shall be on those who change it, for God is he who heareth and knoweth. Howbeit he who apprehendeth from the testator any mistake or injustice, and shall compose the matter between them, that shall be no crime in him, for God is gracious and merciful.

O true believers, a fast is ordained you, as it was ordained unto those before you, that ye may fear God. A certain number of days shall ye fast: but he among you who shall be sick, or on a journey, shall fast an equal number of other days. And those who can keep it, and do not, must redeem their neglect by maintaining of a poor man. And he who voluntarily dealeth better with the poor man than he is obliged, this shall be better for him. But if ye fast it will be better for you, if ye knew it. The month of Ramadan shall ye fast, in which the Koran was sent down from heaven, a direction unto men, and declarations of direction, and the distinction between good and evil.   Therefore let him among you who shall be present in this month fast the same month; but he who shall be sick, or on a journey, shall fast the like number of other days.   God would make this an ease unto you, and would not make it a difficulty unto you; that ye may fufil the number of days, and glorify God, for that he hath directed you, and that ye may give thanks.   When my servants ask thee concerning me, Verily I am near; I will hear the prayer of him that prayeth, when he prayeth unto me: but let them harken unto me, and believe in me, that they may be rightly directed.

It is lawful for you on the night of the fast to go in unto your wives, they are a garment unto you, and ye are a garment unto them.   God knoweth that ye defraud yourselves therein, wherefore he turneth unto you, and forgiveth you. Now therefore go in unto them; and earnestly desire that which God ordaineth you, and eat and drink, until ye can plainly distinguish a white thread from a black thread by the daybreak: then keep the fast until night, and go not in unto them, but be constantly present in the places of worship. These are the prescribed bounds of God, therefore draw not near them to transgress them.   Thus God declareth his signs unto men, that ye may fear him.

Consume not your wealth among yourselves in vain; nor present it unto judges, that ye may devour part of men's substance unjustly, against your own consciences.   They will ask thee concerning the phases of the moon.   Answer, They are times appointed unto men, and to show the season of the pilgrimage to Mecca.   It is not righteousness that ye enter your houses by the back part thereof, but righteousness is of him who feareth God.   Therefore enter your houses by their doors; and fear God, that ye may be happy.

And fight for the religion of God against those who fight against you, but transgress not by attacking them first, for God loveth not the transgressors.   And kill them wherever ye find them, and turn them out of that whereof they have dispossessed you; for temptation to idolatry is more grievous than slaughter: yet fight not against them in the holy temple, until they attack you therein; but if they attack you, slay them there. This shall be the reward of the infidels. But if they desist, God is gracious and merciful. Fight therefore against them, until there be no temptation to idolatry, and the religion be God's: but if they desist, then let there be no hostility, except against the ungodly. A sacred month for a sacred month, and the holy limits of Mecca, if they attack you therein, do ye also attack them therein in retaliation; and whoever transgresseth against you by so doing, do ye transgress against him in like manner as he hath transgressed against you, and fear God, and know that God is with those who fear him. Contribute out of your substance toward the defense of the religion of God, and throw not yourselves with your own hands into perdition; and do good, for God loveth those who do good.

Perform the pilgrimage of Mecca, and the visitation of God; and if ye be besieged, send that offering which shall be the easiest; and shave not your heads, until your offering reacheth the place of sacrifice. But whoever among you is sick, or is troubled with any distemper of the head, must redeem the shaving of his head by fasting, or alms, or some offering. When ye are secure from enemies, he who tarrieth in the visitation of the temple of Mecca until the pilgrimage shall bring that offering which shall be the easiest. But he who findeth not anything to offer shall fast three days in the pilgrimage, and seven when ye are returned; they shall be ten days complete. This is incumbent on him whose family shall not be present at the holy temple. And fear God, and know that God is severe in punishing. The pilgrimage must be performed in the known months; whosoever therefore purposeth to go on pilgrimage therein, let him not know a woman, nor transgress, nor quarrel in the pilgrimage. The good which ye do, God knoweth it. Make provision for your journey; but the best provision is piety: and fear me, O ye of understanding. It shall be no crime in you, if ye seek an increase from your Lord, by trading during the pilgrimage. And when ye go in procession from Arafat, remember God near the holy monument; [15] and remember him for that he hath directed you, although ye were before this of the number of those who go astray. Therefore go in procession from whence the people go in procession, and ask pardon of God, for God is gracious and merciful. And when ye have finished your holy ceremonies, remember God, according as ye remember your fathers, or with a more reverent commemoration.

There are some men who say, O Lord, give us our portion in this world; but such shall have no portion in the next life: and there are others who say, O Lord, give us good in this world, and also good in the next world, and deliver us from the torment of hell fire. They shall have a portion of that which they have gained: God is swift in taking an account. Remember God appointed the number of days: but if any haste to depart from the valley of Mina in two days, it shall be no crime in him. And if any tarry longer, it shall be no crime in him, in him who feareth God. Therefore fear God, and know that unto him ye shall be gathered.

There is a man who causeth thee to marvel [16] by his speech concerning this present life, and calleth God to witness that which is in his heart, yet he is most intent in opposing thee; and when he turneth away from thee, he hasteth to act corruptly in the earth, and to destroy that which is sown, and springeth up: but God loveth not corrupt doing. And if one say unto him, Fear God; pride seizeth him, together with wickedness; but hell shall be his reward, and an unhappy couch shall it be. There is also a man who selleth his soul for the sake of those things which are pleasing unto God; and God is gracious unto his servants. O true believers, enter into the true religion wholly, and follow not the steps of

[15] In Arabic, *al Masher al haram*. It is a mountain in the farther part of Mozdalifa, where it is said Mohammed stood praying and praising God, till his face became extremely shining.

[16] This person was Al Akhnas Ebn Shoraik, a fair-spoken dissembler, who swore that he believed in Mohammed, and pretended to be one of his friends, and to contemn this world. But God here reveals to the prophet his hypocrisy and wickedness.

Satan, for he is your open enemy. If ye have slipped after the declarations of our will have come unto you, know that God is mighty and wise. Do the infidels expect less than that God should come down to them overshadowed with clouds, and the angels also? but the thing is decreed, and to God shall all things return. Ask the children of Israel how many evident signs we have showed them; and whoever shall change the grace of God, after it shall have come unto him, verily God will be severe in punishing him. The present life was ordained for those who believe not, and they laugh the faithful to scorn; but they who fear God shall be above them, on the day of the resurrection: for God is bountiful unto whom he pleaseth without measure.

Mankind was of one faith, and God sent prophets bearing good tidings, and denouncing threats, and sent down with them the scripture in truth, that it might judge between men of that concerning which they disagreed: and none disagreed concerning it, except those to whom the same scriptures were delivered, after the declarations of God's will had come unto them, out of envy among themselves. And God directed those who believed to that truth concerning which they disagreed, by his will: for God directeth whom he pleaseth into the right way. Did ye think ye should enter paradise, when as yet no such thing had happened unto you, as hath happened unto those who have been before you? They suffered calamity and tribulation, and were afflicted; so that the apostle, and they who believed with him, said, When will the help of God come? Is not the help of God nigh? They will ask thee what they shall bestow in alms: Answer, The good which ye bestow, let it be given to parents, and kindred, and orphans, and the poor, and the stranger. Whatsoever good ye do, God knoweth it.

War is enjoined you against the infidels; but this is hateful unto you: yet perchance ye hate a thing which is better for you, and perchance ye love a thing which is worse for you: but God knoweth and ye know not. They will ask thee concerning the sacred month, whether they may war therein: Answer, To war therein is grievous; but to obstruct the way of God, and infidelity toward him, and to keep men from the holy temple, and to drive out his people thence, is more grievous in the sight of God, and the temptation to idolatry is more grievous than to kill in the sacred months. They will not cease to war against you, until they turn you from your religion, if they be able: but whoever among you shall turn back from his religion, and die an infidel, their works shall be in vain in this world and the next; they shall be the companions of hell fire, they shall remain therein forever. But they who believe, and who fly for the sake of religion, and fight in God's cause, they shall hope for the mercy of God; for God is gracious and merciful.

They will ask thee concerning wine and lots: Answer, in both there is great sin, and also some things of use unto men; but their sinfulness is greater than their use. They will ask thee also what they shall bestow in alms: Answer, What ye have to spare. Thus God showeth his signs unto you, that peradventure ye might seriously think of this present world, and of the next. They will also ask thee concerning orphans: Answer, To deal righteously with them is best; and if ye intermeddle with the management of what belongs to them, do them no wrong; they are your brethren: God knoweth the corrupt dealer from the righteous; and if God please, he will surely distress you, for God is mighty and wise.

Marry not women who are idolaters, until they believe: verily a maid-servant who believeth is better than an idolatress, although she please you more. And give not women who believe in marriage to the idolaters, until they believe; for verily a servant who is a true believer is better than an idolater, though he please you more. They invite unto hell fire, but God inviteth unto paradise and pardon through his will, and declareth his signs unto men, that they may remember. They will ask thee also concerning the courses of women: Answer, They are a pollution: therefore separate yourselves from women in their courses, and go not near them until they be cleansed. But when they are cleansed, go in unto them as God hath commanded you, for God loveth those who repent, and loveth those who are clean. Your wives are your tillage; go in therefore unto your tillage in what manner soever ye will: and do first some act that may be profitable unto your souls; and fear God, and know that ye must meet him; and bear good tidings unto the faithful.

Make not God the object of your oaths, that ye will deal justly, and be devout, and make peace among men; for God is he who heareth and knoweth. God will not punish you for an inconsiderate word in your oaths; but he will punish you for that which your hearts have assented unto: God is merciful and gracious. They who vow to abstain from their wives are allowed to wait four months: but if they go back from their vow, verily God is gracious and merciful; and if they resolve on a divorce, God is he who heareth and knoweth.

The women who are divorced shall wait concerning themselves until they have their courses thrice, and it shall not be lawful for them to conceal that which God hath created in their wombs, if they believe in God and the last day; and their husbands will act more justly to bring them back at this time, if they desire a reconciliation. The women ought also to behave toward their husbands in like manner as their husbands should behave toward them, according to what is just: but the men ought to have a superiority over them. God is mighty and wise. Ye may divorce your wives twice; and then either retain them with humanity, or dismiss them with kindness. But it is not lawful for you to take away anything of what ye have given them, unless both fear that they can not observe the ordinances of God. And if ye fear that they can not observe the ordinances of God, it shall be no crime in either of them on account of that for which the wife shall redeem herself. These are the ordinances of God; therefore transgress them not, for whoever transgresseth the ordinances of God, they are unjust doers. But if the husband divorce her a third time, she shall not be lawful for him again, until she marry another husband. But if he also divorce her, it shall be no crime in them, if they return to each other, if they think they can observe the ordinances of God; and these are the ordinances of God, he declareth them to people of understanding.

But when ye divorce women, and they have fulfilled their prescribed time, either retain them with humanity, or dismiss them with kindness; and retain them not by violence, so that ye transgress; for he who doth this surely injureth his own soul. And make not the signs of God a jest: but remember God's favor toward you, and that he hath sent down unto you the book of the Koran, and wisdom, admonishing you thereby; and fear God, and know that God is omniscient.

But when ye have divorced your wives, and they have fulfilled their prescribed time, hinder them not from marrying their husbands, when they have agreed among themselves according to what is honorable. This is given in admonition unto him among you who believeth in God, and the last day. This is most righetous for you, and most pure. God knoweth, but yet know not. Mothers after they are divorced shall give suck unto their children two full years, to him who desireth the time of giving such to be completed; and the father shall be obliged to maintain them and clothe them in the meantime, according to that which shall be reasonable. No person shall be obliged beyond his ability. A mother shall not be compelled to what is unreasonable on account of her child, nor her father on account of his child. And the heir of the father shall be obliged to do in like manner. But if they choose to wean the child before the end of two years, by common consent and on mutual consideration, it shall be no crime in them. And if ye have a mind to provide a nurse for your children, it shall be no crime in you, in case ye fully pay what ye offer her, according to that which is just. And fear God, and know that God seeth whatever ye do.

Such of you as die, and leave wives, their wives must wait concerning themselves four months and ten days, and when they shall have fulfilled their term it shall be no crime in you, for that which they shall do with themselves, according to what is reasonable. God well knoweth that which ye do. And it shall be no crime in you, whether ye make public overtures of marriage unto such women, within the said four months and ten days, or whether ye conceal such your designs in your minds: God knoweth that ye will remember them.

But make no promise unto them privately, unless ye speak honorable words; and resolve not on the knot of marriage, until the prescribed time be accomplished; and know that God knoweth that which is in your minds, therefore beware of him, and know that God is gracious and merciful. It shall be no crime in you, if ye divorce your wives, so long as ye have not touched them, nor settled any dowry on them. And provide for them (he who is at his ease must provide according to his circumstances, and he who is straitened according to his circumstances) necessaries, according to what shall be reasonable. This is a duty incumbent on the righteous. But if ye divorce them before ye have touched them, and have already settled a dowry on them, ye shall give them half of what ye have settled, unless they release any part, or he release part in whose hand the knot of marriage is; and if ye release the whole, it will approach nearer unto piety.

And forget not liberality among you, for God seeth that which ye do. Carefully observe the appointed prayers, and the middle prayer, and be assiduous therein, with devotion toward God. But if ye fear any danger, pray on foot or on horseback; and when ye are safe, remember God, how he hath taught you what as yet ye knew not. And such of you as shall die and leave wives ought to bequeath their wives a year's maintenance, without putting them out of their houses; but if they go out voluntarily, it shall be no crime in you, for that which they shall do with themselves, according to what shall be reasonable; God is mighty and wise. And unto those who are divorced, a reasonable provision is also due; this is a duty incumbent on those who fear God. Thus God declareth his signs unto you, that ye may understand.

Hast thou not considered those who left their habitations (and they were thousands) for fear of death? [17] And God

17 These were some of the children of Israel, who abandoned their dwellings because of a pestilence, or, as others say, to avoid serving in a religious war; but, as they fled, God struck them all dead in a certain valley. About eight days or more after, when their bodies were corrupted, the prophet Ezekiel, the son of Buzi, happening to pass that way, at the sight of their bones wept; whereupon God said to him, " Call to them, O Ezekiel, and I will restore them to life." And accordingly

said unto them, Die; then he restored them to life, for God is gracious toward mankind; but the greater part of men do not give thanks. Fight for the religion of God, and know that God is he who heareth and knoweth. Who is he that will lend unto God on good usury? verily he will double it unto him manifold; for God contracteth and extendeth his hand as he pleaseth, and to him shall ye return.

Hast thou not considered the assembly of the children of Israel, after the time of Moses; when they said unto their prophet Samuel, Set a king over us, that we may fight for the religion of God? The prophet answered, If ye are enjoined to go to war, will ye be near refusing to fight? They answered, And what should ail us that we should not fight for the religion of God, seeing we are dispossessed of our habitations, and deprived of our children? But when they were enjoined to go to war, they turned back, except a few of them: and God knew the ungodly. And their prophet said unto them, Verily God hath set Talut king over you: they answered, How shall he reign over us, seeing we are more worthy of the kingdom than he, neither is he possessed of great riches? Samuel said, Verily God hath chosen him before you, and hath caused him to increase in knowledge and stature, for God giveth his kingdom unto whom he pleaseth; God is bounteous and wise. And their prophet said unto them, Verily the sign of his kingdom shall be, that the ark shall come unto you: therein shall be tranquillity from your Lord, and the relics which have been left by the family of Moses, and the family of Aaron; the angels shall bring it. Verily this shall be a sign unto you, if ye believe. And when Talut departed with his soldiers, he said, Verily God will prove you by the river: for he who drinketh thereof shall not be on my side (but he who shall not taste thereof he shall be on my side) except he who drinketh a draught out of his hand. And they drank thereof, except a few of them. And

on the prophet's call they all arose, and lived several years after; but they retained the color and stench of dead corpses as long as they lived, and the clothes they wore changed as black as pitch, which qualities they transmitted to their posterity.

when they had passed the river, he and those who believed with him, they said, We have no strength to-day against Jalut and his forces. But they who considered that they should meet God at the resurrection, said, How often hath a small army discomfited a great army, by the will of God? and God is with those who patiently persevere. And when they went forth to battle against Jalut and his forces, they said, O Lord, pour on us patience, and confirm our feet, and help us against the unbelieving people. Therefore they discomfited them, by the will of God, and David slew Jalut. And God gave him the kingdom and wisdom, and taught him his will; and if God had not prevented men, the one by the other, verily the earth had been corrupted: but God is beneficent toward his creatures. These are the signs of God: we rehearse them unto thee with truth, and thou art surely one of those who have been sent by God.

These are the apostles; we have preferred some of them before others: some of them hath God spoken unto, and hath exalted the degree of others of them. And he gave unto Jesus the son of Mary manifest signs, and strengthened him with the holy spirit. And if God had pleased, they who came after those apostles would not have contended among themselves, after manifest signs had been shown unto them. But they fell to variance; therefore some of them believed, and some of them believed not; and if God had so pleased, they would not have contended among themselves, but God doth what he will. O true believers, give alms of that which we have bestowed on you, before the day cometh wherein there shall be no merchandizing, nor friendship, nor intercession. The infidels are unjust doers.

God! there is no God but he; the living, the self-subsisting: neither slumber nor sleep seizeth him; to him belongeth whatsoever is in heaven, and on earth. Who is he that can intercede with him, but through his good pleasure? He knoweth that which is past, and that which is to come unto them, and they shall not comprehend anything of his knowledge, but so far as he pleaseth. His throne is extended over heaven and earth, and the preservation of both is no burden unto him. He is the high, the mighty.[18]

Let there be no violence in religion. Now is right direction manifestly distinguished from deceit: whoever therefore shall deny Tagut, and believe in God, he shall surely take hold on a strong handle, which shall not be broken; God is he who heareth and seeth. God is the patron of those who believe; he shall lead them out of darkness into light: but as to those who believe not, their patrons are Tagut; they shall lead them from the light into darkness; they shall be the companions of hell fire, they shall remain therein forever.

Hast thou not considered him who disputed with Abraham concerning his Lord, because God had given him the kingdom? When Abraham said, My Lord is he who giveth life, and killeth: he answered, I give life, and I kill. Abraham said, Verily God bringeth the sun from the east, now do thou bring it from the west. Whereupon the infidel was confounded; for God directeth not the ungodly people. Or hast thou not considered how he behaved who passed by a city which had been destroyed, even to her foundations? He said, How shall God quicken this city, after she hath been dead? And God caused him to die for an hundred years, and afterward raised him to life. And God said, How long hast thou tarried here? He answered, A day, or part of a day. God said, Nay, thou hast tarried here an hundred years. Now look on thy food and the drink, they are not yet corrupted; and look on thine ass: and this have we done that we might make thee a sign unto men. And look on the bones of thine ass, how we raise them, and afterward clothe them with flesh. And when this was shown unto him, he said, I know that God is able to do all things. And when Abraham said, O Lord, show me how thou wilt raise the dead; God said, Dost thou not yet believe? He answered, Yea; but I ask this

[18.] This paragraph contains a magnificent description of the divine majesty and providence; but it must not be supposed the translation comes up to the dignity of the original. This passage is justly admired by the Mohammedans, who recite it in their prayers; and some of them wear it about them, engraved on an agate or other precious stone.

that my heart may rest at ease. God said, take therefore four birds and divide them; then lay a part of them on every mountain; then call them, and they shall come swiftly unto thee: and know that God is mighty and wise. The similitude of those who lay out their substance for advancing the religion of God is as a grain of corn which produceth seven ears, and in every ear an hundred grains; for God giveth twofold unto whom he pleaseth: God is bounteous and wise.

They who lay out their substance for the religion of God, and afterward follow not what they have so laid out by reproaches or mischief, they shall have their reward with their Lord; upon them shall no fear come, neither shall they be grieved. A fair speech, and to forgive, is better than alms followed by mischief. God is rich and merciful.

O true believers, make not your alms of none effect by reproaching, or mischief, as he who layeth out what he hath to appear unto me to give alms, and believeth not in God and the last day. The likeness of such a one is as a flint covered with earth, on which a violent rain falleth, and leaveth it hard. They can not prosper in anything which they have gained, for God directeth not the unbelieving people. And the likeness of those who lay out their substance from a desire to please God, and for an establishment for their souls, is as a garden on a hill, on which a violent rain falleth, and it bringeth forth its fruits twofold; and if a violent rain falleth not on it, yet the dew falleth thereon: and God seeth that which ye do. Doth any of you desire to have a garden of palm-trees and vines, through which rivers flow, wherein he may have all kinds of fruits, and that he may attain to old age, and have a weak offspring? then a violent fiery wind shall strike it, so that it shall be burned. Thus God declareth his signs unto you, that ye may consider.

O true believers, bestow alms of the good things which ye have gained, and of that which we have produced for you out of the earth, and choose not the bad thereof, to give it in alms, such as ye would not accept yourselves, otherwise than by connivance: and know that God is rich and worthy to be praised. The devil threateneth you with poverty, and commandeth you filthy covetousness; but God promiseth you pardon from himself and abundance: God is bounteous and wise. He giveth wisdom unto whom he pleaseth; and he unto whom wisdom is given hath received much good: but none will consider, except the wise of heart. And whatever alms ye shall give, or whatever vow ye shall vow, verily, God knoweth it; but the ungodly shall have none to help them. If ye make your alms to appear, it is well; but if ye conceal them and give them unto the poor, this will be better for you, and will atone for your sins: and God is well informed of that which ye do. The direction of them belongeth not unto thee; but God directeth whom he pleaseth. The good that ye shall give in alms shall redound unto yourselves; and ye shall not give unless out of desire of seeing the face of God. And what good thing ye shall give in alms, it shall be repaid you, and ye shall not be treated unjustly; unto the poor who are wholly employed in fighting for the religion of God, and can not go to and fro in the earth; whom the ignorant man thinketh rich, because of their modesty: thou shalt know them by this mark, they ask not men with importunity; and what good ye shall give in alms, verily God knoweth it. They who distribute alms of their substance night and day, in private and in public, shall have their reward with the Lord; on them shall no fear come, neither shall they be grieved.

They who devour usury shall not arise from the dead, but as he ariseth whom Satan hath infected by a touch: this shall happen to them because they say, Truly selling is but as usury: and yet God hath permitted selling and forbidden usury. He therefore who, when there cometh unto him an admonition from his Lord, abstaineth from usury for the future, shall have what is past forgiven him, and his affair belongest unto God. But whoever returneth to usury, they shall be the companions of hell fire, they shall continue therein forever. God shall take his blessing from usury, and shall increase alms: for God loveth no infidel, or ungodly person. But they who believe and do that which is right, and observe the stated times of prayer, and pay their legal alms, they shall have their reward with their Lord: there shall come no fear on them, neither shall they be grieved.   O true believers, fear God, and remit that which remaineth of usury, if ye really believe; but if ye do it not, harken unto war, which is declared against you from God and his apostle: yet if ye repent, ye shall have the capital of your money.   Deal not unjustly with others, and ye shall not be dealt with unjustly.   If there be any debtor under a difficulty of paying his debt, let his creditor wait till it be easy for him to do it; but if ye remit it as alms, it will be better for you, if ye knew it.   And fear the day wherein ye shall return unto God; then shall every soul be paid what it hath gained, and they shall not be treated unjustly.

O true believers, when ye bind yourselves one to the other in a debt for a certain time, write it down; and let a writer write between you according to justice, and let not the writer refuse writing according to what God hath taught him; but let him write, and let him who oweth the debt dictate, and let him fear God his Lord, and not diminish ought thereof.   But if he who oweth the debt be foolish, or weak, or be not able to dictate himself, let his agent dictate according to equity; and call to witness two witnesses of your neighboring men; but if there be not two men, let there be a man and two women of those whom ye shall choose for witnesses: if one of those women should mistake, the other of them will cause her to recollect.   And the witnesses shall not refuse, whensoever they shall be called.   And disdain not to write it down, be it a large debt, or be it a small one, until its time of payment: this will be more just in the sight of God, and more right for bearing witness, and more easy, that ye may not doubt.   But if it be a present bargain which ye transact between yourselves, it shall be no crime in you, if ye write it not down. And take witness when ye sell one to the other, and let no harm be done to the writer, nor to the witness; which if ye do, it will surely be injustice in you: and fear God, and God will instruct you, for God knoweth all things.   And if ye be on a journey, and find no writer, let pledges be taken: but if one of you trust the other, let him who is trusted return what he is trusted with, and fear God his Lord.   And conceal not the testimony, for he who concealeth it hath surely a wicked heart: God knoweth that which ye do.

Whatever is in heaven and on earth is God's; and whether ye manifest that which is in your minds, or conceal it, God will call you to account for it, and will forgive whom he pleaseth, and will punish whom he pleaseth; for God is almighty. The apostle believeth in that which hath been sent down unto him from his Lord, and the faithful also. Every one of them believeth in God, and his angels, and his scriptures, and his apostles: we make no distinction at all between his apostles. And they say, We have heard, and do obey: we implore thy mercy, O Lord, for unto thee must we return.

God will not force any soul beyond its capacity: it shall have the good which it gaineth, and it shall suffer the evil which it gaineth. O Lord, punish us not, if we forget, or act sinfully: O Lord, lay not on us a burden like that which thou hast laid on those who have been before us; neither make us, O Lord, to bear what we have not strength to bear, but be favorable unto us, and spare us, and be merciful unto us. Thou art our patron, help us therefore against the unbelieving nations.

CHAPTER III

ENTITLED, THE FAMILY OF IMRAN;[1] REVEALED AT MEDINA

IN THE NAME OF THE MOST MERCIFUL GOD

Al. M. There is no God but God, the living, the self-subsisting: He hath sent down unto thee the book of the Koran with truth, confirming that which was revealed before it; for he had formerly sent down the law and the gospel, a direction unto men; and he had also sent down the distinction between good and evil. Verily those who believe not the signs of God shall suffer a grievous punishment; for God is mighty, able to revenge. Surely nothing is hidden from God, of that which is on earth, or in heaven: it is he who formeth you in

---

[1] This name is given in the Koran to the father of the Virgin Mary, mentioned in the chapter.

the wombs, as he pleaseth; there is no God but he, the mighty, the wise.

It is he who hath sent down unto thee the book, wherein are some verses clear to be understood, they are the foundation of the book; and others are parabolical. But they whose hearts are perverse will follow that which is parabolical therein, out of love of schism, and a desire of the interpretation thereof; yet none knoweth the interpretation thereof, except God. But they who are well grounded in knowledge say, We believe therein, the whole is from our Lord; and none will consider except the prudent.

O Lord, cause not our hearts to swerve from truth, after thou hast directed us: and give us from thee mercy, for thou art he who giveth. O Lord, thou shalt surely gather mankind together, unto a day of resurrection: there is no doubt of it, for God will not be contrary to the promise.

As for the infidels, their wealth shall not profit them anything, nor their children, against God: they shall be the fuel of hell fire. According to the wont of the people of Pharaoh, and of those who went before them, they charged our signs with a lie; but God caught them in their wickedness, and God is severe in punishing. Say unto those who believe not, Ye shall be overcome, and thrown together into hell; an unhappy couch shall it be. Ye have already had a miracle shown you in two armies, which attacked each other: one army fought for God's true religion, but the other were infidels; they saw the faithful twice as many as themselves in their eyesight; for God strengtheneth with his help whom he pleaseth. Surely herein was an example unto men of understanding.

The love and eager desire of wives, and children, and sums heaped up of gold and silver, and excellent horses, and cattle, and land, are prepared for men: this is the provision of the present life; but unto God shall be the most excellent return. Say, Shall I declare unto you better things than this? For those who are devout are prepared with their Lord, gardens through which rivers flow; therein shall they continue forever: and they shall enjoy wives free from impurity, and the favor of God; for God regardeth his servants; who say, O Lord, we do sincerely believe; forgive us therefore our sins, and deliver us from the pain of hell fire: the patient, and the lovers of truth, and the devout, and the almsgivers, and those who ask pardon early in the morning.

God hath borne witness that there is no God but he; and the angels, and those who are endowed with wisdom, profess the same; who executeth righteousness; there is no God but he; the mighty, the wise. Verily the true religion, in the sight of God, is Islam;[2] and they who had received the scriptures dissented not therefrom, until after the knowledge of God's unity had come unto them, out of envy among themselves; but whosoever believeth not in the signs of God, verily God will be swift in bringing him to account. If they dispute with thee, say, I have resigned myself unto God, and he who followeth me doth the same: and say unto them who have received the scriptures, and to the ignorant, Do ye profess the religion of Islam? Now if they embrace Islam, they are surely directed; but if they turn their backs, verily unto thee belongeth preaching only; for God regardeth his servants.

And unto those who believe not in the signs of God, and slay the prophets without a cause, and put those men to death who teach justice; denounce unto them a painful punishment. These are they whose works perish in this world, and in that which is to come; and they shall have none to help them. Hast thou not observed those unto whom part of the scripture was given? They were called unto the book of God, that it might judge between them; then some of them turned their backs, and retired afar off. This they did because they said, The fire of hell shall by no means touch us, but for a certain number of days: and that which they had falsely devised hath deceived them in their religion. How then will it with them, when we shall gather them together at the day of judgment,

[2] The proper name of the Mohammedan religion, which signifies the "resigning or devoting one's self" entirely to God and his service. This they say is the religion which all the prophets were sent to teach, being founded on the unity of God.

of which there is no doubt; and every soul shall be paid that which it hath gained, neither shall they be treated unjustly.

Say, O God, who possessest the kingdom; thou givest the kingdom unto whom thou wilt, and thou takest away the kingdom from whom thou wilt: thou exaltest whom thou wilt, and thou humblest whom thou wilt: in thy hand is good, for thou art almighty. Thou makest the night to succeed the day: thou bringest forth the living out of the dead, and thou bringest forth the dead out of the living; and providest food for whom thou wilt without measure. Let not the faithful take the infidels for their protectors, rather than the faithful: he who doth this shall not be protected of God at all; unless ye fear any danger from them: but God warneth you to beware of himself; for unto God must ye return.

Say, Whether ye conceal that which is in your breasts, or whether ye declare it, God knoweth it: for he knoweth whatever is in heaven, and whatever is on earth: God is almighty. On the last day every soul shall find the good which it hath wrought, present; and the evil which it hath wrought, it shall wish that between itself and that were a wide distance: but God warneth you to beware of himself; for God is gracious unto his servants. Say, If ye love God, follow me: then God shall love you, and forgive you your sins; for God is gracious and merciful. Say, Obey God, and his apostle: but if ye go back, verily, God loveth not the unbelievers. God hath surely chosen Adam, and Noah, and the family of Abraham, and the family of Imran above the rest of the world; a race descending the one from the other: God is he who heareth and knoweth.

Remember when the wife of Imran [3] said, Lord, verily I have vowed unto thee that which is in my womb, to be dedicated to thy service: accept it therefore of me; for thou art he who heareth and knoweth. And when she was delivered

[3] The Imran here mentioned was the father of the Virgin Mary, and his wife's name was Hannah, or Ann, the daughter of Fakudh. This woman, say the commentators, being aged and barren, on seeing a bird feed her young ones, became very desirous of issue, and begged a child of God, promising to consecrate it to his service in the temple; whereupon she had a child, but it proved a daughter.

of it, she said, Lord, verily I have brought forth a female (and God well knew what she brought forth), and a male is not as a female: I have called her Mary; and I commend her to thy protection, and also her issue, against Satan driven away with stones. Therefore the Lord accepted her with a gracious acceptance, and caused her to bear an excellent offspring. And Zacharias took care of the child; whenever Zacharias went into the chamber to her, he found provisions with her: and he said, O Mary, whence hadst thou this? she answered, This is from God: for God provideth for whom he pleaseth without measure. There Zacharias called on his Lord and said, Lord, give me from thee a good offspring, for thou art the hearer of prayer. And the angels called to him, while he stood praying in the chamber, saying, Verily God promiseth thee a son·named John, who shall bear witness to the Words which cometh from God; an honorable person, chaste, and one of the righteous prophets. He answered, Lord, how shall I have a son, when old age hath overtaken me, and my wife is barren? The angel said, So God doth that which he pleaseth. Zacharias answered, Lord, give me a sign. The angel said, Thy sign shall be, that thou shalt speak unto no man for three days, otherwise than by gesture: remember thy Lord often, and praise him evening and morning. And when the angels said, O Mary, verily God hath chosen thee, and hath purified thee, and hath chosen thee above all the women of the world: O Mary, be devout toward thy Lord, and worship, and bow down with those who bow down.

This is a secret history: we reveal it unto thee, although thou wast not present with them when they threw in their rods to cast lots which of them should have the education of Mary. Neither wast thou with them, when they strove among themselves. When the angels said, O Mary, verily God sendeth thee good tidings, that thou shalt bear the Word, proceeding from himself; his name shall be Christ Jesus the son of Mary, honorable in this world and in the world to come, and one of those who approach near to the presence of God; and he shall speak unto men in the cradle, and when he is grown up; and he shall be one of the righteous: she answered, Lord, how shall I have a son, since a man hath not touched me? the angel said, So God createth that which he pleaseth: when he decreeth a thing, he only saith unto it, Be, and it is: God shall teach him the scripture, and wisdom, and the law, and the gospel; and shall appoint him his apostle to the children of Israel; and he shall say, Verily I come unto you with a sign from your Lord; for I will make before you, of clay, as it were the figure of a bird; then I will breathe thereon, and it shall become a bird, by the permission of God: and I will heal him that hath been blind from his birth, and the leper: and I will raise the dead by the permission of God: and I will prophesy unto you what ye eat, and what ye lay up for store in your houses. Verily herein will be a sign unto you, if ye believe. And I come to confirm the Law which was revealed before me, and to allow unto you as lawful, part of that which hath been forbidden you: and I come unto you with a sign from your Lord; therefore fear God, and obey me. Verily God is my Lord, and your Lord: therefore serve him. This is the right way. But when Jesus perceived their unbelief, he said, Who will be my helpers toward God? The apostles answered, We will be the helpers of God; we believe in God, and do thou bear witness that we are true believers. O Lord, we believe in that which thou hast sent down, and we have followed thy apostle; write us down therefore with those who bear witness of him. And the Jews devised a stratagem against him, but God devised a stratagem against them; [4] and God is the best deviser of stratagems. When God said, O Jesus, verily I will cause

[4] This stratagem of God's was the taking of Jesus up into heaven, and stamping his likeness on another person, who was apprehended and crucified in his stead. For it is the constant doctrine of the Mohammedans that it was not Jesus himself who underwent that ignominious death, but somebody else in his shape and resemblance. The person crucified some will have to be a spy that was sent to entrap him; others that it was one Titian, who by the direction of Judas entered in at a window of the house where Jesus was, to kill him; and others that it was Judas himself, who agreed with the rulers of the Jews to betray him for thirty pieces of silver, and led those who were sent to take him.

thee to die, and I will take thee up unto me, and I will deliver thee from the unbelievers; and I will place those who follow thee above the unbelievers, until the day of resurrection: then unto me shall ye return, and I will judge between you of that concerning which ye disagree.

Moreover, as for the infidels, I will punish them with a grievous punishment in this world, and in that which is to come; and there shall be none to help them. But they who believe, and do that which is right, he shall give them their reward; for God loveth not the wicked doers. These signs and this prudent admonition do we rehearse unto thee. Verily the likeness of Jesus in the sight of God is as the likeness of Adam: he created him out of the dust, and then said unto him, Be; and he was. This is the truth from thy Lord; be not therefore one of those who doubt: and whoever shall dispute with thee concerning him, after the knowledge which hath been given unto thee, say unto them, Come, let us call together our sons, and your sons, and our wives, and your wives, and ourselves, and yourselves; then let us make imprecations, and lay the curse of God on those who lie.[5] Verily this is a true history: and there is no God but God; and God is most mighty, and wise. If they turn back, God well knoweth the evil-doers.

Say, O ye who have received the scripture, come to a just determination between us and you; that we worship not any except God, and associate no creature with him; and that the one of us take not the other for lords, beside God. But if they turn back, say, Bear witness that we are true believers.

O ye to whom the scriptures have been given, why do ye

[5] To explain this passage their commentators tell the following story. That some Christians, with their bishop named Abu Hareth, coming to Mohammed as ambassadors from the inhabitants of Najran, and entering into some disputes with him touching religion and the history of Jesus Christ, they agreed the next morning to abide the trial here mentioned, as a quick way of deciding which of them were in the wrong. Mohammed met them accordingly, accompanied by his daughter Fatima, his son-in-law Ali, and his two grandsons, Hassan and Hosein, and desired them to wait till he had said his prayers. But when they saw him kneel down, their resolution failed them, and they durst not venture to curse him, but submitted to pay him tribute.

dispute concerning Abraham, since the Law and the Gospel were not sent down until after him? Do ye not therefore understand? Behold ye are they who dispute concerning that which ye have some knowledge in; why therefore do ye dispute concerning that which ye have no knowledge of? God knoweth, but ye know not. Abraham was neither a Jew, nor a Christian; but he was of the true religion, one resigned unto God, and was not of the number of the idolaters. Verily the men who are the nearest of kin unto Abraham, are they who follow him; and this prophet, and they who believe on him: God is the patron of the faithful. Some of those who have received the scriptures desire to seduce you; but they seduce themselves only, and they perceive it not. O ye who have received the scriptures, why do ye not believe in the signs of God, since ye are witnesses of them? O ye who have received the scriptures, why do ye clothe truth with vanity, and knowingly hide the truth?

And some of those to whom the scriptures were given, say, Believe in that which hath been sent down unto those who believe, in the beginning of the day, and deny it in the end thereof; that they may go back from their faith:[6] and believe him only who followeth your religion. Say, Verily the true direction is the direction of God, that there may be given unto some other a revelation like unto what hath been given unto you. Will they dispute with you before your Lord? Say, Surely excellence is in the hand of God, he giveth it unto whom he pleaseth; God is bounteous and wise: he will confer

[6] The commentators, to explain this passage, say that Caab Ebn al Ashraf and Malec Ebn al Seif (two Jews of Medina) advised their companions, when the *Keblah* was changed, to make as if they believed it was done by the divine direction, and to pray toward the Kaaba in the morning, but that in the evening they should pray, as formerly, toward the temple of Jerusalem; that Mohammed's followers, imagining the Jews were better judges of this matter than themselves, might imitate their example. But others say these were certain Jewish priests of Khaibar, who directed some of their people to pretend in the morning that they had embraced Mohammedanism, but in the close of the day to say that they had looked into their books of scripture, and consulted their Rabbins, and could not find that Mohammed was the person described and intended in the law, by which trick they hoped to raise doubts in the minds of the Mohammedans.

peculiar mercy on whom he pleaseth; for God is endued with great beneficence. There is of those who have received the scriptures, unto whom if thou trust a talent, he will restore it unto thee; and there is also of them, unto whom if thou trust a dinar, he will not restore it unto thee, unless thou stand over him continually with great urgency. This they do because they say, We are not obliged to observe justice with the heathen: but they utter a lie against God, knowingly. Yea; whoso keepeth his covenant, and feareth God, God surely loveth those who fear him. But they who make merchandise of God's covenant, and of their oaths, for a small price shall have no portion in the next life, neither shall God speak to them or regard them on the day of resurrection, nor shall he cleanse them; but they shall suffer a grievous punishment.

And there are certainly some of them, who read the scriptures perversely, that ye may think what they read to be really in the scriptures, yet it is not in the scripture; and they say, This is from God; but it is not from God: and they speak that which is false concerning God, against their own knowledge. It is not fit for a man, that God should give him a book of revelations, and wisdom, and prophecy; and then he should say unto men, Be ye worshipers of me, besides God; but he ought to say, Be ye perfect in knowledge and in works, since ye know the scriptures, and exercise yourselves therein.[7] God hath not commanded you to take the angels and the prophets for your Lords: Will he command you to become infidels, after ye have been true believers?

And remember when God accepted the covenant of the prophets, saying, This verily is the scripture and the wisdom which I have given you: hereafter shall an apostle come unto you, confirming the truth of that scripture which is with you; ye shall surely believe on him, and ye shall assist him. God

[7] This passage was revealed, say the commentators, in answer to the Christians, who insisted that Jesus had commanded them to worship him as God. Al Beidawi adds that two Christians named Abu Rafé al Koradhi and al Seyid al Najrani, offered to acknowledge Mohammed for their Lord, and to worship him; to which he answered, "God forbid that we should worship any besides God."

said, Are ye firmly resolved, and do ye accept my covenant on this condition? They answered, We are firmly resolved: God said, Be ye therefore witnesses; and I also bear witness with you: and whosoever turneth back after this, they are surely the transgressors. Do they therefore seek any other religion but God's? since to him is resigned whosoever is in heaven or on earth, voluntarily, or of force: and to him shall they return. Say, We believe in God, and that which hath been sent down unto us, and that which was sent down unto Abraham, and Ismael, and Isaac, and Jacob, and the tribes, and that which was delivered to Moses, and Jesus, and the prophets from their Lord; we make no distinction between any of them; and to him are we resigned. Whoever followeth any other religion than Islam, it shall not be accepted of him: and in the next life he shall be of those who perish.

How shall God direct men who have become infidels after they had believed, and borne witness that the apostle was true, and manifest declarations of the divine will had come unto them? for God directeth not the ungodly people. Their reward shall be, that on them shall fall the curse of God, and of angels, and of all mankind: they shall remain under the same forever; their torment shall not be mitigated, neither shall they be regarded; except those who repent after this, and amend; for God is gracious and merciful. Moreover they who become infidels after they have believed, and yet increase in infidelity, their repentance shall in no wise be accepted, and they are those who go astray. Verily they who believe not, and die in their unbelief, the world full of gold shall in no wise be accepted from any of them, even though he should give it for his ransom; they shall suffer a grievous punishment, and they shall have none to help them. Ye will never attain unto righteousness, until ye give in alms of that which ye love: and whatever ye give, God knoweth it. All food was permitted unto the children of Israel, except what Israel forbade unto himself [8] before the Pentateuch was sent

[8] This passage was revealed on the Jews reproaching Mohammed and his followers with their eating of the flesh and milk of camels, which they said was forbidden Abraham, whose religion Mohammed pretended

down. Say unto the Jews, Bring hither the Pentateuch and read it, if ye speak truth. Whoever therefore contriveth a lie against God after this, they will be evil-doers. Say, God is true: follow ye therefore the religion of Abraham the orthodox; for he was no idolater. Verily the first house appointed unto men to worship in was that which is in Mecca; blessed, and a direction to all creatures. Therein are manifest signs: the place where Abraham stood; and whoever entereth therein shall be safe. And it is a duty toward God, incumbent on those who are able to go thither, to visit this house; but whosoever disbelieveth, verily God needeth not the service of any creature. Say, O ye who have received the scriptures, why do ye not believe in the signs of God? Say, O ye who have received the scriptures, why do ye keep back from the way of God him who believeth? Ye seek to make it crooked, and yet are witnesses that it is the right: but God will not be unmindful of what ye do.

O true believers, if ye obey some of those who have received the scripture, they will render you infidels, after ye have believed: [9] and how can ye be infidels, when the signs of God are read unto you, and his apostle is among you? But he who cleaveth firmly unto God is already directed into the right way. O believers, fear God with his true fear; and die not unless ye also be true believers. And cleave all of you

to follow. In answer to which he tells him that God ordained no distinction of meats before he gave the law to Moses, though Jacob voluntarily abstained from the flesh and milk of camels; which some commentators say was the consequence of a vow made by that patriarch, when afflicted with the sciatica, that if he were cured he would eat no more of that meat which he liked best.

[9] This passage was revealed on occasion of a quarrel excited between the tribes of al Aws and al Khazraj, by one Shas Ebn Kais, a Jew; who, passing by some of both tribes as they were sitting and discoursing familiarly together, and being inwardly vexed at the friendship and harmony which reigned among them on their embracing Mohammedanism, whereas they had been, for 120 years before, most inveterate and mortal enemies, though descendants of two brothers; in order to set them at variance, sent a young man to sit down by them, directing him to relate the story of the battle of Boath (a place near Medina), wherein, after a bloody fight, al Aws had the better of al Khazraj, and to repeat some verses on that subject. A bloody battle nearly resulted.

unto the covenant of God, and depart not from it, and remember the favor of God toward you: since ye were enemies, and he reconciled your hearts, and ye became companions and brethren by his favor: and ye were on the brink of a pit of fire, and he delivered you thence. Thus God declareth unto you his signs, that ye may be directed. Let there be people among you, who invite to the best religion; and command that which is just, and forbid that which is evil; and they shall be happy. And be not as they who are divided, and disagree in matters of religion, after manifest proofs have been brought unto them: they shall suffer a great torment. On the day of resurrection some faces shall become white, and other faces shall become black. And unto them whose faces shall become black, God will say, Have ye returned unto your unbelief, after ye had believed? therefore taste the punishment, for that ye have been unbelievers: but they whose faces shall become white shall be in the mercy of God, therein shall they remain forever. These are the signs of God: we recite them unto thee with truth. God will not deal unjustly with his creatures. And to God belongeth whatever is in heaven and on earth; and to God shall all things return. Ye are the best nation that hath been raised up unto mankind: ye command that which is just, and ye forbid that which is unjust, and ye believe in God. And if they who have received the scriptures had believed, it had surely been the better for them: there are believers among them, but the greater part of them are transgressors. They shall not hurt you, unless with a slight hurt; and if they fight against you, they shall turn their backs to you, and they shall not be helped. They are smitten with vileness wheresoever they are found: unless they obtain security by entering into a treaty with God, and a treaty with men: and they draw on themselves indignation from God, and they are afflicted with poverty. This they suffer, because they disbelieved the signs of God, and slew the prophets unjustly; this, because they were rebellious, and transgressed. Yet they are not all alike: there are of those who have received the scriptures, upright people; they meditate on the signs of God in the night season, and worship; they believe

in God and the last day; and command that which is just, and
forbid that which is unjust, and zealously strive to excel in
good works: these are of the righteous. And ye shall not be
denied the reward of the good which ye do; for God knoweth
the pious. As for the unbelievers, their wealth shall not
profit them at all, neither their children, against God: they
shall be the companions of hell fire; they shall continue
therein forever. The likeness of that which they lay out in
this present life is as a wind wherein there is a scorching cold:
it falleth on the standing corn of those men who have injured
their own souls, and destroyeth it. And God dealeth not unjustly with them; but they injure their own souls.

O true believers, contract not an intimate friendship with
any besides yourselves: they will not fail to corrupt you.
They wish for that which may cause you to perish: their hatred hath already appeared from out of their mouths; but
what their breasts conceal is yet more inveterate. We have
already shown you signs of their ill-will toward you, if ye
understand. Behold, ye love them, and they do not love you:
ye believe in all the scriptures, and when they meet you, they
say, We believe; but when they assemble privately together,
they bite their fingers' ends out of wrath against you. Say
unto them, Die in your wrath: verily God knoweth the innermost part of your breasts. If good happen unto you, it
grieveth them; and if evil befall you, they rejoice at it. But
if ye be patient, and fear God, their subtlety shall not hurt
you at all; for God comprehendeth whatever they do. Call
to mind when thou wentest forth early from thy family, that
thou mightest prepare the faithful a camp for war, and God
heard and knew it; when two companies of you were anx-
iously thoughtful, so that ye became faint-hearted; but God
was the supporter of them both; and in God let the faithful
trust. And God had already given you the victory at Bedr,
when ye were inferior in number; therefore fear God, that ye
may be thankful. When thou saidst unto the faithful, Is it
not enough for you that your Lord should assist you with
three thousand angels, sent down from heaven? Verily if ye
persevere, and fear God, and your enemies come upon you

suddenly, your Lord will assist you with five thousand angels, distinguished by their horses and attire. And this God designed only as good tidings for you that your hearts might rest secure: for victory is from God alone, the mighty, the wise. That he should cut off the uttermost part of the unbelievers, or cast them down, or that they should be overthrown and unsuccessful, is nothing to thee. It is no business of thine; whether God be turned unto them, or whether he punish them; they are surely unjust doers. To God belongeth whatsoever is in heaven and on earth: he spareth whom he pleaseth, and he punisheth whom he pleaseth; for God is merciful.

O true believers, devour not usury, doubling it twofold; but fear God, that ye may prosper; and fear the fire which is prepared for the unbelievers; and obey God, and his apostle, that ye may obtain mercy. And run with emulation to obtain remission from your Lord, and paradise, whose breath equaleth the heavens and the earth, which is prepared for the godly; who give alms in prosperity and adversity; who bridle their anger and forgive men: for God loveth the beneficent. And who, after they have committed a crime, or dealt unjustly with their own souls, remember God, and ask pardon for their sins (for who forgiveth sins except God?) and persevere not in what they have done knowingly: their reward shall be pardon from their Lord, and gardens wherein rivers flow, they shall remain therein forever: and how excellent is the reward of those who labor! There have already been before you examples of punishment of infidels, therefore go through the earth, and behold what hath been the end of those who accuse God's apostles of imposture. This book is a declaration unto men, and a direction, and an admonition to the pious. And be not dismayed, neither be ye grieved; for ye shall be superior to the unbelievers if ye believe. If a wound hath happened unto you in war, a like wound hath already happened unto the unbelieving people: and we cause these days of different success interchangeably to succeed each other among men; that God may know those who believe, and may have martyrs from among you (God loveth not the workers of iniquity) ; and that God might prove those who believe, and destroy the infidels.

Did ye imagine that ye should enter paradise, when as yet God knew not those among you who fought strenuously in his cause; nor knew those who persevered with patience? Moreover ye did sometime wish for death before that ye met it; but ye have now seen it, and ye looked on, but retreated from it. Mohammed is no more than an apostle; the other apostles have already deceased before him: if he die therefore, or be slain, will ye turn back on your heels? but he who turneth back on his heels will not hurt God at all; and God will surely reward the thankful. No soul can die unless by the permission of God, according to what is written in the book containing the determinations of things. And whoso chooseth the reward of this world, we will give him thereof: but whoso chooseth the reward of the world to come, we will give him thereof; and we will surely reward the thankful. How many prophets have encountered those who had many myriads of troops: and yet they desponded not in their mind for what had befallen them in fighting for the religion of God, and were not weakened, neither behaved themselves in an abject manner? God loveth those who persevere patiently. And their speech was no other than that they said, Our Lord forgive us our offenses, and our transgressions in our business; and confirm our feet, and help us against the unbelieving people. And God gave them the reward of this world, and a glorious reward in the life to come; for God loveth the welldoers. O ye who believe, if ye obey the infidels, they will cause you to turn back on your heels, and ye will be turned back and perish: but God is your Lord; and he is the best helper. We will surely cast a dread into the hearts of the unbelievers, because they have associated with God that concerning which he sent them down no power: their dwelling shall be the fire of hell; and the receptacle of the wicked shall be miserable. . . .

And let not the unbelievers think, because we grant them lives long and prosperous, that it is better for their souls: we grant them long and prosperous lives only that their iniquity may be increased; and they shall suffer an ignominious punishment. God is not disposed to leave the faithful in the condition which ye are now in, until he sever the wicked from the good; nor is God disposed to make you acquainted with what is a hidden secret, but God chooseth such of his apostles as he pleaseth, to reveal his mind unto: believe therefore in God, and his apostles; and if ye believe, and fear God, ye shall receive a great reward. And let not those who are covetous of what God of his bounty hath granted them, imagine that their avarice is better for them: nay, rather it is worse for them. That which they have covetously reserved shall be bound as a collar about their neck, on the day of the resurrection: unto God belongeth the inheritance of heaven and earth; and God is well acquainted with what ye do.

God hath already heard the saying of those who said, Verily God is poor, and we are rich: we will surely write down what they have said, and the slaughter which they have made of the prophets without a cause; and we will say unto them, Taste ye the pain of burning. This shall they suffer for the evil which their hands have sent before them, and because God is not unjust toward mankind; who also say, Surely God hath commanded us, that we should not give credit to any apostle, until one should come unto us with a sacrifice, which should be consumed by fire. Say, Apostles have already come unto you before me, with plain proofs, and with the miracle which ye mention: why therefore have ye slain them, if ye speak truth? If they accuse thee of imposture, the apostles before thee have also been accounted impostors, who brought evident demonstrations, and the scriptures, and the book which enlightened the understanding. Every soul shall taste of death, and ye shall have your rewards on the day of resurrection; and he who shall be far removed from hell fire, and shall be admitted into paradise, shall be happy: but the present life is only a deceitful provision. Ye shall surely be proved in your possessions, and in your persons; and ye shall bear from those unto whom the scripture was delivered before you, and from the idolaters, much hurt: but if ye be patient, and fear God, this is a matter that is absolutely determined.

And when God accepted the covenant of those to whom the book of the law was given, saying, Ye shall surely publish it unto mankind, ye shall not hide it; yet they threw it behind their backs, and sold it for a small price; but woeful is the price for which they have sold it. Think not that they who rejoice at what they have done, and expect to be praised for what they have not done; think not, O prophet, that they shall escape from punishment, for they shall suffer a painful punishment; and unto God belongeth the kingdom of heaven and earth; God is almighty.

Now in the creation of heaven and earth, and the vicissitude of night and day, are signs unto those who are endued with understanding; who remember God standing, and sitting, and lying on their sides; and meditate on the creation of heaven and earth, saying, O Lord, thou hast not created this in vain; far be it from thee: therefore deliver us from the torment of hell fire: O Lord, surely whom thou shalt throw into the fire, thou wilt also cover with shame; nor shall the ungodly have any to help them. O Lord, we have heard of a preacher inviting us to the faith, and saying, Believe in your Lord: and we believed. O Lord, forgive us therefore our sins, and expiate our evil deeds from us, and make us to die with the righteous. O Lord, give us also the reward which thou hast promised by thy apostles; and cover us not with shame on the day of resurrection; for thou art not contrary to the promise. Their Lord therefore answereth them, saying, I will not suffer the work of him among you who worketh to be lost, whether he be male or female:[10] the one of you is from the other. They therefore who have left their country, and have been turned out of their houses, and have suffered for my sake, and have been slain in battle; verily I will expiate their evil deeds from them, and I will surely bring them into gardens watered by rivers; a reward from God: and with God is the most excellent reward.

[10] These words were added, as some relate, on Omm Salma, one of the prophet's wives, telling him that she had observed God often made mention of the men who fled their country for the sake of their faith, but took no notice of the women.

Let not the prosperous dealing of the unbelievers in the land deceive thee: it is but a slender provision; and then their receptacle shall be hell; an unhappy couch shall it be. But they who fear their Lord shall have gardens through which rivers flow, they shall continue therein forever: this is the gift of God; for what is with God shall be better for the righteous than short-lived worldly prosperity. There are some of those who have received the scriptures, who believe in God, and that which hath been sent down unto you, and that which hath been sent down to them, submitting themselves unto God; they tell not the signs of God for a small price: these shall have their reward with their Lord; for God is swift in taking an account. O true believers, be patient, and strive to excel in patience, and be constant-minded, and fear God, that ye may be happy.

CHAPTER IV

ENTITLED, WOMEN; REVEALED AT MEDINA

IN THE NAME OF THE MOST MERCIFUL GOD

O men, fear your Lord, who hath created you out of one man, and out of him created his wife, and from those two hath multiplied many men and women: and fear God by whom ye beseech one another; and respect women who have borne you, for God is watching over you. And give the orphans when they come to age their substance; and render them not in exchange bad for good: and devour not their substance by adding it to your substance; for this is a great sin. And if ye fear that ye shall not act with equity toward orphans of the female sex, take in marriage of such other women as please you, two, or three, or four, and not more. But if ye fear that ye can not act equitably toward so many, marry one only, or the slaves which ye shall have acquired. This will be easier, that ye swerve not from righteousness.

And give women their dowry freely; but if they voluntarily remit unto you any part of it, enjoy it with satisfaction and advantage. And give not unto those who are weak of understanding the substance which God hath appointed you to preserve for them; but maintain them thereout, and clothe them, and speak kindly unto them. And examine the orphans in religion until they attain the age of marriage: but if ye perceive they are able to manage their affairs well, deliver their substance unto them; and waste it not extravagantly or hastily, because they grow up. Let him who is rich abstain entirely from the orphan's estates; and let him who is poor take thereof according to what shall be reasonable. And when ye deliver their substance unto them, call witnesses thereof in their presence: God taketh sufficient account of your actions.

Men ought to have a part of what their parents and kindred leave behind them when they die: and women also ought to have a part of what their parents and kindred leave, whether it be little, or whether it be much; a determinate part is due to them. And when they who are of kin are present at the dividing of what is left, and also the orphans, and the poor; distribute unto them some part thereof; and if the estate be too small, at least speak comfortably unto them.

And let those fear to abuse orphans, who if they leave behind them a weak offspring, are solicitous for them: let them therefore fear God, and speak that which is convenient. Surely they who devour the possessions of orphans unjustly, shall swallow down nothing but fire into their bellies, and shall broil in raging flames. God hath thus commanded you concerning your children.

A male shall have as much as the share of two females: but if they be females only, and above two in number, they shall have two-third parts of what the deceased shall leave; and if there be but one, she shall have the half. And the parents of the deceased shall have each of them a sixth part of what he shall leave, if he have a child: but if he have no child, and his parents be his heirs, then his mother shall have the third part. And if he have brethren, his mother shall have a sixth part, after the legacies which he shall bequeath, and his debts be paid. Ye know not whether your parents or your children be of greater use unto you. This is an ordinance from God, and God is knowing and wise.

Moreover ye may claim half of what your wives shall leave, if they have no issue; but if they have issue, then ye shall have the fourth part of what they shall leave, after the legacies which they shall bequeath, and the debts be paid. They also shall have the fourth part of what ye shall leave, in case ye have no issue; but if ye have issue, then they shall have the eighth part of what ye shall leave, after the legacies which ye shall bequeath and your debts be paid. And if a man or woman's substance be inherited by a distant relation, and he or she have a brother or sister; each of these two shall have a sixth part of the estate. But if there be more than this number, they shall be equal sharers in a third part, after payment of the legacies which shall be bequeathed, and the debts, without prejudice to the heirs. This is an ordinance from God: and God is knowing and gracious.

These are the statutes of God. And whoso obeyeth God and his apostle, God shall lead him into gardens wherein rivers flow, they shall continue therein forever; and this shall be great happiness. But whoso disobeyeth God, and his apostle, and transgresseth his statutes, God shall cast him into hell fire; he shall remain therein forever, and he shall suffer a shameful punishment.

If any of your women be guilty of whoredom, produce four witnesses from among you against them, and if they bear witness against them, imprison them in separate apartments until death release them, or God affordeth them a way to escape. And if two of you commit the like wickedness, punish them both: but if they repent and amend, let them both alone; for God is easy to be reconciled and merciful. Verily repentance will be accepted with God, from those who do evil ignorantly, and then repent speedily; unto them will God be turned: for God is knowing and wise. But no repentance shall be accepted from those who do evil until the time when death presenteth itself unto one of them, and he saith, Verily I repent now; nor unto those who die unbelievers: for them have we prepared a grievous punishment.

O true believers, it is not lawful for you to be heirs of women against their will, nor to hinder them from marrying others, that ye may take away part of what ye have given them in dowry; unless they have been guilty of a manifest crime: but converse kindly with them. And if ye hate them, it may happen that ye may hate a thing wherein God hath placed much good. If ye be desirous to exchange a wife for another wife, and ye have already given one of them a talent; take not away anything therefrom: will ye take it by slandering her, and doing her manifest injustice? And how can ye take it, since the one of you hath gone in unto the other, and they have received from you a firm covenant?

Marry not women whom your fathers have had to wife (except what is already past): for this is uncleanness, and an abomination, and an evil way. Ye are forbidden to marry your mothers, and your daughters, and your sisters, and your aunts both on the father's and on the mother's side, and your brother's daughters, and your sister's daughters, and your mothers who have given you suck, and your foster-sisters, and your wives' mothers, and your daughters-in-law which are under your tuition, born of your wives unto whom ye have gone in (but if ye have not gone in unto them, it shall be no sin in you to marry them), and the wives of your sons who proceed out of your loins; and ye are also forbidden to take to wife two sisters; except what is already past: for God is gracious and merciful.

Ye are also forbidden to take to wife free women who are married, except those women whom your right hands shall possess as slaves. This is ordained you from God. Whatever is beside this is allowed you; that ye may with your substance provide wives for yourselves, acting that which is right, and avoiding whoredom. And for the advantage which ye receive from them, give them their reward, according to what is ordained: but it shall be no crime in you to make any other agreement among yourselves, after the ordinance shall be complied with; for God is knowing and wise.

Whoso among you hath not means sufficient that he may marry free women, who are believers, let him marry with such of your maid-servants whom your right hands possess, as are true believers; for God well knoweth your faith. Ye are the one from the other: therefore marry them with the consent of their masters; and give them their dower according to justice; such as are modest, not guilty of entertaining lovers. And when they are married, if they be guilty of adultery, they shall suffer half the punishment which is appointed for the free women. This is allowed unto him among you, who feareth to sin by marrying free women; but if ye abstain from marrying slaves, it will be better for you; God is gracious and merciful. God is willing to declare these things unto you, and to direct you according to the ordinances of those who have gone before you, and to be merciful unto you. God is knowing and wise. God desireth to be gracious unto you; but they who follow their lusts, desire that ye should turn aside from the truth with great deviation. God is minded to make his religion light unto you: for man was created weak.

O true believers, consume not your wealth among yourselves in vanity; unless there be merchandizing among you by mutual consent: neither slay yourselves; for God is merciful toward you: and whoever doth this maliciously and wickedly, he will surely cast him to be broiled in hell fire; and this is easy with God. If ye turn aside from the grievous sins,[1] of those which ye are forbidden to commit, we will cleanse you from your smaller faults; and will introduce you into paradise with an honorable entry. Covet not that which God hath bestowed on some of you preferably to others. Unto the men shall be given a portion of what they shall have gained, and unto the women shall be given a portion of what they shall have gained: therefore ask God of his bounty; for God is

[1] These sins al Beidawi, from a tradition of Mohammed, reckons to be seven (equaling in number the sins called deadly by Christians), that is to say, idolatry, murder, falsely accusing modest women of adultery, wasting the substance of orphans, taking of usury, desertion in a religious expedition, and disobedience to parents. But Ebn Abbas says they amount to near seven hundred; and others suppose that idolatry only, of different kinds, in worshiping idols or any creature, either in opposition to or jointly with the true God, is here intended; that sin being generally esteemed by Mohammedans, and in a few lines after declared by the Koran itself, to be the only one which God will not pardon.

omniscient. We have appointed unto every one kindred, to inherit part of what their parents and relations shall leave at their deaths. And unto those with whom your right hands have made an alliance, give their part of the inheritance; for God is witness of all things.

Men shall have the pre-eminence above women, because of those advantages wherein God hath caused the one of them to excel the other, and for that which they expend of their substance in maintaining their wives. The honest women are obedient, careful in the absence of their husbands, for that God preserveth them, by committing them to the care and protection of the men. But those whose perverseness ye shall be apprehensive of, rebuke; and remove them into separate apartments, and chastise them. But if they shall be obedient unto you, seek not an occasion of quarrel against them; for God is high and great. And if ye fear a breach between the husband and wife, send a judge out of his family, and a judge out of her family: if they shall desire a reconciliation, God will cause them to agree; for God is knowing and wise.

Serve God, and associate no creature with him; and show kindness unto parents, and relations, and orphans, and the poor, and your neighbor who is of kin to you, and also your neighbor who is a stranger, and to your familiar companion, and the traveler, and the captives whom your right hands shall possess; for God loveth not the proud or vainglorious, who are covetous, and recommend covetousness unto men, and conceal that which God of his bounty hath given them (we have prepared a shameful punishment for the unbelievers); and who bestow their wealth in charity to be observed of men, and believe not in God, nor in the last day; and whoever hath Satan for a companion, an evil companion hath he! And what harm would befall them if they should believe in God and the last day, and give alms out of that which God hath bestowed on them? since God knoweth them who do this. Verily God will not wrong any one even the weight of an ant: and if it be a good action, he will double it, and will recompense it in his sight with a great reward. How will it be with the unbelievers when we shall bring a witness out of each nation against itself,[2] and shall bring thee, O Mohammed, a witness against these people?[3] In that day they who have not believed, and have rebelled against the apostle of God, shall wish the earth was leveled with them; and they shall not be able to hide any matter from God.

O true believers, come not to prayers when ye are drunk, until ye understand what ye say; nor when ye are polluted by emission of seed, unless ye be traveling on the road, until ye wash yourselves. But if ye be sick, or on a journey, or any of you come from easing nature, or have touched women, and find no water; take fine clean sand and rub your faces and your hands therewith; for God is merciful and inclined to forgive.

Hast thou not observed those unto whom part of the scripture was delivered? they sell error, and desire that ye may wander from the right way; but God well knoweth your enemies. God is a sufficient patron, and God is a sufficient helper. Of the Jews there are some who pervert words from their places; and say, We have heard, and have disobeyed; and do thou hear without understanding our meaning, and look upon us: perplexing with their tongues, and reviling the true religion. But if they had said, We have heard, and do obey; and do thou hear, and regard us: certainly it were better for them, and more right. But God hath cursed them by reason of their infidelity; therefore a few of them only shall believe.

O ye to whom the scriptures have been given, believe in the revelation which we have sent down, confirming that which is with you; before we deface your countenances, and render them as the back parts thereof;[4] or curse them, as we cursed those who transgressed on the sabbath day;[5] and the com-

---

[2] When the prophet who was sent to each nation in particular, shall on the last day be produced to give evidence against such of them as refused to believe on him, or observed not the laws which he brought.

[3] That is, the Arabians, to whom Mohammed was, as he pretended, more peculiarly sent.

[4] That is, perfectly plain, without eyes, nose, or mouth. The original, however, may also be translated, "and turn them behind," by wringing their necks backward.

[5] And were therefore changed into apes.

mand of God was fulfilled. Surely God will not pardon the giving him an equal; but will pardon any other sin, except that, to whom he pleaseth: and whoso giveth a companion unto God hath devised a great wickedness. Hast thou not observed those who justify themselves? But God justifieth whomsoever he pleaseth, nor shall they be wronged a hair. Behold, how they imagine a lie against God; and therein is iniquity sufficiently manifest.

Hast thou not considered those to whom part of the scripture hath been given? They believe in false gods and idols, and say to those who believe not, These are more rightly directed in the way of truth than they who believe on Mohammed. Those are the men whom God hath cursed; and unto him whom God shall curse, thou shalt surely find no helper. Shall they have a part of the kingdom, since even then they would not bestow the smallest matter on them.

Do they envy other men that which God of his bounty hath given them? We formerly gave unto the family of Abraham a book of revelations and wisdom; and we gave them a great kingdom. There is of them who believeth on him; and there is of them who turneth aside from him: but the raging fire of hell is a sufficient punishment. Verily, those who disbelieve our signs, we will surely cast to be broiled in hell fire; so often as their skins shall be well burned, we will give them other skins in exchange, that they may taste the sharper torment; for God is mighty and wise. But those who believe and do that which is right, we will bring into gardens watered by rivers, therein shall they remain forever, and there shall they enjoy wives free from all impurity; and we will lead them into perpetual shades.

Moreover God commandeth you to restore what ye are trusted with, to the owners;[6] and when ye judge between

[6] This passage, it is said, was revealed on the day of the taking of Mecca, the primary design of it being to direct Mohammed to return the keys of the Kaaba to Othman Ebn Telha Ebn Abdaldar, who had then the honor to be keeper of that holy place, and not to deliver them to his uncle al Abbas, who having already the custody of the well Zemzem, would fain have had also that of the Kaaba. The prophet obeying the divine order, Othman was so affected with the justice of the action, notwithstanding he had at first refused him entrance, that he imme-

men, that ye judge according to equity: and surely an excellent virtue it is to which God exhorteth you; for God both heareth and seeth.

O true believers, obey God, and obey the apostle, and those who are in authority among you: and if ye differ in anything, refer it unto God and the apostle, if ye believe in God and the last day: this is better, and a fairer method of determination. Hast thou not observed those who pretend they believe in what hath been revealed unto thee, and what hath been revealed before thee? They desire to go to judgment before Taghut,[7] although they have been commanded not to believe in him; and Satan desireth to seduce them into a wide error. And when it is said unto them, Come unto the book which God hath sent down, and to the apostle; thou seest the ungodly turn aside from thee, with great aversion. But how will they behave when a misfortune shall befall them, for that which their hands have sent before them? Then will they come unto thee, and swear by God, saying, If we intended any other than to do good, and to reconcile the parties. God knoweth what is in the hearts of these men; therefore let them alone, and admonish them, and speak unto them a word which may affect their souls. We have not sent any apostle, but that he might be obeyed by the permission of God: but if they, after they have injured their own souls, come unto thee, and ask pardon of God, and the apostle ask pardon for them, they

diately embraced Mohammedanism; whereupon the guardianship of the Kaaba was confirmed to this Othman and his heirs forever.

[7] That is, before the tribunals of infidels. This passage was occasioned by the following remarkable incident. A certain Jew having a dispute with a wicked Mohammedan, the latter appealed to the judgment of Caab Ebn al Ashraf, a principal Jew, and the former to Mohammed. But at length they agreed to refer the matter to the prophet singly, who, giving it in favor of the Jew, the Mohammedan refused to acquiesce in his sentence, but would needs have it re-heard by Omar, afterward Calif. When they came to him, the Jew told him that Mohammed had already decided the affair in his favor, but that the other would not submit to his determination; and the Mohammedan confessing this to be true, Omar bid them stay a little, and fetching his sword, struck off the obstinate Moslem's head, saying aloud, "This is the reward of him who refuseth to submit to the judgment of God and his apostle."

shall surely find God easy to be reconciled and merciful. And by thy Lord they will not perfectly believe, until they make thee judge of their controversies; and shall not afterward find in their own minds any hardship in what thou shalt determine, but shall acquiesce therein with entire submission. And if we had commanded them, saying, Slay yourselves, or depart from your houses; they would not have done it, except a few of them. And if they had done what they were admonished, it would certainly have been better for them, and more efficacious for confirming their faith; and we should then have surely given them in our sight an exceeding great reward, and we should have directed them in the right way. Whoever obeyeth God and the apostle, they shall be with those unto whom God hath been gracious, of the prophets, and the sincere, and the martyrs, and the righteous; and these are the most excellent company. This is bounty from God; and God is sufficiently knowing.

O true believers, take your necessary precaution against your enemies, and either go forth to war in separate parties, or go forth all together in a body. There is of you who tarrieth behind; and if a misfortune befall you, he saith, Verily God hath been gracious unto me, that I was not present with them: but if success attend you from God, he will say (as if there was no friendship between you and him), Would to God I had been with them, for I should have acquired great merit. . . .

Those believers who sit still at home, not having any hurt, and those who employ their fortunes and their persons for the religion of God, shall not be held equal. God hath preferred those who employ their fortunes and their persons in that cause, to a degree of honor above those who sit at home: God hath indeed promised every one paradise, but God hath preferred those who fight for the faith before those who sit still, by adding unto them a great reward, by degrees of honor conferred on them from him, and by granting them forgiveness and mercy; for God is indulgent and merciful. Moreover unto those whom the angels put to death, having injured their own souls, the angels said, Of what religion were ye? they answered, We were weak in the earth. The angels replied, Was not God's earth wide enough, that ye might fly therein to a place of refuge? Therefore their habitation shall be hell; and an evil journey shall it be thither: except the weak among men, and women, and children, who were not able to find means, and were not directed in the way; these peradventure God will pardon, for God is ready to forgive and gracious. Whosoever flieth from his country for the sake of God's true religion shall find in the earth many forced to do the same, and plenty of provisions. And whoever departeth from his house, and flieth unto God and his apostle, if death overtake him in the way, God will be obliged to reward him, for God is gracious and merciful.

When ye march to war in the earth, it shall be no crime in you if ye shorten your prayers, in case ye fear the infidels may attack you; for the infidels are your open enemy. But when thou, O prophet, shalt be among them, and shalt pray with them, let a party of them arise to prayer with thee, and let them take their arms; and when they shall have worshiped, let them stand behind you, and let another party come that hath not prayed, and let them pray with thee, and let them be cautious and take their arms. The unbelievers would that ye should neglect you arms and your baggage while ye pray, that they might turn upon you at once. It shall be no crime in you, if ye be incommoded by rain, or be sick, that ye lay down your arms; but take your necessary precaution: God hath prepared for the unbelievers an ignominious punishment. And when ye shall have ended your prayer, remember God, standing, and sitting, and lying on your sides. But when ye are secure from danger, complete your prayers; for prayer is commanded the faithful, and appointed to be said at the stated times.

Be not negligent in seeking out the unbelieving people, though ye suffer some inconvenience; for they also shall suffer as ye suffer, and ye hope for a reward from God which they can not hope for; and God is knowing and wise. We have sent down unto thee the book of the Koran with truth, that thou mayest judge between men through that wisdom which

God showeth thee therein; and be not an advocate for the fraudulent; but ask pardon of God for thy wrong intention, since God is indulgent and merciful.

Dispute not for those who deceive one another, for God loveth not him who is a deceiver or unjust. Such conceal themselves from men, but they conceal not themselves from God; for he is with them when they imagine by night a saying which pleaseth him not, and God comprehendeth what they do. Behold, ye are they who have disputed for them in this present life; but who shall dispute with God for them on the day of resurrection, or who will become their patron? yet he who doth evil, or injureth his own soul, and afterward asketh pardon of God, shall find God gracious and merciful.

Whoso committeth wickedness committeth it against his own soul: God is knowing and wise. And whoso committeth a sin or iniquity, and afterward layeth it on the innocent, he shall surely bear the guilt of calumny and manifest injustice. If the indulgence and mercy of God had not been upon thee, surely a part of them had studied to seduce thee; but they shall seduce themselves only, and shall not hurt thee at all. God hath sent down unto thee the book of the Koran and wisdom, and hath taught thee that which thou knowest not; for the favor of God hath been great toward thee.

There is no good in the multitude of their private discourses, unless in the discourse of him who recommendeth alms, or that which is right, or agreement amongst men; whoever doth this out of a desire to please God, we will surely give him a great reward. But whoso separateth himself from the apostle, after true direction hath been manifested unto him, and followeth any other way than that of the true believers, we will cause him to obtain that to which he is inclined, and will cast him to be burned in hell; and an unhappy journey shall it be thither. Verily God will not pardon the giving him a companion, but he will pardon any crime besides that, unto whom he pleaseth: and he who giveth a companion unto God is surely led aside into a wide mistake: the infidels invoke beside him only female deities, and only invoke rebellious Satan. God cursed him; and he said,

Verily I will take of thy servants a part cut off from the rest, and I will seduce them, and will insinuate vain desires into them, and I will command them, and they shall cut off the ears of cattle; and I will command them, and they shall change God's creature. But whoever taketh Satan for his patron, besides God, shall surely perish with a manifest destruction. He maketh them promises, and insinuateth into them vain desires; yet Satan maketh them only deceitful promises. The receptacle of these shall be hell, they shall find no refuge from it. But they who believe, and do good works, we will surely lead them into gardens, through which rivers flow; they shall continue therein forever, according to the true promise of God; and who is more true than God in what he saith? It shall not be according to your desires, nor according to the desires of those who have received the scriptures.

Whoso doth evil, shall be rewarded for it; and shall not find any patron or helper, beside God; but whoso doth good works, whether he be male or female, and is a true believer, they shall be admitted into paradise, and shall not in the least be unjustly dealt with. Who is better in point of religion than he who resigneth himself unto God, and is a worker of righteousness, and followeth the law of Abraham the orthodox? since God took Abraham for his friend; and to God belongeth whatsoever is in heaven and on earth; God comprehendeth all things.

They will consult thee concerning women; Answer, God instructeth you concerning them, and that which is read unto you in the book of the Koran concerning female orphans, to whom ye give not that which is ordained them, neither will ye marry them, and concerning weak infants, and that ye observe justice toward orphans: whatever good ye do, God knoweth it. If a woman fear ill usage, or aversion, from her husband, it shall be no crime in them if they agree the matter amicably between themselves; for a reconciliation is better than a separation. Men's souls are naturally inclined to covetousness: but if ye be kind toward women, and fear to wrong them, God is well acquainted with what ye do. Ye can by no means carry yourselves equally between women in all respects, although ye study to do it; therefore turn not from a wife with all manner of aversion, nor leave her like one in suspense: if ye agree, and fear to abuse your wives, God is gracious and merciful; but if they separate, God will satisfy them both of his abundance; for God is extensive and wise, and unto God belongeth whatsoever is in heaven and on earth. . . .

O ye who have received the scriptures, exceed not the just bounds in your religion, neither say of God any other than the truth. Verily Christ Jesus the son of Mary is the apostle of God, and his Word, which he conveyed into Mary, and a spirit proceeding from him. Believe therefore in God, and his apostles, and say not, There are three Gods; forbear this; it will be better for you. God is but one God. Far be it from him that he should have a son! unto him belongeth whatsoever is in heaven and on earth; and God is a sufficient protector. Christ doth not proudly disdain to be a servant unto God; neither the angels who approach near to his presence: and whoso disdaineth his service, and is puffed up with pride, God will gather them all to himself, on the last day.

Unto those we believe, and do that which is right, he shall give their rewards, and shall superabundantly add unto them of his liberality: but those who are disdainful and proud, he will punish with a grievous punishment; and they shall not find any to protect or to help them, besides God. O men, now is an evident proof come unto you from your Lord, and we have sent down unto you manifest light. They who believe in God and firmly adhere to him, he will lead them into mercy from him, and abundance; and he will direct them in the right way to himself. They will consult thee for thy decision in certain cases; say unto them, God giveth you these determinations, concerning the more remote degrees of kindred. If a man die without issue, and have a sister, she shall have the half of what he shall leave: and he shall be heir to her, in case she have no issue. But if there be two sisters, they shall have between them two third parts of what he shall leave; and if there be several, both brothers and sisters, a male shall have

VOL. V.—8.

as much as the portion of two females.   God declareth unto
you these precepts, lest ye err: and God knoweth all things.

CHAPTER V

ENTITLED, THE TABLE;[1] REVEALED AT MEDINA

O true believers, perform your contracts.   Ye are allowed
to eat the brute cattle, other than what ye are commanded to
abstain from; except the game which ye are allowed at other
times, but not while ye are on pilgrimage to Mecca; God
ordaineth that which he pleaseth.   O true believers, violate
not the holy rites of God, nor the sacred month, nor the offering, nor the ornaments hung thereon,[2] nor those who are
traveling to the holy house, seeking favor from their Lord, and
to please him.   But when ye shall have finished your pilgrimage, then hunt.

And let not the malice of some, in that they hindered you
from entering the sacred temple, provoke you to transgress,
by taking revenge on them in the sacred months.   Assist one
another according to justice and piety, but assist not one
another in injustice and malice: therefore fear God; for God
is severe in punishing.

Ye are forbidden to eat that which dieth of itself, and
blood, and swine's flesh, and that on which the name of any
besides God hath been invoked; and that which hath been
strangled, or killed by a blow, or by a fall, or by the horns of
another beast, and that which hath been eaten by a wild beast,
except what ye shall kill yourselves; and that which hath been
sacrificed unto idols.

It is likewise unlawful for you to make division by casting

---

[1] This title is taken from the Table, which, toward the end of the
chapter, is fabled to have been let down from heaven to Jesus.   It is
sometimes also called the chapter of "Contracts," which word occurs
in the first verse.

[2] The offering here meant is the sheep led to Mecca, to be there sacrificed, about the neck of which they used to hang garlands, green boughs,
or some other ornament, that it may be distinguished as a thing sacred.

lots with arrows. This is an impiety. On this day,[3] woe be unto those who have apostatized from their religion; therefore fear not them, but fear me. This day have I perfected your religion for you,[4] and have completed my mercy upon you; and I have chosen for you Islam, to be your religion. But whosoever shall be driven by necessity through hunger to eat of what we have forbidden, not designing to sin, surely God will be indulgent and merciful unto him. They will ask thee what is allowed them as lawful to eat? Answer, Such things as are good are allowed you; and what ye shall teach animals of prey to catch, training them up for hunting after the manner of dogs, and teaching them according to the skill which God hath taught you. Eat therefore of that which they shall catch for you; and commemorate the name of God thereon; and fear God, for God is swift in taking an account. This day are ye allowed to eat such things as are good, and the food of those to whom the scriptures were given is also allowed as lawful unto you; and your food is allowed as lawful unto them.

And ye are also allowed to marry free women that are believers, and also free women of those who have received the scriptures before you, when ye shall have assigned them their dower; living chastely with them, neither committing fornication, nor taking them for concubines. Whoever shall renounce the faith, his work shall be vain, and in the next life he shall be of those who perish.

O true believers, when ye prepare yourselves to pray, wash your faces, and your hands unto the elbows; and rub your heads, and your feet unto the ankles; and if ye be polluted by having lain with a woman, wash yourself all over. But if ye be sick, or on a journey, or any of you cometh from the privy, or if ye have touched women, and ye find no water, take fine clean sand, and rub your faces and your hands therewith;

[3] This passage, it is said, was revealed on Friday evening, being the day of the pilgrims visiting Mount Arafat, the last time Mohammed visited the temple of Mecca, therefore called the " pilgrimage of valediction."

[4] And therefore the commentators say, that after this time, no positive or negative precept was given.

God would not put a difficulty upon you; but he desireth to purify you, and to complete his favor upon you, that ye may give thanks. Remember the favor of God toward you, and his covenant which he hath made with you, when ye said, We have heard, and will obey. Therefore fear God, for God knoweth the innermost parts of the breasts of men.

O true believers, observe justice when ye appear as witnesses before God, and let not hatred toward any induce you to do wrong: but act justly; this will approach nearer unto piety; and fear God, for God is fully acquainted with what ye do. God hath promised unto those who believe, and do that which is right, that they shall receive pardon and a great reward. But they who believe not, and accuse our signs of falsehood, they shall be the companions of hell.

O true believers, remember God's favor toward you, when certain men designed to stretch forth their hands against you, but he restrained their hands from hurting you; therefore fear God, and in God let the faithful trust. God formerly accepted the covenant of the children of Israel, and we appointed out of them twelve leaders: and God said, Verily, I am with you: if ye observe prayer, and give alms, and believe in my apostles, and assist them, and lend unto God on good usury, I will surely expiate your evil deeds from you, and I will lead you into gardens, wherein rivers flow: but he among you who disbelieveth after this erreth from the straight path. Wherefore because they have broken their covenant, we have cursed them, and hardened their hearts; they dislocate the words of the Pentateuch from their places, and have forgotten part of what they were admonished; and thou wilt not cease to discover deceitful practises among them, except a few of them. But forgive them, and pardon them, for God loveth the beneficent. And from those who say, We are Christians, we have received their covenant; but they have forgotten part of what they were admonished; wherefore we have raised up enmity and hatred among them, till the day of resurrection; and God will then surely declare unto them what they have been doing. O ye who have received the scriptures, now is our apostle come unto you, to make manifest unto you many things which ye concealed in the scriptures; and to pass over many things. Now is light and a perspicuous book of revelations come unto you from God. Thereby will God direct him who shall follow his good pleasure, into the paths of peace; and shall lead them out of darkness into light, by his will, and shall direct them in the right way. . . .

The Jews say, The hand of God is tied up. Their hands shall be tied up, and they shall be cursed for that which they have said. Nay, his hands are both stretched forth; he bestoweth as he pleaseth: that which hath been sent down unto thee from thy Lord shall increase the transgression and infidelity of many of them; and we have put enmity and hatred between them, until the day of resurrection. So often as they shall kindle a fire for war, God shall extinguish it; and they shall set their minds to act corruptly in the earth, but God loveth not the corrupt doers. Moreover, if they who have received the scriptures believe, and fear God, we will surely expiate their sins from them, and we will lead them into gardens of pleasure; and if they observe the law, and the gospel, and the other scriptures which have been sent down unto them from their Lord, they shall surely eat of good things both from above them and from under their feet. Among them there are people who act uprightly; but how evil is that which many of them do work!

O apostle, publish the whole of that which hath been sent down unto thee from thy Lord: for if thou do not, thou dost not in effect publish any part thereof, and God will defend thee against wicked men; for God directeth not the unbelieving people. Say, O ye who have received the scriptures, ye are not grounded on anything, until ye observe the law and the gospel, and that which hath been sent down unto you from your Lord. That which hath been sent down unto thee from thy Lord shall surely increase the transgression and infidelity of many of them: but be not thou solicitous for the unbelieving people. Verily they who believe, and those who Judaize, and the Sabians, and the Christians, whoever of them believeth in God and the last day, and doth that which is right, there shall come no fear on them, neither shall they be grieved. We formerly accepted the covenant of the children of Israel, and sent apostles unto them. So often as an apostle came unto them with that which their souls desired not, they accused some of them of imposture, and some of them they killed: and they imagined that there should be no punishment for those crimes, and they became blind and deaf. Then was God turned unto them; afterward many of them again became blind and deaf; but God saw what they did.

They are surely infidels, who say, Verily God is Christ the son of Mary; since Christ said, O children of Israel, serve God, my Lord and your Lord; whoever shall give a companion unto God, God shall exclude him from paradise, and his habitation shall be hell fire; and the ungodly shall have none to help them. They are certainly infidels, who say, God is the third of three; for there is no God besides one God; and if they refrain not from what they say, a painful torment shall surely be inflicted on such of them as are unbelievers. Will they not therefore be turned unto God, and ask pardon of him? since God is gracious and merciful. Christ the son of Mary is no more than an apostle; other apostles have preceded him; and his mother was a woman of veracity: they both ate food. Behold, how we declare unto them the signs of God's unity; and then behold, how they turn aside from the truth. Say unto them, Will ye worship, besides God, that which can cause you neither harm nor profit? God is he who heareth and seeth. Say, O ye who have received the scriptures, exceed not the just bounds in your religion, by speaking beside the truth; neither follow the desires of people who have heretofore erred, and who have seduced many, and have gone astray from the straight path. Those among the children of Israel who believed not were cursed by the tongue of David, and of Jesus the son of Mary. This befell them because they were rebellious and transgressed: they forbade not one another the wickedness which they committed; and woe unto them for what they committed. Thou shalt see many of them take for their friends those who believe not. Woe unto them for what their souls have sent before them, for that God is incensed against them, and they shall remain in torment forever. But, if they had believed in God, and the prophet, and that which hath been revealed unto him, they had not taken them for their friends; but many of them are evil-doers. Thou shalt surely find the most violent of all men in enmity against the true believers, to be the Jews and the idolaters: and thou shalt surely find those among them to be the most inclinable to entertain friendship for the true believers, who say, We are Christians. This cometh to pass, because there are priests and monks among them; and because they are not elated with pride.[5] And when they hear that which hath been sent down to the apostle read unto them, thou shalt see their eyes overflow with tears, because of the truth which they perceive therein,[6] saying, O Lord, we believe; write us down therefore with those who bear witness to the truth: and what should hinder us from believing in God, and the truth which hath come unto us, and from earnestly desiring that our Lord would introduce us into paradise with the righteous people? Therefore hath God rewarded them, for what they have said, with gardens through which rivers flow; they shall continue therein forever; and this is the reward of the righteous. But they who believe not, and accuse our signs of falsehood, they shall be the companions of hell.

O true believers, forbid not the good things which God hath allowed you; but transgress not, for God loveth not the transgressors. And eat of what God hath given you for food that

[5] Having not that high conceit of themselves, as the Jews have; but being humble and well disposed to receive the truth; qualities, says al Beidawi, which are to be commended even in infidels.

[6] The persons directly intended in this passage were, either Ashama, king of Ethiopia, and several bishops and priests, who, being assembled for that purpose, heard Jaafar Ebn Abi Taleb, who fled to that country in the first flight, read the 29th and 30th, and afterwards the 18th and 19th chapters of the Koran; on hearing of which the king and the rest of the company burst into tears, and confessed what was delivered therein to be conformable to truth; that prince himself, in particular, becoming a proselyte to Mohammedanism: or else, thirty, or as others say, seventy persons, sent ambassadors to Mohammed by the same king of Ethiopia, to whom the prophet himself read the 36th chapter, entitled Y. S. Whereupon they began to weep, saying, " How like is this to that which was revealed unto Jesus! " and immediately professed themselves Moslems.

which is lawful and good: and fear God, in whom ye believe.

God will not punish you for an inconsiderate word in your oaths; but he will punish you for what ye solemnly swear with deliberation. And the expiation of such an oath shall be the feeding of ten poor men with such moderate food as ye feed your own families withal; or to clothe them; or to free the neck of a true believer from captivity: but he who shall not find wherewith to perform one of these three things shall fast three days. This is the expiation of your oaths, when ye swear inadvertently. Therefore keep your oaths. Thus God declareth unto you his signs, that ye may give thanks.

O true believers, surely wine, and lots, and images, and divining arrows are an abomination of the work of Satan; therefore avoid them, that ye may prosper. Satan seeketh to sow dissension and hatred among you, by means of wine and lots, and to divert you from remembering God, and from prayer; will ye not therefore abstain from them? Obey God, and obey the apostle, and take heed to yourselves: but if ye turn back, know that the duty of our apostle is only to preach publicly. In those who believe and do good works, it is no sin that they have tasted wine or gaming before they were forbidden; if they fear God, and believe, and do good works, and shall for the future fear God, and believe, and shall persevere to fear him, and to do good; for God loveth those who do good.

O true believers, God will surely prove you in offering you plenty of game, which ye may take with your hands or your lances, that God may know who feareth him in secret; but whoever transgresseth after this shall suffer a grievous punishment. O true believers, kill no game while ye are on pilgrimage; whosoever among you shall kill any designedly shall restore the like of what ye shall have killed, in domestic animals, according to the determination of two just persons among you, to be brought as an offering to the Kaaba; or in atonement thereof shall feed the poor; or instead thereof shall fast, that he may taste the heinousness of his deed. . God hath forgiven what is past, but whoever returneth to transgress, God will take vengeance on him; for God is mighty and able

to avenge. It is lawful for you to fish in the sea, and to eat
what ye shall catch, as a provision for you and for those who
travel; but it is unlawful for you to hunt by land, while ye
are performing the rites of pilgrimage; therefore fear God,
before whom ye shall be assembled at the last day.

God hath appointed the Kaaba, the holy house, an establishment for mankind; and hath ordained the sacred month,
and the offering, and the ornaments hung thereon. This hath
he done that ye might know that God knoweth whatsoever is
in heaven and on earth, and that God is omniscient. Know
that God is severe in punishing, and that God is also ready to
forgive and merciful. The duty of our apostle is to preach
only; and God knoweth that which ye discover, and that
which ye conceal. Say, Evil and good shall not be equally
esteemed of, though the abundance of evil pleaseth thee;
therefore fear God, O ye of understanding, that ye may be
happy.

O true believers, inquire not concerning things which, if
they be declared unto you, may give you pain; [7] but if ye ask
concerning them when the Koran is sent down, they will be
declared unto you: God pardoneth you as to these matters;
for God is ready to forgive and gracious. People who have
been before you formerly inquired concerning them; and
afterward disbelieved therein. God hath not ordained anything concerning Bahira, nor Saiba, nor Wasila, nor Hami;
but the unbelievers have invented a lie against God: and the
greater part of them do not understand. And when it was
said unto them, Come unto that which God hath revealed, and

[7] The Arabs continually teasing their prophet with questions, which
probably he was not always prepared to answer, they are here ordered
to wait, till God should think fit to declare his pleasure by some further
revelation; and, to abate their curiosity, they are told, at the same
time, that very likely the answers would not be agreeable to their in-
clinations. Al Beidawi says that when the pilgrimage was first commanded, Soraka Ebn Malec asked Mohammed whether they were obliged
to perform it every year? To this question the prophet at first turned
a deaf ear, but being asked it a second and a third time, he at last
said, " No; but if I had said yes it would have become a duty, and, if it
were a duty, ye would not be able to perform it; therefore give me no
trouble as to things wherein I give you none ": whereupon this passage
was revealed.

to the apostle; they answered, That religion which we found our fathers to follow is sufficient for us. What though their fathers knew nothing, and were not rightly directed?

O true believers, take care of your souls. He who erreth shall not hurt you, while ye are rightly directed: unto God shall ye all return, and he will tell you that which ye have done.

O true believers, let witnesses be taken between you, when death approaches any of you, at the time of making the testament; let there be two witnesses, just men, from among you; or two others of a different tribe or faith from yourselves, if ye be journeying in the earth, and the accident of death befall you. Ye shall shut them both up, after the afternoon prayer, and they shall swear by God, if ye doubt them, and they shall say, We will not sell our evidence for a bribe, although the person concerned be one who is related to us, neither will we conceal the testimony of God, for then should we certainly be of the number of the wicked. But if it appear that both have been guilty of iniquity, two others shall stand up in their place, of those who have convicted them of falsehood, the two nearest in blood, and they shall swear by God, saying, Verily our testimony is more true than the testimony of these two, neither have we prevaricated; for then should we become of the number of the unjust. This will be easier, that men may give testimony according to the plain intention thereof, or fear least a different oath be given, after their oath. Therefore fear God, and harken; for God directeth not the unjust people.

On a certain day shall God assemble the apostles, and shall say unto them, What answer was returned you when ye preached unto the people to whom ye were sent? They shall answer, We have no knowledge but thou art the knower of secrets. When God shall say, O Jesus son of Mary, remember my favor toward thee, and toward thy mother; when I strengthened thee with the holy spirit, that thou shouldest speak unto men in the cradle, and when thou wast grown up; and when I taught thee the scripture, and wisdom, and the law, and the gospel; and when thou didst create of clay as it

were the figure of a bird, by my permission, and didst breathe
thereon, and it became a bird by my permission; and thou
didst heal one blind from his birth, and the leper, by my permission; and when thou didst bring forth the dead from their
graves, by my permission; and when I withheld the children
of Israel from killing thee, when thou hadst come unto them
with evident miracles, and such of them as believed not, said,
This is nothing but manifest sorcery. And when I commanded the apostles of Jesus, saying, Believe in me and in my
messenger; they answered, We do believe; and do thou bear
witness that we are resigned unto thee.

Remember when the apostles said, O Jesus, son of Mary, is
thy Lord able to cause a table to descend unto us from
heaven?[8] He answered, Fear God, if ye be true believers.
They said, We desire to eat thereof, and that our hearts may

[8] This miracle is thus related by the commentators. Jesus having,
at the request of his followers, asked it of God, a red table immediately
descended, in their sight, between two clouds, and was set before them;
whereupon he rose up, and having made the ablution, prayed, and then
took off the cloth which covered the table, saying, " In the name of God,
the best provider of food." What the provisions were with which this
table was furnished is a matter wherein the expositors are not agreed;
but the most received tradition is that when the table was uncovered
there appeared a fish ready dressed, without scales or prickly fins, drop-
ping with fat, having salt placed at its head and vinegar at its tail, and
round it all sorts of herbs, except leeks, and five loaves of bread, on
one of which there were olives, on the second honey, on the third butter,
on the fourth cheese, and on the fifth dried flesh. They add that Jesus,
at the request of the apostles, showed them another miracle, by restoring
the fish to life, and causing its scales and fins to return to it, at which
the standers-by being affrighted, he caused it to become as it was before;
that 1,300 men and women, all afflicted with bodily infirmities or poverty, ate of these provisions, and were satisfied, the fish remaining
whole as it was at first; that then the table flew up to heaven in the
sight of all; and all who had partaken of this food were delivered from
their infirmities and misfortunes; and that it continued to descend for
forty days together at dinner-time, and stood on the ground till the sun
declined, and was then taken up into the clouds. Some of the Mohammedan writers are of opinion that this table did not really descend,
but that the incident was only a parable; but most think the words of
the Koran are plain to the contrary. A further tradition is, that several
men were changed into swine for disbelieving this miracle, and attributing it to magic art; or, as others pretend, for stealing some of the
victuals from it.

rest at ease, and that we may know that thou hast told us the truth, and that we may be witnesses thereof. Jesus, the son of Mary, said, O God our Lord, cause a table to descend unto us from heaven, that the day of its descent may become a festival day unto us, unto the first of us, and unto the last of us, and a sign from thee; and do thou provide food for us, for thou art the best provider. God said, Verily I will cause it to descend unto you; but whoever among you shall disbelieve hereafter, I will surely punish him with a punishment wherewith I will not punish any other creature. And when God shall say unto Jesus, at the last day, O Jesus, son of Mary, hast thou said unto men, Take me and my mother for two gods, beside God? He shall answer, Praise be unto thee! it is not for me to say that which I ought not; if I had said so, thou wouldst surely have known it: thou knowest what is in me, but I know not what is in thee; for thou art the knower of secrets. I have not spoken to them any other than what thou didst command me; namely, Worship God, my Lord and your Lord: and I was a witness of their actions while I stayed among them; but since thou hast taken me to thyself, thou hast been the watcher over them; for thou art witness of all things. If thou punish them, they are surely thy servants; and if thou forgive them, thou art mighty and wise. God will say, This day shall their veracity be of advantage unto those who speak truth; they shall have gardens wherein rivers flow, they shall remain therein forever: God hath been well pleased in them, and they have been well pleased in him. This shall be great felicity.

CHAPTER VI

ENTITLED, CATTLE;[1] REVEALED AT MECCA

IN THE NAME OF THE MOST MERCIFUL GOD

Praise be unto God, who hath created the heavens and the earth, and hath ordained the darkness and the light; nevertheless they who believe not in the Lord equalize other gods with

[1] This chapter is so entitled, because some superstitious customs of the Meccans, as to certain cattle, are therein incidentally mentioned.

him.   It is he who hath created you of clay; and then decreed the term of your lives; and the prefixed term is with him: yet do we doubt thereof.   He is God in heaven and in earth; he knoweth what ye keep secret, and what ye publish, and knoweth what ye deserve.   There came not unto them any sign, of the signs of their Lord, but they retired from the same; and they have gainsaid the truth, after that it hath come unto them: but a message shall come unto them, concerning that which they have mocked at.   Do they not consider how many generations we have destroyed before them?   We had established them in the earth in a manner wherein we have not established you; we sent the heaven to rain abundantly upon them, and we gave them rivers which flowed under their feet; yet we destroyed them in their sins, and raised up other generations after them.

Although we had caused to descend unto thee a book written on paper, and they had handled it with their hands, the unbelievers had surely said, This is no other than manifest sorcery.   They said, Unless an angel be sent down unto him, we will not believe.   But if we had sent down an angel, verily the matter had been decreed, and they should not have been borne with, by having time granted them to repent.   And if we had appointed an angel for our messenger, we should have sent him in the form of a man and have clothed him before them, as they are clothed.   Other apostles have been laughed to scorn before thee; but the judgment which they made a jest of encompassed those who laughed them to scorn.   Say, Go through the earth, and behold what hath been the end of those who accused our prophets of imposture.   Say, Unto whom belongeth whatsoever is in heaven and earth?   Say, Unto God.   He hath prescribed unto himself mercy.   He will surely gather you together on the day of resurrection; there is no doubt of it.   They who destroy their own souls are those who will not believe.   Unto him is owing whatsoever happeneth by night or by day; it is he who heareth and knoweth. Say, Shall I take any other protector than God, the creator of heaven and earth, who feedeth all and is not fed by any? Say, Verily I am commanded to be the first who professeth

Islam, and it was said unto me, Thou shalt by no means be one of the idolaters. Say, Verily I fear, if I should rebel against my Lord, the punishment of the great day: from whomsoever it shall be averted on that day, God will have been merciful unto him; this will be manifest salvation.

If God afflict thee with any hurt, there is none who can take it off from thee, except himself; but if he cause good to befall thee, he is almighty; he is the supreme Lord over his servants; and he is wise and knowing. Say, What thing is the strongest in bearing testimony?[2] Say, God; he is witness between me and you. And this Koran was revealed unto me, that I should admonish you thereby, and also those unto whom it shall reach. Do ye really profess that there are other gods together with God? Say, I do not profess this. Say, Verily he is one God; and I am guiltless of what ye associate with him. They unto whom we have given the scripture know our apostle, even as they know their own children; but they who destroy their own souls will not believe.

Who is more unjust than he who inventeth a lie against God, or chargeth his signs with imposture? Surely the unjust shall not prosper. And on the day of resurrection we will assemble them all; then will we say unto those who associated others with God, Where are your companions, whom ye imagined to be those of God? But they shall have no other excuse, than that they shall say, By God our Lord, we have not been idolaters. Behold, how they lie against themselves, and what they have blasphemously imagined to be the companion of God flieth from them. There is of them who harkeneth unto thee when thou readest the Koran; but we have cast veils over their hearts, that they should not understand it, and a deafness in their ears: and though they should see all kinds of signs, they will not believe therein; and their infidelity will arrive to that height that they will even come unto thee, to dispute with thee. The unbelievers will say, This is nothing

[2] This passage was revealed when the Koreish told Mohammed that they had asked the Jews and Christians concerning him, who assured them they found no mention or description of him in their books of scripture, "Therefore," said they, "who bears witness to thee, that thou art the apostle of God?"

but silly fables of ancient times. And they will forbid others from believing therein, and will retire afar off from it; but they will destroy their own souls only, and they are not sensible thereof. If thou didst see, when they shall be set over the fire of hell! and they shall say, Would to God we might be sent back into the world; we would not charge the signs of our Lord with imposture, and we would become true believers: nay, but that is become manifest unto them, which they formerly concealed; and though they should be sent back into the world, they would surely return to that which was forbidden them; and they are surely liars. And they said, There is no other life than our present life; neither shall we be raised again. But if thou couldst see, when they shall be set before their Lord! He shall say unto them, Is not this in truth come to pass? They shall answer, Yea, by our Lord. God shall say, Taste therefore the punishment due unto you, for that ye have disbelieved. They are lost who reject as falsehood the meeting of God in the next life, until the hour cometh suddenly upon them. Then will they say, Alas! for that we have behaved ourselves negligently in our lifetime; and they shall carry their burdens on their backs;[3] will it not be evil which they shall be laden with?

This present life is no other than a play and a vain amusement; but surely the future mansion shall be better for those who fear God: will they not therefore understand? Now we know that what they speak grieveth thee: yet they do not accuse thee of falsehood; but the ungodly contradict the signs of God. And apostles before thee have been accounted liars: but they patiently bore their being accounted liars, and their

---

[3] When an infidel comes forth from his grave, says Jallalo'ddin, his works shall be represented to him under the ugliest form that ever he beheld, having a most deformed countenance, a filthy smell, and a disagreeable voice; so that he shall cry out, "God defend me from thee, what art thou? I never saw anything more detestable!" To which the figure will answer, "Why dost thou wonder at my ugliness? I am thy evil works; thou didst ride upon me while thou wast in the world; but now will I ride upon thee, and thou shalt carry me." And immediately it shall get upon him; and whatever he shall meet shall terrify him, and say, "Hail, thou enemy of God, thou art he who was meant by these words of the Koran, and they shall carry their burdens," etc.

being vexed, until our help came unto them; for there is none
who can change the words of God: and thou hast received some
information concerning those who have been formerly sent
from him.   If their aversion to thy admonitions be grievous
unto thee, if thou canst seek out a den whereby thou mayest
penetrate into the inward parts of the earth, or a ladder by
which thou mayest ascend into heaven, that thou mayest show
them a sign, do so, but thy search will be fruitless; for if God
pleased he would bring them all to the true direction: be not
therefore one of the ignorant.   He will give a favorable answer unto those only who shall harken with attention: and
God will raise the dead; then unto him shall they return.

The infidels say, Unless some sign be sent down unto him
from his Lord, we will not believe: answer, Verily God is able
to send down a sign: but the greater part of them know it not.
There is no kind of beast on earth, nor fowl which flieth with
its wings, but the same is a people like unto you; we have not
omitted anything in the book of our decrees: then unto their
Lord shall they return.   They who accuse our signs of falsehood are deaf and dumb, walking in darkness: God will lead
into error whom he pleaseth, and whom he pleaseth he will
put in the right way.   Say, What think ye? if the punishment of God come upon you, or the hour of the resurrection
come upon you, will ye call upon any other than God, if ye
speak truth? yea, him shall ye call upon, and he shall free
you from that which ye shall ask him to deliver you from, if
he pleaseth; and ye shall forget that which ye associated with
him.   We have already sent messengers unto sundry nations
before thee, and we afflicted them with trouble and adversity
that they might humble themselves: yet when the affliction
which we sent came upon them, they did not humble themselves: but their hearts became hardened, and Satan prepared
for them that which they committed.   And when they had
forgotten that concerning which they had been admonished,
we opened unto them the gates of all things; until, while they
were rejoicing for that which had been given them, we suddenly laid hold on them, and behold, they were seized with
despair; and the utmost part of the people which had acted

wickedly, was cut off: praise be unto God, the Lord of all creatures! Say, what think ye? if God should take away your hearing and your sight, and should seal up your hearts; what god besides God will restore them unto you? . . .

Verily herein are signs, unto people who believe. Yet they have set up the genii as partners with God, although he created them: and they have falsely attributed unto him sons and daughters, without knowledge. Praise be unto him; and far be that from him which they attribute unto him! He is the maker of heaven and earth: how should he have issue, since he hath no consort? he hath created all things, and he is omniscient. This is God your Lord; there is no God but he, the creator of all things: therefore serve him; for he taketh care of all things. The sight comprehendeth him not, but he comprehendeth the sight; he is the gracious, the wise. Now have evident demonstrations come unto you from your Lord; whoso seeth them, the advantage thereof will redound to his own soul: and whoso is wilfully blind, the consequence will be to himself. I am not a keeper over you. Thus do we variously explain our signs; that they may say, Thou hast studied diligently; and that we may declare them unto people of understanding.

Follow that which hath been revealed unto thee from thy Lord; there is no God but he: retire therefore from the idolaters. If God had so pleased, they had not been guilty of idolatry. We have not appointed thee a keeper over them; neither art thou a guardian over them. Revile not the idols which they invoke besides God, lest they maliciously revile God, without knowledge.

Thus have we prepared for every nation their works: hereafter unto God shall they return, and he shall declare unto them that which they have done. They have sworn by God, by the most solemn oath, that if a sign came unto them, they would certainly believe therein: Say, Verily signs are in the power of God alone; and he permitteth you not to understand that when they come, they will not believe.[4] And we will

[4] In this passage Mohammed excuses his inability of working a miracle, as had been demanded of him; declaring that God did not think fit

turn aside their hearts and their sight from the truth, as they believed not therein the first time; and we will leave them to wander in their error. And though we had sent down angels unto them, and the dead had spoken unto them, and we had gathered together before them all things in one view; [5] they would not have believed, unless God had so pleased: but the greater part of them know it not. Thus have we appointed unto every prophet an enemy; the devils of men, and of genii: who privately suggested the one to the other specious discourses to deceive; but if thy Lord pleased, they would not have done it. Therefore leave them, and that which they have falsely imagined; and let the hearts of those be inclined thereto, who believe not in the life to come; and let them please themselves therein, and let them gain that which they are gaining.

Shall I seek after any other judge besides God to judge between us? It is he who hath sent down unto you the book of the Koran, distinguishing between good and evil; and they to whom we gave the scripture know that it is sent down from thy Lord, with truth. Be not therefore one of those who doubt thereof. The words of thy Lord are perfect in truth and justice; there is none who can change his words: he both heareth and knoweth. But if thou obey the greater part of them who are in the earth, they will lead thee aside from the path of God: they follow an uncertain opinion only, and speak nothing but lies; verily thy Lord well knoweth those who go astray from his path, and well knoweth those who are rightly directed.

Eat of that whereon the name of God hath been commemorated, if ye believe in his signs: and why do ye not eat of that whereon the name of God hath been commemorated? since he hath plainly declared unto you what he hath forbidden you;

to comply with their desires; and that if he had so thought fit, yet it had been in vain, because if they were not convinced by the Koran, they would not be convinced by the greatest miracle.

[5] For the Meccans required that Mohammed should either show them an angel descending from heaven in their sight, or raise their dead fathers, that they might discourse with them, or prevail on God and his angels to appear to them in a body.

except that which ye be compelled to eat of by necessity:
many lead others into error, because of their appetites being
void of knowledge; but thy Lord well knoweth who are the
transgressors. Leave both the outside of iniquity, and the
inside thereof; for they who commit iniquity shall receive the
reward of that which they shall have gained. Eat not therefore of that whereon the name of God hath not been commemorated; for this is certainly wickedness: but the devils will
suggest unto their friends, that they dispute with you concerning this precept; but if ye obey them, ye are surely
idolaters.

Shall he who hath been dead, and whom we have restored
unto life, and unto whom we have ordained a light, whereby
he may walk among men, be as he whose similitude is in
darkness, from whence he shall not come forth? Thus was
that which the infidels are doing, prepared for them. And
thus have we placed in every city chief leaders of the wicked
men thereof, that they may act deceitfully therein; but they
shall act deceitfully against their own souls only; and they
know it not. And when a sign cometh unto them, they say,
We will by no means believe until a revelation be brought
unto us, like unto that which hath been delivered unto the
messengers of God. God best knoweth whom he will appoint
for his messenger. Vileness in the sight of God shall fall
upon those who deal wickedly, and a grievous punishment, for
that they have dealt deceitfully. And whomsoever God shall
please to direct, he will open his breast to receive the faith of
Islam: but whomsoever he shall please to lead into error, he
will render his breast straight and narrow, as though he were
climbing up to heaven. Thus doth God inflict a terrible punishment on those who believe not. This is the right way of
thy Lord.

Now have we plainly declared our signs unto those people
who will consider. They shall have a dwelling of peace with
their Lord, and he shall be their patron, because of that which
they have wrought. Think on the day whereon God shall
gather them all together, and shall say, O company of genii,
ye have been much concerned with mankind; and their friends

from among mankind shall say, O Lord, the one of us hath received advantage from the other, and we are arrived at our limited term which thou hast appointed us. God will say, Hell fire shall be your habitation, therein shall ye remain forever; unless as God shall please to mitigate your pains, for thy Lord is wise and knowing. Thus do we set some of the unjust over others of them, because of that which they have deserved.

O company of genii and men, did not messengers from among yourselves come unto you,[6] rehearsing my signs unto you, and forewarning you of the meeting of this your day? They shall answer, We bear witness against ourselves: the present life deceived them: and they shall bear witness against themselves that they were unbelievers. This hath been the method of God's dealing with his creatures, because thy Lord would not destroy the cities in their iniquity, while their inhabitants were careless. Every one shall have degrees of recompense of that which they shall do; for thy Lord is not regardless of that which they do, and thy Lord is self-sufficient and endued with mercy. If he pleaseth he can destroy you, and cause such as he pleaseth to succeed you, in like manner as he produced you from the posterity of other people. Verily that which is threatened you shall surely come to pass; neither shall ye cause it to fail.

Say unto those of Mecca, O my people, act according to your power; verily I will act according to my duty: and hereafter shall ye know whose will be the reward of paradise. The ungodly shall not prosper. Those of Mecca set apart unto God a portion of that which he hath produced of the fruits of the earth, and of cattle; and say, This belongeth unto God (according to their imagination), and this unto our companions. And that which is destined for their companions cometh not unto God; yet that which is set apart unto

[6] It is the Mohammedan belief that apostles were sent by God for the conversion both of genii and of men; being generally of human race (as Mohammed, in particular, who pretended to have a commission to preach to both kinds); according to this passage, it seems there must have been prophets of the race of genii also, though their mission be a secret to us.

God cometh unto their companions.   How ill do they judge!
In like manner have their companions induced many of the
idolaters to slay their children, that they might bring them
to perdition, and that they might render their religion ob-
scure and confused unto them.   But if God had pleased, they
had not done this: therefore leave them, and that which they
falsely imagine. . . .

Say, Come; I will rehearse that which your Lord hath
forbidden you; that is to say, that ye be not guilty of idolatry, and that ye show kindness to your parents, and that ye
murder not your children for fear lest ye be reduced to poverty: we will provide for you and them; and draw not near
unto heinous crimes, neither openly nor in secret; and slay
not the soul which God hath forbidden you to slay, unless for
a just cause.   This hath he enjoined you that ye may understand.   And meddle not with the substance of the orphan,
otherwise than for the improving thereof, until he attain his
age of strength; and use a full measure and a just balance.
We will not impose a task on any soul, beyond its ability.
And when ye pronounce judgment observe justice, although
it be for or against one who is near of kin, and fulfil the covenant of God.   This hath God commanded you, that ye may
be admonished; and that ye may know that this is my right
way: therefore follow it, and follow not the paths of others,
lest ye be scattered from the path of God.   This hath he
commanded you, that ye may take heed.

We gave also unto Moses the book of the law; a perfect
rule unto him who should do right, and a determination
concerning all things needful, and a direction, and mercy;
that the children of Israel might believe the meeting of their
Lord.   And this book which we have now sent down is
blessed; therefore follow it and fear God, that ye may obtain
mercy: lest ye should say, The scriptures were only sent down
unto two people before us; and we neglected to peruse them
with attention: or lest ye should say, If a book of divine revelations had been sent down unto us, we would surely have
been better directed than they.   And now hath a manifest
declaration come unto you from your Lord, and a direction

and mercy: and who is more unjust than he who deviseth lies against the signs of God, and turneth aside from them? We will reward those who turn aside from our signs with a grievous punishment, because they have turned aside. Do they wait for any other than that the angels should come unto them, to part their souls from their bodies; or that thy Lord should come to punish them; or that some of the signs of thy Lord should come to pass, showing the day of judgment to be at hand?[7] On the day whereon some of thy Lord's signs shall come to pass, its faith shall not profit a soul which believed not before, or wrought not good in its faith. Say, Wait ye for this day; we surely do wait for it.

They who make a division in their religion, and become sectaries, have thou nothing to do with them; their affair belongeth unto God. Hereafter shall he declare unto them that which they have done. He who shall appear with good works shall receive a tenfold recompense for the same; but he who shall appear with evil works shall receive only an equal punishment for the same; and they shall not be treated unjustly. Say, Verily my Lord hath directed me into a right way, a true religion, the sect of Abraham the orthodox; and he was no idolater. Say, Verily, my prayers, and my worship, and my life, and my death are dedicated unto God, the Lord of all creatures: he hath no companion. This have I been commanded: I am the first Moslem. Say, Shall I desire any other Lord besides God? since he is the Lord of all things; and no soul shall acquire any merits or demerits but for itself; and no burdened soul shall bear the burden of another. Moreover unto your Lord shall ye return; and he shall declare unto you that concerning which ye now dispute. It is he who hath appointed you to succeed your predecessors in the earth, and hath raised some of you above others by

---

[7] Al Beidawi, from a tradition of Mohammed, says that ten signs will precede the last day, viz., the smoke, the beast of the earth, an eclipse in the east, another in the west, and a third in the peninsula of Arabia, the appearance of Antichrist, the sun's rising in the west, the eruption of Gog and Magog, the descent of Jesus on earth, and fire which shall break forth from Aden.

various degrees of worldly advantages, that he might prove you by that which he hath bestowed on you. Thy Lord is swift in punishing; and he is also gracious and merciful.

CHAPTER VII

ENTITLED, AL ARAF;[1] REVEALED AT MECCA

IN THE NAME OF THE MOST MERCIFUL GOD

A. L. M. S. A book hath been sent down unto thee: and therefore let there be no doubt in thy breast concerning it; that thou mayest preach the same, and that it may be an admonition unto the faithful. Follow that which hath been sent down unto you from your Lord; and follow no guides besides him: how little will ye be warned! How many cities have we destroyed; which our vengeance overtook by night, or while they were reposing themselves at noonday! And their supplication, when our punishment came upon them, was no other than that they said, Verily we have been unjust. We will surely call those to an account, unto whom a prophet hath been sent; and we will also call those to account who have been sent unto them. And we will declare their actions unto them with knowledge; for we are not absent from them. The weighing of men's actions on that day shall be just; and they whose balances laden with their good works shall be heavy are those who shall be happy; but they whose balances shall be light are those who have lost their souls, because they abjured our signs.

And now have we placed you on the earth, and have provided you food therein: but how little are ye thankful! We created you, and afterward formed you; and then said unto the angels, Worship Adam; and they all worshiped him, except Eblis, who was not one of those who worshiped. God said unto him, What hindered thee from worshiping Adam,

---

[1] Al Araf signifies the partition between paradise and hell, which is mentioned in this chapter.

since I had commanded thee? He answered, I am more excellent than he: thou hast created me of fire, and hast created him of clay. God said, Get thee down therefore from paradise; for it is not fit that thou behave thyself proudly therein: get thee hence; thou shalt be one of the contemptible. He answered, Give me respite until the day of resurrection. God said, Verily thou shalt be one of those who are respited. The devil said, Because thou hast depraved me, I will lay in wait for men in thy strait way; then will I come upon them from before, and from behind, and from their right hands, and from their left; and thou shalt not find the greater part of them thankful. God said unto him, Get thee hence, despised, and driven far away: verily whoever of them shall follow thee, I will surely fill hell with you all: but as for thee, O Adam, dwell thou and thy wife in paradise; and eat of the fruit thereof wherever ye will; but approach not this tree, lest ye become of the number of the unjust. And Satan suggested to them both, that he would discover unto them their nakedness, which was hidden from them; and he said, Your Lord hath not forbidden you this tree, for any other reason but lest ye should become angels, or lest ye become immortal. And he sware unto them, saying, Verily I am one of those who counsel you aright. And he caused them to fall through deceit. And when they had tasted of the tree, their nakedness appeared unto them; and they began to join together the leaves of paradise, to cover themselves. And their Lord called to them, saying, Did I not forbid you this tree; and did I not say unto you, Verily Satan is your declared enemy? They answered, O Lord, we have dealt unjustly with our own souls; and if thou forgive us not, and be not merciful unto us, we shall surely be of those who perish. God said, Get ye down, the one of you an enemy unto the other; and ye shall have a dwelling-place upon earth, and a provision for a season. He said, Therein shall ye live, and therein shall ye die, and from thence shall ye be taken forth at the resurrection. O children of Adam, we have sent down unto you apparel, to conceal your nakedness, and fair garments; but the clothing of piety is better. This is one of the signs of God; that peradventure ye may consider.

O children of Adam, let not Satan seduce you, as he expelled your parents out of paradise, by stripping them of their clothing, that he might show them their nakedness: verily he seeth you, both he and his companions, whereas ye see not them. We have appointed the devils to be the patrons of those who believe not: and when they commit a filthy action, they say, We found our fathers practising the same; and God hath commanded us to do it. Say, Verily God commandeth not filthy actions. Do ye speak concerning God that which ye know not? Say, My Lord hath commanded me to observe justice; therefore set your faces to pray at every place of worship, and call upon him, approving unto him the sincerity of your religion. As he produced you at first, so unto him shall ye return. A part of mankind hath he directed; and a part hath been justly led into error, because they have taken the devils for their patrons besides God, and imagine that they are rightly directed.

O children of Adam, take your decent apparel at every place of worship, and eat and drink, but be not guilty of excess; for he loveth not those who are guilty of excess. Say, Who hath forbidden the decent apparel of God, which he hath produced for his servants, and the good things which he hath provided for food? Say, These things are for those who believe, in this present life, but peculiarly on the day of resurrection. Thus do we distinctly explain our signs unto people who understand. Say, Verily my Lord hath forbidden filthy actions, both that which is discovered thereof, and that which is concealed, and also iniquity, and unjust violence; and hath forbidden you to associate with God that concerning which he hath sent you down no authority, or to speak of God that which ye know not. Unto every nation there is a prefixed term; therefore when their term is expired, they shall not have respite for an hour, neither shall they be anticipated.

O children of Adam, verily apostles from among you shall come unto you, who shall expound my signs unto you: who-

soever therefore shall fear God and amend, there shall come
no fear on them, neither shall they be grieved. But they
who shall accuse our signs of falsehood, and shall proudly
reject them, they shall be the companions of hell fire; they
shall remain therein forever. And who is more unjust than
he who deviseth a lie concerning God, or accuseth his signs
of imposture? Unto these shall be given their portion of
worldly happiness, according to what is written in the book
of God's decrees, until our messengers come unto them, and
shall cause them to die; saying, Where are the idols which
ye called upon, besides God? They shall answer, They have
disappeared from us. And they shall bear witness against
themselves, that they were unbelievers. God shall say unto
them at the resurrection, Enter ye with the nations which
have preceded you, of genii and of men, into hell fire; so
often as one nation shall enter, it shall curse its sister, until
they shall all have successively entered therein. The latter
of them shall say of the former of them, O Lord, these have
seduced us; therefore inflict on them a double punishment
of the fire of hell. God shall answer, It shall be doubled
unto all; but ye know it not. And the former of them shall
say unto the latter of them, Ye have not therefore any favor
above us; taste the punishment for that which ye have gained.
Verily they who shall charge our signs with falsehood, and
shall proudly reject them, the gates of heaven shall not be
opened unto them, neither shall they enter into paradise,
until a camel pass through the eye of a needle; and thus will
we reward the wicked doers. Their couch shall be in hell,
and over them shall be coverings of fire; and thus will we
reward the unjust. But they who believe and do that which
is right (we will not load any soul but according to its ability), they shall be the companions of paradise; they shall
remain therein forever. And we will remove all grudges
from their minds; rivers shall run at their feet, and they
shall say, Praised be God, who hath directed us unto this
felicity! for we should not have been rightly directed, if
God had not directed us: now are we convinced by demonstration that the apostles of our Lord came unto us with truth.

And it shall be proclaimed unto them, This is paradise, whereof ye are made heirs, as a reward for that which ye have wrought. And the inhabitants of paradise shall call out to the inhabitants of hell fire, saying, Now have we found that which our Lord promised us to be true; have ye also found that which your Lord promised you to be true? They shall answer, Yea. And a crier shall proclaim between them, The curse of God shall be on the wicked; who turn men aside from the way of God, and seek to render it crooked, and who deny the life to come. And between the blessed and the damned there shall be a veil; and men shall stand on al Araf,[2] who shall know every one of them by their marks; and shall call unto the inhabitants of paradise, saying, Peace be upon you: yet they shall not enter therein, although they earnestly desire it. And when they shall turn their eyes toward the companions of hell fire, they shall say, O Lord, place us not with the ungodly people! And those who stand on al Araf shall call unto certain men, whom they shall know by their marks, and shall say, What hath your gathering of riches availed you, and that ye were puffed up with pride? Are these the men on whom ye swear that God would not bestow mercy? Enter ye unto paradise; there shall come no fear on you, neither shall ye be grieved. And the inhabitants of hell fire shall call unto the inhabitants of paradise, saying, Pour upon us some water, or of those refreshments which God hath bestowed on you. They shall answer, Verily God hath forbidden them unto the unbelievers; who made a laughing-stock and a sport of their religion, and whom the life of the world hath deceived: therefore this day will we forget them, as they did forget the meeting of this day, and for that they denied our signs to be from God.

And now we have brought unto those of Mecca a book of divine revelations: we have explained it with knowledge; a direction and mercy unto people who shall believe. Do they wait for any other than the interpretation thereof? On the day whereon the interpretation thereof shall come, they who

---

[2] Al Araf is the name of the wall or partition which, as Mohammed taught, will separate paradise from hell.

had forgotten the same before shall say, Now are we convinced by demonstration that the messengers of our Lord came unto us with truth: shall we therefore have any intercessors, who will intercede for us? or shall we be sent back into the world, that we may do other works than what we did in our lifetime? But now have they lost their souls; and that which they impiously imagined hath fled from them.

Verily your Lord is God, who created the heavens and the earth in six days; and then ascended his throne: he causeth the night to cover the day; it succeedeth the same swiftly: he also created the sun and the moon, and the stars, which are absolutely subject unto his command. Is not the whole creation, and the empire thereof, his? Blessed be God, the Lord of all creatures! Call upon your Lord humbly and in secret; for he loveth not those who transgress. And act not corruptly in the earth, after its reformation; and call upon him with fear and desire: for the mercy of God is near unto the righteous. It is he who sendeth the winds, spread abroad before his mercy, until they bring a cloud heavy with rain, which we drive unto a dead country, and we cause water to descend thereon, by which we cause all sorts of fruits to spring forth. Thus will we bring forth the dead from their graves; that peradventure ye may consider. From a good country shall its fruit spring forth abundantly, by the permission of its Lord; but from the land which is bad, it shall not spring forth otherwise than scarcely. Thus do we explain the signs of divine providence unto the people who are thankful.

We formerly sent Noah unto his people: and he said, O my people, worship God: ye have no other God than him. Verily I fear for you the punishment of the great day. The chiefs of his people answered him, We surely perceive thee to be in a manifest error. He replied, O my people, there is no error in me; but I am a messenger from the Lord of all creatures. I bring unto you the messages of my Lord; and I counsel you aright: for I know from God that which ye know not. Do ye wonder that an admonition hath come unto you from your Lord by a man from among you, to warn you, that ye may take heed to yourselves, and that peradventure ye may obtain mercy? And they accused him of imposture: but we delivered him and those who were with him in the ark, and we drowned those who charged our signs with falsehood; for they were a blind people.

And unto the tribe of Ad [3] we sent their brother Hud. He said, O my people, worship God: ye have no other God than him; will ye not fear him? The chiefs of those among his people who believed not answered, Verily we perceive that thou art guided by folly; and we certainly esteem thee to be one of the liars. He replied, O my people, I am not guided by folly; but I am a messenger unto you from the Lord of all creatures: I bring unto you the messages of my Lord; and I am a faithful counselor unto you. Do ye wonder that an admonition hath come unto you from your Lord, by a man from among you, that he may warn you? Call to mind how he hath appointed you successors unto the people of Noah, and hath added unto you in stature largely. Remember the benefits of God, that ye may prosper. They said, Art thou come unto us, that we should worship God alone, and leave the deities which our fathers worshiped? Now bring down that judgment upon us, with which thou threatenest us, if thou speakest truth. Hud answered, Now shall there suddenly fall upon you from your Lord vengeance and indignation. Will ye dispute with me concerning the names which ye have named, and your fathers; as to which God hath not revealed unto you any authority? Do ye wait therefore, and I will be one of those who wait with you. And we delivered him, and them who believed with him, by our mercy; and we cut off the uttermost part of those who charged our signs with falsehood, and were not believers.

And unto the tribe of Thamud we sent their brother Saleh. He said, O my people, worship God: ye have no God besides

---

[3] Ad was an ancient and potent tribe of Arabs, and zealous idolaters. They chiefly worshiped four deities, Sakia, Hafedha, Razeka, and Salema; the first, as they imagined, supplying them with rain, the second preserving them from all dangers abroad, the third providing food for their sustenance, and the fourth restoring them to health when afflicted with sickness, according to the signification of the several names.

him. Now hath a manifest proof come unto you from your Lord. This she-camel of God is a sign unto you: [4] therefore dismiss her freely, that she may feed in God's earth; and do her no hurt, lest a painful punishment seize you. And call to mind how he hath appointed you successors unto the tribe of Ad, and hath given you a habitation on earth; ye build yourselves castles on the plains thereof, and cut out the mountains into houses. Remember therefore the benefits of God, and commit not violence in the earth, acting corruptly. The chiefs among his people who were puffed up with pride said unto those who were esteemed weak, namely, unto those who believed among them, Do ye know that Selah hath been sent from his Lord? They answered, We do surely believe in that wherewith he hath been sent. Those who were elated with pride replied, Verily we believe not in that wherein ye believe. And they cut off the feet of the camel, and insolently transgressed the command of their Lord, and said, O Saleh, cause that to come upon us, with which thou hast threatened us, if thou art one of those who have been sent by God. Whereupon a terrible noise from heaven assailed them; and in the morning they were found in their dwellings prostrate on their beasts and dead. And Saleh departed from them, and said, O my people, now have I delivered unto you the

---

[4] The Thamudites, insisting on a miracle, proposed to Saleh that he should go with them to their festival, and, that they should call on their gods, and he on his, promising to follow that deity which should answer. But after they had called on their idols a long time to no purpose, Jonda Ebn Amru, their prince, pointed to a rock standing by itself, and bade Saleh cause a she-camel big with young to come forth from it, solemnly engaging that, if he did, he would believe, and his people promised the same. Whereupon Saleh asked it of God, and presently the rock, after several throes as if in labor, was delivered of a she-camel answering the description of Jonda, which immediately brought forth a young one, ready weaned, and, as some say, as big as herself. Jonda, seeing this miracle, believed on the prophet, and some few with him; but the greater part of the Thamudites remained, notwithstanding, incredulous. Of this camel the commentators tell several stories: as that, when she went to drink, she never raised her head from the well or river till she had drunk up all the water in it, and then she offered herself to be milked, the people drawing from her as much milk as they pleased; and some say that she went about the town crying aloud, "If any wants milk let him come forth."

message of my Lord; and I advised you well, but ye love not those who advise you well.

And remember Lot, when he said unto his people, Do ye commit a wickedness, wherein no creature hath set you an example? Do ye approach lustfully unto men, leaving the women? Certainly ye are people who transgress all modesty. But the answer of his people was no other than that they said the one to the other, Expel them your city; for they are men who preserve themselves pure from the crimes which ye commit. Therefore we delivered him and his family, except his wife; she was one of those who stayed behind: and we rained a shower of stones upon them. Behold therefore what was the end of the wicked. And unto Madian we sent their brother Shoaib. He said unto them, O my people, worship God; ye have no God besides him. Now hath an evident demonstration come unto you from your Lord. Therefore give full measure and just weight, and diminish not unto men aught of their matters; neither act corruptly in the earth, after its reformation. This will be better for you, if ye believe. And beset not every way, threatening the passenger, and turning aside from the path of God him who believeth in him, and seeking to make it crooked. And remember, when ye were few, and God multiplied you: and behold, what hath been the end of those who acted corruptly. And if part of you believeth that wherewith I am sent, and part believe not, wait patiently until God judge between us; for he is the best judge. . . .

Say, O men, Verily I am the messenger of God unto you all: unto him belongeth the kingdom of heaven and earth; there is no God but he; he giveth life, and he causeth to die. Believe therefore in God and his apostle, the illiterate prophet, who believeth in God and his word; and follow him, that ye may be rightly directed. Of the people of Moses there is a party who direct others with truth, and act justly according to the same. And we divided them into twelve tribes, as into so many nations. And we spake by revelation unto Moses, when his people asked drink of him, and we said, Strike the rock with thy rod; and there gushed thereout twelve fountains, and men knew their respective drinking-place. And we caused clouds to overshadow them, and manna and quails to descend upon them, saying, Eat of the good things which we have given you for food: and they injured not us, but they injured their own souls. And call to mind when it was said unto them, Dwell in this city, and eat of the provisions thereof wherever ye will, and say, Forgiveness! and enter the gate worshiping: we will pardon you your sins, and will give increase unto the well-doers. But they who were ungodly among them changed the expression into another, which had not been spoken unto them. Wherefore we sent down upon them indignation from heaven, because they had transgressed. And ask them concerning the city, which was situate on the sea, when they transgressed on the Sabbath day: when their fish came unto them on their Sabbath day, appearing openly on the water; but on the day whereon they celebrated no Sabbath, they came not unto them. Thus did we prove them, because they were wicked doers. And when a party of them said unto the others, Why do ye warn a people whom God will destroy, or will punish with a grievous punishment? They answered, This is an excuse for us unto your Lord; and peradventure they will beware. But when they had forgotten the admonitions which had been given them, we delivered those who forbade them to do evil; and we inflicted on those who had transgressed a severe punishment, because they had acted wickedly. And when they proudly refused to desist from what had been forbidden them, we said unto them, Be ye transformed into apes, driven away from the society of men. And remember when thy Lord declared that he would surely send against the Jews, until the day of resurrection, some nation who should afflict them with a grievous oppression: for thy Lord is swift in punishing, and he is also ready to forgive and merciful: and we dispersed them among the nations in the earth. Some of them are upright persons, and some of them are otherwise. And we proved them with prosperity and with adversity, that they might return from their disobedience; and a succession of their posterity hath succeeded

THE KAABA, OR SACRED TEMPLE, IN THE HEART
OF MECCA.

The chief shrine of the Mohammedans.

after them, who have inherited the book of the law, who receive the temporal goods of this world, and say, It will surely be forgiven us: and if a temporal advantage like the former be offered them, they accept it also. Is not the covenant of the book of the law established with them, that they should not speak of God aught but the truth? Yet they diligently read that which is therein. But the enjoyment of the next life will be better for those who fear God than the wicked gains of these people (Do ye not therefore understand?) and for those who hold fast the book of the law, and are constant at prayer: for we will by no means suffer the reward of the righteous to perish. And when we shook the mountain of Sinai over them, as though it had been a covering, and they imagined that it was falling upon them; and we said, Receive the law which we have brought you, with reverence; and remember that which is contained therein, that ye may take heed. And when thy Lord drew forth their posterity from the loins of the sons of Adam,[5] and took them to witness against themselves, saying, Am not I your Lord? They answered, Yea: we do bear witness. This was done lest ye should say, at the day of resurrection, Verily we were negligent as to this matter, because we were not apprised thereof: or lest ye should say, Verily our fathers were formerly guilty of idolatry, and we are their posterity who have succeeded them; wilt thou therefore destroy us for that which vain men have committed? Thus do we explain our signs, that they may return from their vanities. And relate unto the Jews the history of him unto whom we brought our signs,

[5] This was done in the plain of Dahia in India, or, as others imagine, in a valley near Mecca. The commentators tell us that God stroked Adam's back, and extracted from his loins his whole posterity, which should come into the world until the resurrection, one generation after another; that these men were actually assembled all together in the shape of small ants, which were endued with understanding; and that after they had, in the presence of the angels, confessed their dependence on God, they were again caused to return into the loins of their great ancestor. From this fiction it appears that the doctrine of pre-existence is not unknown to the Mohammedans; and there is some little conformity between it and the modern theory of generation *ex animalculis in semine marium.*

and he departed from them; wherefore Satan followed him, and he became one of those who were seduced. And if we had pleased, we had surely raised him thereby unto wisdom; but he inclined unto the earth, and followed his own desire. Wherefore his likeness is as the likeness of a dog, which, if thou drive him away, putteth forth his tongue, or, if thou let him alone, putteth forth his tongue also. This is the likeness of the people who accuse our signs of falsehood. Rehearse therefore this history unto them, that they may consider.

Evil is the similitude of those people who accuse our signs of falsehood and injure their own souls. Whomsoever God shall direct, he will be rightly directed; and whomsoever he shall lead astray, they shall perish. Moreover we have created for hell many of the genii and of men; they have hearts by which they understand not, and they have eyes by which they see not, and they have ears by which they hear not. These are like the brute beasts; yea, they go more astray: these are the negligent. God hath most excellent names: therefore call on him by the same; and withdraw from those who use his names perversely: they shall be rewarded for that which they shall have wrought. . . .

And if an evil suggestion from Satan be suggested unto thee, to divert thee from thy duty, have recourse unto God; for he heareth and knoweth. Verily they who fear God, when a temptation from Satan assaileth them, remember the divine commands, and behold, they clearly see the danger of sin, and the wiles of the devil. But as for the brethren of the devils, they shall continue them in error; and afterward they shall not preserve themselves therefrom. And when thou bringest not a verse of the Koran unto them, they say, Hast thou not put it together? Answer, I follow that only which is revealed unto me from my Lord. This book containeth evident proofs from your Lord, and is a direction and mercy unto people who believe. And when the Koran is read, attend thereto, and keep silence; that ye may obtain mercy. And meditate on thy Lord in thine own mind, with humility and fear, and without loud speaking, evening and morning; and be not one of the negligent. Moreover the angels who are with my Lord do not proudly disdain his service, but they celebrate his praise and worship him.

CHAPTER VIII

ENTITLED, THE SPOILS;[1] REVEALED AT MEDINA

IN THE NAME OF THE MOST MERCIFUL GOD

They will ask thee concerning the spoils: Answer, The division of the spoils belongeth unto God and the apostle. Therefore fear God, and compose the matter amicably among you; and obey God and his apostle, if ye are true believers. Verily the true believers are those whose hearts fear when God is mentioned, and whose faith increaseth when his signs are rehearsed unto them, and who trust in their Lord; who observe the stated times of prayer, and give alms out of that which we have bestowed on them. These are really believers: they shall have superior degrees of felicity with their Lord, and forgiveness, and an honorable provision. As thy Lord brought thee forth from thy house with truth; and part of the believers were averse to thy directions:[2] they disputed

[1] This chapter was occasioned by the high disputes which happened about the division of the spoils taken at the battle of Bedr, between the young men who had fought and the old men who had stayed under the ensigns; the former insisting they ought to have the whole, and the latter that they deserved a share. To end the contention, Mohammed pretended to have received orders from heaven to divide the booty among them equally, having first taken thereout a fifth part for the purposes which will be mentioned hereafter.

[2] For the better understanding of this passage, it will be necessary to mention some further particulars relating to the expedition of Bedr. Mohammed having received private information (for which he pretended he was obliged to the angel Gabriel) of the approach of a caravan belonging to the Koreish, which was on its return from Syria with a large quantity of valuable merchandise, guarded by no more than thirty, or, as others say, forty men, set out with a party to intercept it. Abu Sofian, who commanded the little convoy, having notice of Mohammed's motions, sent to Mecca for succors; upon which Abu Jahl, and all the principal men of the city, except only Abu Laheb, marched to his assistance, with a body of nine hundred and fifty men. Mohammed had no sooner received advice of this, than Gabriel descended with a promise that he should either take the caravan or beat the succors; whereupon he consulted with his companions which of the two he should attack. Some of them were

with thee concerning the truth, after it had been made known
unto them; no otherwise than as if they had been led forth to
death, and had seen it with their eyes. And call to mind
when God promised you one of the two parties, that it should
be delivered unto you; and ye desired that the party which
was not furnished with arms should be delivered unto you;
but God purposed to make known the truth in his words,
and to cut off the uttermost part of the unbelievers; that he
might verify the truth, and destroy falsehood, although the
wicked were averse thereto. When ye asked assistance of
your Lord, and he answered you, Verily I will assist you
with a thousand angels, following one another in order. And
this God designed only as good tidings for you, and that your
hearts might thereby rest secure: for victory is from God
alone; and God is mighty and wise. When a sleep fell on
you as a security from him, and he sent down upon you
water from heaven, that he might thereby purify you, and
take from you the abomination of Satan,[3] and that he might
confirm your hearts, and establish your feet thereby. Also
when thy Lord spake unto the angels, saying, Verily I am

for setting upon the caravan, saying that they were not prepared to fight
such a body of troops as were coming with Abu Jahl: but this proposal
Mohammed rejected, telling them that the caravan was at a considerable
distance by the seaside, whereas Abu Jahl was just upon them. The
others, however, insisted so obstinately on pursuing the first design of
falling on the caravan, that the prophet grew angry, but by the inter-
position of Abu Becr, Omar, Saad Ebn Obadah, and Mokdad Ebn Amru,
they at length acquiesced in his opinion. Mokdad in particular assured
him they were all ready to obey his orders, and would not say to him, as
the children of Israel did to Moses, " Go thou and thy Lord to fight, for
we will sit here"; but, " Go thou and thy Lord to fight, and we will fight
with you." At this Mohammed smiled, and again sat down to consult
with them, applying himself chiefly to the Ansars or " helpers," because
they were the greater part of his forces, and he had some apprehension
lest they should not think themselves obliged by the oath they had taken
to him at al Akaba, to assist him against any other than such as should
attack him in Medina. But Saad Ebn Moadh, in the name of the rest,
told him that they had received him as the apostle of God, and had
promised him obedience, and were therefore all to a man ready to follow
him where he pleased, though it were into the sea. Upon which the
prophet ordered them in God's name to attack the succors, assuring them
of the victory.

[3] It is related that the spot where Mohammed's little army lay was a

with you; wherefore confirm those who believe. I will cast a dread into the hearts of the unbelievers. Therefore strike off their heads, and strike off all the ends of their fingers. This shall they suffer, because they have resisted God and his apostle: and whosoever shall oppose God and his apostle, verily God will be severe in punishing him. This shall be your punishment; taste it therefore: and the infidels shall also suffer the torment of hell fire.

O true believers, when ye meet the unbelievers marching in great numbers against you, turn not your backs unto them: for whoso shall turn his back unto them on that day, unless he turneth aside to fight, or retreateth to another party of the faithful, shall draw on himself the indignation of God, and his abode shall be hell; an ill journey shall it be thither! And ye slew not those who were slain at Bedr yourselves, but God slew them. Neither didst thou, O Mohammed, cast the gravel into their eyes, when thou didst seem to cast it; but God cast it, that he might prove the true believers by a gracious trial from himself; for God heareth and knoweth. This was done that God might also weaken the crafty devices of the unbelievers. If ye desire a decision of the matter between us, now hath a decision come unto you: and if ye desist from opposing the apostle, it will be better for you. But if ye return to attack him, we will also return to his assistance; and your forces shall not be of advantage unto you at all, although they be numerous; for God is with the faithful.

O true believers, obey God and his apostle, and turn not back from him, since ye hear the admonitions of the Koran.

dry and deep sand, into which their feet sank as they walked, the enemy having the command of the water; and that having fallen asleep, the greater part of them were disturbed with dreams, wherein the devil suggested to them that they could never expect God's assistance in the battle, since they were cut off from the water, and besides suffering the inconvenience of thirst, must be obliged to pray without washing, though they imagined themselves to be the favorites of God, and that they had his apostle among them. But in the night rain fell so plentifully that it formed a little brook, and not only supplied them with water for all their uses, but made the sand between them and the infidel army firm enough to bear them; whereupon the diabolical suggestions ceased.

And be not as those who say, We hear, when they do not hear. Verily the worst sort of beasts in the sight of God are the deaf and the dumb, who understand not. If God had known any good in them, he would certainly have caused them to hear: and if he had caused them to hear, they would surely have turned back, and have retired afar off. O true believers, answer God and his apostle, when he inviteth you unto that which giveth you life; and know that God goeth between a man and his heart, and that before him ye shall be assembled. Beware of sedition; it will not affect those who are ungodly among you particularly, but all of you in general; and know that God is severe in punishing. And remember when ye were few, and reputed weak in the land; ye feared lest men should snatch you away; but God provided you a place of refuge, and he strengthened you with his assistance, and bestowed on you good things, that ye might give thanks.

O true believers, deceive not God and his apostle; neither violate your faith, against your own knowledge. And know that your wealth, and your children are a temptation unto you; and that with God is a great reward.

O true believers, if ye fear God, he will grant you a distinction, and will expiate your sins from you, and will forgive you; for God is endued with great liberality. And call to mind when the unbelievers plotted against thee, that they might either detain thee in bonds, or put thee to death, or expel thee the city; [4] and they plotted against thee: but God laid a plot against them; and God is the best layer of plots. And when our signs are repeated unto them, they say, We have heard; if we pleased we could certainly pronounce a composition like unto this: this is nothing but fables of the ancients. And when they said, O God, if this be the truth

[4] When the Meccans heard of the league entered into by Mohammed with those of Medina, being apprehensive of the consequence, they held a council, whereat they say the devil assisted in the likeness of an old man of Najd. The point under consideration being what they should do with Mohammed, Abu'lbakhtari was of opinion that he should be imprisoned, and the room walled up, except a little hole, through which he should have necessaries given him, till he died. This the devil opposed, saying

from thee, rain down stones upon us from heaven, or inflict on us some other grievous punishment. But God was not disposed to punish them, while thou wast with them; nor was God disposed to punish them when they asked pardon. But they have nothing to offer in excuse why God should not punish them, since they hindered the believers from visiting the holy temple, although they are not the guardians thereof. The guardians thereof are those only who fear God; but the greater part of them know it not. And their prayer at the house of God is no other than whistling and clapping of the hands. Taste therefore the punishment, for that ye have been unbelievers. They who believe not expend their wealth to obstruct the way of God: they shall expend it, but afterward it shall become matter of sighing and regret unto them, and at length they shall be overcome; and the unbelievers shall be gathered together into hell; that God may distinguish the wicked from the good, and may throw the wicked one upon the other, and may gather them all in a heap, and cast them into hell. These are they who shall perish.

Say unto the unbelievers, that if they desist from opposing thee, what is already past shall be forgiven them; but if they return to attack thee, the exemplary punishment of the former opposers of the prophets is already past, and the like shall be inflicted on them. Therefore fight against them until there be no opposition in favor of idolatry, and the religion be wholly God's. If they desist, verily God seeth that which they do: but if they turn back, know that God is your patron; he is the best patron, and the best helper.

And know that whenever ye gain any spoils, a fifth part thereof belongeth unto God, and to the apostle, and his kindred, and the orphans, and the poor, and the traveler; if ye believe in God, and that which we have sent down unto our servant on the day of distinction, on the day whereon the two armies met: and God is almighty. When ye were en-

that he might probably be released by some of his own party. Hesham Ebn Amru was for banishing him, but his advice also the devil rejected, insisting that Mohammed might engage some other tribes in his interest, and make war on them. At length Abu Jahl gave his opinion for putting him to death, and proposed the manner, which was unanimously approved.

camped on the hithermost side of the valley, and they were
encamped on the farther side, and the caravan was below you;
and if ye had mutually appointed to come to a battle, ye
would certainly have declined the appointment; but ye were
brought to an engagement without any previous appointment,
that God might accomplish the thing which was decreed to be
done, that he who perisheth hereafter may perish after demonstrative evidence, and that he who liveth may live by the
same evidence; God both heareth and knoweth. When thy
Lord caused the enemy to appear unto thee in thy sleep, few
in number; and if he had caused them to appear numerous
unto thee, ye would have been disheartened and would have
disputed concerning the matter: but God preserved you from
this; for he knoweth the innermost parts of the breasts of
men. And when he caused them to appear unto you, when
ye met, to be few in your eyes; and diminished your numbers
in their eyes;[5] that God might accomplish the thing which
was decreed to be done: and unto God shall all things
return. . . .

As to those who enter into a league with thee, and afterward violate their league at every convenient opportunity,
and fear not God; if thou take them in war, disperse, by
making an example, those who shall come after them, that
they may be warned; or if thou apprehend treachery from
any people, throw back their league unto them, with like
treatment; for God loveth not the treacherous. And think
not that the unbelievers have escaped God's vengeance, for
they shall not weaken the power of God. Therefore prepare
against them what force ye are able, and troops of horse,
whereby ye may strike a terror into the enemy of God, and
your enemy, and into other infidels besides them, whom ye

[5] This seeming contradictory to a passage in the third chapter, where it
is said that the Moslems appeared to the infidels to be twice their own
number, the commentators reconcile the matter by telling us that, just
before the battle began, the prophet's party seemed fewer than they really
were, to draw the enemy to an engagement; but that so soon as the
armies were fully engaged, they appeared superior, to terrify and dismay
their adversaries. It is related that Abu Jahl at first thought them so
inconsiderable a handful, that he said one camel would be as much as
they could all eat.

know not, but God knoweth them. And whatsoever ye shall expend in the defense of the religion of God, it shall be repaid unto you, and ye shall not be treated unjustly. And if they incline unto peace, do thou also incline thereto; and put thy confidence in God, for it is he who heareth and knoweth. But if they seek to deceive thee, verily God will be thy support. It is he who hath strengthened thee with his help, and with that of the faithful; and hath united their hearts. If thou hadst expended whatever riches are in the earth, thou couldst not have united their hearts, but God united them; for he is mighty and wise. O prophet, God is thy support, and such of the true believers who followeth thee.

O prophet, stir up the faithful to war: if twenty of you persevere with constancy they shall overcome two hundred, and if there be one hundred of you they shall overcome a thousand of those who believe not; because they are a people which do not understand. Now hath God eased you, for he knew that ye were weak. If there be a hundred of you who persevere with constancy they shall overcome two hundred; and if there be a thousand of you, they shall overcome two thousand, by the permission of God; for God is with those who persevere.

It hath not been granted unto any prophet that he should possess captives, until he had made a great slaughter of the infidels in the earth. Ye seek the accidental goods of this world, but God regardeth the life to come; and God is mighty and wise. Unless a revelation had been previously delivered from God, verily a severe punishment had been inflicted on you, for the ransom which ye took from the captives at Bedr. Eat therefore of what ye have acquired, that which is lawful and good; for God is gracious and merciful.

O prophet, say unto the captives who are in your hands, If God shall know any good to be in your hearts, he will give you better than what hath been taken from you; and he will forgive you, for God is gracious and merciful. But if they seek to deceive thee, verily they have deceived God before; wherefore he hath given thee power over them: and God is knowing and wise.

Moreover they who have believed, and have fled their country, and employed their substance and their persons in fighting for the religion of God, and they who have given the prophet a refuge among them, and have assisted him, these shall be deemed the one nearest of kin to the other. But they who have believed, but have not fled their country, shall have no right of kindred at all with you, until they also fly. Yet if they ask assistance of you on account of religion, it belongeth unto you to give them assistance; except against a people between whom and yourselves there shall be a league subsisting: and God seeth that which ye do. And as to the infidels, let them be deemed of kin the one to the other. Unless ye do this, there will be a sedition in the earth, and grievous corruption. But as for them who have believed, and left their country, and have fought for God's true religion, and who have allowed the prophet a retreat among them, and have assisted him, these are really believers; they shall receive mercy, and an honorable provision. And they who have believed since, and have fled their country, and have fought with you, these also are of you. And those who are related by consanguinity shall be deemed the nearest of kin to each other, preferably to strangers, according to the book of God; God knoweth all things.

CHAPTER IX

ENTITLED, THE DECLARATION OF IMMUNITY; [1] REVEALED AT MEDINA

A declaration of immunity from God and his apostle, unto the idolaters with whom ye have entered into league. Go to and fro in the earth securely four months; and know that ye shall not weaken God, and that God will disgrace the unbelievers. And a declaration from God and his apostle unto the people, on the day of the greater pilgrimage, that God is clear of the idolaters, and his apostle also. Wherefore if ye

[1] The reason why the chapter had this title appears from the opening lines. Some, however, give it other titles, and particularly that of

repent, this will be better for you; but if ye turn back, know that ye shall not weaken God: and denounce unto those who believe not, a painful punishment. Except such of the idolaters with whom ye shall have entered into a league, and who afterwards shall not fail you in any instance, nor assist any other against you. Wherefore perform the covenant which ye shall have made with them, until their time shall be elapsed; for God loveth those who fear him. And when the months wherein ye are not allowed to attack them shall be past, kill the idolaters wheresoever ye shall find them, and take them prisoners, and besiege them, and lay wait for them in every convenient place. But if they shall repent, and observe the appointed times of prayer, and pay the legal alms, dismiss them freely; for God is gracious and merciful. And if any of the idolaters shall demand protection of thee, grant him protection, that he may hear the word of God; and afterward let him reach the place of his security. This shalt thou do, because they are people which know not the excellency of the religion thou preachest.

How shall the idolaters be admitted into a league with God and with his apostle; except those with whom ye entered into a league at the holy temple? So long as they behave with fidelity toward you, do ye also behave with fidelity toward them; for God loveth those who fear him. How can they be admitted into a league with you, since, if they prevail

"Repentance," which is mentioned immediately after. It is observable that this chapter alone has not the auspiciatory form, "In the name of the most merciful God," prefixed to it; the reason of which omission, as some think, was, because these words imply a concession of security, which is utterly taken away by this chapter, after a fixed time; wherefore some have called it the chapter of "Punishment"; others say that Mohammed (who died soon after he had received this chapter), having given no direction where it should be placed, nor for the prefixing the Bismillah to it, as had been done to the other chapters; and the argument of this chapter bearing a near resemblance to that of the preceding, his companions differed about it, some saying that both chapters were but one, and together made the seventh of the seven long ones, and others that they were two distinct chapters; whereupon, to accommodate the dispute, they left a space between them, but did not interpose the distinction of the Bismillah. It is agreed that this chapter was the last which was revealed; and the only one, as Mohammed declared, which was revealed entire and at once, except the 110th.

against you, they will not regard in you either consanguinity or faith? They will please you with their mouths, but their hearts will be averse from you; for the greater part of them are wicked doers. They sell the signs of God for a small price, and obstruct his way; it is certainly evil which they do. They regard not in a believer either consanguinity or faith; and these are the transgressors. Yet if they repent, and observe the appointed times of prayer, and give alms, they shall be deemed your brethren in religion. We distinctly propound our signs unto people who understand. But if they violate their oaths, after their league, and revile your religion, oppose the leaders of infidelity (for there is no trust in them), and they may desist from their treachery. Will ye not fight against people who have violated their oaths, and conspired to expel the apostle of God; and who of their own accord assaulted you the first time? Will ye fear them? But it is more just that ye should fear God, if ye are true believers. Attack them therefore; God shall punish them by your hands, and will cover them with shame, and will give you the victory over them; and he will heal the breasts of the people who believe, and will take away the indignation of their hearts: for God will be turned unto whom he pleaseth; and God is knowing and wise. Did ye imagine that ye should be abandoned, whereas God did not yet know those among you who sought for his religion, and took not any besides God, and his apostle, and the faithful for their friends? God is well acquainted with that which ye do. It is not fitting that the idolaters should visit the temples of God, being witnesses against their own souls of their infidelity. The works of these men are vain; and they shall remain in hell fire forever. But he only shall visit the temples of God, who believeth in God and the last day, and is constant at prayer, and payeth the legal alms, and feareth God alone. These perhaps may become of the number of those who are rightly directed.

Do ye reckon the giving drink to the pilgrims, and the visiting of the holy temple, to be actions as meritorious as those performed by him who believeth in God and the last day, and fighteth for the religion of God? They shall not be held equal with God: for God directeth not the unrighteous people. They who have believed, and fled their country, and employed their substance and their persons in the defense of God's true religion, shall be in the highest degree of honor with God; and these are they who shall be happy. Their Lord sendeth them good tidings of mercy from him, and good will, and of gardens wherein they shall enjoy lasting pleasure; they shall continue therein forever: for God is a great reward.

O true believers, take not your fathers or your brethren for friends, if they love infidelity above faith; and whosoever among you shall take them for his friends, they will be unjust doers. Say, If your fathers, and your sons, and your brethren, and your wives, and your relations, and your substance which ye have acquired, and your merchandise which ye apprehend may not be sold off, and your dwellings wherein ye delight, be more dear unto you than God, and his apostle, and the advancement of his religion; wait, until God shall send his command: for God directeth not the ungodly people.

Now hath God assisted you in many engagements, and particularly in the battle of Honein; [2] when ye pleased yourselves in your multitude, but it was no manner of advantage

---

[2] This battle was fought in the eighth year of the Hegira, in the valley of Honein, which lies about three miles from Mecca toward Tayef, between Mohammed, who had an army of twelve thousand men, and the tribes of Hawazen and Thakif, whose forces did not exceed four thousand. The Mohammedans, seeing themselves so greatly superior to their enemies, made sure of the victory; a certain person, whom some suppose to have been the prophet himself, crying out, " These can never be overcome by so few." But God was so highly displeased with this confidence, that in the first encounter the Moslems were put to flight, some of them running away quite to Mecca, so that none stood their ground except Mohammed himself, and some few of his family; and they say the prophet's courage was so great, that his uncle al Abbas, and his cousin Abu Sofian Ebn al Hareth, had much ado to prevent his spurring his mule into the midst of the enemy, by laying hold of the bridle and stirrup. Then he ordered al Abbas, who had the voice of a Stentor, to recall his flying troops; upon which they rallied, and the prophet throwing a handful of dust against the enemy, they attacked them a second time, and by the divine assistance gained the victory.

unto you, and the earth became too strait for you,[3] notwithstanding it was spacious; then did ye retreat and turn your backs. Afterward God sent down his security upon his apostle and upon the faithful, and sent down troops of angels which ye saw not; and he punished those who disbelieved: and this was the reward of the unbelievers. Nevertheless God will hereafter be turned unto whom he pleaseth; for God is gracious and merciful.

O true believers, verily the idolaters are unclean; let them not therefore come near unto the holy temple after this year. And if ye fear want, by the cutting off trade and communication with them, God will enrich you of his abundance, if he pleaseth; for God is knowing and wise. Fight against them who believe not in God, nor in the last day, and forbid not that which God and his apostle have forbidden, and profess not the true religion, of those unto whom the scriptures have been delivered, until they pay tribute by right of subjection, and they be reduced low.

The Jews say, Ezra is the son of God;[4] and the Christians say, Christ is the son of God. This is their saying in their mouths: they imitate the saying of those who were unbelievers in former times. May God resist them. How are they infatuated! They take their priests and their monks for their lords, besides God, and Christ the son of Mary; although they are commanded to worship one God only: there is no God but he; far be that from him, which they associate with him! They seek to extinguish the light of God with their mouths; but God willeth no other than to perfect his light, although the infidels be averse thereto. It is he who hath sent his apostle with the direction and true religion; that he may cause it to appear superior to every other religion; although the idolaters be averse thereto.

[3] For the valley being very deep, and encompassed by craggy mountains, the enemy placed themselves in ambush on every side, attacking in the straits and narrow passages, and from behind the rocks, with great advantage.

[4] This charge against the Jews the commentators endeavor to support by telling us that it is meant of some ancient heterodox Jews, or else of some Jews of Medina; who said so for no other reason than for that the

O true believers, verily many of the priests and monks devour the substance of men in vanity, and obstruct the way of God. But unto those who treasure up gold and silver, and employ it not for the advancement of God's true religion, denounce a grievous punishment. On the day of judgment their treasures shall be intensely heated in the fire of hell, and their foreheads, and their sides, and their backs shall be stigmatized therewith; and their tormentors shall say, This is what ye have treasured up for your souls; taste therefore that which ye have treasured up.

Moreover, the complete number of months with God is twelve months, which were ordained in the book of God, on the day whereon he created the heavens and the earth: of these, four are sacred. This is the right religion: therefore deal not unjustly with yourselves therein. But attack the idolaters in all the months, as they attack you in all; and know that God is with those who fear him. Verily the transferring of a sacred month to another month is an additional infidelity. The unbelievers are led into an error thereby: they allow a month to be violated one year, and declare it sacred another year, that they may agree in the number of months which God hath commanded to be kept sacred; and they allow that which God hath forbidden. The evil of their actions hath been prepared for them: for God directeth not the unbelieving people.

O true believers, what ailed you, that, when it was said unto you, Go forth to fight for the religion of God, ye inclined heavily toward the earth? Do ye prefer the present life to that which is to come? But the provision of this life, in respect of that which is to come, is but slender. Unless ye go forth when ye are summoned to war, God will punish you with a grievous punishment; and he will place another people

law being utterly lost and forgotten during the Babylonish captivity, Ezra, having been raised to life after he had been dead one hundred years, dictated the whole anew to the scribes, out of his own memory; at which they greatly marveled, and declared that he could not have done it unless he were the son of God. Al Beidawi adds that the imputation must be true, because this verse was read to the Jews, and they did not contradict it; which they were ready enough to do in other instances.

in your stead, and ye shall not hurt him at all; for God is almighty. If ye assist not the prophet, verily God will assist him, as he assisted him formerly, when the unbelievers drove him out of Mecca, the second of two: when they were both in the cave: when he said unto his companion, Be not grieved, for God is with us. And God sent down his security upon him, and strengthened him with armies of angels, whom ye saw not. And he made the word of those who believed not to be abased, and the word of God was exalted; for God is mighty and wise.

Go forth to battle, both light and heavy, and employ your substance and your persons for the advancement of God's religion. This will be better for you, if ye know it. If it had been a near advantage and a moderate journey, they had surely followed thee; but the way seemed tedious unto them: and yet they will swear by God, saying, If we had been able, we had surely gone forth with you. They destroy their own souls; for God knoweth that they are liars. God forgive thee! why didst thou give them leave to stay at home, until they who speak the truth, when they excuse themselves, had become manifested unto thee, and thou hadst known the liars? They who believe in God and the last day will not ask leave of thee to be excused from employing their substance and their persons for the advancement of God's true religion; and God knoweth those who fear him. Verily they only will ask leave of thee to stay behind, who believe not in God and the last day, and whose hearts doubt concerning the faith: wherefore they are tossed to and fro in their doubting. If they had been willing to go forth with thee, they had certainly prepared for that purpose a provision of arms and necessaries: but God was averse to their going forth; wherefore he rendered them slothful, and it was said unto them, Sit ye still with those who sit still. If they had gone forth with you, they had only been a burden unto you, and had run to and fro between you, stirring you up to sedition; and there would have been some among you who would have given ear unto them: and God knoweth the wicked. They formerly sought to raise a sedition, and they disturbed thy affairs, until the truth came, and the decree of God was made manifest; although they were averse thereto. There is of them who saith unto thee, Give me leave to stay behind, and expose me not to temptation. Have they not fallen into temptation at home? But hell will surely encompass the unbelievers. If good happen unto thee, it grieveth them: but if a misfortune befall thee, they say, We ordered our business before; and they turn their backs, and rejoice at thy mishap. Say, Nothing shall befall us, but what God hath decreed for us: he is our patron: and on God let the faithful trust. Say, Do ye expect any other should befall us than one of the two most excellent things; either victory or martyrdom? But we expect concerning you, that God inflict a punishment on you, either from himself, or by our hands. Wait therefore to see what will be the end of both; for we will wait with you.

Say, Expend your money in pious uses, either voluntarily or by constraint; it shall not be accepted of you, because ye are wicked people. And nothing hindereth their contributions from being accepted of them, but that they believe not in God and his apostle, and perform not the duty of prayer, otherwise than sluggishly; and expend not their money for God's service, otherwise than unwillingly. Let not therefore their riches or their children cause thee to marvel. Verily God intendeth only to punish them by these things in this world; and that their souls may depart while they are unbelievers. They swear by God that they are of you; yet they are not of you, but are people who stand in fear. If they find a place of refuge, or caves, or a retreating hole, they surely turn toward the same, and in a headstrong manner haste thereto.

There is of them also who spreadeth ill reports of thee, in relation to thy distribution of the alms: yet if they receive part thereof, they are well pleased; but if they receive not a part thereof, behold, they are angry. But if they had been pleased with that which God and his apostle had given them, and had said, God is our support; God will give unto us of his abundance and his prophet also; verily unto God do we make our supplications: it would have been more decent. Alms are to be distributed only unto the poor and needy, and those who are employed in collecting and distributing the same, and unto those whose hearts are reconciled, and for the redemption of captives, and unto those who are in debt and insolvent, and for the advancement of God's religion, and unto the traveler. This is an ordinance from God: and God is knowing and wise.

There are some of them who injure the prophet, and say, He is an ear: Answer, He is an ear of good unto you: he believeth in God, and giveth credit to the faithful, and is a mercy unto such of you who believe. But they who injure the apostle of God shall suffer a painful punishment. They swear unto you by God that they may please you; but it is more just that they should please God and his apostle, if they are true believers. Do they not know that he who opposeth God and his apostle shall without doubt be punished with the fire of hell; and shall remain therein forever? This will be great ignominy. . . .

There are some who have built a temple to hurt the faithful, and to propagate infidelity, and to foment division among the true believers, and for a lurking-place for him who hath fought against God and his apostle in time past; and they swear, saying, Verily we intended no other than to do for the best: but God is witness that they do certainly lie. Stand not up to pray therein forever. There is a temple founded on piety, from the first day of its building. It is more just that thou stand up to pray therein: therein are men who love to be purified; for God loveth the clean. Whether therefore is he better, who hath founded his building on the fear of God and his good-will; or he who hath founded his building on the brink of a bank of earth which is washed away by waters, so that it falleth with him into the fire of hell? God directeth not the ungodly people. Their building which they have built will not cease to be an occasion of doubting in their hearts until their hearts be cut in pieces; and God is knowing and wise.

Verily God hath purchased of the true believers their souls and their substance, promising them the enjoyment of paradise; on condition that they fight for the cause of God:

whether they slay or be slain, the promise for the same is assuredly due by the law, and the gospel, and the Koran.

And who performeth his contract more faithfully than God? Rejoice therefore in the contract which ye have made. This shall be great happiness. The penitent, and those who serve God, and praise him, and who fast, and bow down, and worship; and who command that which is just, and forbid that which is evil, and keep the ordinances of God, shall likewise be rewarded with paradise: wherefore bear good tidings unto the faithful.

It is not allowed unto the prophet, nor those who are true believers, that they pray for idolaters, although they be of kin, after it is become known unto them, that they are inhabitants of hell. Neither did Abraham ask forgiveness for his father, otherwise than in pursuance of a promise which he had made unto him: but when it became known unto him that he was an enemy unto God, he declared himself clear of him. Verily Abraham was pitiful and compassionate.

Nor is God disposed to lead people into error, after he hath directed them, until that which they ought to avoid is become known unto them; for God knoweth all things. Verily unto God belongeth the kingdom of heaven and of earth; he giveth life, and he causeth to die; and ye have no patron or helper besides God.

God is reconciled unto the prophet, and unto the Mohajerin, and the Ansars, who followed him in the hour of distress, after it had wanted little but that the hearts of a part of them had swerved from their duty: afterward was he turned unto them; for he was compassionate and merciful toward them. And he is also reconciled unto the three who were left behind, so that the earth became too strait for them, notwithstanding its spaciousness, and their souls became straitened within them, and they considered that there was no refuge from God, otherwise than by having recourse unto him. Then was he turned unto them, that they might repent; for God is easy to be reconciled and merciful.

O true believers, fear God, and be with the sincere. There was no reason why the inhabitants of Medina, and the Arabs of the desert who dwell around them, should stay behind the apostle of God, or should prefer themselves before him. This is unreasonable: because they are not distressed either by thirst, or labor, or hunger, for the defense of God's true religion; neither do they stir a step, which may irritate the unbelievers; neither do they receive from the enemy any damage, but a good work is written down unto them for the same; for God suffereth not the reward of the righteous to perish. And they contribute not any sum either small or great, nor do they pass a valley, but it is written down unto them, that God may reward them with a recompense exceeding that which they have wrought.

The believers are not obliged to go forth to war all together: if a part of every band of them go not forth, it is that they may diligently instruct themselves in their religion; and may admonish their people, when they return unto them, that they may take heed to themselves.

O true believers, wage war against such of the infidels as are near you; and let them find severity in you: and know that God is with those who fear him. Whenever a Sura is sent down, there are some of them who say, Which of you hath this caused to increase in faith? It will increase the faith of those who believe, and they shall rejoice: but unto those in whose hearts there is an infirmity, it will add further doubt unto their present doubt; and they shall die in their infidelity. Do they not see that they are tried every year once or twice? yet they repent not, neither are they warned. And whenever a Sura is sent down, they look at one another, saying, Doth any one see you? then do they turn aside. God shall turn aside their hearts from the truth; because they are a people who do not understand. Now hath an apostle come unto you of our own nation, an excellent person: it is grievous unto him that ye commit wickedness; he is careful over you, and compassionate and merciful towards the believers. If they turn back, say, God is my support: there is no God but he. On him do I trust; and he is the Lord of the magnificent throne.

CHAPTER X

ENTITLED, JONAS;[1] REVEALED AT MECCA

IN THE NAME OF THE MOST MERCIFUL GOD

A. L. R.   These are the signs of the wise book.   Is it a strange thing unto the men of Mecca, that we have revealed our will unto a man from among them, saying, Denounce threats unto men if they believe not; and bear good tidings unto those who believe, that on the merit of their sincerity they have an interest with their Lord?   The unbelievers say, This is manifest sorcery.   Verily your Lord is God who hath created the heavens and the earth in six days; and then ascended his throne, to take on himself the government of all things.   There is no intercessor, but by his permission.   This is God, your Lord; therefore serve him.   Will ye not consider?   Unto him shall ye all return, according to the certain promise of God; for he produceth a creature, and then causeth it to return again; that he may reward those who believe and do that which is right with equity.   But as for the unbelievers, they shall drink boiling water, and they shall suffer a grievous punishment, for that they have disbelieved.   It is he who hath ordained the sun to shine by day, and the moon for a light by night; and hath appointed her stations, that ye might know the number of years, and the computation of time.   God hath not created this, but with truth.   He explaineth his signs unto people who understand.   Moreover in the vicissitude of night and day, and whatever God hath created in heaven and earth, are surely signs unto men who fear him.

Verily they who hope not to meet us at the last day, and delight in this present life, and rest securely in the same, and who are negligent of our signs; their dwelling shall be hell fire, for that which they have deserved.   But as to those who believe, and work righteousness, their Lord will direct them because of their faith; they shall have rivers flowing through

[1] This prophet is mentioned toward the end of the chapter.

gardens of pleasure. Their prayer therein shall be, Praise be unto thee, O God! and their salutation therein shall be, Peace! and the end of their prayer shall be, Praise be unto God, the Lord of all creatures!

If God should cause evil to hasten unto men, according to their desire of hastening good, verily their end had been decreed. Wherefore we suffer those who hope not to meet us at the resurrection to wander amazedly in their error. When evil befalleth a man, he prayeth unto us lying on his side, or sitting, or standing: but when we deliver him from his affliction, he continueth his former course of life, as though he had not called upon us to defend him against the evil which had befallen him. Thus was that which the transgressors committed prepared for them. We have formerly destroyed the generations who were before you, O men of Mecca, when they had acted unjustly, and our apostles had come unto them with evident miracles, and they would not believe. Thus do we reward the wicked people. Afterward did we cause you to succeed them in the earth; that we might see how ye would act. When our evident signs are recited unto them, they who hope not to meet us at the resurrection say, Bring a different Koran from this; or make some change therein. Answer, It is not fit for me, that I should change it at my pleasure: I follow that only which is revealed unto me. Verily I fear, if I should be disobedient unto my Lord, the punishment of the great day. Say, If God had so pleased, I had not read it unto you, neither had I taught you the same. I have already dwelt among you to the age of forty years before I received it. Do ye not therefore understand? And who is more unjust than he who deviseth a lie against God, or accuseth his signs of falsehood? Surely the wicked shall not prosper. They worship besides God, that which can neither hurt them nor profit them, and they say, These are our intercessors with God. Answer, Will ye tell God that which he knoweth not, neither in heaven nor in earth? Praise be unto him! and far be that from him, which they associate with him!

Men were professors of one religion only, but they dissented therefrom; and if a decree had not previously issued from thy

Lord, deferring their punishment, verily the matter had been decided between them, concerning which they disagreed. They say, Unless a sign be sent down unto him from his Lord, we will not believe. Answer, Verily that which is hidden is known only unto God: wait therefore the pleasure of God; and I also will wait with you. And when we caused the men of Mecca to taste mercy, after an affliction which had befallen them, behold, they devised a stratagem against our signs. Say unto them, God is more swift in executing a stratagem than ye. Verily our messengers write down that which ye deceitfully devise. It is he who hath given you conveniences for traveling by land and by sea; so that ye be in ships, which sail with them with a favorable wind, and they rejoice therein. And when a tempestuous wind overtaketh them, and waves come upon them from every side, and they think themselves to be encompassed with inevitable dangers; they call upon God, exhibiting the pure religion unto him, and saying, Verily, if thou deliver us from this peril, we will be of those who give thanks. But when he hath delivered them, behold, they behave themselves insolently in the earth, without justice.

O men, Verily the violence which ye commit against your own souls is for the enjoyment of this present life only; afterward unto us shall ye return, and we will declare unto you that which ye have done. Verily the likeness of this present life is no other than as water, which we send down from heaven, and wherewith the productions of the earth are mixed, of which men eat, and cattle also, until the earth receive its vesture, and be adorned with various plants: the inhabitants thereof imagine that they have power over the same; but our command cometh unto it by night or by day, and we render it as though it had been mown, as though it had not yesterday abounded with fruits. Thus do we explain our signs unto people who consider.

God inviteth unto the dwelling of peace, and directeth whom he pleaseth into the right way. They who do right shall receive a most excellent reward, and a superabundant addition; neither blackness nor shame shall cover their faces. These shall be the inhabitants of paradise; they shall continue therein forever. But they who commit evil shall receive the reward of evil, equal thereunto, and they shall be covered with shame (for they shall have no protector against God); as though their faces were covered with the profound darkness of the night. These shall be the inhabitants of hell fire; they shall remain therein forever. On the day of the resurrection we will gather them all together; then will we say unto the idolaters, Get ye to your place, ye and your companions: and we will separate them from one another; and their companions shall say unto them, Ye did not worship us; and God is a sufficient witness between us and you; neither did we mind your worshiping of us. There shall every soul experience that which it shall have sent before it; and they shall be brought before God, their true Lord; and the false deities which they vainly imagined shall disappear from before them.

Say, who provideth you food from heaven and earth? or who hath the absolute power over the hearing and sight? and who bringeth forth the living from the dead, and bringeth forth the dead from the living? and who governeth all things? They will surely answer, God. Say, Will ye not therefore fear him? This is therefore God, your true Lord: and what remaineth there after truth, except error? How therefore are ye turned aside from the truth? Thus is the word of thy Lord verified upon them who do wickedly; that they believe not. Say, Is there any of your companions who produceth a creature, and then causeth it to return unto himself? Say, God produceth a creature, and then causeth it to return unto himself. How therefore are ye turned aside from his worship? Say, Is there any of your companions who directeth unto the truth? Say, God directeth unto the truth. Whether is he therefore, who directeth unto the truth, more worthy to be followed; or he who directeth not, unless he be directed? What aileth you, therefore, that ye judge as ye do? And the greater part of them follow an uncertain opinion only; but a mere opinon attaineth not unto any truth. Verily God knoweth that which they do.

This Koran could not have been composed by any except

God; but it is a confirmation of that which was revealed before it, and an explanation of the scripture; there is no doubt thereof; sent down from the Lord of all creatures. Will they say, Mohammed hath forged it? Answer, Bring therefore a chapter like unto it; and call whom ye may to your assistance, besides God, if ye speak truth. But they have charged that with falsehood, the knowledge whereof they do not comprehend, neither hath the interpretation thereof come unto them. In the same manner did those who were before them accuse their prophets of imposture; but behold what was the end of the unjust. There are some of them who believe therein; and there are some of them who believe not therein: and thy Lord well knoweth the corrupt doers. If they accuse thee of imposture, say, I have my work, and ye have your work; ye shall be clear of that which I do, and I will be clear of that which ye do.

There are some of them who harken unto thee; but wilt thou make the deaf to hear, although they do not understand? And there are some of them who look at thee; but wilt thou direct the blind, although they see not? Verily God will not deal unjustly with men in any respect: but men deal unjustly with their own souls. On a certain day he will gather them together, as though they had not tarried above an hour of a day: they shall know one another. Then shall they perish who have denied the meeting of God, and were not rightly directed. Whether we cause thee to see a part of the punishment wherewith we have threatened them, or whether we cause thee to die before thou see it; unto us shall they return: then shall God be witness of that which they do. Unto every nation hath an apostle been sent: and when their apostle came, the matter was decided between them with equity; and they were not treated unjustly. . . .

Do ye speak of God that which ye know not? Say, Verily they who imagine a lie concerning God shall not prosper. They may enjoy a provision in this world; but afterward unto us shall they return, and we will then cause them to taste a grievous punishment, for that they were unbelievers. Rehearse unto them the history of Noah: when he said unto his people, O my people, if my standing forth among you, and my warning you of the signs of God, be grievous unto you; in God do I put my trust. Therefore lay your designs against me, and assemble your false gods; but let not your design be carried on by you in the dark: then come forth against me, and delay not. And if ye turn aside from my admonitions, I ask not any reward of you for the same; I expect my reward from God alone, and I am commanded to be one of those who are resigned unto him. But they accused him of imposture; wherefore we delivered him, and those who were with him in the ark, and we caused them to survive the flood, but we drowned those who charged our signs with falsehood. Behold, therefore, what was the end of those who were warned by Noah. Then did we send, after him, apostles unto their respective people, and they came unto them with evident demonstrations: yet they were not disposed to believe in that which they had before rejected as false. Thus do we seal up the hearts of the transgressors. Then did we send, after them, Moses and Aaron unto Pharaoh and his princes with our signs: but they behaved proudly, and were a wicked people. And when the truth from us had come unto them, they said, Verily this is manifest sorcery. Moses said unto them, Do ye speak this of the truth, after it hath come unto you? Is this sorcery? but sorcerers shall not prosper. They said, Art thou come unto us to turn us aside from that religion which we found our fathers practised; and that ye two may have the command in the land? But we do not believe you. And Pharaoh said, Bring unto me every expert magician. And when the magicians were come, Moses said unto them, Cast down that which ye are about to cast down. And when they had cast down their rods and cords, Moses said unto them, The enchantment which ye have performed shall God surely render vain; for God prospereth not the work of the wicked doers. And God will verify the truth of his words, although the wicked be averse thereto. And there believed not any on Moses, except a generation of his people, for fear of Pharaoh and of his princes, lest he should afflict them. And Pharaoh was lifted up with pride in the earth, and was surely one of the transgressors. And Moses said, O my people, if ye believe in God, put your trust in him, if ye be resigned to his will. They answered, We put our trust in God: O Lord, suffer us not to be afflicted by unjust people; but deliver us, through thy mercy, from the unbelieving people. And we spake by inspiration unto Moses and his brother, saying, Provide habitations for your people in Egypt, and make your houses a place of worship, and be constant at prayer; and bear good news unto the true believers. And Moses said, O Lord, verily thou hast given unto Pharaoh and his people pompous ornaments, and riches in this present life, O Lord, that they may be seduced from thy way; O Lord, bring their riches to nought, and harden their hearts; that they may not believe, until they see their grievous punishment. God said, Your petition is heard: be ye upright therefore, and follow not in the way of those who are ignorant. And we caused the children of Israel to pass through the sea; and Pharaoh and his army followed them in a violent and hostile manner; until, when he was drowning, he said, I believe that there is no God but he on whom the children of Israel believe; and I am one of the resigned.[2] Now dost thou believe; when thou hast been hitherto rebellious, and one of the wicked doers? This day will we raise the body[3] from the bottom of the sea, that thou mayest be a sign unto those who shall be after thee; and verily a great number of men are negligent of our signs. And we prepared for the children of Israel an established dwelling in the land of Canaan, and we provided good things for their sustenance: and they differed not in point of religion, until knowledge had come unto them; verily thy Lord will judge

[2] These words, it is said, Pharaoh repeated often in his extremity, that he might be heard. But his repentance came too late; for Gabriel soon stopped his mouth with mud, lest he should obtain mercy; reproaching him at the same time in the words which follow.

[3] Some of the children of Israel doubting whether Pharaoh was really drowned, Gabriel, by God's command, caused his naked corpse to swim to shore, that they might see it. The word here translated, "body," signifying also a "coat of mail," some imagine the meaning to be, that his corpse floated armed with his coat of mail, which they tell us was of gold, by which they knew that it was he.

between them on the day of resurrection, concerning that wherein they disagreed.

If thou art in a doubt concerning any part of that which we have sent down unto thee, ask them who have read the book of the law before thee. Now hath the truth come unto thee from thy Lord; be not, therefore, one of those who doubt: neither be thou one of those who charge the signs of God with falsehood, lest thou become one of those who perish. Verily those against whom the word of thy Lord is decreed shall not believe, although there come unto them every kind of miracle; until they see the grievous punishment prepared for them. And if it were not so, some city, among the many which have been destroyed, would have believed; and the faith of its inhabitants would have been of advantage unto them: but none of them believed before the execution of their sentences, except the people of Jonas. When they believed, we delivered them from the punishment of shame in this world, and suffered them to enjoy their lives and possessions for a time. But if thy Lord had pleased, verily all who are in the earth would have believed in general. Wilt thou therefore forcibly compel men to be true believers? No soul can believe but by the permission of God: and he shall pour out his indignation on those who will not understand. Say, Consider whatever is in heaven and on earth: but signs are of no avail, neither preachers, unto people who will not believe. Do they therefore expect any other than some terrible judgment, like unto the judgments which have fallen on those who have gone before them? Say, Wait ye the issue; and I also will wait with you: then will we deliver our apostles and those who believe. Thus is it a justice due from us, that we should deliver the true believers.

Say, O men of Mecca, if ye be in doubt concerning my religion, verily I worship not the idols which ye worship, besides God; but I worship God, who will cause you to die: and I am commanded to be one of the true believers. And it was said unto me, Set thy face toward the true religion, and be orthodox; and by no means be one of those who attribute companions unto God; neither invoke, besides God, that which can neither profit thee nor hurt thee: for if thou do, thou wilt then certainly become one of the unjust. If God afflict thee with hurt, there is none who can relieve thee from it, except he; and if he willeth thee any good, there is none who can keep back his bounty: he will confer it on such of his servants as he pleaseth; and he is gracious and merciful.

Say, O men, now hath the truth come unto you from your Lord. He therefore who shall be directed will be directed to the advantage of his own soul: but he who shall err will err only against the same. I am no guardian over you. Do thou, O prophet, follow that which is revealed unto thee: and persevere with patience, until God shall judge; for he is the best judge.

CHAPTER XI

ENTITLED, HUD; [1] REVEALED AT MECCA

IN THE NAME OF THE MOST MERCIFUL GOD

A. L. R. This book, the verses whereof are guarded against corruption, and are also distinctly explained, is a revelation from the wise, the knowing God: that ye serve not any other than God (verily I am a denouncer of threats, and a bearer of good tidings unto you from him); and that ye ask pardon of your Lord, and then be turned unto him. He will cause you to enjoy a plentiful provision, until a prefixed time: and unto every one that hath merit by good works will he give his abundant reward. But if ye turn back, verily I fear for you the punishment of the great day: unto God shall ye return; and he is almighty. Do they not double the folds of their breasts, that they may conceal their designs from him? When they cover themselves with their garments, doth not he know that which they conceal, and that which they discover? For he knoweth the innermost parts of the breasts of men.

There is no creature which creepeth on the earth, but God provideth its food; and he knoweth the place of its retreat,

[1] The story of the prophet Hud is repeated in this chapter.

and where it is laid up. The whole is written in the perspicuous book of his decrees. It is he who hath created the heavens and the earth in six days (but his throne was above the waters before the creation thereof), that he might prove you, and see which of you would excel in works.

If thou say, Ye shall surely be raised again after death; the unbelievers will say, This is nothing but manifest sorcery. And verily if we defer their punishment unto a determined season, they will say, What hindereth it from falling on us? Will it not come upon them on a day wherein there shall be none to avert it from them; and that which they scoffed at shall encompass them?

Verily, if we cause man to taste mercy from us, and afterward take it away from him, he will surely become desperate, and ungrateful. And if we cause him to taste favor, after an affliction hath befallen him, he will surely say, The evils which I suffered are passed from me; and he will become joyful and insolent: except those who persevere with patience, and do that which is right: they shall receive pardon and a great reward. Peradventure thou wilt omit to publish part of that which hath been revealed unto thee, and thy breast will become straitened, lest they say, Unless a treasure be sent down unto him, or an angel come with him, to bear witness unto him, we will not believe. Verily thou art a preacher only; and God is the governor of all things. Will they say, He hath forged the Koran? Answer, Bring therefore ten chapters like unto it, forged by yourselves; and call on whomsoever ye may to assist you, except God, if ye speak truth. But if they whom ye call to your assistance hear you not, know that this book hath been revealed by the knowledge of God only, and that there is no God but he. Will ye therefore become Moslems?

Whoso chooseth the present life, and the pomp thereof, unto them will we give the recompense of their works therein, and the same shall not be diminished unto them. These are they for whom no other reward is prepared in the next life, except the fire of hell: that which they have done in this life shall perish; and that which they have wrought shall be vain.

Shall he therefore be compared with them, who followeth the evident declaration of his Lord, and whom a witness from him attendeth, preceded by the book of Moses, which was revealed for a guide, and out of mercy to mankind? These believe in the Koran: but whosoever of the confederate infidels believeth not therein is threatened with the fire of hell, which threat shall certainly be executed: be not therefore in a doubt concerning it; for it is the truth from thy Lord: but the greater part of men will not believe.

Who is more unjust than he who imagineth a lie concerning God? They shall be set before their Lord, at the day of judgment, and the witnesses shall say, These are they who devised lies against their Lord. Shall not the curse of God fall on the unjust; who turn men aside from the way of God, and seek to render it crooked, and who believe not in the life to come? These were not able to prevail against God on earth, so as to escape punishment; neither had they any protectors besides God: their punishment shall be doubled unto them. They could not hear, neither did they see. These are they who have lost their souls; and the idols which they falsely imagined have abandoned them. There is no doubt but they shall be most miserable in the world to come. But as for those who believe, and do good works, and humble themselves before their Lord, they shall be the inhabitants of paradise; they shall remain therein forever. The similitude of the two parties is as the blind and the deaf, and as he who seeth and heareth: shall they be compared as equal? Will ye not therefore consider?

We formerly sent Noah unto his people; and he said, Verily I am a public preacher unto you; that ye worship God alone: verily I fear for you the punishment of the terrible day. But the chiefs of his people, who believed not, answered, We see thee to be no other than a man, like unto us; and we do not see that any follow thee, except those who are the most abject among us, who have believed on thee by a rash judgment; neither do we perceive any excellence in you above us: but we esteem you to be liars. Noah said, O my people, tell me; if I have received an evident declaration from my Lord, and he hath bestowed on me mercy from himself, which is hidden from you, do we compel you to receive the same, in case ye be averse thereto? O my people, I ask not of you any riches, for my preaching unto you: my reward is with God alone. I will not drive away those who have believed: verily they shall meet their Lord, at the resurrection; but I perceive that ye are ignorant men. O my people, who shall assist me against God, if I drive them away? Will ye not therefore consider? I say not unto you, The treasures of God are in my power; neither do I say, I know the secrets of God; neither do I say, Verily I am an angel; neither do I say of those whom your eyes do contemn, God will by no means bestow good on them (God best knoweth that which is in their souls); for then should I certainly be one of the unjust. They answered, O Noah, thou hast already disputed with us, and hast multiplied disputes with us; now therefore do thou bring that punishment upon us wherewith thou hast threatened us, if thou speakest truth. Noah said, Verily God alone shall bring it upon you, if he pleaseth; and ye shall not prevail against him, so as to escape the same. Neither shall my counsel profit you, although I endeavor to counsel you aright, if God shall please to lead you into error. He is your Lord, and unto him shall ye return.

Will the Meccans say, Mohammed hath forged the Koran? Answer, If I have forged it, on me be my guilt; and let me be clear of that which ye are guilty of. And it was revealed unto Noah, saying, Verily none of thy people shall believe, except he who hath already believed: be not therefore grieved for that which they are doing. But make an ark in our presence, according to the form and dimensions which we have revealed unto thee: and speak not unto me in behalf of those who have acted unjustly; for they are doomed to be drowned. And he built the ark; and so often as a company of his people passed by him, they derided him: but he said, Though ye scoff at us now, we will scoff at you hereafter, as ye scoff at us; and ye shall surely know on whom a punishment shall be inflicted, which shall cover him with shame, and on whom a lasting punishment shall fall. Thus were they employed until our sentence was put in execution, and the oven poured forth water. And we said unto Noah, Carry into the ark of every species of animals one pair; and thy family (except him on whom a previous sentence of destruction hath passed), and those who believe. But they believed not with him, except a few. And Noah said, Embark thereon, in the name of God; while it moveth forward, and while it standeth still; for my Lord is gracious and merciful. And the ark swam with them between waves like mountains: and Noah called unto his son, who was separated from him, saying, Embark with us, my son, and stay not with the unbelievers. He answered, I will get on a mountain, which will secure me from the water. Noah replied, There is no security this day from the decree of God, except for him on whom he shall have mercy. And a wave passed between them, and he became one of those who were drowned. And it was said, O earth, swallow up thy waters, and thou, O heaven, withhold thy rain. And immediately the water abated, and the decree was fulfilled, and the ark rested on the mountain Al Judi; ' and it was said, Away with the ungodly people! And Noah called upon his Lord, and said, O Lord, verily my son is of my family; and thy promise is true; for thou art the most just of those who exercise judgment. God answereth, O Noah, verily he is not of thy family: this intercession of thine for him is not a righteous work. Ask not of me therefore that wherein thou hast no knowledge: I admonish thee that thou become not one of the ignorant. Noah said, O Lord, I have recourse unto thee for the assistance of thy grace, that I ask not of thee that wherein I have no knowledge: and unless thou forgive me, and be merciful unto me, I shall be one of those who perish. It was said unto him, O Noah, come down from the ark, with peace from us, and blessings upon thee and upon a part of those who are with thee: but as for a part of them, we will suffer them to enjoy the provision of this world; and afterward shall a grievous punishment from us be inflicted on them, in the life to come. This is a secret history, which we reveal unto thee: thou didst not know it, neither did thy people before this. Wherefore persevere with patience: for the prosperous issue shall attend the pious.

And unto the tribe of Ad we sent their brother Hud. He said, O my people, worship God; ye have no God besides him: ye only imagine falsehood, in setting up idols and intercessors of your own making. O my people, I ask not of you for this my preaching, any recompense: my recompense do I expect from him only who hath created me. Will ye not therefore understand? O my people, ask pardon of your Lord; and be turned unto him: he will send the heaven to pour forth rain plentifully upon you, and he will increase your strength by giving unto you further strength: therefore turn not aside to commit evil. They answered, O Hud, thou hast brought us no proof of what thou sayest; therefore we will not leave our gods for thy saying, neither do we believe thee. We say no other than that some of our gods have afflicted thee with evil. He replied, Verily I call God to witness, and do ye also bear witness, that I am clear of that which ye associate with God, besides him. Do ye all therefore join to devise a plot against me, and tarry not; for I put my confidence in God, my Lord and your Lord. There is no beast, but he holdeth it by its forelock: verily my Lord proceedeth in the right way. But if ye turn back, I have already declared unto you that with which I was sent unto you; and my Lord shall substitute another nation in your stead; and ye shall not hurt him at all: for my Lord is guardian over all things. And when our sentence came to be put in execution, we delivered Hud, and those who had believed with him, through our mercy; and we delivered them from a grievous punishment. And this tribe of Ad wittingly rejected the signs of their Lord, and were disobedient unto his messengers, and they followed the command of every rebellious perverse person. Wherefore they were followed in this world by a curse, and they shall be followed by the same on the day of resurrection. Did not Ad disbelieve in their Lord? Was it not said, Away with Ad, the people of Hud?

And unto the tribe of Thamud we sent their brother Saleh. He said unto them, O my people, worship God; ye have no

God besides him.   It is he who hath produced you out of the
earth, and hath given you an habitation therein.   Ask pardon of him, therefore, and be turned unto him; for my Lord
is near, and ready to answer.   They answered, O Saleh, thou
wast a person on whom we placed our hopes before this.   Dost
thou forbid us to worship that which our fathers worshiped?
But we are certainly in doubt concerning the religion to
which thou dost invite us, as justly to be expected.   Saleh
said, O my people, tell me; if I have received an evident declaration from my Lord, and he hath bestowed on me mercy
from himself; who will protect me from the vengeance of
God, if I be disobedient unto him?   For ye shall not add
unto me, other than loss.   And he said, O my people, this
she-camel of God is a sign unto you; therefore dismiss her
freely that she may feed in God's earth, and do her no harm,
lest a swift punishment seize you.   Yet they killed her;
and Saleh said, Enjoy yourselves in your dwellings for three
days, after which ye shall be destroyed.   This is an infallible
prediction.   And when our decree came to be executed, we
delivered Saleh and those who believed with him, through
our mercy, from the disgrace of that day; for thy Lord is
the strong, the mighty God.   But a terrible noise from
heaven assailed those who had acted unjustly; and in the
morning they were found in their houses, lying dead and
prostrate; as though they had never dwelt therein.   Did not
Thamud disbelieve in their Lord?   Was not Thamud cast
far away?

Our messengers also came formerly unto Abraham, with
good tidings: they said, Peace be upon thee.   And he answered, And on you be peace! and he tarried not, but brought
a roasted calf.   And when he saw that their hands did not
touch the meat, he misliked them, and entertained a fear of
them.   But they said, Fear not: for we are sent unto the
people of Lot.   And his wife Sarah was standing by, and
she laughed; and we promised her Isaac, and after Isaac,
Jacob.   She said, Alas! shall I bear a son, who am old; this
my husband also being advanced in years?   Verily this
would be a wonderful thing.   The angels answered, Dost

thou wonder at the effect of the command of God? The mercy of God and his blessings be upon you, the family of the house: for he is praiseworthy, and to be glorified. And when his apprehension had departed from Abraham, and the good tidings of Isaac's birth had come unto him, he disputed with us concerning the people of Lot: for Abraham was a pitiful, compassionate, and devout person. The angels said unto him, O Abraham, abstain from this; for now is the command of thy Lord come, to put their sentence in execution, and an inevitable punishment is ready to fall upon them. And when our messengers came unto Lot, he was troubled for them, and his arm was straitened concerning them, and he said, This is a grievous day. And his people came unto him, rushing upon him: and they had formerly been guilty of wickedness. Lot said unto them, O my people, these my daughters are more lawful for you: therefore fear God, and put me not to shame by wronging my guests. Is there not a man of prudence among you? They answered, Thou knowest that we have no need of thy daughters; and thou well knowest what we would have. He said, If I had strength sufficient to oppose you, or I could have recourse unto a powerful support, I would certainly do it. The angels said, O Lot, verily we are the messengers of thy Lord; they shall by no means come in unto thee. Go forth therefore with thy family, in some part of the night, and let not any of you turn back; but as for thy wife, that shall happen unto her, which shall happen unto them. Verily the prediction of their punishment shall be fulfilled in the morning: is not the morning near? And when our command came, we turned those cities upside down, and we rained upon them stones of baked clay, one following another, and being marked, from thy Lord; and they are not far distant from those who act unjustly.

And unto Madian we sent their brother Shoaib: he said, O my people, worship God; ye have no God but him: and diminish not measure and weight. Verily I see you to be in a happy condition: but I fear for you the punishment of the day which will encompass the ungodly. O my people, give full measure and just weight; and diminish not unto men aught of their matters; neither commit injustice in the earth, acting corruptly.   The residue which shall remain unto you as the gift of God, after ye shall have done justice to others, will be better for you than wealth gotten by fraud; if ye be true believers.   I am no guardian over you.   They answered, O Shoaib, do thy prayers enjoin thee, that we should leave the gods which our fathers worshiped; or that we should not do what we please with our substance?   Thou only, it seems, art the wise person, and fit to direct.   He said, O my people, tell me; if I have received an evident declaration from my Lord, and he hath bestowed on me an excellent provision, and I will not consent unto you in that which I forbid you; do I seek any other than your reformation, to the utmost of my power?   My support is from God alone; on him do I trust, and unto him do I turn me.

O my people, let not your opposing of me draw on you a vengeance like unto that which fell on the people of Noah, or the people of Hud, or the people of Saleh: neither was the people of Lot far distant from you.   Ask pardon therefore of your Lord; and be turned unto him: for my Lord is merciful and loving.   They answered, O Shoaib, we understand not much of what thou sayest; and we see thee to be a man of no power among us: if it had not been for the sake of thy family, we had surely stoned thee, neither couldst thou have prevailed against us.   Shoaib said, O my people, is my family more worthy in your opinion than God? and do ye cast him behind you with neglect?   Verily my Lord comprehendeth that which ye do.   O my people, do ye work according to your condition; I will surely work according to my duty. And ye shall certainly know on whom will be inflicted a punishment which shall cover him with shame, and who is a liar.   Wait therefore the event; for I also will wait it with you.   Wherefore when our decree came to be executed, we delivered Shoaib and those who believed with him, through our mercy: and a terrible noise from heaven assailed those who had acted unjustly; and in the morning they were found in their houses lying dead and prostrate, as though they had never dwelt therein. Was not Madian removed from off the earth, as Thamud had been removed? . . .

We formerly gave unto Moses the book of the law; and disputes arose among his people concerning it: and unless a previous decree had proceeded from thy Lord, to bear with them during this life, the matter had been surely decided between them. And thy people are also jealous and in doubt concerning the Koran. But unto every one of them will thy Lord render the reward of their works; for he well knoweth that which they do. Be thou steadfast, therefore, as thou hast been commanded; and let him also be steadfast who shall be converted with thee; and transgress not: for he seeth that which ye do. And incline not unto those who act unjustly, lest the fire of hell touch you: for ye have no protectors, except God; neither shall ye be assisted against him. Pray regularly morning and evening; and in the former part of the night, for good works drive away evils. This is an admonition unto those who consider: wherefore persevere with patience; for God suffereth not the reward of the righteous to perish. Were such of the generations before you, endued with understanding and virtue, who forbade the acting corruptly in the earth, any more than a few only of those whom we delivered? But they who were unjust followed the delights which they enjoyed in this world and were wicked doers: and thy Lord was not of such a disposition as to destroy the cities unjustly, while their inhabitants behaved themselves uprightly. And if thy Lord pleased, he would have made all men of one religion: but they shall not cease to differ among themselves, unless those on whom thy Lord shall have mercy: and unto this hath he created them; for the word of thy Lord shall be fulfilled, when he said, Verily I will fill hell altogether with genii and men.

The whole which we have related of the histories of our apostles do we relate unto thee, that we may confirm thy heart thereby; and herein is the truth come unto thee, and an admonition, and a warning unto the true believers. Say unto those who believe not, Act ye according to your condition; we surely will act according to our duty: and wait the issue; for we certainly wait it also.   Unto God is known that which is secret in heaven and earth; and unto him shall the whole matter be referred.   Therefore worship him, and put thy trust in him; for thy Lord is not regardless of that which ye do.

CHAPTER XII

ENTITLED, JOSEPH;[1] REVEALED AT MECCA

IN THE NAME OF THE MOST MERCIFUL GOD

A. L. R.   These are the signs of the perspicuous book; which we have sent down in the Arabic tongue, that peradventure ye might understand.   We relate unto thee a most excellent history, by revealing unto thee this Koran, whereas thou wast before one of the negligent.

When Joseph said unto his father, O my father, verily I saw in my dream eleven stars, and the sun and the moon: I saw them make obeisance unto me.   Jacob said, O my child, tell not thy vision to thy brethren, lest they devise some plot against thee; for the devil is a professed enemy unto man: and thus, according to thy dream, shall thy Lord choose thee, and teach thee the interpretation of dark sayings, and he shall accomplish his favor upon thee and upon the family of Jacob, as he hath formerly accomplished it upon thy fathers Abraham and Isaac; for thy Lord is knowing and wise. Surely in the history of Joseph and his brethren there are signs of God's providence to the inquisitive; when they said to one another, Joseph and his brother are dearer to our father than we, who are the greater number: our father certainly maketh a wrong judgment.   Wherefore slay Joseph, or drive him into some distant or desert part of the earth,

[1] The Koreish, thinking to puzzle Mohammed, at the instigation and by the direction of certain Jewish Rabbins, demanded of him how Jacob's family happened to go down into Egypt, and that he would relate to them the history of Joseph, with all its circumstances: whereupon he pretended to have received this chapter from heaven, containing the story of that patriarch.   It is said, however, to have been rejected by two Mohammedan sects, branches of the Kharejites, called the Ajaredites and the Maimunians, as apocryphal and spurious.

and the face of your father shall be cleared toward you; and ye shall afterward be people of integrity. One of them spoke and said, Slay not Joseph, but throw him to the bottom of the well; and some travelers will take him up, if ye do this. They said unto Jacob, O father, why dost thou not entrust Joseph with us, since we are sincere well-wishers unto him? Send him with us to-morrow, into the field, that he may divert himself, and sport, and we will be his guardians. Jacob answered, It grieveth me that ye take him away; and I fear lest the wolf devour him, while ye are negligent of him. They said, Surely if the wolf devour him when there are so many of us, we shall be weak indeed. And when they had carried him with them, and agreed to set him at the bottom of the well, they executed their design: and we sent a revelation unto him, saying, Thou shalt hereafter declare this their action unto them; and they shall not perceive thee to be Joseph. And they came to their father at even, weeping, and said, Father, we went and ran races with one another, and we left Joseph with our baggage, and the wolf hath devoured him; but thou wilt not believe us, although we speak the truth. And they produced his inner garment stained with false blood. Jacob answered, Nay, but ye yourselves have contrived the thing for your own sakes: however, patience is most becoming, and God's assistance is to be implored to enable me to support the misfortune which ye relate. And certain travelers came, and sent one to draw water for them: and he let down his bucket, and said, Good news! this is a youth. And they concealed him, that they might sell him as a piece of merchandise: but God knew that which they did. And they sold him for a mean price, for a few pence, and valued him lightly. And the Egyptian who bought him said to his wife, Use him honorably; peradventure he may be serviceable to us, or we may adopt him for our son. Thus did we prepare an establishment for Joseph in the earth, and we taught him the interpretation of dark sayings: for God is well able to effect his purpose; but the greater part of men do not understand.

And when he had attained his age of strength, we bestowed

on him wisdom and knowledge; for thus do we recompense the righteous. And she, in whose house he was, desired him to lie with her; and she shut the doors and said, Come hither. He answered, God forbid! verily my lord hath made my dwelling with him easy; and the ungrateful shall not prosper. But she resolved within herself to enjoy him, and he would have resolved to enjoy her, had he not seen the evident demonstration of his Lord. So we turned away evil and filthiness from him, because he was one of our sincere servants. And they ran to get one before the other to the door; and she rent his inner garment behind. And they met her lord at the door. She said, What shall be the reward of him who seeketh to commit evil in thy family, but imprisonment, and a painful punishment? And Joseph said, She asked me to lie with her. And a witness of her family bore witness, saying, If his garment be rent before, she speaketh truth, and he is a liar; but if his garment be rent behind, she lieth, and he is a speaker of truth. And when her husband saw that his garment was torn behind, he said, This is a cunning contrivance of your sex; for surely your cunning is great. O Joseph, take no further notice of this affair: and thou, O woman, ask pardon for thy crime, for thou art a guilty person. And certain women said publicly in the city, The nobleman's wife asked her servant to lie with her: he hath inflamed her breast with his love; and we perceive her to be in a manifest error. And when she heard of their subtle behavior, she sent unto them, and prepared a banquet for them, and she gave to each of them a knife; and she said unto Joseph, Come forth unto them. And when they saw him they praised him greatly; and they cut their own hands, and said, O God! this is not a mortal; he is no other than an angel, deserving the highest respect. And his mistress said, This is he for whose sake ye blamed me: I asked him to lie with me, but he hath constantly refused. But if he do not perform that which I command him, he shall surely be cast into prison, and he shall be made one of the contemptible. Joseph said, O Lord, a prison is more eligible unto me than the crime to which they invite me; but unless thou turn aside their snares from me, I shall

youthfully incline unto them, and I shall become one of
the foolish. Wherefore his Lord heard him, and turned
aside their snares from him; for he both heareth and
knoweth. . . .

Moreover Joseph's brethren came, and went in unto him;
and he knew them, but they knew not him. And when he
had furnished them with their provisions, he said, Bring
unto me your brother, the son of your father: do ye not see
that I give full measure, and that I am the most hospitable
receiver of guests? But if ye bring him not unto me, there
shall be no corn measured unto you from me, neither shall
ye approach my presence. They answered, We will endeavor to obtain him of his father, and we will certainly perform what thou requirest. And Joseph said to his servants,
Put their money which they have paid for their corn into
their sacks, that they may perceive it, when they shall be
returned to their family: peradventure they will come back
unto us. And when they had returned unto their father,
they said, O father, it is forbidden to measure out corn unto
us any more, unless we carry our brother Benjamin with us:
wherefore send our brother with us, and we shall have corn
measured unto us; and we will certainly guard him from any
mischance. Jacob answered, Shall I trust him with you with
any better success than I trusted your brother Joseph with
you heretofore? But God is the best guardian; and he is the
most merciful of those who show mercy. And when they
opened their provisions, they found their money had been
returned unto them; and they said, O father, what do we
desire further? this our money hath been returned unto us:
we will therefore return, and provide corn for our family: we
will take care of our brother; and we shall receive a camel's
burden more than we did the last time. This is a small
quantity. Jacob said, I will by no means send him with you,
until ye give me a solemn promise, and swear by God that ye
will certainly bring him back unto me, unless ye be encompassed by some inevitable impediment. And when they had
given him their solemn promise, he said, God is witness of
what we say. And he said, My sons, enter not into the city

by one and the same gate; but enter by different gates. But this precaution will be of no advantage unto you against the decree of God; for judgment belongeth unto God alone: in him do I put my trust, and in him let those confide who seek in whom to put their trust.

And when they entered the city as their father had commanded them, it was of no advantage unto them against the decree of God; and the same served only to satisfy the desire of Jacob's soul, which he had charged them to perform: for he was endued with knowledge of that which we had taught him; but the greater part of men do not understand. And when they entered into the presence of Joseph, he received his brother Benjamin as his guest, and said, Verily I am thy brother; be not therefore afflicted for that which they have committed against us. And when he had furnished them with their provisions, he put his cup in his brother Benjamin's sack. Then a crier cried after them, saying, O company of travelers, ye are surely thieves. They said (and turned back unto them), What is it that ye miss? They answered, We miss the prince's cup: and unto him who shall produce it, shall be given a camel's load of corn; and I will be surety for the same. Joseph's brethren replied, By God, ye do well know that we come not to act corruptly in the land, neither are we thieves. The Egyptians said, What shall be the reward of him who shall appear to have stolen the cup, if ye be found liars? Joseph's brethren answered, As to the reward of him in whose sack it shall be found, let him become a bondman in satisfaction for the same: thus do we reward the unjust, who are guilty of theft. Then he began by their sacks, before he searched the sack of his brother; and he drew out the cup from his brother's sack. Thus did we furnish Joseph with a stratagem. It was not lawful for him to take his brother for a bondman, by the law of the King of Egypt, had not God pleased to allow it, according to the offer of his brethren. We exalt to degrees of knowledge and honor whom we please: and there is one who is knowing above all those who are endued with knowledge. His brethren said, If Benjamin be guilty of theft, his brother Joseph hath been also guilty of theft heretofore.[2] But Joseph concealed these things in his mind, and did not discover them unto them; and he said within himself, Ye are in a worse condition than us two; and God best knoweth what ye discourse about. They said unto Joseph, Noble lord, Verily this lad hath an aged father; wherefore take one of us in his stead; for we perceive that thou art a beneficent person. Joseph answered, God forbid that we should take any other than him with whom we found our goods; for then should we certainly be unjust. And when they despaired of obtaining Benjamin, they retired to confer privately together. And the elder of them said, Do ye not know that your father hath received a solemn promise from you, in the name of God; and how perfidiously ye behaved heretofore toward Joseph? Wherefore I will by no means depart the land of Egypt, until my father give me leave to return unto him, or God maketh known his will to me; for he is the best judge. Return ye to your father, and say, O father, verily thy son hath committed theft; we bear witness of no more than what we know, and we could not guard against what we did not foresee: and do thou inquire in the city where we have been, and of the company of merchants with whom we are arrived, and thou wilt find that we speak the truth.

And when they were returned, and had spoken thus to their father, he said, Nay, but rather ye yourselves have contrived the thing for your own sakes: but patience is most proper for me; peradventure God will restore them all unto me; for he is knowing and wise. And he turned from them and said,

[2] The occasion of this suspicion, it is said, was, that Joseph having been brought up by his father's sister, she became so fond of him that, when he grew up, and Jacob designed to take him from her, she contrived the following stratagem to keep him: Having a girdle which had once belonged to Abraham, she girt it about the child, and then, pretending she had lost it, caused strict search to be made for it; and it being at length found on Joseph, he was adjudged, according to the above-mentioned law of the family, to be delivered to her as her property. Some, however, say that Joseph actually stole an idol of gold, which belonged to his mother's father, and destroyed it; a story probably taken from Rachel's stealing the images of Laban: and others tell us that he once stole a goat, or a hen, to give to a poor man.

Oh, how am I grieved for Joseph! And his eyes became white with mourning, he being oppressed with deep sorrow. His sons said, By God, thou wilt not cease to remember Joseph, until thou be brought to death's door, or thou be actually destroyed by excessive affliction. He answered, I only represent my grief, which I am not able to contain, and my sorrow unto God; but I know by revelation from God that which ye know not. O my sons, go and make inquiry after Joseph and his brother; and despair not of the mercy of God; for none despaireth of God's mercy, except the unbelieving people. Wherefore Joseph's brethren returned into Egypt: and when they came into his presence they said, Noble lord, the famine is felt by us and our family, and we are come with a small sum of money: yet give unto us full measure, and bestow corn upon us as alms: for God rewardeth the almsgivers. Joseph said unto them, Do ye know what ye did unto Joseph and his brother, when ye were ignorant of the consequences thereof? They answered, Art thou really Joseph? He replied, I am Joseph; and this is my brother. Now hath God been gracious unto us. For whoso feareth God, and persevereth with patience, shall at length find relief; since God will not suffer the reward of the righteous to perish. They said, By God, now hath God chosen thee above us; and we have surely been sinners. Joseph answered, Let there be no reproach cast on you this day. God forgiveth you; for he is the most merciful of those who show mercy. Depart ye with this my inner garment, and throw it on my father's face; and he shall recover his sight: and then come unto me with all your family. And when the company of travelers was departed from Egypt on their journey toward Canaan, their father said unto those who were about him, Verily I perceive the smell of Joseph: although ye think that I dote. They answered, By God, thou art in thy old mistake. But when the messenger of good tidings was come with Joseph's inner garment, he threw it over his face; and he recovered his eyesight. And Jacob said, Did I not tell you that I knew from God that which ye knew not? They answered, O father, ask pardon of our sins for us, for we have surely been sinners. He replied, I will surely ask pardon for you of my Lord; for he is gracious and merciful.

And when Jacob and his family arrived in Egypt and were introduced unto Joseph, he received his parents unto him, and said, Enter ye into Egypt, by God's favor, in full security. And he raised his parents to the seat of state, and they, together with his brethren, fell down and did obeisance unto him. And he said, O my father, this is the interpretation of my vision, which I saw heretofore: now hath my Lord rendered it true. And he hath surely been gracious unto me, since he took me forth from the prison, and hath brought me hither from the desert; after that the devil had sown discord between me and my brethren: for my Lord is gracious unto whom he pleaseth; and he is the knowing, the wise God. O Lord, thou hast given me a part of the kingdom, and hast taught me the interpretation of dark sayings. The Creator of heaven and earth! thou art my protector in this world, and in that which is to come: make me to die a Moslem, and join me with the righteous.

This is a secret history, which we reveal unto thee, O Mohammed, although thou wast not present with the brethren of Joseph, when they concerted their design, and contrived a plot against him. But the greater part of men, although thou earnestly desire it, will not believe. Thou shalt not demand of them any reward for thy publishing the Koran; it is no other than an admonition unto all creatures. And how many signs soever there be of the being, unity, and providence of God, in the heavens and the earth; they will pass by them, and will retire afar off from them. And the greater part of them believe not in God, without being also guilty of idolatry. Do they not believe that some overwhelming affliction shall fall on them, as a punishment from God; or that the hour of judgment shall overtake them suddenly, while they consider not its approach?

Say unto those of Mecca, This is my way: I invite you unto God, by an evident demonstration; both I and he who followeth me; and, praise be unto God! I am not an idolater. We sent not any apostles before thee, except men unto whom we revealed our will, and whom we chose out of those who dwelt in cities. Will they not go through the earth, and see what hath been the end of those who have preceded them? But the dwelling of the next life shall surely be better for those who fear God. Will they not therefore understand? Their predecessors were borne with for a time, until, when our apostles despaired of their conversion, and they thought that they were liars, our help came unto them, and we delivered whom we pleased; but our vengeance was not turned away from the wicked people. Verily in the histories of the prophets and their people there is an instructive example unto those who are endued with understanding. The Koran is not a new invented fiction; but a confirmation of those scriptures which have been revealed before it, and a distinct explication of everything necessary, in respect either to faith or practise, and a direction and mercy unto people who believe.

CHAPTER XIII

ENTITLED, THUNDER; REVEALED AT MECCA

IN THE NAME OF THE MOST MERCIFUL GOD

A. L. M. R. These are the signs of the book of the Koran: and that which hath been sent down unto thee from thy Lord is the truth; but the greater part of men will not believe. It is God who hath raised the heavens without visible pillars; and then ascended his throne, and compelled the sun and the moon to perform their services: every of the heavenly bodies runneth an appointed course. He ordereth all things. He showeth his signs distinctly, that ye may be assured ye must meet your Lord at the last day. It is he who hath stretched forth the earth, and placed therein steadfast mountains, and rivers; and hath ordained therein of every fruit two different kinds. He causeth the night to cover the day. Herein are certain signs unto people who consider. And in the earth are tracts of land of different natures, though bordering on each other; and also vineyards, and seeds, and palm-trees springing several from the same root, and singly from distinct roots. They are watered with the same water, yet we render some of them more excellent than others to eat. Herein are surely signs unto people who understand.

If thou dost wonder at the infidels denying the resurrection, surely wonderful is their saying, After we shall have been reduced to dust, shall we be restored in a new creature? These are they who believe not in their Lord; these shall have collars on their necks, and these shall be the inhabitants of hell fire: therein shall they abide forever. They will ask of thee to hasten evil rather than good: although there have already been examples of the divine vengeance before them. Thy Lord is surely endued with indulgence toward men, notwithstanding their iniquity; but thy Lord is also severe in punishing. The infidels say, Unless a sign be sent down unto him from his Lord, we will not believe. Thou art commissioned to be a preacher only, and not a worker of miracles; and unto every people hath a director been appointed. God knoweth what every female beareth in her womb; and what the wombs want or exceed of their due time, or number of young. With him is everything regulated according to a determined measure. He knoweth that which is hidden, and that which is revealed. He is the great, the most high. He among you who concealeth his words, and he who proclaimeth them in public; he also who seeketh to hide himself in the night, and he who goeth forth openly in the day, is equal in respect to the knowledge of God. Each of them hath angels mutually succeeding each other, before him, and behind him; they watch him by the command of God.

Verily God will not change his grace which is in men, until they change the disposition in their souls by sin. When God willeth evil on a people, there shall be none to avert it; neither shall they have any protector beside him. It is he who causeth the lightning to appear unto you, to strike fear, and to raise hope, and who formeth the pregnant clouds. The thunder celebrateth his praise, and the angels also, for fear of him.

He sendeth his thunderbolts, and striketh therewith whom

he pleaseth, while they dispute concerning God;[1] for he is mighty in power. It is he who ought of right to be invoked; and the idols which they invoke besides him shall not hear them all; otherwise than as he is heard, who stretcheth forth his hand to the water that it may ascend to his mouth, when it can not ascend thither: the supplication of the unbelievers is utterly erroneous. Whatsoever is in heaven and on earth worshipeth God, voluntarily or of force; and their shadows also, morning and evening.

Say, Who is the Lord of heaven and earth? Answer, God. Say, Have ye therefore taken unto yourselves protectors beside him, who are unable either to help, or to defend themselves from hurt? Say, Shall the blind and the seeing be esteemed equal? or shall darkness and light be accounted the same? or have they attributed companions unto God, who have created as he hath created, so that their creation bear any resemblance unto his? Say, God is the creator of all things; he is the one, the victorious God. He causeth water to descend from heaven, and the brooks flow according to their respective measure, and the floods bear the floating froth: and from the metals which they melt in the fire, seeking to cast ornaments or vessels for use, there ariseth a scum like unto it. Thus God setteth forth truth and vanity. But the scum is thrown off, and that which is useful to mankind remaineth on the earth. Thus doth God put forth parables.

Unto those who obey their Lord shall be given the most excellent reward: but those who obey him not, although they

[1] This passage was revealed on the following occasion: Amer Ebn al Tofail and Arbad Ebn Rabiah, the brother of Labid, went to Mohammed with an intent to kill him; and Amer began to dispute with him concerning the chief points of his doctrine, while Arbad, taking a compass, went behind him to dispatch him with his sword; but the prophet, perceiving his design, implored God's protection; whereupon Arbad was immediately struck dead by thunder, and Amer was struck with a pestilential boil, of which he died in a short time, in a miserable condition. Jallalo'ddin, however, tells another story, saying that Mohammed, having sent one to invite a certain man to embrace his religion, the person put this question to the missionary, " Who is this apostle, and what is God? Is he of gold, or of silver, or of brass? " Upon which a thunderbolt struck off his skull, and killed him.

were possessed of whatever is in the whole earth and as much more, they would give it all for their ransom. These will be brought to a terrible account: their abode shall be hell; an unhappy couch shall it be! Shall he, therefore, who knoweth that what hath been sent down unto thee from thy Lord, is truth, be rewarded as he who is blind? The prudent only will consider; who fulfil the covenant of God, and break not their contract; and who join that which God hath commanded to be joined, and who fear their Lord, and dread an ill account; and who persevere out of a sincere desire to please their Lord, and observe the stated times of prayer, and give alms out of what we have bestowed on them, in secret and openly, and who turn away evil with good: the reward of these shall be paradise, gardens of eternal abode, which they shall enter, and also whoever shall have acted uprightly, of their fathers, and their wives, and their posterity; and the angels shall go in unto them by every gate, saying, Peace be upon you, because ye have endured with patience; how excellent a reward is paradise!

But as for those who violate the covenant of God, after the establishment thereof, and who cut in sunder that which God hath commanded to be joined, and act corruptly in the earth, on them shall a curse fall, and they shall have a miserable dwelling in hell. God giveth provision in abundance unto whom he pleaseth, and is sparing unto whom he pleaseth. Those of Mecca rejoice in the present life; although the present life, in respect to the future, is but a precarious provision. The infidels say, Unless a sign be sent down unto him from his Lord, we will not believe. Answer, Verily God will lead into error whom he pleaseth, and will direct unto himself him who repenteth, and those who believe, and whose hearts rest securely in the meditation of God; shall not men's hearts rest securely in the meditation of God? They who believe and do that which is right shall enjoy blessedness, and partake of a happy resurrection.

Thus have we sent thee to a nation which other nations have preceded, unto whom prophets have likewise been sent, that thou mayest rehearse unto them that which we have revealed unto thee, even while they believe not in the merciful God. Say unto them, He is my Lord; there is no God but he: in him do I trust, and unto him must I return. Though a Koran were revealed by which mountains should be removed, or the earth cleaved in sunder, or the dead be caused to speak, it would be in vain. But the matter belongeth wholly unto God. Do not therefore the believers know that if God pleased, he would certainly direct all men? Adversity shall not cease to afflict the unbelievers for that which they have committed, or to sit down near their habitations, until God's promise come: for God is not contrary to the promise. Apostles before thee have been laughed to scorn; and I permitted the infidels to enjoy a long and happy life: but afterward I punished them; and how severe was the punishment which I inflicted on them! Who is it therefore that standeth over every soul, to observe that which it committeth? They attribute companions unto God. Say, Name them: will ye declare unto him that which he knoweth not in the earth? or will ye name them in outward speech only? But the deceitful procedure of the infidels was prepared for them; and they are turned aside from the right path: for he whom God shall cause to err shall have no director. They shall suffer a punishment in this life; but the punishment of the next shall be more grievous: and there shall be none to protect them against God.

This is the description of paradise, which is promised to the pious. It is watered by rivers; its food is perpetual, and its shade also: this shall be the reward of those who fear God. But the reward of the infidels shall be hell fire. Those to whom we have given the scriptures, rejoice at what hath been revealed unto thee. Yet there are some of the confederates who deny part thereof. Say unto them, Verily I am commanded to worship God alone; and to give him no companion: upon him do I call, and unto him shall I return. To this purpose have we sent down the Koran, a rule of judgment, in the Arabic language. And verily if thou follow their desires, after the knowledge which hath been given thee, there shall be none to defend or protect thee against God. We have formerly sent apostles before thee, and bestowed on them wives and children; [2] and no apostle had the power to come with a sign, unless by permission of God. Every age hath its book of revelation: God shall abolish and shall confirm what he pleaseth. With him is the original of the book. Moreover, whether we cause thee to see any part of that punishment wherewith we have threatened them, or whether we cause thee to die before it be inflicted on them, verily unto thee belongeth preaching only, but unto us inquisition. Do they not see that we come into their land, and straiten the borders thereof, by the conquests of the true believers? When God judgeth, there is none to reverse his judgment; and he will be swift in taking an account. Their predecessors formerly devised subtle plots against their prophets; but God is master of every subtle device. He knoweth that which every soul deserveth: and the infidels shall surely know, whose will be the reward of paradise. The unbelievers will say, Thou art not sent of God. Answer, God is a sufficient witness between me and you, and he who understandeth the scriptures.

CHAPTER XIV

ENTITLED, ABRAHAM; [1] REVEALED AT MECCA

IN THE NAME OF THE MOST MERCIFUL GOD

A. L. R. This book have we sent down unto thee, that thou mayest lead men forth from darkness into light, by the permission of their Lord, into the glorious and laudable way. God is he unto whom belongeth whatsoever is in heaven and on earth: and woe be to the infidels, because a grievous punishment waiteth them; who love the present life above that which is to come, and turn men aside from the way of God,

[2] "As we have on thee." This passage was revealed in answer to the reproaches which were cast on Mohammed, on account of the great number of his wives. For the Jews said that if he was a true prophet, his care and attention would be employed about something else than women and the getting of children.

[1] Mention is made of this patriarch toward the end of the chapter.

and seek to render it crooked: these are in an error far distant from the truth.

We have sent no apostle but with the language of his people, that he might declare their duty plainly unto them: for God causeth to err whom he pleaseth, and directeth whom he pleaseth; and he is the mighty, the wise. We formerly sent Moses with our signs, and commanded him, saying, Lead forth thy people from darkness into light, and remind them of the favors of God: verily therein are signs unto every patient and grateful person. And call to mind when Moses said unto his people, Remember the favor of God toward you, when he delivered you from the people of Pharaoh: they grievously oppressed you; and they slew your male children, but let your females live: therein was a great trial from your Lord. And when your Lord declared by the mouth of Moses, saying, If ye be thankful, I will surely increase my favors toward you; but if ye be ungrateful, verily my punishment shall be severe. And Moses said, if ye be ungrateful, and all who are in the earth likewise; verily God needeth not your thanks, though he deserveth the highest praise.

Hath not the history of the nations your predecessors reached you; namely, of the people of Noah, and of Ad, and of Thamud, and of those who succeeded them; whose number none knoweth except God? Their apostles came unto them with evident miracles; but they clapped their hands to their mouths out of indignation, and said, We do not believe the message with which ye pretend to be sent; and we are in a doubt concerning the religion to which ye invite us, as justly to be suspected. Their apostles answered, Is there any doubt concerning God, the creator of heaven and earth? He inviteth you to the true faith that he may forgive you part of your sins, and may respite your punishment, by granting you space to repent, until an appointed time. They answered, Ye are but men, like unto us: ye seek to turn us aside from the gods which our fathers worshiped: wherefore bring us an evident demonstration by some miracle, that ye speak truth. Their apostles replied unto them, We are no other than men like unto you; but God is bountiful unto such of his servants as he pleaseth: and it is not in our power to give you a miraculous demonstration of our mission, unless by the permission of God; in God therefore let the faithful trust. And what excuse have we to allege that we should not put our trust in God; since he hath directed us our paths? Wherefore we will certainly suffer with patience the persecution wherewith ye shall afflict us: in God therefore let those put their confidence who seek in whom to put their trust. And those who believed not said unto their apostles, We will surely expel you out of our land; or ye shall return unto our religion. And their Lord spake unto them by revelation, saying, We will surely destroy the wicked doers; and we will cause you to dwell in the earth, after them. This shall be granted unto him who shall dread the appearance at my tribunal, and shall fear my threatening. And they asked assistance of God, and every rebellious perverse person failed of success. Hell lieth unseen before him, and he shall have filthy water given him to drink: he shall sup it up by little and little, and he shall not easily let it pass his throat, because of its nauseousness; death also shall come upon him from every quarter, yet he shall not die; and before him shall there stand prepared a grievous torment. This is the likeness of those who believe not in their Lord. Their works are as ashes, which the wind violently scattereth in a stormy day: they shall not be able to obtain any solid advantage from that which they have wrought. This is an error most distant from truth.

Dost thou not see that God hath created the heavens and the earth in wisdom? If he please he can destroy you, and produce a new creature in your stead: neither will this be difficult with God. And they shall all come forth into the presence of God at the last day: and the weak among them shall say' unto those who behaved themselves arrogantly, Verily we were your followers on earth; will ye not therefore avert from us some part of the divine vengeance? They shall answer, If God had directed us aright, we had certainly directed you. It is equal unto us whether we bear our torments impatiently, or whether we endure them with patience: for we have no way to escape. And Satan shall say, after judgment shall have been given, Verily God promised you a promise of truth: and I also made you a promise; but I deceived you. Yet I had not any power over you to compel you; but I called you only, and ye answered me: wherefore accuse not me, but accuse yourselves. I can not assist you; neither can ye assist me. Verily I do now renounce your having associated me with God heretofore.

A grievous punishment is prepared for the unjust. But they who shall have believed and wrought righteousness shall be introduced into gardens, wherein rivers flow; they shall remain therein forever, by the permission of their Lord; and their salutation therein shall be, Peace!

Dost thou not see how God putteth forth a parable; representing a good word, as a good tree, whose root is firmly fixed in the earth, and whose branches reach unto heaven; which bringeth forth its fruit in all seasons, by the will of its Lord? God propoundeth parables unto men, that they may be instructed. And the likeness of an evil word is as an evil tree; which is torn up from the face of the earth, and hath no stability.[2] God shall confirm them who believe, by the steadfast word of faith, both in this life and in that which is to come:[3] but God shall lead the wicked into error, for God doth that which he pleaseth.

Hast thou not considered those who have changed the grace of God to infidelity, and cause their people to descend into the house of perdition, namely, into hell? They shall be thrown to burn therein; and an unhappy dwelling shall it be. They also set up idols as copartners with God, that they might cause men to stray from his path. Say unto them, Enjoy the pleasures of this life for a time; but your departure hence

[2] What is particularly intended in this passage by the good word, and the evil word, the expositors differ. But the first seems to mean the profession of God's unity, the inviting others to the true religion, or the Koran itself; and the latter, the acknowledging a plurality of gods, the seducing of others to idolatry, or the obstinate opposition of God's prophets.

[3] Jallalo'ddin supposes the sepulcher to be here understood; in which place when the true believers come to be examined by the two angels concerning their faith, they will answer properly and without hesitation; which the infidels will not be able to do.

shall be into hell fire. Speak unto my servants who have believed, that they be assiduous at prayer, and give alms out of that which we have bestowed on them, both privately and in public; before the day cometh, wherein there shall be no buying nor selling, neither any friendship.

It is God who hath created the heavens and the earth; and causeth water to descend from heaven, and by means thereof produceth fruits for your sustenance: and by his command he obligeth the ships to sail in the sea for your service; and he also forceth the rivers to supply your uses: he likewise compelleth the sun and the moon, which diligently perform their courses, to serve you; and hath subjected the day and the night to your service. He giveth you of everything which ye ask him; and if ye attempt to reckon up the favors of God, ye shall not be able to compute the same.

Surely man is unjust and ungrateful. Remember when Abraham said, O Lord, make this land a place of security; and grant that I and my children may avoid the worship of idols; for they, O Lord, have seduced a great number of men. whoever therefore shall follow me, he shall be of me: and whosoever shall disobey me; verily thou wilt be gracious and merciful. O Lord, I have caused some of my offspring to settle in an unfruitful valley, near thy holy house, O Lord, that they may be constant at prayer. Grant, therefore, that the hearts of some men may be affected with kindness toward them; and do thou bestow on them all sorts of fruits; that they may give thanks. O Lord, thou knowest whatsoever we conceal, and whatsoever we publish; for nothing is hidden from God, either on earth, or in heaven. Praise be unto God, who hath given me, in my old age, Ismael and Isaac: for my Lord is the hearer of supplication. O Lord, grant that I may be an observer of prayer, and a part of my posterity also, O Lord; and receive my supplication. O Lord, forgive me, and my parents, and the faithful, on the day whereon an account shall be taken.

Think not, O prophet, that God is regardless of what the ungodly do. He only deferreth their punishment unto the day whereon men's eyes shall be fixed: they shall hasten forward, at the voice of the angel calling to judgment, and shall lift up their heads; they shall not be able to turn their sight from the object whereon it shall be fixed, and their hearts shall be void of sense, through excessive terror. Wherefore do thou threaten men with the day, whereon their punishment shall be inflicted on them, and whereon those who have acted unjustly shall say, O Lord, give us respite unto a term near at hand; and we will obey thy call, and we will follow thy apostles. But it shall be answered unto them, Did ye not swear heretofore, that no reverse should befall you? yet ye dwelt in the dwellings of those who had treated their own souls unjustly; and it appeared plainly unto you how we had dwelt with them; and we propounded their destruction as examples unto you. They employ their utmost subtlety to oppose the truth; but their subtlety is apparent unto God, who is able to frustrate their designs; although their subtlety were so great, that the mountains might be moved thereby.

Think not therefore, O prophet, that God will be contrary to his promise of assistance, made unto his apostles; for God is mighty, able to avenge. The day will come, when the earth shall be changed into another earth, and the heavens into other heavens; [4] and men shall come forth from their graves to appear before the only, the mighty God. And thou shalt see the wicked on that day bound together in fetters: their inner garments shall be of pitch, and fire shall cover their faces; that God may reward every soul, according to what it shall have deserved; for God is swift in taking an account. This is a sufficient admonition unto men, that they may be warned thereby, and that they may know that there is but one God; and that those who are endued with understanding may consider.

[4] This the Mohammedans suppose will come to pass at the last day; the earth becoming white and even, or, as some will have it, of silver; and the heavens of gold.

CHAPTER XV

ENTITLED, AL HEJR;[1] REVEALED AT MECCA

IN THE NAME OF THE MOST MERCIFUL GOD

A. L. R. These are the signs of the book, and of the perspicuous Koran. The time may come when the unbelievers shall wish that they had been Moslems. Suffer them to eat and to enjoy themselves in this world; and let hope entertain them, but they shall hereafter know their folly. We have not destroyed any city, but a fixed term of repentance was appointed them. No nation shall be punished before their time shall be come; neither shall they be respited after.

The Meccans say, O thou to whom the admonition hath been sent down, thou art certainly possessed with a devil: wouldest thou not have come unto us with an attendance of angels, if thou hadst spoken truth? Answer, We sent not down the angels, unless on a just occasion; nor should they be then respited any longer. We have surely sent down the Koran; and we will certainly preserve the same from corruption. We have heretofore sent apostles before thee, among the ancient sects: and there came no apostle unto them, but they laughed him to scorn. In the same manner will we put it into the hearts of the wicked Meccans to scoff at their prophet: they shall not believe on him; and the sentence of the nations of old hath been executed heretofore. If we should open a gate in the heaven above them, and they should ascend thereto all the day long, they would surely say, Our eyes are only dazzled; or rather we are a people deluded by enchantments. We have placed the twelve signs in the heaven, and have set them out in various figures, for the observation of spectators: and we guard them from every devil[2] driven away with stones; except him who listeneth by

[1] Al Hejr is a territory in the province of Hejaz, between Medina and Syria, where the tribe of Thamud dwelt, and is mentioned toward the end of the chapter.

[2] For the Mohammedans imagine that the devils endeavor to ascend to the constellations, to pry into the actions and overhear the discourse of the inhabitants of heaven, and to tempt them. They also pretend that

stealth, at whom a visible flame is darted.[3] We have also spread forth the earth, and thrown thereon stable mountains; and we have caused every kind of vegetables to spring forth in the same, according to a determinate weight: and we have provided therein necessaries of life for you, and for him whom ye do not sustain. There is no one thing but the storehouses thereof are in our hands; and we distribute not the same otherwise than in a determinate measure. We also send the winds driving the pregnant clouds, and we send down from heaven water, whereof we give you to drink, and which ye keep not in store. Verily we give life, and we put to death; and we are the heirs of all things. We know those among you who go before; and we know those who stay behind. And thy Lord shall gather them together at the last day; for he is knowing and wise.

We created man of dried clay, of black mud, formed into shape: and we had before created the devil of subtle fire. And remember when thy Lord said before the angels, Verily I am about to create man of dried clay, of black mud, wrought into shape; when therefore I shall have completely formed him, and shall have breathed of my spirit into him; do ye fall down and worship him. And all the angels worshiped Adam together, except Eblis, who refused to be with those who worshiped him. And God said unto him, O Eblis, what hindered thee from being with those who worshiped Adam ? He answered, It is not fit that I should worship man, whom thou hast created of dried clay, of black mud, wrought into shape. God said, Get thee therefore hence; for thou shalt be driven away with stones: and a curse shall be on thee, until the day of judgment. The devil said, O Lord, give me respite until the day of resurrection. God answered, Verily thou shalt be one of those who are respited until the day of the appointed time. The devil replied, O Lord, because thou hast seduced

these evil spirits had the liberty of entering any of the heavens till the birth of Jesus, when they were excluded three of them; but that on the birth of Mohammed they were forbidden the other four.

[3] For when a star seems to fall or shoot, the Mohammedans suppose the angels, who keep guard in the constellations, dart them at the devils who approach too near.

me, I will surely tempt them to disobedience in the earth; and I will seduce them all, except such of them as shall be thy chosen servants. God said, This is the right way with me. Verily as to my servants, thou shalt have no power over them; but over those only who shall be seduced, and who shall follow thee. And hell is surely denounced unto them all: it hath seven gates; unto every gate a distinct company of them shall be assigned. But those who fear God shall dwell in gardens, amidst fountains. The angels shall say unto them, Enter ye therein in peace and security. And we will remove all grudges from their breasts; they shall be as brethren, sitting over against one another on couches: weariness shall not affect them therein, neither shall they be cast out thence forever. Declare unto my servants that I am gracious, the merciful God; and that my punishment is a grievous punishment. And relate unto them the history of Abraham's guests. When they went in unto him, and said, Peace be unto thee, he answered, Verily we are afraid of you: and they replied, Fear not; we bring thee the promise of a wise son. He said, Do ye bring me the promise of a son now old age hath overtaken me? what is it therefore that ye tell me? They said, We have told thee the truth; be not therefore one of those who despair. He answered, And who despaireth of the mercy of God, except those who err? And he said, What is your errand therefore, O messengers of God? They answered, Verily we are sent to destroy a wicked people: but as for the family of Lot, we will save them all, except his wife; we have decreed that she shall be one of those who remain behind to be destroyed with the infidels. And when the messengers came to the family of Lot, he said unto them, Verily ye are people who are unknown to me. They answered, But we are come unto thee to execute that sentence, concerning which your fellow-citizens doubted: we tell thee a certain truth; and we are messengers of veracity. Therefore lead forth thy family, in some time of the night; and do thou follow behind them, and let none of you turn back; but go whither ye are commanded. And we gave him this command; because the utmost remnant of those people was to be cut off in the morning. And the inhabitants of the city came unto Lot rejoicing at the news of the arrival of some strangers. And he said unto them, Verily these are my guests: wherefore do not disgrace me by abusing them; but fear God, and put me not to shame. They answered, Have we not forbidden thee from entertaining or protecting any man? Lot replied, These are my daughters; therefore rather make use of them, if ye be resolved to do what ye purpose. As thou livest they wander in their folly. Wherefore a terrible storm from heaven assailed them at sunrise: and we turned the city upside down, and we rained on them stones of baked clay. Verily herein are signs unto men of sagacity, and those cities were punished, to point out a right way for men to walk in. Verily herein is a sign unto the true believers.

The inhabitants of the wood near Midian were also ungodly: wherefore we took vengeance on them. And both of them were destroyed, to serve as a manifest rule for men to direct their actions by. And the inhabitants of Al Hejr likewise heretofore accused the messengers of God of imposture: and we produced our signs unto them, but they retired afar off from the same. And they hewed houses out of the mountains, to secure themselves. But a terrible noise from heaven assailed them in the morning: neither was what they had wrought of any advantage unto them.

We have not created the heavens and the earth, and whatever is contained between them otherwise than in justice: and the hour of judgment shall surely come. Wherefore, O Mohammed, forgive thy people with a gracious forgiveness.[4] Verily thy Lord is the creator of thee and of them, and knoweth what is most expedient. We have already brought unto thee seven verses which are frequently to be repeated,[5] and the glorious Koran. Cast not thine eyes on the good things which we have bestowed on several of the unbelievers, so as to covet the same;[6] neither be thou grieved on their

[4] This verse, it is said, was abrogated by that of the sword.

[5] That is, the first chapter of the Koran, which consists of so many verses; though some suppose the seven long chapters are here intended.

[6] That is, Do not envy or covet their worldly prosperity, since thou hast received, in the Koran, a blessing, in comparison whereof all that

account. Behave thyself with meekness toward the true believers; and say, I am a public preacher. If they believe not, we will inflict a like punishment on them, as we have inflicted on the dividers, who distinguished the Koran into different parts; for by thy Lord, we will demand an account from them all, of that which they have wrought. Wherefore publish that which thou hast been commanded, and withdraw from the idolaters. We will surely take thy part against the scoffers, who associate with God another god; they shall surely know their folly. And now we well know that thou art deeply concerned on account of that which they say: but do thou celebrate the praise of thy Lord; and be one of those who worship; and serve thy Lord, until death shall overtake thee.

CHAPTER XVI

ENTITLED, THE BEE; REVEALED AT MECCA

IN THE NAME OF THE MOST MERCIFUL GOD

The sentence of God will surely come to be executed; wherefore do not hasten it. Praise be unto him! and far be that from him which they associated with him! He shall cause the angels to descend with a revelation by his command, unto such of his servants as he pleaseth, saying, Preach that there is no God, except myself; therefore fear me.

He hath created the heavens and the earth to manifest his justice: far be that from him which they associate with him! He hath created man of seed; and yet behold, he is a professed disputer against the resurrection. He hath likewise created the cattle for you: from them ye have wherewith to

we have bestowed on them ought to be contemned as of no value. Al Beidawi mentions a tradition, that Mohammed meeting at Adhriat (a town of Syria) seven caravans, very richly laden, belonging to some Jews of the tribes of Koreidha and al Nadir, his men had a great mind to plunder them, saying, "That those riches would be of great service for the propagation of God's true religion." But the prophet represented to them, by this passage, that they had no reason to repine, God having given them the seven verses, which were infinitely more valuable than those seven caravans.

keep yourselves warm, and other advantages; and of them do ye also eat. And they are likewise a credit unto you, when ye drive them home in the evening, and when ye lead them forth to feed in the morning: and they carry your burdens to a distant country, at which ye could not otherwise arrive, unless with great difficulty to yourselves; for your Lord is compassionate and merciful. And he hath also. created horses, and mules, and asses, that ye may ride thereon, and for an ornament unto you; and he likewise createth other things which ye know not.

It appertaineth unto God to instruct men in the right way; and there is who turneth aside from the same: but if he had pleased, he would certainly have directed you all. It is he who sendeth down from heaven rain water, whereof ye have to drink, and from which plants, whereon ye feed your cattle, receive their nourishment. And by means thereof he causeth corn, and olives, and palm-trees, and grapes, and all kinds of fruits to spring forth for you. Surely herein is a sign of the divine power and wisdom unto people who consider. And he hath subjected the night and the day to your service; and the sun, and the moon, and the stars, which are compelled to serve by his command. Verily herein are signs unto people of understanding. And he hath also given you dominion over whatever he hath created for you in the earth, distinguished by its different color. Surely herein is a sign unto people who reflect. It is he who hath subjected the sea unto you, that ye might eat fish thereout, and take from thence ornaments for you to wear: and thou seest the ships plowing the waves thereof, that ye may seek to enrich yourselves of his abundance, by commerce; and that ye might give thanks. And he hath thrown upon the earth mountains firmly rooted, lest it should move with you,[1] and also rivers, and paths, that ye might be directed: and he hath likewise ordained marks whereby men may know their way; and they are directed by

[1] The Mohammedans suppose that the earth, when first created, was smooth and equal, and thereby liable to a circular motion as well as the celestial orbs; and that the angels asking, who could be able to stand on so tottering a frame, God fixed it the next morning by throwing the mountains on it.

the stars. Shall God therefore who createth be as he who createth not? Do ye not therefore consider?

If ye attempt to reckon up the favors of God, ye shall not be able to compute their number: God is surely gracious, and merciful; and God knoweth that which ye conceal and that which ye publish. But the idols which ye invoke, besides God, create nothing, but are themselves created. They are dead, and not living; neither do they understand when they shall be raised. Your God is one God. As to those who believe not in the life to come, their hearts deny the plainest evidence, and they proudly reject the truth. . . .

On a certain day we will raise up in every nation a witness against them, from among themselves; and we will bring thee, O Mohammed, as a witness against these Arabians. We have sent down unto thee the book of the Koran, for an explication of everything necessary both as to faith and practise, and a direction, and mercy, and good tidings unto the Moslems. Verily God commandeth justice, and the doing of good, and the giving unto kindred what shall be necessary; and he forbiddeth wickedness, and iniquity, and oppression: he admonisheth you that ye may remember.[2]

Perform your covenant with God, when ye enter into covenant with him; and violate not your oaths, after the ratification thereof; since ye have made God a witness over you. Verily God knoweth that which ye do. And be not like unto her who undoeth that which she hath spun, untwisting it after she hath twisted it strongly; taking your oaths between you deceitfully, because one party is more numerous than another party. Verily God only tempteth you therein; and he will make that manifest unto you, on the day of resurrec-

[2] This verse, which was the occasion of the conversion of Othman Ebn Matun, the commentators say, containeth the whole which it is a man's duty either to perform or to avoid; and is alone a sufficient demonstration of what is said in the foregoing verse. Under the three things here commanded, they understand the belief of God's unity, without inclining to atheism, on the one hand, or polytheism, on the other; obedience to the commands of God; and charity toward those in distress. And under the three things forbidden, they comprehend all corrupt and carnal affections; all false doctrines and heretical opinions; and all injustice toward man.

tion, concerning which ye now disagree. If God had pleased, he would surely have made you one people: but he will lead into error whom he pleaseth, and he will direct whom he pleaseth; and ye shall surely give an account of that which ye have done. Therefore take not your oaths between you deceitfully, lest your foot slip, after it hath been steadfastly fixed, and ye taste evil in this life, for that ye have turned aside from the way of God; and ye suffer a grievous punishment in the life to come. And sell not the covenant of God for a small price; for with God is a better recompense prepared for you, if ye be men of understanding. That which is with you will fail; but that which is with God is permanent: and we will surely reward those who shall persevere, according to the utmost merit of their actions. Whoso worketh righteousness, whether he be male or female, and is a true believer, we will surely raise him to a happy life; and we will give them their reward, according to the utmost merit of their actions. When thou readest the Koran, have recourse unto God, that he may preserve thee from Satan driven away with stones:[3] he hath no power over those who believe, and who put their confidence in their Lord; but his power is over those only, who take him for their patron, and who give companions unto God. When we substitute in the Koran an abrogating verse in lieu of a verse abrogated, (and God best knoweth the fitness of that which he revealeth,) the infidels say, Thou art only a forger of these verses: but the greater part of them know not truth from falsehood. Say, The holy spirit hath brought the same down from thy Lord with truth; that he may confirm those who believe, and for a direction and good tidings unto the Moslems. We also know that they say, Verily, a certain man teacheth him to compose

[3] Mohammed one day reading in the Koran, uttered a horrid blasphemy, to the great scandal of those who were present, as will be observed in Chapter XXII; to excuse which he assured them that those words were put into his mouth by the devil; and to prevent any such accident for the future, he is here taught to beg God's protection before he entered on that duty. Hence, the Mohammedans, before they begin to read any part of this book, repeat these words, " I have recourse unto God for assistance against Satan driven away with stones."

the Koran. The tongue of the person unto whom they incline is a foreign tongue; but this, wherein the Koran is written, is the perspicuous Arabic tongue.[4]

Moreover as for those who believe not in the signs of God, God will not direct them, and they shall suffer a painful torment: verily they imagine a falsehood who believe not in the signs of God, and they are really the liars. Whoever denieth God, after he hath believed, except him who shall be compelled against his will, and whose heart continueth steadfast in the faith, shall be severely chastised: but whoever shall voluntarily profess infidelity, on those shall the indignation of God fall, and they shall suffer a grievous punishment. This shall be their sentence, because they have loved the present life above that which is to come, and for that God directeth not the unbelieving people. These are they whose hearts, and hearing, and sight God hath sealed up; and these are the negligent: there is no doubt but that in the next life they shall perish.

Moreover thy Lord will be favorable unto those who have fled their country, after having suffered persecution, and been compelled to deny the faith by violence, and who have since fought in defense of the true religion, and have persevered with patience; verily unto these will thy Lord be gracious and merciful, after they shall have shown their sincerity. On a certain day shall every soul come to plead for itself, and

---

[4] This was a great objection made by the Meccans to the authority of the Koran; for when Mohammed insisted, as a proof of its divine origin, that it was impossible a man so utterly unacquainted with learning as himself could compose such a book, they replied, that he had one or more assistants in the forgery; but as to the particular person or persons suspected of this confederacy, the traditions differ. One says it was Jabar, a Greek, servant to Amer Ebn al Hadrami, who could read and write well; another, that they were Jabar and Yesar, two slaves who followed the trade of sword-cutlers at Mecca, and used to read the Pentateuch and gospel, and had often Mohammed for their auditor, when he passed that way. Another tells us, it was one Aish, or Yaish, a domestic of al Haweiteb Ebn Abd al Uzza, who was a man of some learning, and had embraced Mohammedanism. Another supposes it was one Kais, a Christian, whose house Mohammed frequented; another, that it was Addas, a servant of Otba Ebn Rabia; and another, that it was Salman the Persian.

every soul shall be repaid that which it shall have wrought; and they shall not be treated unjustly. God propoundeth as a parable a city which was secure and quiet, unto which her provisions came in abundance from every side; but she ungratefully denied the favors of God: wherefore God caused her to taste the extreme famine, and fear, because of that which they had done. And now is an apostle come unto the inhabitants of Mecca from among themselves; and they accuse him of imposture: wherefore a punishment shall be inflicted on them, while they are acting unjustly. Eat of what God hath given you for food, that which is lawful and good; and be thankful for the favors of God, if ye serve him. He hath only forbidden you that which dieth of itself, and blood, and swine's flesh, and that which hath been slain in the name of any, besides God. But unto him who shall be compelled by necessity to eat of these things, not lusting nor wilfully transgressing, God will surely be gracious and merciful. And say not that wherein your tongues utter a lie; This is lawful, and this is unlawful; that ye may devise a lie concerning God: for they who devise a lie concerning God shall not prosper. They shall have small enjoyment in this world, and in that which is to come they shall suffer a grievous torment. Unto the Jews did we forbid that which we have told thee formally: and we did them no injury in that respect; but they injured their own souls.

Moreover thy Lord will be favorable unto those who do evil through ignorance; and afterward repent and amend: verily unto these will thy Lord be gracious and merciful, after their repentance. Abraham was a model of true religion, obedient unto God, orthodox, and was not an idolater: he was also grateful for his benefits: wherefore God chose him, and directed him into the right way. And we bestowed on him good in this world; and in the next he shall surely be one of the righteous. We have also spoken unto thee, O Mohammed, by revelation, saying, Follow the religion of Abraham, who was orthodox, and was no idolater. The Sabbath was only appointed unto those who differed with their prophet concerning it; and thy Lord will surely judge between them, on the day of resurrection, as to that concerning which they differed. Invite men unto the way of thy Lord by wisdom and mild exhortation; and dispute with them in the most condescending manner: for thy Lord well knoweth him who strayeth from his path, and he well knoweth those who are rightly directed. If ye take vengeance on any, take a vengeance proportionable to the wrong which hath been done unto you; but if ye suffer wrong patiently, verily this will be better for the patient. Wherefore do thou bear opposition with patience; but thy patience shall not be practicable, unless with God's assistance. And be not thou grieved on account of the unbelievers; neither be thou troubled for that which they subtilely devise; for God is with those who fear him and are upright.

CHAPTER XVII

ENTITLED, THE NIGHT-JOURNEY; REVEALED AT MECCA

IN THE NAME OF THE MOST MERCIFUL GOD

Praise be unto him, who transported his servant by night, from the sacred temple of Mecca to the farther temple of Jerusalem,[1] the circuit of which we have blessed, that we might show him some of our signs; for God is he who heareth and seeth. And we gave unto Moses the book of the law, and appointed the same to be a direction unto the children of Israel, commanding them, saying, Beware that ye take not any other patron besides me. O posterity of those whom we carried in the ark with Noah: verily he was a grateful servant. And we expressly declared unto the children of

[1] From whence he was carried through the seven heavens to the presence of God, and brought back again to Mecca the same night. It is a dispute among the Mohammedan divines, whether their prophet's night-journey was really performed by him corporally, or whether it was only a dream or vision. Some think the whole was no more than a vision; and allege and express tradition of Moawivoh, one of Mohammed's successors, to that purpose. Others suppose he was carried bodily to Jerusalem, but no farther; and that he ascended thence to heaven in spirit only. But the received opinion is that it was no vision, but that he was actually transported in the body to his journey's end.

Israel in the book of the law, saying, Ye will surely commit evil in the earth twice, and ye will be elated with great insolence. And when the punishment threatened for the first of those transgressions came to be executed, we sent against you our servants, endued with exceeding strength in war, and they searched the inner apartments of your houses; and the prediction became accomplished. Afterward we gave you the victory over them, in your turn, and we granted you increase of wealth and children, and we made you a more numerous people, saying, If ye do well, ye will do well to your own souls; and if ye do evil, ye will do it unto the same. And when the punishment threatened for your latter transgression come to be executed, we sent enemies against you to afflict you, and to enter the temple, as they entered it the first time, and utterly to destroy that which they had conquered. Peradventure your Lord will have mercy on you hereafter: but if ye return to transgress a third time, we also will return to chastise you; and we have appointed hell to be the prison of the unbelievers.

Verily this Koran directeth unto the way which is most right, and declareth unto the faithful, who do good works, that they shall receive a great reward; and that for those who believe not in the life to come, we have prepared a grievous punishment. Man prayeth for evil, as he prayeth for good; for man is hasty.[2] We have ordained the night and the day for two signs of our power: afterward we blot out the sign of the night, and we cause the sign of the day to shine forth, that ye may endeavor to obtain plenty from your Lord by doing your business therein, and that ye may

[2] It is said that the person here meant is Adam, who, when the breath of life was breathed into his nostrils, and had reached so far as his navel, though the lower part of his body was, as yet, but a piece of clay, must needs try to rise up, and got an ugly fall by the bargain. But others pretend the passage was revealed on the following occasion. Mohammed committed a certain captive to the charge of his wife, Sawda bint Zamaa, who, moved with compassion at the man's groans, unbound him, and let him escape; upon which the prophet, in the first motions of his anger, wished her hand might fall off; but immediately composing himself, said aloud, "O God, I am but a man; therefore turn my curse into a blessing."

know the number of years, and the computation of time; and
everything necessary have we explained by a perspicuous explication. The fate of every man have we bound about his
neck; and we will produce unto him, on the day of resurrection, a book wherein his actions shall be recorded: it shall
be offered him open, and the angels shall say unto him, Read
thy book; thine own soul will be a sufficient accountant
against thee, this day. He who shall be rightly directed shall
be directed to the advantage only of his own soul; and he
who shall err shall err only against the same: neither shall
any laden soul be charged with the burden of another. . . .

Kill not your children for fear of being brought to want;
we will provide for them and for you: verily the killing them
is a great sin. Draw not near unto fornication; for it is
wickedness, and an evil way. Neither slay the soul which
God hath forbidden you to slay, unless for a just cause; and
whosoever shall be slain unjustly, we have given his heir
power to demand satisfaction; but let him not exceed the
bounds of moderation in putting to death the murderer in too
cruel a manner, or by revenging his friend's blood on any
other than the person who killed him; since he is assisted
by this law. And meddle not with the substance of the
orphan, unless it be to improve it, until he attain his age
of strength: and perform your covenant; for the performance
of your covenant shall be inquired into hereafter. And give
full measure, when you measure aught; and weigh with a
just balance. This will be better, and more easy for deter-
mining every man's due.

And follow not that whereof thou hast no knowledge; for
the hearing, and the sight, and the heart, every of these shall
be examined at the last day. Walk not proudly in the land,
for thou canst not cleave the earth, neither shalt thou equal
the mountains in stature. All this is evil, and abominable
in the sight of thy Lord. These precepts are a part of the
wisdom which thy Lord hath revealed unto thee. Set not
up any other god as equal unto God, lest thou be cast into
hell, reproved and rejected. Hath your Lord preferably
granted unto you sons, and taken for himself daughters from

among the angels? Verily in asserting this ye utter a grievous saying. And now have we used various arguments and repetitions in this Koran, that they may be warned; yet it only rendereth them more disposed to fly from the truth. Say unto the idolaters, If there were other gods with him, as ye say, they would surely seek an occasion of making some attempt against the possessor of the throne: God forbid! and far, very far, be that from him which they utter! The seven heavens praise him, and the earth, and all who are therein: neither is there anything which doth not celebrate his praise; but ye understand not their celebration thereof: he is gracious and merciful.

When thou readest the Koran, we place between thee and those who believe not in the life to come a dark veil; and we put coverings over their hearts, lest they should understand it, and in their ears thickness of hearing. And when thou makest mention, in repeating the Koran, of thy Lord only, they turn their backs, flying the doctrine of his unity. We well know with what design they harken, when they harken unto thee, and when they privately discourse together: when the ungodly say, Ye follow no other than a madman. Behold! what epithets they bestow on thee. But they are deceived; neither can they find any just occasion to reproach thee. They also say, After we shall have become bones and dust, shall we surely be raised a new creature? Answer, Be ye stones, or iron, or some creature more improbable in your opinions to be raised to life. But they will say, Who shall restore us to life? Answer, He who created you the first time: and they will wag their heads at thee, saying, When shall this be? Answer, Peradventure it is nigh. On that day shall God call you forth from your sepulchers, and ye shall obey, with celebration of his praise; and ye shall think that ye tarried but a little while.

Speak unto my servants, that they speak mildly unto the unbelievers, lest ye exasperate them; for Satan soweth discord among them, and Satan is a declared enemy unto man. Your Lord well knoweth you; if he pleaseth, he will have mercy on you, or, if he pleaseth, he will punish you: and we have not sent thee to be a steward over them. Thy Lord well knoweth all persons in heaven and on earth. We have bestowed peculiar favors on some of the prophets, preferably to others; and we gave unto David the psalms. Say, Call upon those whom ye imagine to be gods besides him; yet they will not be able to free you from harm, or turn it on others. Those whom ye invoke do themselves desire to be admitted to a near conjunction with their Lord; striving which of them shall approach nearest unto him: they also hope for his mercy, and dread his punishment; for the punishment of thy Lord is terrible. There is no city but we will destroy the same before the day of resurrection, or we will punish it with a grievous punishment. This is written in the book of our eternal decrees. Nothing hindered us from sending thee with miracles, except that the former nations have charged them with imposture. We gave unto the tribe of Thamud, at their demand, the she-camel visible to their sight; yet they dealt unjustly with her: and we sent not a prophet with miracles, but to strike terror.

Remember when we said unto thee, Verily thy Lord encompasseth men by his knowledge and power. We have appointed the vision which we showed thee, and also the tree cursed in the Koran, only for an occasion of dispute unto men, and to strike them with terror; but it shall cause them to transgress only the more enormously. And remember when we said unto the angels, Worship Adam; and they all worshiped him except Eblis, who said, Shall I worship him whom thou hast created of clay? And he said, What thinkest thou, as to this man whom thou hast honored above me? verily, if thou grant me respite until the day of resurrection, I will extirpate his offspring, except a few. God answered, Begone, I grant thee respite; but whosoever of them shall follow thee, hell shall surely be your reward; an ample reward for your demerits! And entice to vanity such of them as thou canst, by thy voice; and assault them on all sides with thy horsemen and thy footmen; and partake with them in their riches, and their children; and make them promises; (but the devil shall make them no other than deceitful promises:) as to my servants, thou shalt have no power over them; for thy Lord is a sufficient protector of those who trust in him. . . .

Regularly perform thy prayer at the declension of the sun, at the first darkness of the night, and the prayer of daybreak; for the prayer of daybreak is borne witness unto by the angels. And watch some part of the night in the same exercise, as a work of supererogation for thee; peradventure thy Lord will raise thee to an honorable station. And say, O Lord, cause me to enter with a favorable entry, and cause me to come forth with a favorable coming forth; and grant me from thee an assisting power. And say, Truth is come, and falsehood is vanished: for falsehood is of short continuance.[3] We send down of the Koran that which is a medicine and a mercy unto the true believers, but it shall only increase the perdition of the unjust. When we bestow favors on man, he retireth and withdraweth himself ungratefully from us: but when evil toucheth him, he despaireth of our mercy. Say, Every one acteth after his own manner: but your Lord best knoweth who is most truly directed in his way.

They will ask thee concerning the spirit: answer, The spirit was created at the command of my Lord: but ye have no knowledge given unto you, except a little. If we pleased, we should certainly take away that which we have revealed unto thee; in such case thou couldest not find any to assist thee therein against us, unless through mercy from thy Lord; for his favor toward thee hath been great. Say, Verily if men and genii were purposely assembled, that they might produce a book like this Koran, they could not produce one like unto it, although the one of them assisted the other. And we have variously propounded unto men in this Koran every kind of figurative argument; but the greater part of men refuse to receive it, merely out of infidelity.

And they say, We will by no means believe on thee, until

[3] These words Mohammed repeated, when he entered the temple of Mecca, after the taking of that city, and cleansed it of the idols; a great number of which are said to have fallen down on his touching them with the end of the stick he held in his hand.

thou cause a spring of water to gush forth for us out of the earth; or thou have a garden of palm-trees and vines, and thou cause rivers to spring forth from the midst thereof in abundance; or thou cause the heaven to fall down upon us, as thou hast given out, in pieces; or thou bring down God and the angels to vouch for thee; or thou have a house of gold; or thou ascend by a ladder to heaven: neither will we believe thy ascending thither alone, until thou cause a book to descend unto us, bearing witness of thee, which we may read. Answer, My Lord be praised! Am I other than a man, sent as an apostle? And nothing hindereth men from believing, when a direction is come unto them, except that they say, Hath God sent a man for his apostle? Answer, If the angels had walked on earth as familiar inhabitants thereof, we had surely sent down unto them from heaven an angel for our apostle. Say, God is a sufficient witness between me and you: for he knoweth and regardeth his servants. Whom God shall direct, he shall be the rightly directed; and whom he shall cause to err, thou shalt find none to assist, besides him. And we will gather them together on the day of resurrection, creeping on their faces, blind, and dumb, and deaf: their abode shall be hell; so often as the fire thereof shall be extinguished, we will rekindle a burning flame to torment them. This shall be their reward, because they disbelieve in our signs, and say, When we shall have been reduced to bones and dust, shall we surely be raised new creatures? Do they not perceive that God, who created the heavens and the earth, is able to create other bodies, like their present? And he hath appointed them a limited term; there is no doubt thereof: but the ungodly reject the truth, merely out of unbelief. Say, If ye possessed the treasures of the mercy of my Lord, ye would surely refrain from using them, for fear of spending them; for man is covetous.

We heretofore gave unto Moses the power of working nine evident signs. And do thou ask the children of Israel as to the story of Moses; when he came unto them, and Pharaoh said unto him, Verily I esteem thee, O Moses, to be deluded by sorcery. Moses answered, Thou well knowest that none hath sent down these evident signs except the Lord of heaven and earth; and I surely esteem thee, O Pharaoh, a lost man. Wherefore Pharaoh sought to drive them out of the land; but we drowned him, and all those who were with him. And we said unto the children of Israel, after his destruction, Dwell ye in the land: and when the promise of the next life shall come to be fulfilled, we will bring you both promiscuously to judgment.

We have sent down the Koran with truth, and it hath descended with truth: and we have not sent thee otherwise than to be a bearer of good tidings, and a denouncer of threats. And we have divided the Koran, revealing it by parcels, that thou mightest read it unto men with deliberation; and we have sent it down, causing it to descend as occasion required. Say, Whether ye believe therein, or do not believe, verily those who have been favored with the knowledge of the scriptures which were revealed before it, when the same is rehearsed unto them, fall down on their faces, worshiping, and say, Our Lord be praised, for that the promise of our Lord is surely fulfilled! And they fall down on their faces, weeping; and the hearing thereof increaseth their humility. Say, Call upon God, or call on the Merciful: by whichsoever of the two names ye invoke him, it is equal; for he hath most excellent names. Pronounce not thy prayer aloud, neither pronounce it with too low a voice, but follow a middle way between these: and say, Praise be unto God, who hath not begotten any child; who hath no partner in the kingdom, nor hath any to protect him from contempt.

CHAPTER XVIII

ENTITLED, THE CAVE; [1] REVEALED AT MECCA

IN THE NAME OF THE MOST MERCIFUL GOD

Praise be unto God, who hath sent down unto his servant the book of the Koran, and hath not inserted therein any

[1] The chapter is thus inscribed because it makes mention of the cave wherein the seven sleepers concealed themselves.

crookedness, but hath made it a straight rule: that he should theaten a grievous punishment unto the unbelievers, from his presence; and should bear good tidings unto the faithful, who work righteousness, that they shall receive an excellent reward, namely, paradise, wherein they shall remain forever: and that he should warn those who say, God hath begotten issue; of which matter they have no knowledge, neither had their fathers. A grievous saying it is, which proceedeth from their mouths: they speak no other than a lie. Peradventure thou wilt kill thyself with grief after them, out of thy earnest zeal for their conversion, if they believe not in this new revelation of the Koran. Verily we have ordained whatsoever is on the earth for the ornament thereof, that we might make trial of men, and see which of them excelleth in works: and we will surely reduce whatever is thereon to dry dust.

Dost thou consider that the companions of the cave,[2] and al Rakim,[3] were one of our signs, as well as a great miracle?

When the young men took refuge in the cave, they said, O Lord, grant us mercy from before thee, and dispose our business for us to a right issue. Wherefore we struck their ears with deafness, so that they slept without disturbance in

[2] These were certain Christian youths, of a good family in Ephesus, who, to avoid the persecution of the emperor Decius, by the Arab writers called Decianus, hid themselves in a cave, where they slept for a great number of years. This apocryphal story was borrowed by Mohammed from the Christian traditions, but has been embellished by him and his followers with several additional circumstances.

[3] What is meant by this word the commentators can not agree. Some will have it to be the name of the mountain, or the valley, wherein the cave was; some say it was the name of their dog; and others (who seem to come nearest the true signification) that it was a brass plate, or stone table, placed near the mouth of the cave, on which the names of the young men were written. There are some, however, who take the companions of al Rakim to be different from the seven sleepers: for they say the former were three men who were driven by ill weather into a cave for shelter, and were shut in there by the falling down of a vast stone, which stopped the cave's mouth; but on their begging God's mercy, and their relating each of them a meritorious action which they hoped might entitle them to it, were miraculously delivered by the rock's rending in sunder to give them passage.

the cave for a great number of years: then we awaked them, that we might know which of the two parties was more exact in computing the space which they had remained there. We will relate unto thee their history with truth. Verily they were young men who had believed in their Lord; and we had abundantly directed them: and we fortified their hearts with constancy when they stood before the tyrant; and they said, Our Lord is the Lord of heaven and earth: we will by no means call on any god besides him; for then should we surely utter an extravagance. These our fellow-people have taken other gods, besides him; although they bring no demonstrative argument for them: and who is more unjust than he who deviseth a lie concerning God? And they said the one to the other, When ye shall separate yourselves from them, and from the deities which they worship, except God, fly into the cave: your Lord will pour his mercy on you abundantly, and will dispose your business for you to advantage. And thou mightest have seen the sun, when it had risen, to decline from their cave toward the right hand; and when it went down, to leave them on the left hand: and they were in the spacious part of the cave. This was one of the signs of God. Whomsoever God shall direct he shall be rightly directed; and whomsoever he shall cause to err, thou shalt not find any to defend or to direct. And thou wouldest have judged them to have been awake, while they were sleeping; and we caused them to turn themselves to the right hand, and to the left. And their dog [4] stretched forth his forelegs in the mouth of the cave: if thou hadst come suddenly upon them, verily thou wouldest have turned thy back and fled from them, and thou wouldest have been filled with fear at the sight of them. And so we awaked them from their sleep, that they might ask questions of one another. One of

[4] The Mohammedans have a great respect for this dog, and allow him a place in paradise with some other favorite brutes: and they have a sort of proverb which they use in speaking of a covetous person, "that he would not throw a bone to the dog of the seven sleepers"; nay, it is said that they have the superstition to write his name, which they suppose to be Katmir, on their letters which go far, or which pass the sea, as a protection, or kind of talisman, to preserve them from miscarriage.

them spake and said, How long have we tarried here? They
answered, We have tarried a day, or part of a day. The
others said, Your Lord best knowest the time ye have tarried:
and now send one of you with this your money into the city,
and let him see which of its inhabitants hath the best and
cheapest food, and let him bring you provision from him;
and let him behave circumspectly, and not discover you to
any one. Verily, if they come up against you, they will
stone you, or force you to return to their religion; and then
shall ye not prosper for ever.

And so we made their people acquainted with what had
happened to them; that they might know that the promise
of God is true, and that there is no doubt of the last hour;
when they disputed among themselves concerning their matter. And they said, Erect a building over them: their Lord
best knoweth their condition. Those who prevailed in their
affair answered, We will surely build a chapel over them.
Some say, The sleepers were three; and their dog was the
fourth: and others say, They were five: and their dog was
the sixth; guessing at a secret matter: and others say, They
were seven; and their dog was the eighth. Say, My Lord
best knoweth their number: none shall know them, except a
few. Wherefore dispute not concerning them, unless with a
clear disputation, according to what hath been revealed unto
thee: and ask not any of the Christians concerning them.
Say not of any matter, I will surely do this to-morrow; unless
thou add, If God please.[5] And remember thy Lord, when
thou forgettest, and say, My Lord is able to direct me with
ease, that I may draw near unto the truth of this matter
rightly. And they remained in their cave three hundred

[5] It is said, that when the Koreish, by the direction of the Jews, put
the three questions above mentioned to Mohammed, he bid them come
to him the next day, and he would give them an answer, but added not,
"if it please God"; for which reason he had the mortification to wait
above ten days before any revelation was vouchsafed him concerning those
matters, so that the Koreish triumphed, and bitterly reproached him as
a liar: but at length Gabriel brought him directions what he should say;
with this admonition, however, that he should not be so confident for
the future.

years, and nine years over. Say, God best knoweth how
long they continued there: unto him are the secrets of heaven
and earth known; do thou make him to see and to hear. . . .

And remember when Moses said unto his servant Joshua,
the son of Nun, I will not cease to go forward, until I come to
the place where the two seas meet; or I will travel for a long
space of time.[6] But when they were arrived at the meeting of
the two seas, they forgot their fish which they had taken with
them; and the fish took its way freely in the sea. And when
they had passed beyond that place, Moses said unto his servant, Bring us our dinner: for now are we fatigued with this
our journey. His servant answered, Dost thou know what
has befallen me? When we took up our lodging at the rock,
verily I forgot the fish: and none made me to forget it, except
Satan, that I should not remind thee of it. And the fish took
its way in the sea, in a wonderful manner. Moses said, This
is what we sought after. And they both went back, returning
by the way they came. And coming to the rock they found
one of our servants,[7] unto whom we had granted mercy from
us, and whom we had taught wisdom from before us. And
Moses said unto him, Shall I follow thee, that thou mayest

[6] The original word properly signifies the space of eighty years and
upward. To explain this long passage the commentators tell the following story. They say that Moses once preaching to the people, they admired his knowledge and eloquence so much that they asked him whether
he knew any man in the world who was wiser than himself; to which he
answered in the negative: whereupon God, in a revelation, having reprehended him for his vanity (though some pretend that Moses asked God
the question of his own accord), acquainted him that his servant al
Khedr was more knowing than he; and, at Moses's request, told him he
might find that person at a certain rock, where the two seas met; directing him to take a fish with him in a basket, and that where he missed the
fish, that was the place. Accordingly Moses set out, with his servant
Joshua, in search of al Khedr; which expedition is here described.

[7] This person, according to the general opinion, was the prophet al
Khedr; whom the Mohammedans usually confound with Phineas, Elias,
and St. George, saying that his soul passed by a metempsychosis successively through all three. Some, however, say his true name was Balya
Ebn Malcan, and that he lived in the time of Afridun, one of the ancient
kings of Persia, and that he preceded Dhu'lkarnein, and lived to the time
of Moses. They suppose al Khedr, having found out the fountain of
life and drunk thereof, became immortal; and that he had therefore this
name from his flourishing and continual youth.

teach me part of that which thou hast been taught, for a direction unto me? He answered, Verily thou canst not bear with me: for how canst thou patiently suffer those things, the knowledge whereof thou dost not comprehend? Moses replied, Thou shalt find me patient, if God please; neither will I be disobedient unto thee in anything. He said, If thou follow me therefore, ask me not concerning anything, until I shall declare the meaning thereof unto thee. So they both went on by the sea-shore, until they went up into a ship; and he made a hole therein. And Moses said unto him, Hast thou made a hole therein, that thou mightest drown those who are on board? now hast thou done a strange thing. He answered, Did I not tell thee that thou couldest not bear with me? Moses said, Rebuke me not, because I did forget; and impose not on me a difficulty in what I am commanded. Wherefore they left the ship and proceeded, until they met with a youth; and he slew him. Moses said, Hast thou slain an innocent person, without his having killed another? Now hast thou committed an unjust action. He answered, Did I not tell thee that thou couldest not bear with me? Moses said, If I ask thee concerning anything hereafter, suffer me not to accompany thee: now hast thou received an excuse from me. They went forward therefore, until they came to the inhabitants of a certain city: and they asked food of the inhabitants thereof; but they refused to receive them. And they found therein a wall, which was ready to fall down; and he set it upright. Whereupon Moses said unto him, If thou wouldest thou mightest doubtless have received a reward for it. He answered, This shall be a separation between me and thee: but I will first declare unto thee the signification of that which thou couldest not bear with patience. The vessel belonged to certain poor men, who did their business in the sea: and I was minded to render it unserviceable, because there was a king behind them, who took every sound ship by force. As to the youth, his parents were true believers, and we feared lest he, being an unbeliever, should oblige them to suffer his perverseness and ingratitude: wherefore we desired that their Lord might give them a more righteous child in exchange for him, and one more affectionate toward them. And the wall belonged to two orphan youths in the city, and under it was a treasure hidden which belonged to them; and their father was a righteous man: and thy Lord was pleased that they should attain their full age, and take forth their treasure, through the mercy of thy Lord. And I did not what thou hast seen of mine own will, but by God's direction. This is the interpretation of that which thou couldest not bear with patience.

The Jews will ask thee concerning Dhu'lkarnein. Answer, I will rehearse unto you an account of him. We made him powerful in the earth, and we gave him means to accomplish everything he pleased. And he followed his way, until he came to the place where the sun setteth; and he found it to set in a spring of black mud; and he found near the same a certain people. And he said, O Dhu'lkarnein, either punish this people, or use gentleness toward them. He answered, Whosoever of them shall commit injustice, we will surely punish him in this world; afterward shall he return unto his Lord, and he shall punish him with a severe punishment. But whosoever believeth, and doth that which is right, shall receive the most excellent reward, and we will give him in command that which is easy. Then he continued his way, until he came to the place where the sun riseth; and he found it to rise on certain people, unto whom he had not given anything wherewith to shelter themselves therefrom. Thus it was; and we comprehended with our knowledge the forces which were with him. And he prosecuted his journey from south to north, until he came between the two mountains; beneath which he found certain people, who could scarce understand what was said. And they said, O Dhu'lkarnein, verily Gog and Magog waste the land; shall we therefore pay the tribute, on condition that thou build a rampart between us and them? He answered, The power wherewith my Lord hath strengthened me is better than your tribute: but assist me strenuously, and I will set a strong wall between you and them. Bring me iron in large pieces, until it fill up the space between the two sides of these mountains. And he said to the workmen, Blow with your bellows, until it make the

iron red hot as fire. And he said further, Bring me molten
brass, that I may pour upon it. Wherefore, when this wall
was finished, Gog and Magog could not scale it, neither could
they dig through it.[8] And Dhu'lkarnein said, This is a
mercy from my Lord: but when the prediction of my Lord
shall come to be fulfilled, he shall reduce the wall to dust; and
the prediction of my Lord is true. On that day we will suffer
some of them to press tumultuously like waves on others; and
the trumpet shall be sounded, and we will gather them in a
body together. And we will set hell, on that day, before the
unbelievers; whose eyes have been veiled from my remembrance, and who could not hear my words.

Do the unbelievers think that I will not punish them, for
that they take my servants for their protectors besides me?
Verily we have prepared hell for the abode of the infidels.
Say, Shall we declare unto you those whose works are vain,
whose endeavor in the present life hath been wrongly directed,
and who think they do the work which is right? These are
they who believe not in the signs of their Lord, or that they
shall be assembled before him; wherefore their works are vain,
and we will not allow them any weight on the day of resurrection. This shall be their reward, namely, hell; for that
they have disbelieved, and have held my signs and my apostles
in derision. But as for those who believe and do good works,
they shall have the gardens of paradise for their abode; they
shall remain therein forever; they shall wish for no change
therein. Say, If the sea were ink to write the words of my
Lord, verily the sea would fail, before the words of my Lord
would fail; although we added another sea like unto it as a
further supply. Say, Verily I am only a man as ye are. It

8 The commentators say the wall was built in this manner. They dug
till they found water, and having laid the foundation of stone and melted
brass, they built the superstructure of large pieces of iron, between which
they laid wood and coals, till they equaled the height of the mountains;
and then setting fire to the combustibles, by the help of large bellows,
they made the iron red hot, and over it poured melted brass, which filling
up the vacancies between the pieces of iron, rendered the whole work as
firm as a rock. Some tell us that the whole was built of stones joined
by cramps of iron, on which they poured melted brass to fasten them.

is revealed unto me that your God is one only God: let him therefore who hopeth to meet his Lord, work a righteous work; and let him not make any other to partake in the worship of his Lord.

CHAPTER XIX

ENTITLED, MARY;[1] REVEALED AT MECCA

IN THE NAME OF THE MOST MERCIFUL GOD

C. H. Y. A. S. A commemoration of the mercy of thy Lord toward his servant Zacharias. When he called upon his Lord, invoking him in secret, and said, O Lord, verily my bones are weakened, and my head is become white with hoariness, and I have never been unsuccessful in my prayers to thee, O Lord. But now I fear my nephews, who are to succeed after me, for my wife is barren: wherefore give me a successor of my own body from before thee; who may be my heir, and may be an heir of the family of Jacob; and grant, O Lord, that he may be acceptable unto thee. And the angel answered him, O Zacharias, verily we bring thee tidings of a son, whose name shall be John; we have not caused any to bear the same name before him. Zacharias said, Lord, how shall I have a son, seeing my wife is barren, and I am now arrived at a great age, and am decrepit? The angel said, So shall it be: thy Lord saith, This is easy with me; since I created thee heretofore, when thou wast nothing. Zacharias answered, O Lord, give me a sign. The angel replied, Thy sign shall be, that thou shalt not speak to men for three nights, although thou be in perfect health. And he went forth unto his people, from the chamber, and he made signs unto them, as if he should say, Praise ye God in the morning and in the evening. And we said unto his son, O John, receive the book of the law, with a resolution to study and observe it. And we bestowed on him wisdom, when he was yet a child, and mercy from us, and purity of life; and he was a devout person, and dutiful toward

[1] Several circumstances relating to the Virgin Mary being mentioned in this chapter, her name was pitched upon for the title.

his parents, and was not proud or rebellious. Peace be on him the day whereon he was born, and the day whereon he shall die, and the day whereon he shall be raised to life.

And remember in the book of the Koran the story of Mary; when she retired from her family to a place toward the east, and took a veil to conceal herself from them; and we sent our spirit Gabriel unto her, and he appeared unto her in the shape of a perfect man. She said, I fly for refuge unto the merciful God, that he may defend me from thee: if thou fearest him, thou wilt not approach me. He answered, Verily I am the messenger of thy Lord, and am sent to give thee a holy son. She said, how shall I have a son, seeing a man hath not touched me, and I am no harlot? Gabriel replied, So shall it be: thy Lord saith, This is easy with me; and we will perform it, that we may ordain him for a sign unto men, and a mercy from us: for it is a thing which is decreed. Wherefore she conceived him: and she retired aside with him in her womb to a distant place; and the pains of childbirth came upon her near the trunk of a palm-tree. She said, Would to God I had died before this, and had become a thing forgotten, and lost in oblivion! And he who was beneath her called to her, saying, Be not grieved: now hath God provided a rivulet under thee; and do thou shake the body of the palm-tree, and it shall let fall ripe dates upon thee, ready gathered. And eat, and drink, and calm thy mind. Moreover if thou see any man, and he question thee, say, Verily I have vowed a fast unto the Merciful; wherefore I will by no means speak to a man this day. So she brought the child to her people, carrying him in her arms. And they said unto her, O Mary, now hast thou done a strange thing: O sister of Aaron, thy father was not a bad man, neither was thy mother a harlot. But she made signs unto the child to answer them; and they said, How shall we speak to him, who is an infant in the cradle? Whereupon the child said, Verily I am the servant of God; he hath given me the book of the gospel, and hath appointed me a prophet. And he hath made me blessed, wheresoever I shall be; and hath commanded me to observe prayer, and to give alms, so long as I shall live; and he hath made me dutiful toward my mother, and hath not made me proud, or unhappy. And peace be on me the day whereon I was born, and the day whereon I shall die, and the day whereon I shall be raised to life.

This was Jesus, the son of Mary; the Word of truth, concerning whom they doubt. It is not meet for God, that he should have any son: God forbid! When he decreeth a thing, he only saith unto it, Be; and it is. And verily God is my Lord, and your Lord; wherefore serve him: this is the right way. Yet the sectaries differ among themselves concerning Jesus; but woe be unto those who are unbelievers, because of their appearance at the great day. Do thou cause them to hear, and do thou cause them to see, on the day whereon they shall come unto us to be judged: but the ungodly are this day in a manifest error. And do thou forewarn them of the day of sighing, when the matter shall be determined, while they are now sunk in negligence and do not believe. Verily we will inherit the earth, and whatever creatures are therein: and unto us shall they all return.

And remember Abraham in the book of the Koran; for he was one of great veracity, and a prophet. When he said unto his father, O my father, why dost thou worship that which heareth not, neither seeth, nor profiteth thee at all? O my father, verily a degree of knowledge hath been bestowed on me, which hath not been bestowed on thee: wherefore follow me; I will lead thee into an even way. O my father, serve not Satan; for Satan was rebellious unto the Merciful. O my father, verily I fear lest a punishment be inflicted on thee from the Merciful, and thou become a companion of Satan. His father answered, Dost thou reject my gods, O Abraham? If thou forbear not, I will surely stone thee: wherefore leave me for a long time. Abraham replied, Peace be on thee: I will ask pardon for thee of my Lord; for he is gracious unto me. And I will separate myself from you, and from the idols which ye invoke besides God; and I will call upon my Lord: it may be that I shall not be unsuccessful in calling on my Lord, as ye are in calling upon them. And when he had separated himself from them, and from the idols which they worshiped besides God, we gave him Isaac and Jacob; and we made each of them a prophet; and we bestowed on them, through our mercy, the gift of prophecy, and children, and wealth; and we caused them to deserve the highest commendations.

And remember Moses in the book of the Koran: for he was sincerely upright, and was an apostle and a prophet. And we called unto him from the right side of Mount Sinai, and caused him to draw near, and to discourse privately with us. And we gave him, through our mercy, his brother Aaron, a prophet, for his assistant. Remember also Ismael in the same book: for he was true to his promise; and was an apostle, and a prophet. And he commanded his family to observe prayer, and to give alms; and he was acceptable unto his Lord. And remember Edris in the same book; for he was a just person, and a prophet; and we exalted him to a high place. These are they unto whom God hath been bounteous, of the prophets of the posterity of Adam, and of those whom we carried in the ark with Noah; and of the posterity of Abraham, and of Israel, and of those whom we have directed and chosen. When the signs of the Merciful were read unto them, they fell down, worshiping, and wept: but a succeeding generation have come after them, who neglect prayer, and follow their lusts; and they shall surely fall into evil: except him who repenteth, and believeth, and doth that which is right; these shall enter paradise, and they shall not in the least be wronged; gardens of perpetual abode shall be their reward, which the Merciful hath promised unto his servants, as an object of faith; for his promise will surely come to be fulfilled. Therein shall they hear no vain discourse, but peace; and their provision shall be prepared for them therein morning and evening.

This is paradise, which we will give for an inheritance unto such of our servants as shall be pious. We descend not from heaven, unless by the command of thy Lord: unto him belongeth whatsoever is before us, and whatsoever is behind us, and whatsoever is in the intermediate space; neither is thy Lord forgetful of thee. He is the Lord of heaven and earth, and of whatsoever is between them: wherefore worship him, and be constant in his worship. Dost thou know any named like him? Man saith, After I shall have been dead, shall I really be brought forth alive from the grave? Doth not man remember that we created him heretofore, when he was nothing? But by thy Lord we will surely assemble them and the devils to judgment; then will we set them round about hell on their knees: afterward we will draw forth from every sect such of them as shall have been a more obstinate rebel against the Merciful; and we best know which of them are more worthy to be burned therein. There shall be none of you but shall approach near the same: this is an established decree with thy Lord. Afterward we will deliver those who shall have been pious, but we will leave the ungodly therein on their knees.

When our manifest signs are read unto them, the infidels say unto the true believers, Which of the two parties is in the more eligible condition and formeth the more excellent assembly? But how many generations have we destroyed before them, which excelled them in wealth, and in outward appearance? Say, Whosoever is in error, the Merciful will grant him a long and prosperous life; until they see that with which they are threatened, whether it be the punishment of this life, or that of the last hour; and hereafter they shall know who is in the worse condition, and the weaker in forces. God shall more fully direct those who receive direction; and the good works which remain forever are better in the sight of thy Lord than worldly possessions, in respect to the reward, and more eligible in respect to the future recompense.

Hast thou seen him who believeth not in our signs, and faith, I shall surely have riches and children bestowed on me? Is he acquainted with the secrets of futurity; or hath he received a covenant from the Merciful that it shall be so? By no means. We will surely write down that which he saith; and increasing we will increase his punishment: and we will be his heir as to that which he speaketh of, and on the last day he shall appear before us alone and naked. They have taken other gods, besides God, that they may be a glory unto them. By no means. Hereafter shall they deny their worship; and

they shall become adversaries unto them. Dost thou not see
that we send the devils against the infidels, to incite them to
sin by their instigations? Wherefore be not in haste to call
down destruction upon them; for we number unto them a
determined number of days of respite. On a certain day we
will assemble the pious before the Merciful in an honorable
manner, as ambassadors come into the presence of a prince;
but we will drive the wicked into hell, as cattle are driven to
water: they shall obtain no intercession, except he only who
hath received a covenant from the Merciful. They say, The
Merciful hath begotten issue. Now have ye uttered an
impious thing: it wanteth little but that on occasion thereof
the heavens be rent, and the earth cleave in sunder, and the
mountains be overthrown and fall, for that they attribute children unto the Merciful; whereas it becometh not God to beget
children.

Verily there is none in heaven or on earth, but shall approach the Merciful as his servant. He encompasseth them
by his knowledge and power, and numbereth them with an
exact computation: and they shall all come unto him on the
day of resurrection, destitute both of helpers and followers.
But as for those who believe and do good works, the Merciful
will bestow on them love. Verily we have rendered the Koran
easy for thy tongue, that thou mayest thereby declare our
promises unto the pious, and mayest thereby denounce threats
unto contentious people. And how many generations have we
destroyed before them? Dost thou find one of them remaining?

CHAPTER XX

ENTITLED, T. H.; [1] REVEALED AT MECCA

IN THE NAME OF THE MOST MERCIFUL GOD

T. H. We have not sent down the Koran unto thee, that
thou shouldest be unhappy; but for an admonition unto him

[1] The signification of these letters, which being prefixed to the chapter
are therefore taken for the title, is uncertain. Some, however, imagine

who feareth God: being sent down from him who created the earth, and the lofty heavens. The Merciful sitteth on his throne: unto him belongeth whatsoever is in heaven and on earth, and whatsoever is between them, and whatsoever is under the earth. If thou pronounce thy prayers with a loud voice, know that it is not necessary in respect to God; for he knoweth that which is secret, and what is yet more hidden. God! there is no god but he: he hath most excellent names.

Hast thou been informed of the history of Moses? [2] When he saw fire, and said unto his family, Tarry ye here; for I perceive fire: peradventure I may bring you a brand thereout, or may find a direction in our way by the fire. And when he was come near into it, a voice called unto him, saying, O Moses! verily I am thy Lord: wherefore put off thy shoes; for thou art in the sacred valley Towa. And I have chosen thee; therefore harken with attention unto that which is revealed unto thee. Verily I am God; there is no god beside me: wherefore worship me, and perform thy prayer in remembrance of me. Verily the hour cometh: I will surely manifest the same, that every soul may receive its reward for that which it hath deliberately done. Let not him who believeth not therein, and who followeth his lust, prevent thee from believing in the same, lest thou perish. Now what is that in thy right hand, O Moses? He answered, It is my rod whereon I lean, and with which I beat down leaves for my flock; and I have other uses for it. God said unto him, Cast it down, O Moses. And he cast it down, and behold, it became

they stand for *Ya rajol*, i.e., "O man!" which interpretation, seeming not easily to be accounted for from the Arabic, is by a certain tradition deduced from the Ethiopic: or for *Ta*, i.e., "tread"; telling us that Mohammed, being employed in watching and prayer the night this passage was revealed, stood on one foot only, but was hereby commanded to ease himself by setting both feet to the ground. Others fancy the first letter stands for *Tuba*, "beatitude"; and the latter for *Hawiyat*, the name of the lower apartment of hell. *Tah* is also an interjection commanding silence, and may properly enough be used in this place.

[2] The relation of the story of Moses, which takes up the greatest part of this chapter, was designed to encourage Mohammed, by his example, to discharge the prophetic office with firmness of mind, as being assured of receiving the like assistance from God: for it is said this chapter was one of the first that were revealed.

a serpent, which ran about. God said, Take hold on it, and fear not: we will reduce it to its former condition. And put thy right hand under thy left arm: it shall come forth white, without any hurt. This shall be another sign: that we may show thee some of our greatest signs. Go unto Pharaoh: for he is exceedingly impious. Moses answered, Lord, enlarge my breast, and make what thou hast commanded me easy unto me: and loose the knot of my tongue, that they may understand my speech.[3] And give me a counselor of my family, namely, Aaron, my brother. Gird up my loins by him, and make him my colleague in the business: that we may praise thee greatly, and may remember thee often; for thou regardest us. God replied, Now hast thou obtained thy request, O Moses: and we have heretofore been gracious unto thee, another time; when we revealed unto thy mother that which was revealed unto her, saying, Put him into the ark, and cast him into the river, and the river shall throw him on the shore; and my enemy and his enemy shall take him and bring him up: and I bestowed on thee love from me, that thou mightest be bred up under my eye. When thy sister went and said, Shall I bring you unto one who will nurse the child? So we returned thee unto thy mother, that her mind might be set at ease, and that she might not be afflicted. And thou slewest a soul, and we delivered thee from trouble; and we proved thee by several trials: and afterward thou didst dwell some years among the inhabitants of Madian. Then thou camest hither according to our decree, O Moses; and I have chosen thee for myself: wherefore go thou and thy brother with my signs; and be not negligent in remembering me.

Go ye unto Pharaoh, for he is excessively impious: and

[3] For Moses had an impediment in his speech, which was occasioned by the following accident. Pharaoh one day carrying him in his arms, when a child, he suddenly laid hold of his beard, and plucked it in a very rough manner, which put Pharaoh into such a passion, that he ordered him to be put to death: but Asia, his wife, representing to him that he was but a child, who could not distinguish between a burning coal and a ruby, he ordered the experiment to be made; and a live coal and a ruby being set before Moses, he took the coal and put it into his mouth, and burned his tongue: and thereupon he was pardoned. This is a Jewish story a little altered.

speak mildly unto him; peradventure he will consider, or will fear our threats.   They answered, O Lord, verily we fear lest he be precipitately violent against us, or lest he transgress more exorbitantly.   God replied, Fear not; for I am with you: I will hear and will see.   Go ye therefore unto him, and say, Verily we are the messengers of thy Lord: wherefore send the children of Israel with us, and do not afflict them.   Now are we come unto thee with a sign from thy Lord: and peace be upon him who shall follow the true direction.   Verily it hath been revealed unto us that a punishment shall be inflicted on him who shall charge us with imposture, and shall turn back.   And when they had delivered their message, Pharaoh said, Who is your Lord, O Moses?   He answered, Our Lord is he who giveth all things: he hath created them, and directeth them by his providence.   Pharaoh said, What therefore is the condition of the former generations?   Moses answered, The knowledge thereof is with my Lord, in the book of his decrees: my Lord erreth not, neither doth he forget.   It is he who hath spread the earth as a bed for you, and hath made you paths therein; and who sendeth down rain from heaven, whereby we cause various kinds of vegetables to spring forth; saying, Eat of part, and feed your cattle with other part thereof.   Verily herein are signs unto those who are indued with understanding.   Out of the ground have we created you; and to the same will we cause you to return, and we will bring you forth from thence another time.   And we showed Pharaoh all our signs which we had empowered Moses to perform: but he accused him of imposture, and refused to believe; and he said, Art thou come unto us that thou mayest dispossess us of our land by thy enchantments, O Moses? Verily we will meet thee with the like enchantment: wherefore fix an appointment between us and thee; we will not fail it, neither shalt thou, in an equal place.   Moses answered, Let your appointment be on the day of your solemn feast; and let the people be assembled in open day.   And Pharaoh turned away from Moses, and gathered together the most expert magicians, to execute his stratagem; and they came to the appointment.   Moses said unto them, Woe be unto you! do not devise a lie against God, lest he utterly destroy you by some judgment: for he shall not prosper who deviseth lies. And the magicians disputed concerning their affair among themselves, and discoursed in private: and they said, These two are certainly magicians: they seek to dispossess you of your land by their sorcery; and to lead away with them your chiefest and most considerable men. Wherefore collect all your cunning, and then come in order: for he shall prosper this day, who shall be superior. They said, O Moses, whether wilt thou cast down thy rod first, or shall we be the first who cast down our rods? He answered, Do ye cast down your rods first. And behold, their cords and their rods appeared unto him, by their enchantment, to run about like serpents; wherefore Moses conceived fear in his heart. But we said unto him, Fear not; for thou shalt be superior: therefore cast down the rod which is in thy right hand; and it shall swallow up the seeming serpents which they have made: for what they have made is only the deceit of an enchanter; and an enchanter shall not prosper, whithersoever he cometh. And the magicians, when they saw the miracle which Moses performed, fell down and worshiped, saying, We believe in the Lord of Aaron and of Moses. Pharaoh said unto them, Do ye believe in him before I give you permission? Verily this is your master, who hath taught you magic. But I will surely cut off your hands and your feet on the opposite sides; and I will crucify you on trunks of palm-trees: and ye shall know which of us is more severe in punishing, and can longer protract your pains. They answered, We will by no means have greater regard unto thee, than unto those evident miracles which have been shown us, or than unto him who hath created us. Pronounce therefore that sentence against us which thou art about to pronounce; for thou canst only give sentence as to this present life. Verily we believe in our Lord, that he may forgive us our sins, and the sorcery which thou hast forced us to exercise: for God is better to reward, and more able to prolong punishment than thou. Verily whosoever shall appear before his Lord on the day of judgment, polluted with crimes, shall have hell for his reward; he shall not die therein, neither shall he live. But whoever shall appear before him, having been a true believer, and shall have worked righteousness, for these are prepared the highest degrees of happiness; namely, gardens of perpetual abode, which shall be watered by rivers; they shall remain therein forever: and this shall be the reward of him who shall be pure.

And we spake by revelation unto Moses, saying, Go forth with my servants out of Egypt by night; and smite the waters with the rod, and make them a dry path through the sea: be not apprehensive of Pharaoh's overtaking thee; neither be thou afraid. And when Moses had done so, Pharaoh followed them with his forces; and the waters of the sea which overwhelmed them, overwhelmed them. And Pharaoh caused his people to err, neither did he direct them aright. Thus, O children of Israel, we delivered you from your enemy; and we appointed you the right side of Mount Sinai to discourse with Moses and to give him the law; and we caused manna and quails to descend upon you; saying, Eat of the good things which we have given you for food; and transgress not therein, lest my indignation fall on you: and on whomsoever my indignation shall fall, he shall go down headlong into perdition. But I will be gracious unto him who shall repent and believe, and shall do that which is right; and who shall be rightly directed. What hath caused thee to hasten from thy people, O Moses, to receive the law? He answered, These follow close on my footsteps; but I have hastened unto thee, O Lord, that thou mightest be well pleased with me. God said, We have already made a trial of thy people, since thy departure; and al Sameri hath seduced them to idolatry. Wherefore Moses returned unto his people in great wrath, and exceedingly afflicted. And he said, O my people, had not your Lord promised you a most excellent promise? Did the time of my absence seem long unto you? Or did ye desire that indignation from your Lord should fall on you, and therefore, fail to keep the promise which ye made me? They answered, We have not failed in what we promised thee of our own authority; but we were made to carry in several loads of gold and silver, of the ornaments of the people, and we cast them into the fire; and in like manner al Sameri also cast in what he had collected, and he produced unto them a corporeal calf, which lowed.   And al Sameri and his companions said, This is your god, and the god of Moses; but he hath forgotten him, and is gone to seek some other.   Did they not therefore see that their idol returned them no answer, and was not able to cause them either hurt or profit?   And Aaron had said unto them before, O my people, verily ye are only proved by this calf; for your Lord is the Merciful: wherefore follow me, and obey my command.   They answered, We will by no means cease to be devoted to its worship, until Moses return unto us.   And when Moses was returned, he said, O Aaron, what hindered thee, when thou sawest that they went astray, that thou didst not follow me?   Hast thou therefore been disobedient to my command?   Aaron answered, O son of my mother, drag me not by my beard, nor by the hair of my head. Verily I feared lest thou shouldest say, Thou hast made a division among the children of Israel, and thou hast not observed my saying.   Moses said unto al Sameri, What was thy design, O Sameri?   He answered, I saw that which they saw not; wherefore I took a handful of dust from the footsteps of the messenger of God, and I cast it into the molten calf; for so did my mind direct me.   Moses said, Get thee gone; for thy punishment in this life shall be that thou shalt say unto those who shall meet thee, Touch me not; and a threat is denounced against thee of more terrible pains, in the life to come, which thou shalt by no means escape.   And behold now thy god, to whose worship thou hast continued assiduously devoted: verily we will burn it; and we will reduce it to powder, and scatter it in the sea.   Your God is the true God, besides whom there is no other god: he comprehendeth all things by his knowledge. . . .

Wherefore do thou, O Mohammed, patiently bear that which they say; and celebrate the praise of thy Lord before the rising of the sun, and before the setting thereof, and praise him in the hours of the night, and in the extremities of the day, that thou mayest be well pleased with the prospect of receiving favor from God.   And cast not thine eyes on that which we have granted divers of the unbelievers to enjoy, namely, the splendor of this present life, that we may prove them thereby: for the provision of thy Lord is better, and more permanent. Command thy family to observe prayer; and do thou persevere therein. We require not of thee that thou labor to gain necessary provisions for thyself and family: we will provide for thee; for the prosperous issue shall attend on piety.[4]

The unbelievers say, Unless he come unto us with a sign from his Lord, we will not believe on him. Hath not a plain declaration come unto them, of that which is contained in the former volumes of scripture, by the revelation of the Koran? If we had destroyed them by a judgment before the same had been revealed, they would have said at the resurrection, O Lord, how could we believe since thou didst not send unto us an apostle, that we might follow thy signs, before we were humbled and covered with shame? Say, Each of us wait the issue: wait therefore; for ye shall surely know hereafter who have been the followers of the even way, and who have been rightly directed.

CHAPTER XXI

ENTITLED, THE PROPHETS; REVEALED AT MECCA

IN THE NAME OF THE MOST MERCIFUL GOD

The time of giving up their account draweth nigh unto the people of Mecca; while they are sunk in negligence, turning aside from the consideration thereof. No admonition cometh unto them from their Lord, being lately revealed in the Koran, but when they hear it they turn it to sport: their hearts are taken up with delights. And they who act unjustly discourse privately together, saying, is this Mohammed any more than a man like yourselves? Will ye therefore come to hear a piece of sorcery, when ye plainly perceive it to be so? Say, My Lord knoweth whatever is spoken in heaven and on earth:

---

[4] It is said that when Mohammed's family were in any strait or affliction, he used to order them to go to prayers, and to repeat this verse.

it is he who heareth and knoweth. But they say, The Koran is a confused heap of dreams: nay, he hath forged it; nay, he is a poet: let him come unto us therefore with some miracle, in like manner as the former prophets were sent. None of the cities which we have destroyed believed the miracles which they saw performed before them: will these therefore believe if they see a miracle? We sent none as our apostles before thee, other than men, unto whom we revealed our will. Ask those who are acquainted with the scripture, if ye know not this. We gave them not a body which could be supported without their eating food; neither were they immortal. But we made good our promise unto them: wherefore we delivered them, and those whom we pleased; but we destroyed the exorbitant transgressors.

Now have we sent down unto you, O Koreish, the book of the Koran; wherein there is honorable mention of you: will ye not therefore understand? And how many cities have we overthrown, which were ungodly; and caused other nations to rise up after them? And when they felt our severe vengeance, behold, they fled swiftly from those cities. And the angels said, scoffingly, unto them, Do not fly; but return to that wherein ye delighted, and to your habitations: peradventure ye will be asked. They answered, Alas for us! verily we have been unjust. And this their lamentation ceased not, until we had rendered them like corn which is mowed down, and utterly extinct. We created not the heavens and the earth, and that which is between them, by way of sport. If we had pleased to take diversion, verily we had done it with which beseemeth us; if we had resolved to have done this. But we will oppose truth to vanity, and it shall confound the same; and behold, it shall vanish away. . . .

We formerly gave unto Moses and Aaron the Law, being a distinction between good and evil, and a light and admonition unto the pious; who fear their Lord in secret, and who dread the hour of judgment. And this book also is a blessed admonition; which we have sent down from heaven: will ye therefore deny it? And we gave unto Abraham his direction heretofore, and we knew him to be worthy of the revelations wherewith he was favored. Remember when he said unto his father, and his people, What are these images, to which ye are so entirely devoted? They answered, We found our fathers worshiping them. He said, Verily both ye and your fathers have been in a manifest error. They said, Dost thou seriously tell us the truth, or art thou one who jestest with us? He replied, Verily your Lord is the Lord of the heavens and the earth; it is he who hath created them: and I am one of those who bear witness thereof. By God, I will surely devise a plot against your idols, after ye shall have retired from them, and shall have turned your backs. And in the people's absence he went into the temple where the idols stood, and he brake them all in pieces, except the biggest of them; that they might lay the blame upon that. And when they were returned, and saw the havoc which had been made, they said, Who hath done this to our gods? He is certainly an impious person. And certain of them answered, We heard a young man speak reproachfully of them: he is named Abraham. They said, Bring him therefore before the eyes of the people, that they may bear witness against him. And when he was brought before the assembly, they said unto him, Hast thou done this unto our gods, O Abraham? He answered, Nay, that biggest of them hath done it: but ask them, if they can speak. And they returned unto themselves, and said the one to the other, Verily ye are the impious persons. Afterward they relapsed into their former obstinacy and said, Verily thou knowest that these speak not. Abraham answered, Do ye therefore worship, besides God, that which can not profit you at all, neither can it hurt you? Fie on you; and upon that which ye worship besides God! Do ye not understand? They said, Burn him, and avenge your gods; if ye do this it will be well. And when Abraham was cast into the burning pile, we said, O fire, be thou cold, and a preservation unto Abraham.[1] And they sought to lay a plot against him: but we caused them to be the sufferers. And we deliv-

[1] The commentators relate that, by Nimrod's order, a large space was enclosed at Cutha, and filled with a vast quantity of wood, which being set on fire burned so fiercely that none dared to venture near it: then

ered him, and Lot, by bringing them into the land wherein we have blessed all creatures. And we bestowed on him Isaac, and Jacob, as an additional gift: and we made all of them righteous persons. We also made them models of religion, that they might direct others by our command: and we inspired into them the doing of good works, and the observance of prayer, and the giving of alms; and they served us. And unto Lot we gave wisdom and knowledge, and we delivered him out of the city which committed filthy crimes; for they were a wicked and insolent people: and we led him into our mercy; for he was an upright person.

And remember Noah, when he called for destruction on his people, before the prophets above mentioned; and we heard him, and delivered him and his family from a great strait: and we protected him from the people who accused our signs of falsehood; for they were a wicked people, wherefore we drowned them all. And remember David and Solomon, when they pronounced judgment concerning a field, when the sheep of certain people had fed therein by night, having no shepherd; and we were witnesses of their judgment: and we gave the understanding thereof unto Solomon.[2] And on all of

they bound Abraham, and putting him into an engine (which some suppose to have been of the devil's invention), shot him into the midst of the fire; from which he was preserved by the angel Gabriel who was sent to his assistance; the fire burning only the cords with which he was bound. They add that the fire having miraculously lost its heat, in respect to Abraham, became an odoriferous air, and that the pile changed to a pleasant meadow, though it raged so furiously otherwise, that, according to some writers, about two thousand of the idolaters were consumed by it.

[2] Some sheep, in their shepherd's absence, having broken into another man's field (or vineyard, say others), by night, and eaten up the corn, a dispute arose thereupon: and the cause being brought before David and Solomon, the former said that the owner of the land should take the sheep, in compensation of the damage which he had sustained; but Solomon, who was then but eleven years old, was of opinion that it would be more just for the owner of the field to take only the profit of the sheep, viz., their milk, lambs, and wool, till the shepherd should, by his own labor and at his own expense, put the field into as good condition as when the sheep entered it; after which the sheep might be returned to their master. And this judgment of Solomon was approved by David himself as better than his own.

them we bestowed wisdom, and knowledge. And we compelled the mountains to praise us with David; and the birds also: and we did this. And we taught him the art of making coats of mail for you, that they may defend you in your wars: will ye therefore be thankful? And unto Solomon we subjected a strong wind; it ran at his command to the land whereon we had bestowed our blessing: and we knew all things. And we also subjected unto his command divers of the devils, who might dive to get pearls for him, and perform other work besides this; and we watched over them. And remember Job; when he cried unto his Lord, saying, Verily evil hath afflicted me: but thou art the most merciful of those who show mercy. Wherefore we heard him, and relieved him from the evil which was upon him: and we restored unto him his family, and as many more with them, through our mercy, and for an admonition unto those who serve God. And remember Ismael, and Edris, and Dhu'lkefl. All these were patient persons: wherefore we led them into our mercy; for they were righteous doers. And remember Dhu'lnun, when he departed in wrath, and thought that we could not exercise our power over him. And he cried out in the darkness, saying, There is no God, besides thee: praise be unto thee! Verily I have been one of the unjust. Wherefore we heard him, and delivered him from affliction: for so do we deliver the true believers. And remember Zacharias, when he called upon his Lord, saying, O Lord, leave me not childless: yet thou art the best heir. Wherefore we heard him, and we gave him John; and we rendered his wife fit for bearing a child unto him. These strove to excel in good works, and called upon us with love, and with fear; and humbled themselves before us. And remember her who preserved her virginity, and into whom we breathed of our spirit; ordaining her and her son for a sign unto all creatures. Verily, this your religion is one religion; and I am your Lord; wherefore serve me. But the Jews and Christian have made schisms in the affair of their religion among themselves: but all of them shall appear before us.

Whosoever shall do good works, being a true believer, there

shall be no denial of the reward due to his endeavors; and we will surely write it down unto him. An inviolable prohibition is laid on every city which we shall have destroyed; for that they shall not return any more into the world; until Gog and Magog shall have a passage opened for them, and they shall hasten from every high hill; and the certain promise shall draw near to be fulfilled: and behold, the eyes of the infidels shall be fixed with astonishment, and they shall say, Alas for us! we were formerly regardless of this day; yea, we were wicked doers. Verily both ye, O men of Mecca, and the idols which ye worship besides God, shall be cast as fuel into hell fire: ye shall go down into the same. If these were really gods, they would not go down into the same: and all of them shall remain therein forever. In that place shall they groan for anguish; and they shall not hear aught therein. As for those unto whom the most excellent reward of paradise hath been predestinated by us, they shall be transported far off from the same; they shall not hear the least sound thereof: and they shall continue forever in the felicity which their souls desire. The greatest terror shall not trouble them; and the angels shall meet them to congratulate them, saying, This is your day which ye were promised. On that day we will roll up the heavens, as the angel al Sijil rolleth up the book wherein every man's actions are recorded. As we made the first creature out of nothing, so we will also reproduce it at the resurrection. This is a promise which it lieth on us to fulfil: we will surely perform it.

And now have we written in the psalms, after the promulgation of the law, that my servants the righteous shall inherit the earth. Verily in this book are contained sufficient means of salvation unto people who serve God. We have not sent thee, O Mohammed, but as a mercy unto all creatures. Say, No other hath been revealed unto me, than that your God is one God: will ye therefore be resigned unto him? But if they turn their backs to the confession of God's unity, say I proclaim war against you all equally: but I know not whether that which ye are threatened with be nigh, or whether it be far distant. Verily, God knoweth the discourse which is spoken in public; and he also knoweth that which ye hold in private. I know not but peradventure the respite granted you is for a trial of you; and that he may enjoy the prosperity of this world for a time. Say, Lord, judge between me and my adversaries with truth. Our Lord is the Merciful; whose assistance is to be implored against the blasphemies and calumnies which ye utter.

CHAPTER XXII

ENTITLED, THE PILGRIMAGE;[1] REVEALED AT MECCA

IN THE NAME OF THE MOST MERCIFUL GOD

O men of Mecca, fear your Lord. Verily the shock of the last hour will be a terrible thing. On the day whereon ye shall see it, every woman who giveth suck shall forget the infant which she sucketh, and every female that is with young shall cast her burden; and thou shalt see men seemingly drunk, yet they shall not be really drunk: but the punishment of God will be severe. There is a man who disputeth concerning God without knowledge,[2] and followeth every rebellious devil: against whom it is written that, whoever shall take him for his patron, he shall surely seduce him, and shall lead him into the torment of hell.

O men, if ye be in doubt concerning the resurrection, consider that we first created you of the dust of the ground; afterward of seed; afterward of a little coagulated blood; afterward, of a piece of flesh, perfectly formed in part, and in part imperfectly formed; that we might make our power manifest unto you: and we cause that which we please to rest in the wombs, until the appointed time of delivery. Then we bring you forth infants; and afterward we permit you to attain your age of full strength: and one of you dieth in his youth,

[1] Some ceremonies used at the pilgrimage of Mecca being mentioned in this chapter, gave occasion to the inscription.

[2] This passage was revealed on account of al Nodar Ebn al Hareth, who maintained that the angels were the daughters of God, that the Koran was a fardel of old fables, and denied the resurrection.

and another of you is postponed to a decrepit age, so that he forgetteth whatever he knew. Thou seest the earth sometimes dried up and barren: but when we send down rain thereon, it is put in motion, and swelleth, and produceth every kind of luxuriant vegetable. This showest that God is the truth, and that he raiseth the dead to life, and that he is almighty; and that the hour of judgment will surely come (there is no doubt thereof), and that God will raise again those who are in the graves.

There is a man who disputeth concerning God without either knowledge, or a direction, or an enlightening book; proudly turning his side, that he may seduce men from the way of God. Ignominy shall attend him in this world; and on the day of resurrection we will make him take the torment of burning, when it shall be said unto him, This thou sufferest because of that which thy hands have formerly committed; for God is not unjust toward mankind. There are some men who serve God in a wavering manner, standing, as it were, on the verge of the true religion. If good befall one of them, he resteth satisfied therein; but if any tribulation befall him, he turneth himself round, with the loss both of this world, and of the life to come. This is manifest perdition. He will call upon that besides God, which can neither hurt him nor profit him. This is an error remote from truth. He will invoke him who will sooner be of hurt to his worshiper than of advantage. Such is surely a miserable patron, and a miserable companion. But God will introduce those who shall believe, and do righteous works, into gardens through which rivers flow; for God doth that which he pleaseth. Whoso thinketh that God will not assist his apostle in this world and in the world to come, let him strain a rope toward heaven, then let him put an end to his life, and see whether his devices can render that ineffectual, for which he was angry. Thus do we send down the Koran, being evident signs; for God directeth whom he pleaseth.

As to the true believers, and those who Judaize, and the Sabians, and the Christians, and the Magians, and the idolaters; verily God shall judge between them on the day of resurrection; for God is witness of all things. Dost thou not perceive that all creatures both in heaven and on earth adore God; and the sun, and the moon, and the stars, and the mountains, and the trees, and the beasts, and many men? But many are worthy of chastisement: and whomsoever God shall render despicable, there shall be none to honor; for God doth that which he pleaseth. These are two opposite parties, who dispute concerning their Lord. And they who believe not shall have garments of fire fitted unto them: boiling water shall be poured on their heads; their bowels shall be dissolved thereby, and also their skins; and they shall be beaten with maces of iron. So often as they shall endeavor to get out of hell, because of the anguish of their torments, they shall be dragged back into the same; and their tormentors shall say unto them, Taste ye the pain of burning. God will introduce those who shall believe, and act righteously, into gardens through which rivers flow: they shall be adorned therein with bracelets of gold, and pearls; and their vestures therein shall be silk. They are directed unto a good saying; and are directed into the honorable way. But they who shall disbelieve, and obstruct the way of God, and hinder men from visiting the holy temple of Mecca, which we have appointed for a place of worship unto all men: the inhabitant thereof, and the stranger have an equal right to visit it: and whosoever shall seek impiously to profane it, we will cause him to taste a grievous torment.

Call to mind when we gave the site of the house of the Kaaba for an abode unto Abraham, saying, Do not associate anything with me; and cleanse my house for those who compass it, and who stand up, and who bow down to worship, and proclaim unto the people a solemn pilgrimage; let them come unto thee on foot, and on every lean camel, arriving from every distant road; that they may be witnesses of the advantages which accrue to them from the visiting this holy place, and may commemorate the name of God on the appointed days, in gratitude for the brute cattle which he hath bestowed on them. Wherefore eat thereof, and feed the needy, and the poor. Afterward let them put an end to the neglect of their persons; and let them pay their vows, and compass the ancient house.[3] This let them do.

And who ever shall regard the sacred ordinances of God; this will be better for him in the sight of his Lord. All sorts of cattle are allowed you to eat, except what hath been read unto you, in former passages of the Koran, to be forbidden. But depart from the abomination of idols, and avoid speaking that which is false: being orthodox in respect to God, associating no other god with him: for whosoever associateth any other with God is like that which falleth from heaven, and which the birds snatch away, or the wind bloweth to a far distant place. This is so. And whoso maketh valuable offerings unto God; verily they proceed from the piety of men's hearts. Ye receive various advantages from the cattle designed for sacrifices, until a determined time for slaying them: then the place of sacrificing them is at the ancient house. Unto the possessors of every religion have we appointed certain rites, that they may commemorate the name of God on slaying the brute cattle which he hath provided for them. Your God is one God: wherefore resign yourselves wholly unto him. And do thou bear good tidings unto those who humble themselves; whose hearts, when mention is made of God, are struck with fear; and unto those who patiently endure that which befalleth them; and who duly perform their prayers, and give alms out of what we have bestowed on them.

The camels slain for sacrifice have we appointed for you as symbols of your obedience unto God: ye also receive other advantages from them. Wherefore commemorate the name of God over them, when ye slay them, standing on their feet disposed in right order: and when they are fallen down dead, eat of them; and give to eat thereof both unto him who is content with what is given him, without asking, and unto

[3] *I.e.*, The Kaaba; which the Mohammedans pretend was the first edifice built and appointed for the worship of God. The going round this chapel is a principal ceremony of the pilgrimage, and is often repeated; but the last time of their doing it, when they take their farewell of the temple, seems to be more particularly meant in this place.

him who asketh. Thus have we given you dominion over
them, that ye might return us thanks. Their flesh is not
accepted of God, neither their blood; but your piety is accepted of him. Thus have we given you dominion over them,
that ye might magnify God, for the revelations whereby he
hath directed you.

And bear good tidings unto the righteous, that God will
repel the ill designs of the infidels from the true believers;
for God loveth not every perfidious unbeliever. Permission
is granted unto those who take arms against the unbelievers,
for that they have been unjustly persecuted by them (and
God is certainly able to assist them): who have been turned
out of their habitations injuriously, and for no other reason
than because they say, Our Lord is God.[4] And if God did
not repel the violence of some men by others, verily monas-
teries, and churches, and synagogues, and the temples of the
Moslems, wherein the name of God is frequently commemorated, would be utterly demolished. And God will certainly assist him who shall be on his side: for God is strong
and mighty. And he will assist those who, if we establish
them in the earth, will observe prayer, and give alms, and
command that which is just, and forbid that which is unjust. And unto God shall be the end of all things.

If they accuse thee, O Mohammed, of imposture; consider
that, before them, the people of Noah, and the tribes of Ad
and Thamud, and the people of Abraham, and the people of
Lot, and the inhabitants of Madian, accused their prophets of
imposture: and Moses was also charged with falsehood. And
I granted a long respite unto the unbelievers; but afterward
I chastised them; and how different was the change I made in
their condition! How many cities have we destroyed, which
were ungodly, and which are now fallen to ruin on their
roofs? And how many wells have been abandoned, and

[4] This was the first passage of the Koran which allowed Mohammed
and his followers to defend themselves against their enemies by force,
and was revealed a little before the flight to Medina; till which time the
prophet had exhorted his Moslems to suffer the injuries offered them with
patience, which is also commanded in more than seventy different places
in the Koran.

lofty castles? Do they not therefore journey through the land? And have they not hearts to understand with, or ears to hear with? Surely as to these things their eyes are not blind, but the hearts are blind which are in their breasts. They will urge thee to hasten the threatened punishment; but God will not fail to perform what he hath threatened: and verily one day with thy Lord is as a thousand years, of those which ye compute. Unto how many cities have I granted respite, though they were wicked? Yet afterward I chastised them: and unto me shall they come to be judged, at the last day.

Say, O men, verily I am only a public preacher unto you. And they who believe, and do good works, shall obtain forgiveness and an honorable provision. But those who endeavor to make our signs of none effect shall be the inhabitants of hell. We have sent no apostle, or prophet, before thee, but, when he read, Satan suggested some error in his reading.[5] But God shall make void that which Satan hath suggested: then shall God confirm his signs; for God is knowing and wise. But this he permitteth, that he may make that which Satan hath suggested, a temptation unto those in whose hearts there is an infirmity, and whose hearts are hardened: (for the ungodly are certainly in a wide disagreement from the truth:) and that they on whom knowledge hath been bestowed may know that this book is the truth from thy Lord, and may believe therein; and that their hearts may acquiesce in the same: for God is surely the director of those who believe, into the right way. But the infidels

[5] The occasion of the passage is thus related. Mohammed one day reading the 53d chapter of the Koran, when he came to this verse, "What think ye of Allat, and al Uzza, and of Manah, the other third goddess?" the devil put the following words into his mouth, which he pronounced through inadvertence, or, as some tell us, because he was then half asleep, viz., "These are the most high and beauteous damsels, whose intercession is to be hoped for." The Koreish, who were sitting near Mohammed, greatly rejoiced at what they had heard, and when he had finished the chapter, joined with him and his followers in making their adoration: but the prophet, being acquainted by the angel Gabriel with the reason of their compliance, and with what he had uttered, was deeply concerned at his mistake, till this verse was revealed for his consolation.

will not cease to doubt concerning it, until the hour of judgment cometh suddenly upon them; or until the punishment of a grievous day overtake them. On that day the kingdom shall be God's: he shall judge between them. And they who shall have believed, and shall have wrought righteousness, shall be in gardens of pleasure: but they who shall have disbelieved, and shall have charged our signs with falsehood, those shall suffer a shameful punishment. And as to those who shall have fled their country for the sake of God's true religion, and afterward shall have been slain, or shall have died; on them will God bestow an excellent provision; and God is the best provider. He will surely introduce them with an introduction with which they shall be well pleased: for God is knowing and gracious. This is so. . . .

O true believers, bow down, and prostrate yourselves, and worship your Lord; and work righteousness, that ye may be happy: and fight in defense of God's true religion, as it behoveth you to fight for the same. He hath chosen you, and hath not imposed on you any difficulty in the religion which he hath given you, the religion of your father Abraham: he hath named you Moslems heretofore, and in this book; that our apostle may be a witness against you at the day of judgment, and that ye may be witnesses against the rest of mankind. Wherefore be ye constant at prayer; and give alms: and adhere firmly unto God. He is your master; and he is the best master; and the best protector.

CHAPTER XXIII

ENTITLED, THE TRUE BELIEVERS; REVEALED AT MECCA

IN THE NAME OF THE MOST MERCIFUL GOD

Now are the true believers happy: who humble themselves in their prayer, and who eschew all vain discourse, and who are doers of alms-deeds; and who keep themselves from carnal knowledge of any woman except their wives, or the captives which their right hands possess; (for as to them they shall be blameless: but whoever coveteth any woman beyond these, they are transgressors: and who acquit themselves faithfully of their trust, and justly perform their covenant; and who observe their appointed times of prayer:) these shall be the heirs, who shall inherit paradise; they shall continue therein forever.

We formerly created man of a finer sort of clay; afterward we placed him in the form of seed in a sure receptacle: afterward we made the seed coagulated blood; and we formed the coagulated blood into a piece of flesh: then we formed the piece of flesh into bones; and we clothed those bones with flesh: then we produced the same by another creation. Wherefore blessed be God, the most excellent Creator! After this shall ye die: and afterward shall ye be restored to life, on the day of resurrection. And we have created over you seven heavens: and we are not negligent of what we have created. And we sent down rain from heaven, by measure; and we cause it to remain on the earth: we are also certainly able to deprive you of the same. And we cause gardens of palm-trees, and vineyards, to spring forth for you by means thereof; wherein ye have many fruits, and whereof ye eat. And we also raise for you a tree springing from Mount Sinai; which produceth oil, and a sauce for those who eat. Ye have likewise an instruction in the cattle: we give you to drink of the milk which is in their bellies, and ye receive many advantages from them; and of them do ye eat: and on them, and on ships, are ye carried.

We sent Noah heretofore unto his people, and he said, O my people, serve God: ye have no God besides him; will ye not therefore fear the consequence of your worshiping other gods? And the chiefs of his people, who believed not, said, This is no other than a man, as ye are: he seeketh to raise himself to a superiority over you. If God had pleased to have sent a messenger unto you, he would surely have sent angels: we have not heard this of our forefathers. Verily he is no other than a man disturbed with frenzy: wherefore wait concerning him for a time. Noah said, O Lord, do thou protect me; for that they accuse me of falsehood. And we revealed our orders unto him, saying, Make the ark in our sight; and according to our revelation. And when our decree cometh to be executed, and the oven shall boil and pour forth water, carry into it of every species of animals one pair; and also thy family, except such of them on whom a previous sentence of destruction hath passed: and speak not unto me in behalf of those who have been unjust; for they shall be drowned. And when thou and they who shall be with thee shall go up into the ark, say, Praise be unto God, who hath delivered us from the ungodly people! And say, O Lord, cause me to come down from this ark with a blessed descent; for thou art best able to bring me down from the same with safety. Verily herein were signs of our omnipotence; and we proved mankind thereby.

Afterward we raised up another generation after them; and we sent unto them an apostle from among them, who said, Worship God: ye have no God besides him; will ye not therefore fear his vengeance? And the chiefs of his people, who believed not, and who denied the meeting of the life to come, and on whom we had bestowed affluence in this present life, said, This is no other than a man, as ye are; he eateth of that whereof ye eat, and he drinketh of that whereof ye drink; and if ye obey a man like unto yourselves, ye will surely be sufferers. Doth he threaten you that after ye shall be dead, and shall become dust and bones, ye shall be brought forth alive from your graves? Away, away with that ye are threatened with! There is no other life besides our present life: we die, and we live; and we shall not be raised again. This is no other than a man, who deviseth a lie concerning God: but we will not believe him. Their apostle said, O Lord, defend me; for that they have accused me of imposture. God answered, After a little while they shall surely repent their obstinacy. Wherefore a severe punishment was justly inflicted on them, and we rendered them like the refuse which is carried down by a stream. Away therefore with the ungodly people!

Afterward we raised up other generations after them. No nation shall be punished before their determined time;

neither shall they be respited after. Afterward we sent our apostles, one after another. So often as their apostle came unto any nation they charged him with imposture: and we caused them successively to follow one another to destruction; and we made them only subjects of traditional stories. Away therefore with the unbelieving nations! Afterward we sent Moses, and Aaron his brother, with our signs and manifest power, unto Pharaoh and his princes: but they proudly refused to believe on him; for they were a haughty people. And they said, Shall we believe on two men like unto ourselves; whose people are our servants? And they accused them of imposture: wherefore they became of the number of those who were destroyed. And we heretofore gave the book of the law unto Moses, that the children of Israel might be directed thereby. And we appointed the son of Mary, and his mother, for a sign: and we prepared an abode for them in an elevated part of the earth, being a place of quiet and security, and watered with running springs.

O apostles, eat of those things which are good; and work righteousness: for I well know that which ye do. This your religion is one religion; and I am your Lord: wherefore fear me. But men have rent the affair of their religion into various sects: every party rejoiceth in that which they follow. Wherefore leave them in their confusion, until a certain time. Do they think that we hasten unto them the wealth and children which we have abundantly bestowed on them, for their good? But they do not understand. Verily they who stand in awe, for fear of their Lord, and who believe in the signs of their Lord, and who attribute not companions unto their Lord; and who give that which they give in alms, their hearts being struck with dread, for that they must return unto their Lord: these hasten unto good, and are foremost to obtain the same. We will not impose any difficulty on a soul, except according to its ability; with us is a book, which speaketh the truth; and they shall not be injured. But their hearts are drowned in negligence, as to this matter; and they have works different from those we have mentioned; which they will continue to do, until, when we chastise such of them as enjoy an affluence of fortune, by a severe punishment, behold, they cry aloud for help: but it shall be answered them, Cry not for help to-day: for ye shall not be assisted by us. My signs were read unto you, but ye turned back on your heels: proudly elating yourselves because of your possessing the holy temple; discoursing together by night, and talking foolishly. Do they not therefore attentively consider that which is spoken unto them; whether a revelation is come unto them which came not unto their forefathers? Or do they not know their apostle; and therefore reject him? Or do they say, He is a madman? Nay, he hath come unto them with the truth; but the greater part of them detest the truth. If the truth had followed their desires, verily the heavens and the earth, and whoever therein is, had been corrupted. But we have brought them their admonition; and they turn aside from their admonition. Dost thou ask of them any maintenance for thy preaching? since the maintenance of thy Lord is better; for he is the most bounteous provider. Thou certainly invitest them to the right way: and they who believe not in the life to come do surely deviate from that way. If we had had compassion on them, and had taken off from them the calamity which had befallen them, they would surely have more obstinately persisted in their error, wandering in confusion. We formerly chastised them with a punishment: yet they did not humble themselves before their Lord, neither did they make supplications unto him; until, when we have opened upon them a door, from which a severe punishment hath issued, behold, they are driven to despair thereat.

It is God who hath created in you the senses of hearing and of sight, that ye may perceive our judgments, and hearts, that ye may seriously consider them: yet how few of you give thanks! It is he who hath produced you in the earth; and before him shall ye be assembled. It is he who giveth life, and putteth to death; and to him is to be attributed the vicissitude of night and day: do ye not therefore understand? But the unbelieving Meccans say as their predecessors said: they say, When we shall be dead, and shall have become dust and bones, shall we really be raised to life? We have al-

ready been threatened with this, and our fathers also heretofore: this is nothing but fables of the ancients. Say,
Whose is the earth, and whoever therein is; if ye know?
They will answer, God's. Say, Will ye not therefore consider? Say, Who is the Lord of the seven heavens, and the
Lord of the magnificent throne? They will answer, They are
God's. Say, Will ye not therefore fear him? Say, In
whose hand is the kingdom of all things; who protecteth
whom he pleaseth, but is himself protected of none; if ye
know? They will answer, In God's. Say, How therefore
are ye bewitched? Yea, we have brought them the truth;
and they are certainly liars in denying the same. God hath
not begotten issue; neither is there any other god with him:
otherwise every god had surely taken away that which he had
created; and some of them had exalted themselves above the
others. Far be that from God, which they affirm of him.
He knoweth that which is concealed, and that which is made
public; wherefore far be it from him to have those sharers
in his honor, which they attribute to him! Say, O Lord,
If thou wilt surely cause me to see the vengeance with which
they have been threatened; O Lord, set me not among the
ungodly people: for we are surely able to make thee to see
that with which we have threatened them. Turn aside evil
with that which is better: we well know the calumnies which
they utter against thee. And say, O Lord, I fly unto thee
for refuge, against the suggestions of the devils: and I have
recourse unto thee, O Lord, to drive them away, that they be
not present with me.

The gainsaying of the unbelievers ceaseth not until, when
death overtaketh any of them, he saith, O Lord, suffer me to
return to life, that I may do that which is right; in profess-
ing the true faith which I have neglected. By no means.
Verily these are the words which he shall speak: but behind
them there shall be a bar, until the day of resurrection.
When therefore the trumpet shall be sounded there shall be
no relation between them which shall be regarded on that
day; neither shall they ask assistance of each other. They
whose balances shall be heavy with good works shall be happy:

but they whose balances shall be light are those who shall lose their souls, and shall remain in hell forever. The fire shall scorch their faces, and they shall writhe their mouths therein for anguish: and it shall be said unto them, Were not my signs rehearsed unto you; and did ye not charge them with falsehood? They shall answer, O Lord, our happiness prevailed over us, and we were people who went astray. O Lord, take us forth from this fire: if we return to our former wickedness, we shall surely be unjust. God will say unto them, Be ye driven away with ignominy thereinto: and speak not unto me to deliver you. Verily there were a party of my servants, who said, O Lord, we believe: wherefore forgive us, and be merciful unto us; for thou art the best of those who show mercy. But ye received them with scoffs, so that they suffered you to forget my admonition, and ye laughed them to scorn. I have this day rewarded them, for that they suffered the injuries ye offered them with patience: verily they enjoy great felicity. God will say, What number of years have ye continued on earth? They will answer, We have continued there a day, or part of a day: but ask those who keep account. God will say, Ye have tarried but a little, if ye knew it. Did ye think that we had created you in sport, and that ye should not be brought again before us? Wherefore let God be exalted, the King, the Truth! There is no God besides him, the Lord of the honorable throne. Whoever together with the true God shall invoke another god, concerning whom he hath no demonstrative proof, shall surely be brought to an account for the same before his Lord.

CHAPTER XXIV

ENTITLED, LIGHT;[1] REVEALED AT MEDINA

IN THE NAME OF THE MOST MERCIFUL GOD

This Sura have we sent down from heaven; and have ratified the same: and we have revealed therein evident signs, that

[1] This title is taken from an allegorical comparison made between light and God, or faith in him, about the middle of the chapter.

ye may be warned. The whore, and the whoremonger, shall
ye scourge with an hundred stripes.[2] And let not compassion
toward them prevent you from executing the judgment of
God; if ye believe in God and the last day: and let some of
the true believers be witnesses of their punishment. The
whoremonger shall not marry any other than a harlot, or an
idolatress. And a harlot shall no man take in marriage,
except a whoremonger, or an idolater. And this kind of
marriage is forbidden the true believers. But as to those who
accuse women of reputation of whoredom, and produce not
four witnesses of the fact, scourge them with fourscore
stripes, and receive not their testimony forever; for such are
infamous prevaricators: excepting those who shall afterward repent, and amend; for unto such will God be gracious
and merciful. They who shall accuse their wives of adultery,
and shall have no witnesses thereof besides themselves; the
testimony which shall be required of one of them shall be
that he swear four times by God that he speaketh the truth:
and the fifth time that he imprecate the curse of God on him,
if he be a liar. And it shall avert the punishment from the
wife, if she swear four times by God that he is a liar; and if
the fifth time she imprecate the wrath of God on her, if he
speaketh the truth. If it were not for the indulgence of God
toward you, and his mercy, and that God is easy to be reconciled, and wise; he would immediately discover your
crimes.

As to the party among you who have published the falsehood concerning Ayesha,[3] think it not to be an evil unto you:
on the contrary, it is better for you. Every man of them

[2] This law is not to be understood to relate to married people, who are
of free condition; because adultery in such, according to the Sonna, is
to be punished by stoning.

[3] Mohammed having undertaken an expedition against the tribe of
Mostalek, in the sixth year of the Hegira, took his wife Ayesha with him,
to accompany him. In their return, when they were not far from
Medina, the army removing by night, Ayesha, on the road, alighted from
her camel, and stepped aside on a private occasion: but, on her return,
perceiving she had dropped her necklace, which was of onyxes of Dhafar,
she went back to look for it; and in the meantime her attendants, taking
it for granted that she was got into her pavilion (or little tent sur-

shall be punished according to the injustice of which he hath
been guilty; and he among them who hath undertaken to
aggravate the same shall suffer a grievous punishment. Did
not the faithful men, and the faithful women, when ye heard
this, judge in their own minds for the best; and say, This
is a manifest falsehood? Have they produced four witnesses
thereof? wherefore since they have not produced the witnesses, they are surely liars in the sight of God. Had it not
been for the indulgence of God toward you, and his mercy,
in this world and in that which is to come, verily a grievous
punishment had been inflicted on you, for the calumny which
ye have spread: when ye published that with your tongues,
and spoke that with your mouths, of which ye had no knowledge; and esteemed it to be light, whereas it was a matter of
importance in the sight of God. When ye heard it, did ye
say, It belongeth not unto us, that we should talk of this
matter: God forbid! this is a grievous calumny? God warneth you, that ye return not to the like crime forever; if ye be
true believers. And God declareth unto you his signs; for
God is knowing and wise. Verily they who love that scandal
be published of those who believe shall receive a severe punishment both in this world and in the next. God knoweth,

rounded with curtains, wherein women are carried in the East) set it
again on the camel, and led it away. When she came back to the road,
and saw her camel was gone, she sat down there, expecting that when
she was missed some would be sent back to fetch her; and in a little
time she fell asleep. Early in the morning, Safwan Ebn al Moattel, who
had stayed behind to rest himself, coming by, and perceiving somebody
asleep, went to see who it was, and knew her to be Ayesha; upon which
he waked her, by twice pronouncing with a low voice these words, "We
are God's, and unto him must we return." Then Ayesha immediately
covered herself with her veil; and Safwan set her on his own camel,
and led her after the army, which they overtook by noon, as they were
resting. This accident had like to have ruined Ayesha, whose reputation was publicly called in question, as if she had been guilty of adultery
with Safwan; and Mohammed himself knew not what to think, when he
reflected on the circumstances of the affair, which were improved by
some malicious people very much to Ayesha's dishonor; and notwithstanding his wife's protestation of her innocence, he could not get rid of
his perplexity, nor stop the mouths of the censorious, till about a month
after, when this passage was revealed, declaring the accusation to be
unjust.

but ye know not. Had it not been for the indulgence of God toward you, and his mercy, and that God is gracious and merciful, ye had felt his vengeance.

O true believers, follow not the steps of the devil: for whosoever shall follow the steps of the devil, he will command him filthy crimes, and that which is unlawful. If it were not for the indulgence of God, and his mercy toward you, there had not been so much as one of you cleansed from his guilt forever: but God cleanseth whom he pleaseth; for God both heareth and knoweth. Let not those among you who possess abundance of wealth, and have ability, swear that they will not give unto their kindred, and the poor, and those who have fled their country for the sake of God's true religion: but let them forgive, and act with benevolence toward them. Do ye not desire that God should pardon you? And God is gracious and merciful. Moreover they who falsely accuse modest women, who behave in a negligent manner, and are true believers, shall be cursed in this world, and in the world to come; and they shall suffer a severe punishment. One day their own tongues shall bear witness against them, and their hands, and their feet, concerning that which they have done. On that day shall God render unto them their just due: and they shall know that God is the evident truth. The wicked women should be joined to the wicked men, and the wicked men to the wicked women; but the good women should be married to the good men, and the good men to the good women. These shall be cleared from the calumnies which slanderers speak of them: they shall obtain pardon, and an honorable provision.

O true believers, enter not any houses, besides your own houses, until ye have asked leave, and have saluted the family thereof: this is better for you; peradventure ye will be admonished. And if ye shall find no person in the houses, yet do not enter them, until leave be granted you: and if it be said unto you, Return back; do ye return back. This will be more decent for you; and God knoweth that which ye do. It shall be no crime in you, that ye enter uninhabited houses, wherein ye may meet with a convenience. God knoweth that which ye discover, and that which ye conceal.

Speak unto the true believers, that they restrain their eyes, and keep themselves from immodest actions: this will be more pure for them; for God is well acquainted with that which they do. And speak unto the believing women, that they restrain their eyes, and preserve their modesty, and discover not their ornaments, except what necessarily appeareth thereof: and let them throw their veils over their bosoms, and not show their ornaments, unless to their husbands, or their fathers, or their husbands' fathers, or their sons, or their husbands' sons, or their brothers, or their brothers' sons, or their sisters' sons, or their women, or the captives which their right hands shall possess, or unto such men as attend them, and have no need of women, or unto children, who distinguish not the nakedness of women. And let them not make a noise with their feet, that their ornaments which they hide may thereby be discovered. And be ye all turned unto God, O true believers, that ye may be happy.

Marry those who are single among you, and such as are honest of your men-servants, and your maid-servants: if they be poor, God will enrich them of his abundance; for God is bounteous and wise. And let those who find not a match keep themselves from fornication, until God shall enrich them of his abundance. And unto such of your slaves as desire a written instrument allowing them to redeem themselves on paying a certain sum, write one, if ye know good in them; and give them of the riches of God, which he hath given you. And compel not your maid-servants to prostitute themselves, if they be willing to live chastely; that ye may seek the casual advantage of this present life: but whoever shall compel them thereto, verily God will be gracious and merciful unto such women after their compulsion.

And now have we revealed unto you evident signs, and a history like unto some of the histories of those who have gone before you, and an abomination unto the pious. God is the light of heaven and earth: the similitude of his light is as a niche in a wall, wherein a lamp is placed, and the lamp enclosed in a case of glass; the glass appears as it were a shining star. It is lighted with the oil of a blessed tree, an olive neither of the east, nor of the west: it wanteth little but that the oil thereof would give light, although no fire touched it. This is light added unto light: God will direct unto his light whom he pleaseth. God propoundeth parables unto men; for God knoweth all things. In the houses which God hath permitted to be raised, and that his name be commemorated therein: men celebrate his praise in the same morning and evening, whom neither merchandizing nor selling diverteth from the remembering of God, and the observance of prayer, and the giving of alms; fearing the day whereon men's hearts and eyes shall be troubled; that God may recompense them according to the utmost merit of what they shall have wrought, and may add unto them of his abundance a more excellent reward; for God bestoweth on whom he pleaseth without measure. But as to the unbelievers, their works are like the vapor in a plain, which the thirsty traveler thinketh to be water, until, when he cometh thereto, he findeth it to be nothing; but he findeth God with him, and he will fully pay him his account; and God is swift in taking an account: or, as the darkness in a deep sea, covered by waves riding on waves, above which are clouds, being additions of darkness one over the other; when one stretcheth forth his hand, he is far from seeing it. And unto whomsoever God shall not grant his light, he shall enjoy no light at all.

Dost thou not perceive that all creatures both in heaven and earth praise God; and the birds also, extending their wings? Every one knoweth his prayer, and his praise: and God knoweth that which they do. Unto God belongeth the kingdom of heaven and earth; and unto God shall be the return at the last day. Dost thou not see that God gently driveth forward the clouds, and gathereth them together, and then layeth them on heaps? Thou also seest the rain, which falleth from the midst thereof; and God sendeth down from heaven as it were mountains, wherein there is hail; he striketh therewith whom he pleaseth, and turneth the same away from whom he pleaseth: the brightness of his lightning wanteth but little of taking away the sight. God shifteth the night, and the day: verily herein is an instruction unto those who have sight. . . .

O true believers, let your slaves and those among you who shall not have attained the age of puberty ask leave of you, before they come into your presence three times in the day; namely, before the morning prayer, and when ye lay aside your garments at noon, and after the evening prayer. These are the three times for you to be private: it shall be no crime in you, or in them, if they go in to you without asking permission after these times, while ye are in frequent attendance, the one of you on the other. Thus God declareth his signs unto you; for God is knowing and wise. And when your children attain the age of puberty, let them ask leave to come into your presence at all times, in the same manner as those who have attained that age before them ask leave. Thus God declareth his signs unto you; and God is knowing and wise. As to such women as are past child-bearing, who hope not to marry again, because of their advanced age; it shall be no crime in them, if they lay aside their outer garments, not showing their ornaments; but if they abstain from this, it will be better for them. God both heareth and knoweth.

It shall be no crime in the blind, nor shall it be any crime in the lame, neither shall it be any crime in the sick, or in yourselves, that ye eat in your houses, or in the houses of your fathers, or the houses of your mothers, or in the houses of your brothers, or the houses of your sisters, or the houses of your uncles on the father's side, or the houses of your aunts on the father's side, or the houses of your uncles on the mother's side, or the houses of your aunts on the mother's side, or in those houses the keys whereof ye have in your possession, or in the house of your friend. It shall not be any crime in you whether ye eat together, or separately.

And when ye enter any houses, salute one another on the part of God, with a blessed and a welcome salutation. Thus God declareth his signs unto you, that ye may understand. Verily they only are true believers, who believe in God and his apostle, and when they are assembled with him on any affair, depart not, until they have obtained leave of him.

Verily they who ask leave of thee are those who believe in God and his apostle. When therefore they ask leave of thee to depart, on account of any business of their own, grant leave unto such of them as thou shalt think fit, and ask pardon for them of God; for God is gracious and merciful. Let not the calling of the apostle be esteemed among you, as your calling the one to the other. God knoweth such of you as privately withdraw themselves from the assembly, taking shelter behind one another. But let those who withstand his command take heed; lest some calamity befall them in this world, or a grievous punishment be inflicted on them in the life to come. Doth not whatever is in heaven and on earth belong unto God? He well knoweth what ye are about: and on a certain day they shall be assembled before him; and he shall declare unto them that which they have done; for God knoweth all things.

CHAPTER XXV

ENTITLED, AL FORKAN; REVEALED AT MECCA

IN THE NAME OF THE MOST MERCIFUL GOD

Blessed be he who hath revealed the Forkan [1] unto his servant, that he may be a preacher unto all creatures: unto whom belongeth the kingdom of heaven and of earth: who hath begotten no issue; and hath no partner in his kingdom: who hath created all things; and disposed the same according to his determinate will. Yet have they taken other gods besides him; which have created nothing, but are themselves created, and are able neither to avert evil from, nor to produce good unto themselves; and have not the power of death, or of life, or of raising the dead.

And the unbelievers say, This Koran is no other than a forgery which he hath contrived; and other people have assisted him therein: but they utter an unjust thing, and a falsehood. They also say, These are fables of the ancients, which he hath caused to be written down; and they are dictated

---

[1] Forkan is one of the names of the Koran.

unto him morning and evening. Say, He hath revealed it, who knoweth the secrets in heaven and earth: verily he is gracious and merciful. And they say, What kind of apostle is this? He eateth food, and walketh in the streets, as we do: unless an angel be sent down unto him, and become a fellow-preacher with him; or unless a treasure be cast down unto him; or he have a garden, of the fruit whereof he may eat; we will not believe. The ungodly also say, Ye follow no other than a man who is distracted. Behold, what they liken thee unto. But they are deceived; neither can they find a just occasion to reproach thee.

Blessed be he, who, if he pleaseth, will make for thee a better provision than this which they speak of, namely, gardens through which rivers flow: and he will provide thee palaces. But they reject the belief of the hour of judgment, as a falsehood: and we have prepared for him, who shall reject the belief of that hour, burning fire; when it shall see them from a distant place, they shall hear it furiously raging, and roaring. And when they shall be cast bound together into a strait place thereof, they shall there call for death: but it shall be answered them, Call not this day for one death, but call for many deaths. Say, Is this better, or a garden of eternal duration, which is promised unto the pious? It shall be given unto them for a reward, and a retreat: therein shall they have whatever they please; continuing in the same forever. This is a promise to be demanded at the hands of thy Lord. On a certain day he shall assemble them, and whatever they worship, besides God; and shall say unto the worshiped, Did ye seduce these my servants; or did they wander of themselves from the right way? They shall answer, God forbid! It was not fitting for us, that we should take any protectors besides thee: but thou didst permit them and their fathers to enjoy abundance; so that they forgot thy admonition, and became lost people. And God shall say unto their worshipers, Now have these convinced you of falsehood, in that which ye say: they can neither avert your punishment, nor give you any assistance. And whoever of you shall be guilty of injustice, him will we cause to taste a grievous torment. We have sent no messengers before thee, but they ate food, and walked through the streets: and we make some of you an occasion of trial unto others. Will ye persevere with patience? since your Lord regardeth your perseverance.

They who hope not to meet us at the resurrection say, Unless the angels be sent down unto us, or we see our Lord himself, we will not believe. Verily they behave themselves arrogantly; and have transgressed with an enormous transgression. The day whereon they shall see the angels, there shall be no glad tidings on that day for the wicked; and they shall say, Be this removed far from us! and we will come unto the work which they shall have wrought, and we will make it as dust scattered abroad. On that day shall they who are destined to paradise be more happy in an abode, and have a preferable place of repose at noon. On that day the heaven shall be cloven in sunder by the clouds, and the angels shall be sent down, descending visibly therein. On that day the kingdom shall of right belong wholly unto the Merciful; and that day shall be grievous for the unbelievers. On that day the unjust person shall bite his hands for anguish and despair, and shall say, O that I had taken the way of truth with the apostle! Alas for me! O that I had not taken such a one for my friend! He seduced me from the admonition of God, after it had come unto me: for the devil is the betrayer of man. And the apostle shall say, O Lord, verily my people esteemed this Koran to be a vain composition. In like manner did we ordain unto every prophet an enemy from among the wicked: but thy Lord is a sufficient director, and defender.

The unbelievers say, Unless the Koran be sent down unto him entire at once, we will not believe. But in this manner have we revealed it, that we might confirm thy heart thereby, and we have dictated it gradually, by distinct parcels. They shall not come unto thee with any strange question; but we will bring thee the truth in answer, and a most excellent interpretation. They who shall be dragged on their faces into hell shall be in the worst condition, and shall stray most widely from the way of salvation. We heretofore delivered unto Moses the book of the law; and we appointed him Aaron his brother for a counselor. And we said unto them, Go ye to the people who charge our signs with falsehood. And we destroyed them with a signal destruction. And remember the people of Noah, when they accused our apostles of imposture: we drowned them, and made them a sign unto mankind. And we have prepared for the unjust a painful torment. Remember also Ad, and Thamud, and those who dwelt at al Rass; and many other generations, within this period. Unto each of them did we propound examples for their admonition; and each of them did we destroy with an utter destruction. The Koreish have passed frequently near the city which was rained on by a fatal rain: have they not seen where it once stood? Yet have they not dreaded the resurrection. When they see thee, they will receive thee only with scoffing, saying, Is this he, whom God hath sent as his apostle? Verily he had almost drawn us aside from the worship of our gods; if we had not firmly persevered in our devotion toward them. But they shall know hereafter, when they shall see the punishment prepared for them, who hath strayed more widely from the right path. What thinkest thou? He who taketh his lust for his god; canst thou be his guardian? Dost thou imagine that the greater part of them hear, or understand? They are no other than like the brute cattle; yea, they stray more widely from the true path.

Dost thou not consider the works of thy Lord, how he stretcheth forth the shadow before sunrise? If he had pleased, he would have made it immovable forever. Then we cause the sun to rise, and to show the same; and afterward we contract it by an easy and gradual contraction. It is he who hath ordained the night to cover you as a garment; and sleep to give you rest; and hath ordained the day for waking. It is he who sendeth the winds, driving abroad the pregnant clouds, as the forerunners of his mercy: and we send down pure water from heaven, that we may thereby revive a dead country, and give to drink thereof unto what we have created, both of cattle and men, in great numbers; and we distribute the same among them at various times, that they even may consider: but the greater part of men refuse to consider, only out of ingratitude. If we had pleased, we had sent a preacher unto every city: wherefore do not thou obey the unbelievers; but oppose them herewith, with a strong opposition. It is he who hath let loose the two seas; this fresh and sweet, and that salt and bitter: and hath placed between them a bar, and a bound which can not be passed. It is he who hath created man of water; and hath made him to bear the double relation of consanguinity and affinity; for the Lord is powerful. They worship, besides God, that which can neither profit them nor hurt them: and the unbeliever is an assistant of the devil against his Lord. We have sent thee to be no other than a bearer of good tidings, and a denouncer of threats. Say, I ask not of you any reward for this my preaching; besides the conversion of him who shall desire to take the way unto his Lord. And do thou trust in him who liveth, and dieth not; and celebrate his praise: (he is sufficiently acquainted with the faults of his servants:) who hath created the heavens and the earth, and whatever is between them, in six days; and then ascended his throne; the Merciful.

Ask now the knowing concerning him. When it is said unto the unbelievers, Adore the Merciful; they reply, And who is the Merciful? Shall we adore that which thou commandest us? And this precept causeth them to fly the faster from the faith. Blessed be he who hath placed the twelve signs in the heavens; and hath placed therein a lamp by day, and the moon which shineth by night! It is he who hath ordained the night and the day to succeed each other, for the observation of him who will consider, or desireth to show his gratitude. The servants of the Merciful are those who walk meekly on the earth, and, when the ignorant speak unto them, answer, Peace: and who pass the night adoring their Lord, and standing up to pray unto him; and who say, O Lord, avert from us the torment of hell, for the torment thereof is perpetual; verily the same is a miserable abode, and a wretched station: and who, when they bestow, are neither profuse nor niggardly; but observe a just medium between these; and who invoke not another god together with the true God; neither slay the soul, which God hath forbidden to be slain, unless for a just cause: and who are not guilty of fornication. But he who shall do this shall meet the reward of his wickedness: his punishment shall be doubled unto him on the day of resurrection; and he shall remain therein, covered with ignominy, forever: except him who shall repent, and believe, and shall work a righteous work; unto them will God change their former evils into good; for God is ready to forgive, and merciful. And whoever repenteth, and doth that which is right; verily he turneth unto God with an acceptable conversion. And they who do not bear false witness; and when they pass by vain discourse, pass by the same with decency: and who, when they are admonished by the signs of their Lord, fall not down as if they were deaf and blind, but stand up and are attentive thereto: and who say, O Lord, grant us of our wives and our offspring such as may be the satisfaction of our eyes; and make us patterns unto those who fear thee. These shall be rewarded with the highest apartments in paradise, because they have persevered with constancy; and they shall meet therein with greeting and salutation; they shall remain in the same forever: it shall be an excellent abode and a delightful station. Say, My Lord is not solicitous on your account, if ye do not invoke him: ye have already charged his apostle with imposture; but hereafter shall there be a lasting punishment inflicted on you.

CHAPTER XXVI

ENTITLED, THE POETS;[1] REVEALED AT MECCA

IN THE NAME OF THE MOST MERCIFUL GOD

T. S. M. These are the signs of the perspicuous book. Peradventure thou afflictest thyself unto death, lest the Meccans become not true believers. If we pleased, we could send

[1] The chapter bears this inscription because at the conclusion of it the Arabian poets are severely censured.

down unto them a convincing sign from heaven, unto which their necks would humbly submit. But there cometh unto them no admonition from the Merciful, being newly revealed as occasions require, but they turn aside from the same; and they have charged it with falsehood: but a message shall come unto them, which they shall not laugh to scorn. Do they not behold the earth, how many vegetables we cause to spring up therein, of every noble species? Verily herein is a sign: but the greater part of them do not believe. Verily thy Lord is the mighty, the merciful God.

Remember when thy Lord called Moses, saying, Go to the unjust people, the people of Pharaoh; will they not dread me? Moses answered, O Lord, verily I fear lest they accuse me of falsehood, and lest my breast become straitened, and my tongue be not ready in speaking: send therefore unto Aaron, to be my assistant. Also they have a crime to object against me; and I fear they will put me to death. God said, They shall by no means put thee to death: wherefore go ye with our signs; for we will be with you, and will hear what passes between you and them. Go ye therefore unto Pharaoh, and say, Verily we are the apostle of the Lord of all creatures: send away with us the children of Israel. And when they had delivered their message, Pharaoh answered, Have we not brought thee up among us, when a child; and hast thou not dwelt among us for several years of thy life? Yet hast thou done thy deed which thou hast done: and thou art an ungrateful person. Moses replied, I did it indeed, and I was one of those who erred; wherefore I fled from you, because I feared you: but my Lord hath bestowed on me wisdom, and hath appointed me one of his apostles. And this is the favor which thou hast bestowed on me, that thou hast enslaved the children of Israel. Pharaoh said, And who is the Lord of all creatures? Moses answered, The Lord of heaven and earth, and of whatever is between them: if ye are men of sagacity. Pharaoh said unto those who were about him, Do ye not hear? Moses said, Your Lord, and the Lord of your forefathers. Pharaoh said unto those who were present, Your apostle, who is sent unto you, is certainly distracted.

Moses said, The Lord of the east, and of the west, and of whatever is between them; if ye are men of understanding. Pharaoh said unto him, Verily if thou take any god besides me, I will make thee one of those who are imprisoned. Moses answered, What, although I come unto you with a convincing miracle? Pharaoh replied, Produce it, therefore, if thou speakest truth. And he cast down his rod, and behold, it became a visible serpent: and he drew forth his hand out of his bosom; and behold, it appeared white unto the spectators. . . .

And rehearse unto them the story of Abraham: when he said unto his father and his people, What do ye worship? They answered, We worship idols; and we constantly serve them all the day long. Abraham said, Do they hear you, when ye invoke them? Or do they either profit you, or hurt you? They answered, But we found our fathers do the same. He said, What think ye? The gods which ye worship, and your forefathers worshiped, are my enemy: except only the Lord of all creatures, who hath created me and directeth me; and who giveth me to eat and to drink, and when I am sick, healeth me; and who will cause me to die, and will afterward restore me to life; and who, I hope, will forgive my sins on the day of judgment. O Lord, grant me wisdom; and join me with the righteous; and grant that I may be spoken of with honor among the latest posterity; and make me an heir of the garden of delight: and forgive my father, for that he hath been one of those who go astray. And cover me not with shame on the day of resurrection; on the day in which neither riches nor children shall avail, unless unto him who shall come unto God with a sincere heart: when paradise shall be brought near to the view of the pious, and hell shall appear plainly to those who shall have erred; and it shall be said unto them, Where are your deities which ye served besides God? will they deliver you from punishment, or will they deliver themselves? And they shall be cast into the same, both they, and those who have been seduced to their worship; and all the hosts of Eblis. The seduced shall dispute therein with their false gods, saying, By God, we were in a manifest error, when we equaled you with the Lord of all creatures: and none seduced us but the wicked. We have now no intercessors, nor any friends who careth for us. If we were allowed to return once more into the world, we would certainly become true believers. Verily herein was a sign: but the greater part of them believed not. Thy Lord is the mighty, the merciful.

The people of Noah accused God's messengers of imposture: when their brother Noah said unto them, Will ye not fear God? Verily I am a faithful messenger unto you; wherefore fear God, and obey me. I ask no reward of you for my preaching unto you; I expect my reward from no other than the Lord of all creatures: wherefore fear God, and obey me. They answered, Shall we believe on thee, when only the most abject persons have followed thee? Noah said, I have no knowledge of that which they did; it appertaineth unto my Lord alone to bring them to account, if ye understand; wherefore I will not drive away the believers: I am no more than a public preacher. They replied, Assuredly, unless thou desist, O Noah, thou shalt be stoned. He said, O Lord, verily my people take me for a liar: wherefore judge publicly between me and them; and deliver me and the true believers who are with me. Wherefore we delivered him, and those who were with him, in the ark filled with men and animals; and afterward we drowned the rest. Verily herein was a sign: but the greater part of them believed not. Thy Lord is the mighty, the merciful.

The tribe of Ad charged God's messengers with falsehood: when their brother Hud said unto them, Will ye not fear God? Verily I am a faithful messenger unto you; wherefore fear God, and obey me. I demand not of you any reward for my preaching unto you: I expect my regard from no other than the Lord of all creatures. Do ye build a landmark on every high place, to divert yourselves? And do ye erect magnificent works, hoping that ye may continue in their possession forever? And when ye exercise your power, do ye exercise it with cruelty and rigor? Fear God, by leaving these things; and obey me. And fear him who hath bestowed on you that which ye know: he hath bestowed on you cattle, and children, and gardens, and springs of water. Verily I fear for you the punishment of a grievous day. They answered, It is equal unto us whether thou admonish us, or dost not admonish us: this which thou preachest is only a device of the ancients; neither shall we be punished for what we have done. And they accused him of imposture: wherefore we destroyed them. Verily herein was a sign: but the greater part of them believed not. Thy Lord is the mighty, the merciful.

The tribe of Thamud also charged the messengers of God with falsehood. When their brother Saleh said unto them, Will ye not fear God? Verily I am a faithful messenger unto you: wherefore fear God, and obey me. I demand no reward of you for my preaching unto you; I expect my reward from no other than the Lord of all creatures. Shall ye be left forever secure in the possession of the things which are here; among gardens, and fountains, and corn, and palm-trees, whose branches sheathe their flowers? And will ye continue to cut habitations for yourselves out of the mountains, behaving with insolence? Fear God, and obey me; and obey not the command of the transgressors, who act corruptly in the earth, and reform not the same. They answered, Verily thou art distracted: thou art no other than a man like unto us: produce now some sign, if thou speakest truth. Saleh said, This she-camel shall be a sign unto you: she shall have her portion of water, and ye shall have your portion of water alternately, on a several day appointed for you; and do her no hurt, lest the punishment of a terrible day be inflicted on you. But they slew her; and were made to repent of their impiety: for the punishment which had been threatened overtook them. Verily herein was a sign; but the greater part of them did not believe. Thy Lord is the mighty, the merciful.

The people of Lot likewise accused God's messengers of imposture. When their brother Lot said unto them, Will ye not fear God? Verily I am a faithful messenger unto you: wherefore fear God, and obey me. I demand no reward of you for my preaching: I expect my reward from no other than the Lord of all creatures. Do ye approach unto the males among mankind, and leave your wives which your Lord hath created for you? Surely ye are people who transgress. They answered, Unless thou desist, O Lot, thou shalt certainly be expelled our city. He said, Verily I am one of those who abhor your doings: O Lord, deliver me and my family from that which they act. Wherefore we delivered him, and all his family; except an old woman, his wife, who perished among those who remained behind: then we destroyed the rest; and we rained on them a shower of stones; and terrible was the shower which fell on those who had been warned in vain. Verily herein was a sign; but the greater part of them did not believe. Thy Lord is the mighty, the merciful.

The inhabitants of the wood also accused God's messengers of imposture. When Shoaib said unto them, Will ye not fear God? Verily I am a faithful messenger unto you; wherefore fear God, and obey me. I ask no reward of you for my preaching: I expect my reward from no other than the Lord of all creatures. Give just measure, and be not defrauders; and weigh with an equal balance; and diminish not unto men aught of their matters; neither commit violence in the earth, acting corruptly. And fear him who hath created you, and also the former generations. They answered, Certainly thou art distracted: thou art no more than a man, like unto us; and we do surely esteem thee to be a liar. Cause now a part of the heaven to fall upon us, if thou speakest truth. Shoaib said, My Lord best knoweth that which we do. And they charged him with falsehood: wherefore the punishment of the day of the shadowing cloud overtook them; and this was the punishment of a grievous day. Verily herein was a sign; but the greater part of them did not believe. Thy Lord is the mighty, the merciful.

This book is certainly a revelation from the Lord of all creatures, which the faithful spirit hath caused to descend upon thy heart, that thou mightest be a preacher to thy people, in the perspicuous Arabic tongue: and it is borne witness to in the scriptures of former ages. Was it not a sign unto them, that the wise men among the children of Israel knew it? Had we revealed it unto any of the foreigners, and he had read the same unto them, yet they would not have believed therein. Thus have we caused obstinate infidelity to enter the hearts of the wicked: they shall not believe therein, until they see a painful punishment. It shall come suddenly upon them, and they shall not foresee it: and they shall say, Shall we be respited? Do they therefore desire our punishment to be hastened? What thinkest thou? If we suffer them to enjoy the advantage of this life for several years, and afterward that with which they are threatened come upon them; what will that which they have enjoyed profit them? We have destroyed no city, but preachers were first sent unto it, to admonish the inhabitants thereof; neither did we treat them unjustly. The devils did not descend with the Koran, as the infidels give out: it is not for their purpose, neither are they able to produce such a book; for they are far removed from hearing the discourse of the angels in heaven.

Invoke no other god with the true God, lest thou become one of those who are doomed to punishment. And admonish thy more near relations. And behave thyself with meekness toward the true believers who follow thee: and if they be disobedient unto thee, say, Verily I am clear of that which ye do. And trust in the most mighty and merciful God; who seeth thee when thou risest up, and thy behavior among those who worship; for he both heareth and knoweth. Shall I declare unto you upon whom the devils descend? They descend upon every lying and wicked person: they learn what is heard; but the greater part of them are liars. And those who err follow the steps of the poets: dost thou not see that they rove as bereft of their senses through every valley, and that they say that which they do not?[2] except those who believe, and do good works, and remember God frequently; and who

[2] Their compositions being as wild as the actions of a distracted man: for most of the ancient poetry was full of vain imaginations; as fabulous stories and descriptions, love-verses, flattery, excessive commendations of their patrons, and as excessive reproaches of their enemies, incitements to vicious actions, vainglorious vauntings, and the like.

defend themselves, after they have been unjustly treated.[3]
And they who act unjustly shall know hereafter with what
treatment they shall be treated.

CHAPTER XXVII

ENTITLED, THE ANT;[1] REVEALED AT MECCA

IN THE NAME OF THE MOST MERCIFUL GOD

T. S. These are the signs of the Koran, and of the perspicuous book: a direction, and good tidings unto the true
believers; who regularly perform their prayer, and give alms,
and firmly believe in the life to come. As to those who
believe not in the life to come, we have prepared their works
for them; and they shall be struck with astonishment at their
disappointment, when they shall be raised again; these are
they whom an evil punishment awaiteth in this life; and in
that which is to come they shall be the greatest losers. Thou
hast certainly received the Koran from the presence of a wise,
a knowing God.

Remember when Moses said unto his family, Verily I perceive fire: I will bring you tidings thereof, or I will bring you
a lighted brand, that ye may be warmed. And when he was
come near unto it, a voice cried unto him, saying, Blessed be
he who is in the fire, and whoever is about it; and praise be
unto God, the Lord of all creatures! O Moses, verily I am

[3] That is, such poets as had embraced Mohammedanism; whose works,
free from the profaneness of the former, run chiefly on the praises of
God, and the establishing his unity, and contain exhortations to obedience and other religious and moral virtues, without any satirical invec-
tives, unless against such as have given just provocations, by having first
attacked them, or some others of the true believers, with the same
weapons. In this last case Mohammed saw it was necessary for him
to borrow assistance from the poets of his party, to defend himself and
religion from the insults and ridicule of the others, for which purpose
he employed the pens of Labid Ebn Rabia, Abda'llah Ebn Rawaha, Hassan
Ebn Thabet, and the two Caabs. It is related that Mohammed once said
to Caab Ebn Malec, " Ply them with satires; for, by him in whose hand
my soul is, they wound more deeply than arrows."

[1] In this chapter is related an odd story of the ant, which has therefore been pitched on for the title.

God, the mighty, the wise: cast down now thy rod. And when he saw it, that it moved, as though it had been a serpent, he retreated and fled, and returned not. And God said, O Moses, fear not; for my messengers are not disturbed with fear in my sight: except he who shall have done amiss, and shall have afterward substituted good in lieu of evil; for I am gracious and merciful. Moreover put thy hand into thy bosom; it shall come forth white, without hurt: this shall be one among the nine signs unto Pharaoh and his people; for they are a wicked people. And when our visible signs had come unto them, they said, This is manifest sorcery. And they denied them, although their souls certainly knew them to be from God, out of iniquity and pride; but behold what was the end of the corrupt doers. We heretofore bestowed knowledge on David and Solomon; and they said, Praise be unto God, who hath made us more excellent than many of his faithful servants!

And Solomon was David's heir; and he said, O men, we have been taught the speech of birds, and have had all things bestowed on us; this is manifest excellence. And his armies were gathered together unto Solomon, consisting of genii, and men, and birds; and they were led in distinct bands, until they came unto the valley of ants. And an ant, seeing the hosts approaching, said, O ants, enter ye into your habitations, lest Solomon and his army tread you underfoot, and perceive it not. And Solomon smiled, laughing at her words, and said, O Lord, excite me that I may be thankful for thy favor, wherewith thou hast favored me, and my parents; and that I may do that which is right, and well-pleasing unto thee: and introduce me, through thy mercy, into paradise, among thy servants, the righteous. And he viewed the birds, and said, What is the reason that I see not the lapwing? Is she absent? Verily I will chastise her with a severe chastisement, or I will put her to death, unless she bring me a just excuse. And she tarried not long before she presented herself unto Solomon, and said, I have viewed a country which thou hast not viewed; and I come unto thee from Saba, with a certain piece of news. I found a woman to reign over them, who is provided with everything requisite for a prince, and hath a magnificent throne. I found her and her people to worship the sun, besides God: and Satan hath prepared their works for them, and hath turned them aside from the way of truth (wherefore they are not rightly directed), lest they should worship God, who bringeth to light that which is hidden in heaven and earth, and knoweth whatever they conceal and whatever they discover. God! there is no God but he; the Lord of the magnificent throne. Solomon said, We shall see whether thou hast spoken the truth, or whether thou art a liar. Go with this my letter, and cast it down unto them; then turn aside from them, and wait to know what answer they will return. And when the Queen of Saba had received the letter, she said, O nobles, verily an honorable letter hath been delivered unto me; it is from Solomon, and this is the tenor thereof: In the name of the most merciful God, Rise not up against me: but come, and surrender yourselves unto me. She said, O nobles, advise me in my business: I will not resolve on anything, until ye be witnesses and approve thereof. The nobles answered, We are endued with strength, and are endued with great prowess in war; but the command appertaineth unto thee: see therefore what thou wilt command. She said, Verily kings, when they enter a city by force, waste the same, and abase the most powerful of the inhabitants thereof: and so will these do with us. But I will send gifts unto them; and will wait for what further information those who shall be sent shall bring back. And when the Queen's ambassador came unto Solomon, that prince said, Will ye present me with riches? Verily that which God hath given me is better than what he hath given you: but ye do glory in your gifts. Return unto the people of Saba. We will surely come unto them with forces, which they shall not be able to withstand; and we will drive them out from their city, humbled; and they shall become contemptible. And Solomon said, O nobles, which of you will bring unto me her throne, before they come and surrender themselves unto me? A terrible genius answered, I will bring it unto thee, before thou arise from thy place: for I am able to perform it, and may be trusted. And one with whom was the knowledge of scriptures said, I will bring it unto thee, in the twinkling of an eye. And when Solomon saw the throne placed before him, he said, This is a favor of my Lord, that he may make trial of me, whether I will be grateful, or whether I will be ungrateful: and he who is grateful is grateful to his own advantage, but if any shall be ungrateful verily my Lord is self-sufficient and munificent. And Solomon said unto his servants, Alter her throne, that she may not know it, to the end we may see whether she be rightly directed, or whether she be one of those who are not rightly directed. And when she was come unto Solomon, it was said unto her, Is thy throne like this? She answered, As though it were the same. And we have had knowledge bestowed on us before this, and have been resigned unto God. But that which she worshiped, besides God, had turned her aside from the truth; for she was of an unbelieving people. It was said unto her, Enter the palace. And when she saw it, she imagined it to be a great water; and she discovered her legs, by lifting up her robe to pass through it.[2] Whereupon Solomon said unto her, Verily this is a palace evenly floored with glass. Then said the Queen, O Lord, verily I have dealt unjustly with my own soul; and I resign myself, together with Solomon, unto God, the Lord of all creatures.[3]

Also we heretofore sent unto the tribe of Thamud their brother Saleh; who said unto them, Serve ye God. And behold they were divided into two parties, who disputed among themselves. Saleh said, O my people, why do you hasten evil rather than good? Unless ye ask pardon of God, that ye may obtain mercy, ye are lost. They answered, We presage evil from thee, and from those who are with thee.

[2] Some Arab writers tell us Solomon had been informed that Balkis's legs and feet were covered with hair, like those of an ass, of the truth of which he had hereby an opportunity of being satisfied by ocular demonstration.

[3] The Queen of Saba having by these words professed Islam, and renounced idolatry, Solomon had thoughts of making her his wife. Some, however, will have it that she did not marry Solomon, but a prince of the tribe of Hamdan.

Saleh replied, The evil which ye presage is with God: but ye are a people who are proved by a vicissitude of prosperity and adversity. And there were nine men in the city, who acted corruptly in the earth, and behaved not with integrity. And they said unto one another, Swear ye reciprocally by God, that we will fall upon Saleh and his family by night: and afterward we will say unto him who hath right to avenge his blood, We were not so much as present at the destruction of his family; and we certainly speak the truth. And they devised a plot against him: but we devised a plot against them; and they perceived it not. And see what was the issue of their plot: we utterly destroyed them and their whole people; and these their habitations remain empty, because of the injustice which they committed. Verily herein is a sign, unto people who understand. And we delivered those who believed and feared God.

And remember Lot, when he said unto his people, Do ye commit a wickedness, though ye see the heinousness thereof? Do ye approach lustfully unto men, leaving the women? Ye are surely an ignorant people. But the answer of his people was no other than that they said, Cast the family of Lot out of your city: for they are men who preserve themselves pure from the crimes of which ye are guilty. Wherefore we delivered him and his family, except his wife, whom we decreed to be one of those who remained behind to be destroyed. And we rained on them a shower of stones: and dreadful was the shower which fell on those who had been warned in vain. Say, Praise be unto God; and peace be upon his servants whom he hath chosen!

Is God more worthy, or the false gods which they associate with him? Is not he to be preferred, who hath created the heavens and the earth, and sendeth down rain for you from heaven, whereby we cause delicious groves to spring up? It is not in your power to cause the trees thereof to shoot forth. Is there any other god partner with the true God? Verily these are a people who deviate from the truth. Is not he more worthy to be adored who hath established the earth, and hath caused rivers to flow through the midst thereof, and placed thereon immovable mountains, and set a bar between the two seas? Is there any other god equal with the true God? Yet the greater part of them know it not. Is not he more worthy who heareth the afflicted, when he calleth upon him, and taketh off the evil which distressed him; and who hath made you the successors of your forefathers in the earth? Is there any other god who can be equaled with the true God? How few consider these things! Is not he more worthy who directeth you in the dark paths of the land and of the sea; and who sendeth the winds driving abroad the clouds as the fore-runners of his mercy? Is there any other god who can be equaled with the true God? Far be God from having those partners in his power, which ye associate with him! Is not he more worthy, who produceth a creature, and after it hath been dead restoreth it to life, and who giveth you food from heaven and earth? Is there any other god with the true God, who doth this? Say, produce your proof thereof, if ye speak truth. Say, None either in heaven or earth knoweth that which is hidden, besides God: neither do they understand when they shall be raised. However their knowledge at-taineth some notion of the life to come: yet they are in an uncertainty concerning the same; yea, they are blind as to the real circumstances thereof.

And the unbelievers say, When we and our fathers shall have been reduced to dust, shall we be taken forth from the grave? Verily we have been threatened with this, both we and our fathers, heretofore. This is no other than fables of the ancients. Say unto them, Pass through the earth, and see what hath been the end of the wicked. And be not thou grieved for them; neither be thou in any concern on account of the plots which they are contriving against thee. And they say, When will this threat be accomplished, if ye speak true? Answer, Peradventure some part of that punishment, which ye desire to be hastened, may follow close behind you: verily thy Lord is endued with indulgence toward mankind; but the greater part of them are not thankful. Verily thy Lord knoweth what their breasts conceal, and what they dis-cover: and there is nothing hidden in heaven or on earth, but it is written in a clear book. Verily this Koran declareth unto the children of Israel most of those points concerning which they disagree: and it is certainly a direction, and a mercy unto the true believers. Thy Lord will decide the controversy between them, by his definitive sentence: and he is the mighty, the wise. Therefore put thy trust in God; for thou art in the manifest truth. Verily thou shalt not make the dead to hear, neither shalt thou make the deaf to hear thy call to the true faith, when they retire and turn their backs: neither shalt thou direct the blind to extricate themselves out of their error. Thou shalt make none to hear thee, except him who shall believe in our signs: and they are wholly resigned unto us. When the sentence shall be ready to fall upon them, we will cause a beast [4] to come forth unto them from out of the earth, which shall speak unto them: verily men do not firmly believe in our signs. On the day of resurrection we will assemble, out of every nation, a company of those who shall have charged our signs with falsehood; and they shall be prevented from mixing together, until they shall arrive at the place of judgment. And God shall say unto them, Have ye charged my signs with falsehood, although ye comprehended them not with your knowledge? Or what is it that ye were doing? And the sentence of damnation shall fall on them, for that they have acted unjustly: and they shall not speak in their own excuse. Do they not see that we have ordained the night, that they may rest therein, and the day giving open light? Verily herein are signs unto people who believe.

On that day the trumpet shall be sounded; and whoever are in heaven and on earth shall be struck with terror, except those whom God shall please to exempt therefrom: and all shall come before him, in humble guise. And thou shalt see the mountains, and shalt think them firmly fixed: but they shall pass away, even as the clouds pass away. This will be the work of God, who hath rightly disposed all things: and he is well acquainted with that which ye do. Whoever shall

[4] The Mohammedans call this beast, whose appearance will be one of the approach of the day of judgment, al Jassasa, or the Spy.

have wrought righteousness shall receive a reward beyond the desert thereof; and they shall be secure from the terror of that day; but whoever shall have wrought evil shall be thrown on their faces into hell fire. Shall ye receive the reward of any other than of that which ye shall have wrought? Verily I am commanded to worship the Lord of this territory of Mecca, who hath sanctified the same: unto him belong all things. And I am commanded to be a Moslem, and to rehearse the Koran: he who shall be directed thereby will be directed to his own advantage; and to him who shall go astray, say, Verily, I am a warner only. And say, Praise be unto God! he will show you his signs, and ye shall know them; and thy Lord is not regardless of that which they do.

CHAPTER XXVIII

ENTITLED, THE STORY; [1] REVEALED AT MECCA

IN THE NAME OF THE MOST MERCIFUL GOD

T. S. M. These are the signs of the perspicuous book. We will dictate unto thee, O Mohammed, some parts of the history of Moses and Pharaoh, with truth; for the sake of people who believe. Now Pharaoh lifted himself up in the land of Egypt; and he caused his subjects to be divided into parties: he weakened one party of them, by slaying their male children, and preserving their females alive; for he was an oppressor. And we were minded to be gracious unto those who were weakened in the land, and to make them models of religion; and to make them the heirs of the wealth of Pharaoh and his people, and to establish a place for them in the earth; and to show Pharaoh, and Haman, and their forces, that destruction of their kingdom and nation by them, which they sought to avoid. And we directed the mother of Moses by revelation, saying, Give him suck: and if thou fearest for him, cast him into the river; and fear not, neither be afflicted; for we will restore him unto thee, and we will appoint him

[1] The title is taken from the verse where Moses is said to have related the story of his adventures to Shoaib.

one of our apostles. And when she had put the child in the ark, and had cast it into the river, the family of Pharaoh took him up; providence designing that he should become an enemy and a sorrow unto them. Verily Pharaoh, and Haman, and their forces were sinners. And the wife of Pharaoh said, This child is a delight of the eye to me and to thee: kill him not; peradventure it may happen that he may be serviceable unto us; or we may adopt him for our son. And they perceived not the consequence of what they were doing. And the heart of the mother of Moses became oppressed with fear; and she had almost discovered him, had we not armed her heart with constancy, that she might be one of those who believe the promises of God. And she said unto his sister, Follow him. And she watched him at a distance; and they perceived it not. And we suffered him not to take the breasts of the nurses who were provided before his sister came up: and she said, Shall I direct you unto some of his nation, who may nurse him for you, and will be careful of him? And, at their desire, she brought his mother to them. So we restored him to his mother, that her mind might be set at ease, and that she might not be afflicted; and that she might know that the promise of God was true: but the greater part of mankind know not the truth.

And when Moses had attained his age of full strength, and was become a perfect man, we bestowed on him wisdom and knowledge: and thus do we reward the upright. And he went into the city, at a time when the inhabitants thereof observed not what passed in the streets: and he found therein two men fighting; the one being of his own party, and the other of his enemies. And he who was of his party begged his assistance against him who was of the contrary party; and Moses struck him with his fist, and slew him: but being sorry for what had happened, he said, This is of the work of the devil; for he is a seducing and an open enemy. And he said, O Lord, verily I have injured my own soul; wherefore forgive me. So God forgave him; for he is ready to forgive, and merciful. He said, O Lord, by the favors with which thou hast favored me, I will not be an assistant to the wicked for the future. And the next morning he was afraid in the city, and looked about him, as one apprehensive of danger: and behold, he whom he had assisted the day before cried out unto him for help a second time. But Moses said unto him, Thou art plainly a quarrelsome fellow. And when he sought to lay hold on him who was an enemy unto them both, he said, O Moses, dost thou intend to kill me, as thou killedst a man yesterday? Thou seekest only to be an oppressor in the earth, and seekest not to be a reconciler of quarrels. And a certain man came from the farther part of the city, running hastily, and said, O Moses, verily the magistrates are deliberating concerning thee, to put thee to death: depart therefore; I certainly advise thee well. Wherefore he departed out of the city in great fear, looking this way and that, lest he should be pursued. And he said, O Lord, deliver me from the unjust people. And when he was journeying towards Madian, he said, Peradventure my Lord will direct me in the right way.[2] And when he arrived at the water of Madian, he found about the well a company of men, who were watering their flocks. And he found, besides them, two women, who kept off their sheep at a distance. And he said unto them, What is the matter with you? They answered, We shall not water our flock, until the shepherds shall have driven away theirs: for our father is an old man, stricken in years. So Moses watered their sheep for them; and afterward retired to the shade, saying, O Lord, verily I stand in need of the good which thou shalt send down unto me. And one of the damsels came unto him, walking bashfully, and said, My father calleth thee, that he may recompense thee for the trouble which thou hast taken in watering our sheep for us. And when he was come unto Shoaib, and had told him the story of his adventures, he said unto him, Fear not; thou hast escaped from unjust people. And one of the damsels said, My father, hire him for certain wages; the best servant thou canst hire, is an

[2] For Moses knew not the way and, coming to a place where three roads met, committed himself to the guidance of God, and took the middle road, which was the right; providence likewise so ordering it, that his pursuers took the other two roads, and missed him. Some say he was led by an angel in the appearance of a traveler.

able and trusty person. And Shoaib said unto Moses, Verily I will give thee one of these my two daughters in marriage, on condition that thou serve me for hire eight years: and if thou fulfil ten years, it is in thine own breast; for I seek not to impose a hardship on thee: and thou shalt find me, if God please, a man of probity. Moses answered, Let this be the covenant between me and thee: whichsoever of the two terms I shall fulfil, let it be no crime in me if I then quit thy service; and God is witness of that which we say.

And when Moses had fulfilled the term,[3] and was journeying with his family toward Egypt, he saw fire on the side of Mount Sinai. And he said unto his family, Tarry ye here; for I see fire: peradventure I may bring you thence some tidings of the way, or at least a brand out of the fire, that ye may be warmed. And when he was come thereto, a voice cried unto him from the right side of the valley, in the sacred bottom, from the tree, saying, O Moses, verily I am God, the Lord of all creatures: cast down now thy rod. And when he saw it that it moved, as though it had been a serpent, he retreated and fled, and returned not. And God said unto him, O Moses, draw near, and fear not; for thou art safe. Put thy hand into thy bosom, and it shall come forth white, without any hurt; and draw back thy hand unto thee which thou stretchest forth for fear. These shall be two evident signs from thy Lord, unto Pharaoh and his princes; for they are a wicked people. Moses said, O Lord, verily I have slain one of them; and I fear they will put me to death: but my brother Aaron is of a more eloquent tongue than I am; wherefore send him with me for an assistant, that he may gain me credit; for I fear lest they accuse me of imposture. God said, We will strengthen thine arm by thy brother, and we will give each of you extraordinary power, so that they shall not come up to you, in our signs. Ye two, and whoever shall follow you, shall be the conquerors. And when Moses came

[3] *Viz.*, The longer term of ten years. The Mohammedans say, after the Jews, that Moses received from Shoaib the rod of the prophets (which was a branch of a myrtle of paradise, and had descended to him from Adam) to keep off the wild beasts from his sheep; and that this was the rod with which he performed all those wonders in Egypt.

unto them with our evident signs, they said, This is no other than a deceitful piece of sorcery: neither have we heard of anything like this among our forefathers. And Moses said, My Lord best knoweth who cometh with a direction from him; and who shall have success in this life, as well as the next: but the unjust shall not prosper. And Pharaoh said, O princes, I did not know that ye had any other god besides me. Wherefore do thou, O Haman, burn me clay into bricks; and build me a high tower,[4] that I may ascend unto the God of Moses: for I verily believe him to be a liar. And both he and his forces behaved themselves insolently and unjustly in the earth; and imagined that they should not be brought before us to be judged. Wherefore we took him and his forces, and cast them into the sea. Behold, therefore, what was the end of the unjust. And we made them deceitful guides, inviting their followers to hell fire; and on the day of resurrection they shall not be screened from punishment. We pursued them with a curse in this life, and on the day of resurrection they shall be shamefully rejected. . . .

The Meccans say, If we follow the same direction with thee, we shall be forcibly expelled our land. Have we not established for them a secure asylum; to which fruits of every sort are brought, as a provision of our bounty? but the greater part of them do not understand. How many cities have we destroyed, whose inhabitants lived in ease and plenty? and these their dwellings are not inhabited after them, unless for a little while; and we were the inheritors of their wealth. But thy Lord did not destroy those cities, until he had sent unto their capital an apostle, to rehearse our signs unto them: neither did we destroy those cities, unless their inhabitants were injurious to their apostle. The things which are given

4 It is said that Haman, having prepared bricks and other materials, employed no less than fifty thousand men, besides laborers, in the building; which they carried to so immense a height that the workmen could no longer stand on it: that Pharaoh, ascending this tower, threw a javelin toward heaven, which fell back again stained with blood, whereupon he impiously boasted that he had killed the God of Moses; but at sunset God sent the angel Gabriel, who, with one stroke of his wing, demolished the tower, a part whereof, falling on the King's army, destroyed a million of men.

you are the provisions of this present life, and the pomp
thereof; but that which is with God is better and more durable: will ye not therefore understand? Shall he then, unto
whom we have promised an excellent promise of future happiness, and who shall attain the same, be as he on whom we
have bestowed the provision of this present life, and who, on
the day of resurrection, shall be one of those who are delivered
up to eternal punishment? On that day God shall call unto
them, and shall say, Where are my partners, which ye
imagined to be so? And they upon whom the sentence of
damnation shall be justly pronounced shall answer, These, O
Lord, are those whom we seduced; we seduced them as we also
had been seduced: but now we clearly quit them, and turn
unto thee. They did not worship us, but their own lusts.
And it shall be said unto the idolaters, Call now upon those
whom ye associated with God: and they shall call upon them,
but they shall not answer them; and they shall see the punishment prepared for them, and shall wish that they had submitted to be directed. On that day God shall call unto them,
and shall say, What answer did ye return to our messengers?
But they shall not be able to give an account thereof on that
day; neither shall they ask one another for information.
Howbeit whoso shall repent and believe, and shall do that
which is right, may expect to be happy. Thy Lord createth
what he pleaseth; and chooseth freely: but they have no free
choice.

Praise be unto God; and far be he removed from the idols
which they associate with him! Thy Lord knoweth both the
secret malice which their breasts conceal, and the open hatred
which they discover. He is God; there is no God but he.
Unto him is the praise due, both in this life and in that which
is to come: unto him doth judgment belong, and before him
shall ye be assembled at the last day. Say, What think ye?
If God should cover you with perpetual night, until the day
of resurrection; what god, besides God, would bring you
light? Will ye not therefore harken? Say, What think ye?
If God should give you continual day, until the day of resurrection; what god, besides God, would bring you night, that

ye might rest therein? Will ye not therefore consider? Of his mercy he hath made for you the night and the day, that ye may rest in the one, and may seek to obtain provision for yourselves of his abundance, by your industry, in the other; and that ye may give thanks. On a certain day God shall call unto them, and shall say, Where are my partners, which ye imagined to share the divine power with me? And we will produce a witness out of every nation, and will say, Bring hither your proof of what ye have asserted. And they shall know that the right is God's alone; and the deities which they have devised shall abandon them.

Karun was of the people of Moses;[5] but he behaved insolently toward them: for we had given him so much treasure, that his keys would have loaded several strong men. When

[5] The commentators say Karun was the son of Yeshar (or Izhar), the uncle of Moses, and, consequently, make him the same with the Korah of the scriptures. This person is represented by them as the most beautiful of the Israelites, and so far surpassing them all in opulency that the riches of Karun have become a proverb. The Mohammedans are indebted to the Jews for this last circumstance, to which they have added several other fables: for they tell us that he built a large palace overlaid with gold, the doors whereof were of massy gold; that he became so insolent, because of his immense riches, as to raise a sedition against Moses, though some pretend the occasion of his rebellion to have been his unwillingness to give alms, as Moses had commanded; that one day, when that prophet was preaching to the people, and, among other laws which he published, declared that adulterers should be stoned, Karun asked him what if he should be found guilty of the same crime? To which Moses answered, that in such case he would suffer the same punishment; and thereupon Karun produced a harlot, whom he had hired to swear that Moses had lain with her, and charged him publicly with it; but on Moses adjuring the woman to speak the truth, her resolution failed her, and she confessed that she was suborned by Karun to accuse him wrongfully; that then God directed Moses, who had complained to him of this usage, to command the earth what he pleased, and it should obey him; whereupon he said, "O earth, swallow them up!" and that immediately the earth opened under Karun and his confederates, and swallowed them up, with his palace and all his riches. There goes a tradition that, as Karun sank gradually into the ground, first to his knees, then to his waist, then to his neck, he cried out four several times, "O Moses, have mercy on me!" but that Moses continued to say, "O earth, swallow them up," till at last he wholly disappeared: upon which God said to Moses, "Thou hast no mercy on Karun, though he asked pardon of thee four times; but I would have had compassion on him if he had asked pardon of me but once."

his people said unto him, Rejoice not immoderately; for God loveth not those who rejoice in their riches immoderately: but seek to attain, by means of the wealth which God hath given thee, the future mansion of paradise. And forget not thy portion in this world; but be thou bounteous unto others, as God hath been bounteous unto thee: and seek not to act corruptly in the earth; for God loveth not the corrupt doers. He answered, I have received these riches, only because of the knowledge which is with me. Did he not know that God had already destroyed, before him, several generations, who were mightier than he in strength, and had amassed more abundance of riches? And the wicked shall not be asked to discover their crimes. And Karun went forth unto his people, in his pomp. And they who loved this present life said, Oh that we had the like wealth as hath been given unto Karun! verily he is master of a great fortune. But those on whom knowledge had been bestowed answered, Alas for you! the reward of God in the next life will be better unto him who shall believe and do good works: but none shall attain the same, except those who persevere with constancy. And we caused the ground to cleave in sunder, and to swallow up him and his palace: and he had no forces to defend him, besides God; neither was he rescued from punishment. And the next morning, those who had coveted his condition the day before said, Aha! verily God bestoweth abundant provision on such of his servants as he pleaseth; and he is sparing unto whom he pleaseth. Unless God had been gracious unto us, certainly the earth had swallowed us up also. Aha! the unbelievers shall not prosper.

As to this future mansion of paradise, we will give it unto them who seek not to exalt themselves in the earth, or to do wrong; for the happy issue shall attend the pious. Whoso doth good shall receive a reward which shall exceed the merit thereof: but as to him who doth evil, they who work evil shall be rewarded according to the merit only of that which they shall have wrought. Verily he who hath given thee the Koran for a rule of faith and practise will certainly bring thee back home unto Mecca. Say, My Lord best knoweth who cometh with a true direction, and who is in a manifest error. Thou didst not expect that the book of the Koran should be delivered unto thee: but thou hast received it through the mercy of thy Lord. Be not therefore assisting to the unbelievers; neither let them turn thee aside from the signs of God, after they have been sent down unto thee: and invite men unto thy Lord. And be not thou an idolater; neither invoke any other god, together with the true God: there is no god but he. Everything shall perish, except himself: unto him belongeth judgment; and before him shall ye be assembled at the last day.

CHAPTER XXIX

ENTITLED, THE SPIDER; [1] REVEALED AT MECCA

IN THE NAME OF THE MOST MERCIFUL GOD

A. L. M. Do men imagine that it shall be sufficient for them to say, We believe; while they be not proved? We heretofore proved those who were before them; for God will surely know them who are sincere, and he will surely know the liars. Do they who work evil think that they shall prevent us from taking vengeance on them? An ill judgment do they make. Whoso hopeth to meet God, verily God's appointed time will certainly come; and he both heareth and knoweth. Whoever striveth to promote the true religion striveth for the advantage of his own soul; for God needeth not any of his creatures: and as to those who believe and work righteousness, we will expiate their evil deeds from them; and we will give them a reward according to the utmost merit of their actions.

We have commanded man to show kindness toward his parents: but if they endeavor to prevail with thee to associate with me that concerning which thou hast no knowledge, obey them not. Unto me shall ye return; and I will declare unto you what ye have done. Those who shall believe, and shall

[1] Transient mention is made of this insect toward the middle of the chapter.

work righteousness, we will surely introduce into paradise, among the upright.

There are some men who say, We believe in God: but when such a one is afflicted for God's sake, he esteemeth the persecution of men to be as grievous as the punishment of God. Yet if success cometh from thy Lord, they say, Verily we are with you. Doth not God well know that which is in the breasts of his creatures? Verily God well knoweth the true believers, and he well knoweth the hypocrites. The unbelievers say unto those who believe, Follow our way; and we will bear your sins. Howbeit they shall not bear any part of their sins; for they are liars: but they shall surely bear their own burdens, and other burdens besides their own burdens; and they shall be examined, on the day of resurrection, concerning that which they have falsely devised.

We heretofore sent Noah unto his people; and he tarried among them one thousand years, save fifty years, and the deluge took them away, while they were acting unjustly; but we delivered him and those who were in the ark, and we made the same a sign unto all creatures. We also sent Abraham; when he said unto his people, Serve God, and fear him: this will be better for you, if ye understand. Ye only worship idols besides God, and forge a lie. Verily those which ye worship, besides God, are not able to make any provision for you: seek therefore your provision from God; and serve him and give thanks unto him; unto him shall ye return. If he charge me with imposture, verily sundry nations before you likewise charged their prophets with imposture: but public preaching only is incumbent on an apostle. Do they not see how God produceth creatures, and afterward restoreth them? Verily this is easy with God. Say, Go through the earth, and see how he originally produceth creatures: afterward will God reproduce another production; for God is almighty. He will punish whom he pleaseth, and he will have mercy on whom he pleaseth. Before him shall ye be brought at the day of judgment: and ye shall not escape his reach, either in earth, or in heaven; neither shall ye have any patron or defender besides God. As for those who believe not in the signs of God, or that they shall meet him at the resurrection, they shall despair of my mercy, and for them is a painful punishment prepared. And the answer of his people was no other than that they said, Slay him, or burn him. But God saved him from the fire. Verily herein were signs unto people who believed.

And Abraham said, Ye have taken idols, besides God, to cement affection between you in this life: but on the day of resurrection, the one of you shall deny the other, and the one of you shall curse the other; and your abode shall be hell fire, and there shall be none to deliver you. And Lot believed on him. And Abraham said, Verily I fly from my people, unto the place which my Lord hath commanded me; for he is mighty, the wise. And we gave him Isaac and Jacob; and we placed among his descendants the gift of prophecy and the scriptures: and we gave him his reward in this world; and in the next he shall be one of the righteous. We also sent Lot; when he said unto his people, Do ye commit filthiness which no creature hath committed before you? Do ye approach lustfully unto men, and lay wait in the highways, and commit wickedness in your assembly? And the answer of his people was no other than that they said, Bring down the vengeance of God upon us, if thou speakest truth. Lot said, O Lord, defend me against the corrupt people. And when our messengers came unto Abraham with good tidings, they said, We will surely destroy the inhabitants of this city; for the inhabitants thereof are unjust doers. Abraham answered, Verily Lot dwelleth there. They replied, We well know who dwelleth therein: we will surely deliver him and his family except his wife; she shall be one of those who remain behind. And when our messengers came unto Lot, he was troubled for them, and his arm was straitened concerning them. But they said, Fear not, neither be grieved; for we will deliver thee and thy family, except thy wife; for she shall be one of those who remain behind. We will surely bring down upon the inhabitants of this city vengeance from heaven, for that they have been wicked doers: and we have left thereof a manifest sign unto people who understand.

And unto the inhabitants of Madian we sent their brother Shoaib; and he said unto them, O my people, serve God, and expect the last day; and transgress not, acting corruptly in the earth. But they accused him of imposture; wherefore a storm from heaven assailed them, and in the morning they were found in their dwellings dead and prostrate. And we also destroyed the tribes of Ad and Thamud; and this is well known unto you from what yet remains of their dwellings. And Satan prepared their works for them, and turned them aside from the way of truth; although they were sagacious people. And we likewise destroyed Karun, and Pharaoh, and Haman. Moses came unto them with evident miracles; and they behaved themselves insolently in the earth: but they could not escape our vengeance. Every of them did we destroy in his sin. Against some of them we sent a violent wind: some of them did a terrible noise from heaven destroy: some of them did we cause the earth to swallow up: and some of them we drowned. Neither was God disposed to treat them unjustly; but they dealt unjustly with their own souls.

The likeness of those who take other patrons besides God is as the likeness of the spider, which maketh herself a house: but the weakest of all houses surely is the house of the spider; if they knew this. Moreover God knoweth what things they invoke, besides him; and he is the mighty, the wise. These similitudes do we propound unto men: but none understand them, except the wise. God hath created the heavens and the earth in truth: verily herein is a sign unto the true believers.

Rehearse that which hath been revealed unto thee of the book of the Koran: and be constant at prayer; for prayer preserveth a man from filthy crimes, and from that which is blamable; and the remembering of God is surely a most important duty. God knoweth that which ye do. Dispute not against those who have received the scriptures, unless in the mildest manner; except against such of them as behave injuriously toward you: and say, We believe in the revelation which hath been sent down unto us, and also in that which hath been sent down unto you; our God and your God is one, and unto him are we resigned. Thus have we sent down the book of the Koran unto thee: and they unto whom we have given the former scriptures believe therein; and of these Arabians also there is who believeth therein: and none reject our signs except the obstinate infidels. Thou couldst not read any book before this; neither couldst thou write it with thy right hand: then had the gainsayers justly doubted of the divine original thereof. But the same is evident signs in the breasts of those who have received understanding: for none reject our signs, except the unjust.

They say, Unless a sign be sent down unto him from his Lord, we will not believe. Answer, Signs are in the power of God alone; and I am no more than a public preacher. Is it not sufficient for them that we have sent down unto thee the book of the Koran, to be read unto them? Verily herein is a mercy, and an admonition unto people who believe. Say, God is a sufficient witness between me and you: he knoweth whatever is in heaven and earth; and those who believe in vain idols, and deny God, they shall perish. They will urge thee to hasten the punishment which they defy thee to bring down upon them: if there had not been a determined time for their respite, the punishment had come upon them before this; but it shall surely overtake them suddenly, and they shall not foresee it. They urge thee to bring down vengeance swiftly upon them: but hell shall surely encompass the unbelievers. On a certain day their punishment shall suddenly assail them, both from above them, and from under their feet; and God shall say, Taste ye the reward of that which ye have wrought.

O my servants who have believed, verily my earth is spacious; wherefore serve me. Every soul shall taste death: afterward shall ye return unto us; and as for those who shall have believed, and wrought righteousness, we will surely lodge them in a higher apartment of paradise; rivers shall flow beneath them, and they shall continue therein forever. How excellent will be the reward of the workers of righteousness; who persevere with patience, and put their trust in their Lord! How many beasts are there, which provide not their food? It is God who provideth food for them and for you;

and he both heareth and knoweth. Verily, if thou ask the
Meccans, who hath created the heavens and the earth, and
hath obliged the sun and the moon to serve in their courses;
they will answer, God. How therefore do they lie, in
acknowledging of other gods? God maketh abundant provision for such of his servants as he pleaseth; and is sparing
unto him, if he pleaseth: and is sparing unto him, if he
pleaseth: for God knoweth all things. Verily if thou ask
them, Who sendeth rain from heaven, and thereby quickeneth
the earth, after it hath been dead; they will answer, God.
Say, God be praised! But the greater part of them do not
understand. This present life is no other than a toy and a
plaything; but the future mansion of paradise is life indeed:
if they knew this, they would not prefer the former to the latter. When they sail in a ship, they call upon God, sincerely
exhibiting unto him the true religion: but when he bringeth
them safe to land, behold, they return to their idolatry; to
show themselves ungrateful for that which we have bestowed
on them, and that they may enjoy the delights of this life; but
they shall hereafter know the issue. Do they not see that we
have made the territory of Mecca an inviolable and secure asylum, when men are spoiled in the countries round about them?
Do they therefore believe in that which is vain, and acknowledge not the goodness of God? But who is more unjust than
he who deviseth a lie against God, or denieth the truth, when
it hath come unto him? Is there not in hell an abode for the
unbelievers? Whoever do their utmost endeavor to promote
our true religion, we will direct them into our ways.

CHAPTER XXX

ENTITLED, THE GREEKS;[1] REVEALED AT MECCA

IN THE NAME OF THE MOST MERCIFUL GOD

A. L. M. The Greeks have been overcome by the Per-

[1] The original word is al Rum; by which the later Greeks, or subjects
of the Constantinopolitan empire, are here meant; though the Arabs
give the same name also to the Romans and other Europeans.

sians,[2] in the nearest part of the land; but after their defeat, they shall overcome the others in their turn, within a few years. Unto God belongeth the disposal of this matter, both for what is past, and for what is to come: and on that day shall the believers rejoice in the success granted by God; for he granteth success unto whom he pleaseth, and he is the mighty, the merciful. This is the promise of God: God will not act contrary to his promise; but the greater part of men know not the veracity of God. They know the outward appearance of this present life; but they are careless as to the life to come. Do they not consider within themselves that

[2] The accomplishment of the prophecy contained in this passage, which is very famous among the Mohammedans, being insisted on by their doctors as a convincing proof that the Koran really came down from heaven, it may be excusable to be a little particular.

The passage is said to have been revealed on occasion of a great victory obtained by the Persians over the Greeks, the news whereof coming to Mecca, the infidels became strangely elated, and began to abuse Mohammed and his followers, imagining that this success of the Persians, who, like themselves, were idolaters, and supposed to have no scriptures, against the Christians, who pretended as well as Mohammed to worship one God, and to have divine scriptures, was an earnest of their own future successes against the prophet and those of his religion: to check which vain hopes, it was foretold, in the words of the text, that how improbable soever it might seem, yet the scale should be turned in a few years, and the vanquished Greeks prevail as remarkably against the Persians.

History informs us that the successes of Khosru Parviz, King of Persia, who carried on a terrible war against the Greek Empire, were very great, and continued in an uninterrupted course for two and twenty years. Particularly in the year of Christ 615, about the beginning of the sixth year before the Hegira the Persians, having the preceding year conquered Syria, made themselves masters of Palestine, and took Jerusalem; which seems to be that signal advantage gained over the Greeks mentioned in this passage, as agreeing best with the terms here used, and most likely to alarm the Arabs by reason of their vicinity to the scene of action: and there was so little probability, at that time, of the Greeks being able to retrieve their losses, much less to distress the Persians, that in the following years the arms of the latter made still further and more considerable progresses, and at length they laid siege to Constantinople itself. But in the year 625, in which the fourth year of the Hegira began, about ten years after the taking of Jerusalem, the Greeks, when it was least expected, gained a remarkable victory over the Persians, and not only obliged them to quit the territories of the empire, by carrying the war into their own country, but drove them to the last extremity, and spoiled the capital city al Madayen.

God hath not created the heavens and the earth, and whatever is between them, otherwise than in truth, and hath set them a determined period? Verily a great number of men reject the belief of their future meeting their Lord at the resurrection. Do they not pass through the earth, and see what hath been the end of those who were before them? They excelled the Meccans in strength, and broke up the earth, and inhabited it in greater affluence and prosperity than they inhabit the same: and their apostles came unto them with evident miracles; and God was not disposed to treat them unjustly, but they injured their own souls by their obstinate infidelity; and the end of those who had done evil was evil, because they charged the signs of God with falsehood and laughed the same to scorn. God produceth creatures, and will hereafter restore them to life: then shall ye return unto him. And on the day whereon the hour shall come, the wicked shall be struck dumb for despair; and they shall have no intercessors from among the idols which they associated with God; and they shall deny the false gods which they associated with him. On the day whereon the hour shall come, on that day shall the true believers and the infidels be separated: and they who shall have believed, and wrought righteousness, shall take their pleasure in a delightful meadow: but as for those who shall have disbelieved, and rejected our signs, and the meeting of the next life, they shall be delivered up to punishment.

Wherefore glorify God, when the evening overtaketh you, and when ye rise in the morning: and unto him be praise in heaven and earth; and at sunset, and when ye rest at noon. He bringeth forth the living out of the dead, and he bringeth forth the dead out of the living; and he quickeneth the earth after it hath been dead: and in like manner shall ye be brought forth from your graves. Of his signs one is that he hath created you of dust; and behold, ye are become men, spread over the face of the earth. And of his signs another is that he hath created for you, out of yourselves, wives, that ye may cohabit with them; and hath put love and compassion between you: verily herein are signs unto people who consider. And of his signs are also the creation of the heavens and the earth, and the variety of your languages, and of your complexions: verily herein are signs unto men of understanding. And of his signs are your sleeping by night and by day, and your seeking to provide for yourselves of his abundance: verily herein are signs unto people who harken. Of his signs others are that he showeth you the lightning, to strike terror, and to give hope of rain, and that he sendeth down water from heaven, and quickeneth thereby the earth, after it hath been dead: verily herein are signs unto people who understand.

And of his signs this also is one, namely that the heaven and the earth stand firm at his command: hereafter, when he shall call you out of the earth at one summons, behold, ye shall come forth. Unto him are subject whosoever are in the heavens and on earth: all are obedient unto him. It is he who originally produceth a creature, and afterward restoreth the same to life: and this is most easy with him. He justly challengeth the most exalted comparison, in heaven and earth; and he is the mighty, the wise. He propoundeth unto you a comparison taken from yourselves. Have ye, among the slaves whom your right hands possess, any partner in the substance which we have bestowed on you, so that ye become equal sharers therein with them, or that ye fear them as ye fear one another?

Thus do we distinctly explain our signs, unto people who understand. But those who act unjustly by attributing companions unto God, follow their own lusts, without knowledge: and who shall direct him whom God shall cause to err? They shall have none to help them. Wherefore be thou orthodox, and set thy face toward the true religion, the institution of God, to which he hath created mankind disposed: there is no change in what God hath created. This is the right religion; but the greater part of men know it not. And be ye turned unto him, and fear him, and be constant at prayer, and be not idolaters. Of those who have made a schism in their religion, and are divided into various sects; every sect rejoice in their own opinion. When adversity befalleth men, they call upon their Lord, turning unto him: afterward, when he hath caused them to taste of his mercy, behold, a part of them associate other deities with their Lord; to show themselves ungrateful for the favors which we have bestowed on them. Enjoy therefore the vain pleasures of this life; but hereafter shall ye know the consequence. Have we sent down unto them any authority, which speaketh of the false gods which they associate with him? When we cause men to taste mercy, they rejoice therein; but if evil befalleth them, for that which their hands have before committed, behold, they despair. Do they not see that God bestoweth provision abundantly on whom he pleaseth, and is sparing unto whom he pleaseth? Verily herein are signs unto people who believe.

Give unto him who is of kin to thee his reasonable due; and also to the poor and the stranger: this is better for those who seek the face of God; and they shall prosper. Whatever ye shall give in usury, to be an increase of men's substance, shall not be increased by the blessing of God: but whatever ye shall give in alms, for God's sake, they shall receive a twofold reward. It is God who hath created you, and hath provided food for you: hereafter will he cause you to die; and after that will he raise you again to life. Is there any of your false gods, who is able to do the least of these things? Praise be unto him; and far be he removed from what they associate with him! Corruptions hath appeared by land and by sea, for the crimes which men's hands have committed; that it might make them to taste a part of the fruits of that which they had wrought, that peradventure they might turn from their evil ways. Say, Go through the earth, and see what hath been the end of those who have been before you: the greater part of them were idolaters. Set thy face therefore toward the right religion, before the day cometh, which none can put back from God. On that day shall they be separated into two companies: whoever shall have been an unbeliever, on him shall his unbelief be charged; and whoever shall have done that which is right shall spread themselves couches of repose in paradise; that he may reward those who shall believe and work righteousness, of his abundant liberality; for he loveth not the unbelievers.

Of his signs one is, that he sendeth the winds, bearing welcome tidings of rain, that he may cause you to taste of his mercy; and that ships may sail at his command, that ye may seek to enrich yourselves of his abundance by commerce; and that ye may give thanks. We sent apostles, before thee, unto their respective people, and they came unto them with evident proofs: and we took vengeance on those who did wickedly; and it was incumbent on us to assist the true believers. It is God who sendeth the winds, and raiseth the clouds, and spreadeth the same in the heaven, as he pleaseth; and afterward disperseth the same: and thou mayest see the rain issuing from the midst thereof; and when he poureth the same down on such of his servants as he pleaseth, behold, they are filled with joy; although before it was sent down unto them, before such relief, they were despairing.

Consider therefore the traces of God's mercy; how he quickeneth the earth, after its state of death: verily the same will raise the dead; for he is almighty. Yet if we should send a blasting wind, and they should see their corn yellow and burned up, they would surely become ungrateful, after our former favors. Thou canst not make the dead to hear, neither canst thou make the deaf to hear thy call, when they retire and turn their backs; neither canst thou direct the blind out of their error: thou shalt make none to hear, except him who shall believe in our signs; for they are resigned unto us.

It is God who created you in weakness, and after weakness hath given you strength; and after strength, he will again reduce you to weakness, and gray hairs: he createth that which he pleaseth; and he is the wise, the powerful. On the day whereon the last hour shall come, the wicked will swear that they have not tarried above an hour: in like manner did they utter lies in their lifetime. But those on whom knowledge hath been bestowed, and faith, will say, Ye have tarried, according to the book of God, until the day of resurrection: for this is the day of resurrection; but ye knew it not. On that day their excuse shall not avail those who have acted unjustly; neither shall they be invited any more to make themselves acceptable unto God. And now have we propounded unto men, in this Koran, parables of every kind: yet if thou bring them a verse thereof, the unbelievers will surely say, Ye are no other than publishers of vain falsehoods. Thus hath God sealed up the hearts of those who believe not. But do thou, O Mohammed, persevere with constancy, for the promise of God is true; and let not those induce thee to waver, who have no certain knowledge.

CHAPTER XXXI

ENTITLED, LOKMAN; [1] REVEALED AT MECCA

IN THE NAME OF THE MOST MERCIFUL GOD

A. L. M. These are the signs of the wise book, a direction, and a mercy unto the righteous; who observe the appointed times of prayer, and give alms, and have firm assurance in the life to come: these are directed by their Lord, and they shall prosper. There is a man who purchaseth a ludicrous story,[2] that he may seduce men from the way of God, without knowledge, and may laugh the same to scorn: these shall suffer a shameful punishment. And when our signs are rehearsed unto him, he disdainfully turneth his back, as though he heard them not, as though there were a deafness in his ears: wherefore denounce unto him a grievous punishment. But they who shall believe and work righteousness shall enjoy gardens of pleasure; they shall continue therein forever: this is the certain promise of God; and he is the mighty, the wise. He hath created the heavens without visible pillars to sustain them, and hath thrown on the earth mountains firmly rooted, lest it should move with you; and he hath replenished the

---

[1] The chapter is so entitled from a person of this name mentioned therein.

[2] *I.e.*, Vain and silly fables. The passage was revealed, it is said, on occasion of al Nodar Ebn al Hareth, who, having brought from Persia the romance of Rostam and Isfandiyar, the two heroes of that country, recited it in the assemblies of the Koreish, highly extolling the power and splendor of the ancient Persian kings, and preferring their stories to those of Ad and Thamud, David and Solomon, and the rest which are told in the Koran. Some say that al Nodar bought singing girls, and carried them to those who were inclined to become Moslems to divert them from their purpose by songs and tales.

same with all kinds of beasts: and we send down rain from heaven, and cause every kind of noble vegetable to spring forth therein. This is the creation of God: show me now what they have created, who are worshiped besides him? verily the ungodly are in a manifest error.

We heretofore bestowed wisdom on Lokman,[3] and commanded him, saying, Be thou thankful unto God: for whoever is thankful shall be thankful to the advantage of his own soul; and if any shall be unthankful, verily God is self-sufficient, and worthy to be praised. And remember when Lokman said unto his son, as he admonished him, O my son, Give not a partner unto God; for polytheism is a great impiety. We have commanded man concerning his parents, (his mother carrieth him in her womb with weakness and faintness, and he is weaned in two years), saying, Be grateful unto me and to thy parents. Unto me shall all come to be judged. But if thy parents endeavor to prevail on thee to associate with me that concerning which thou hast no knowledge, obey them not: bear them company in this world in what shall be reasonable; but follow the way of him who sincerely turneth unto me. Hereafter unto me shall ye return, and then will I declare unto you that which ye have done. O my son, verily every matter, whether good or bad, though it be of the weight of a grain of mustard-seed, and be hidden in a rock, or in the

[3] The Arab writers say that Lokman was the son of Baura, who was the son or grandson of a sister or aunt of Job; and that he lived several centuries and to the time of David, with whom he was conversant in Palestine. According to the description they give of his person, he must have been deformed enough; for they say he was of a black complexion (whence some call him an Ethiopian), with thick lips and splay feet: but in return he received from God wisdom and eloquence in a great degree, which some pretend were given him in a vision, on his making choice of wisdom preferably to the gift of prophecy, either of which was offered him. The generality of the Mohammedans, therefore, hold him to have been no prophet, but only a wise man. As to his condition, they say he was a slave, but obtained his liberty on the following occasion: His master having one day given him a bitter melon to eat, he paid him such exact obedience as to eat it all; at which his master being surprised, asked him how he could eat so nauseous a fruit? To which he replied, it was no wonder that he should for once accept a bitter fruit from the same hand from which he had received so many favors.

heavens, or in the earth, God will bring the same to light; for God is clear-sighted and knowing. O my son, be constant at prayer, and command that which is just, and forbid that which is evil: and be patient under the afflictions which shall befall thee; for this is a duty absolutely incumbent on all men. Distort not thy face out of contempt to men, neither walk in the earth with insolence; for God loveth no arrogant, vainglorious person. And be moderate in thy pace: and lower thy voice; for the most ungrateful of all voices surely is the voice of asses.

Do ye not see that God hath subjected whatever is in heaven and on earth to your service, and hath abundantly poured on you his favors, both outwardly and inwardly? There are some men who dispute concerning God without knowledge, and without a direction, and without an enlightening book. And when it is said unto them, Follow that which God hath revealed; they answer, Nay, we will follow that which we found our fathers to practise. What, though the devil invite them to the torment of hell? Whoever resigneth himself unto God, being a worker of righteousness, taketh hold on a strong handle; and unto God belongeth the issue of all things. But whoever shall be an unbeliever, let not his unbelief grieve thee: unto us shall they return; then will we declare unto them that which they have done, for God knoweth the innermost parts of the breasts of men. We will suffer them to enjoy this world for a little while: afterward we will drive them to a severe punishment. If thou ask them who hath created the heavens and the earth, they will surely answer, God. Say, God be praised! But the greater part of them do not understand. Unto God belongeth whatever is in heaven and earth: for God is the self-sufficient, the praiseworthy. If whatever trees are in the earth were pens, and he should after that swell the sea into seven seas of ink, the words of God would not be exhausted; for God is mighty and wise. Your creation and your resuscitation are but as the creation and resuscitation of one soul: verily God both heareth and seeth.

Dost thou not see that God causeth the night to succeed

the day, and causeth the day to succeed the night, and compelleth the sun and the moon to serve you? Each of those luminaries hasteneth in its course to a determined period: and God is well acquainted with that which ye do. This is declared concerning the divine knowledge and power, for that God is the true Being, and for that whatever ye invoke, besides him, is vanity; and for that God is the high, the great God. Dost thou not see that the ships run in the sea, through the favor of God, that he may show you of his signs? Verily herein are signs, unto every patient, grateful person. When waves cover them, like overshadowing clouds, they call upon God, exhibiting the pure religion unto him; but when he bringeth them safe to land, there is of them who halteth between the true faith and idolatry. Howbeit, none rejecteth our signs, except every perfidious, ungrateful person.

O men, fear your Lord, and dread the day whereon a father shall not make satisfaction for his son, neither shall a son make satisfaction for his father at all: the promise of God is assuredly true. Let not this present life, therefore, deceive you; neither let the deceiver deceive you concerning God. Verily the knowledge of the hour of judgment is with God: and he causeth the rain to descend, at his own appointed time; and he knoweth what is in the wombs of females. No soul knoweth what it shall gain on the morrow; neither doth any soul know in what land it shall die: [4] but God is knowing and fully acquainted with all things.

[4] As to the last particular, al Beidawi relates the following story: The angel of death passing once by Solomon in a visible shape, and looking at one who was sitting with him, the man asked who he was, and upon Solomon's acquainting him that it was the angel of death, said, He seems to want me; wherefore order the wind to carry me from hence into India; which being accordingly done, the angel said to Solomon, I looked so earnestly at the man out of wonder; because I was commanded to take his soul in India, and found him.with thee in Palestine.

CHAPTER XXXII

ENTITLED, ADORATION;[1] REVEALED AT MECCA

IN THE NAME OF THE MOST MERCIFUL GOD

A. L. M. The revelation of this book, there is no doubt thereof, is from the Lord of all creatures. Will they say, Mohammed hath forged it? Nay, it is the truth from thy Lord, that thou mayest preach to a people, unto whom no preacher hath come before thee; peradventure they will be directed. It is God who hath created the heavens and the earth, and whatever is between them, in six days; and then ascended his throne. Ye have no patron or intercessor besides him. Will ye not therefore consider? He governeth all things from heaven even to the earth: hereafter shall they return unto him, on the day whose length shall be a thousand years, of those which ye compute. This is he who knoweth the future and the present; the mighty, the merciful. It is he who hath made everything which he hath created exceeding good; and first created man of clay, and afterward made his posterity of an extract of despicable water; and then formed him into proper shape, and breathed of his spirit into him; and hath given you the senses of hearing and seeing, and hearts to understand. How small thanks do ye return! And they say, When we shall lie hidden in the earth, shall we be raised thence a new creature? Yea, they deny the meeting of their Lord at the resurrection. Say, The angel of death, who is set over you, shall cause you to die: then shall ye be brought back unto your Lord. If thou couldst see, when the wicked shall bow down their heads before their Lord, saying, O Lord, we have seen and have heard: suffer us therefore to return into the world, and we will work that which is right; since we are now certain of the truth of what hath been preached to us: thou wouldst see an amazing sight. If we had pleased, we had certainly given unto every soul its direction: but the word which hath proceeded from me

[1] The title is taken from the middle of the chapter, where the believers are said " to fall down adoring."

must necessarily be fulfilled, when I said, Verily I will fill hell with genii and men, altogether. Taste therefore the torment prepared for you, because ye have forgotten the coming of this your day, we also have forgotten you; taste therefore a punishment of eternal duration, for that which ye have wrought.

Verily they only believe in our signs, who, when they are warned thereby, fall down adoring, and celebrate the praise of their Lord, and are not elated with pride: their sides are raised from their beds, calling on their Lord with fear and with hope; and they distribute alms out of what we have bestowed on them. No soul knoweth the complete satisfaction which is secretly prepared for them, as a reward for that which they have wrought. Shall he, therefore, who is a true believer, be as he who is an impious transgressor? They shall not be held equal. As to those who believe and do that which is right, they shall have gardens of perpetual abode, an ample recompense for that which they shall have wrought: but as for those who impiously transgress, their abode shall be hell fire; so often as they shall endeavor to get thereout, they shall be dragged back into the same, and it shall be said unto them, Taste ye the torment of hell fire, which ye rejected as a falsehood. And we will cause them to taste the nearer punishment of this world, besides the more grievous punishment of the next; peradventure they will repent. Who is more unjust than he who is warned by the signs of his Lord, and then turneth aside from the same? We will surely take vengeance on the wicked.

We heretofore delivered the book of the law unto Moses; wherefore be not thou in doubt as to the revelation thereof: and we ordained the same to be a direction unto the children of Israel; and we appointed teachers from among them, who should direct the people at our command, when they had persevered with patience, and had firmly believed in our signs. Verily thy Lord will judge between them, on the day of resurrection, concerning that wherein they have disagreed. Is it not known unto them how many generations we have destroyed before them, through whose dwelling they walk?

Verily herein are signs: will they not therefore harken? Do they not see that we drive rain unto a land bare of grass and parched up, and thereby produce corn, of which their cattle eat, and themselves also? Will they not therefore regard? The infidels say to the true believers, When will this decision be made between us, if ye speak truth? Answer, On the day of that decision, the faith of those who shall have disbelieved shall not avail them; neither shall they be respited any longer. Wherefore avoid them, and expect the issue: verily they expect to obtain some advantage over thee.

CHAPTER XXXIII

ENTITLED, THE CONFEDERATES; [1] REVEALED AT MEDINA

IN THE NAME OF THE MOST MERCIFUL GOD

O prophet, fear God, and obey not the unbelievers and the hypocrites: verily God is knowing and wise. But follow that which is revealed unto thee from thy Lord; for God is well acquainted with that which ye do: and put thy trust in God; for God is a sufficient protector. God hath not given a man two hearts within him; neither hath he made your wives (some of whom ye divorce, regarding them thereafter as your mothers) your true mothers; nor hath he made your adopted sons your true sons.[2] This is your saying in your mouths;

[1] Part of this chapter was revealed on occasion of the war of the ditch, which happened in the fifth year of the Hegira, when Medina was besieged, for above twenty days, by the joint and confederate forces of several Jewish tribes, and of the inhabitants of Mecca, Najd, and Tehama, at the instigation of the Jews of the tribe of Nadhir, who had been driven out of their settlement near Medina, by Mohammed, the year before.

[2] This passage was revealed to abolish two customs among the old Arabs. The first was their manner of divorcing their wives, when they had no mind to let them go out of their house, or to marry again: and this the husband did by saying to the woman, "Thou art henceforward to me as the back of my mother"; after which words pronounced he abstained from her bed, and regarded her in all respects as his mother; and she became related to all his kindred in the same degree as if she had been really so. The other custom was the holding their adopted sons to be as nearly related to them as their natural sons, so that the same impediments of marriage arose from that supposed relation, in the prohibited degrees, as it would have done in the case of a genuine son. The

but God speaketh the truth; and he directeth the right way. Call such as are adopted the sons of their natural fathers: this will be more just in the sight of God. And if ye know not their fathers, let them be as your brethren in religion, and your companions: and it shall be no crime in you, that ye err in this matter; but that shall be criminal which your hearts purposely design; for God is gracious and merciful. The prophet is nigher unto the true believers than their own souls; and his wives are their mothers.[3] Those who are related by consanguinity are nigher of kin the one of them unto the others, according to the book of God, than the other true believers, and the Mohajerun: unless that ye do what is fitting and reasonable to your relations in general. This is written in the book of God.[4] . . .

O prophet, say unto thy wives, If ye seek this present life, and the pomp thereof, come, I will make a handsome provision for you, and I will dismiss you with an honorable dismission;[5] but if ye seek God and his apostle, and the life to come, verily God hath prepared for such of you as work righteousness a great reward. O wives of the prophet, who-

latter Mohammed had a peculiar reason to abolish — *viz.*, his marrying the divorced wife of his freedman Zeid, who was also his adopted son. By the declaration which introduces this passage, that God "has not given a man two hearts," is meant, that a man can not have the same affection for supposed parents and adopted children as for those who are really so.

[3] Though the spiritual relation between Mohammed and his people, declared in the preceding words, created no impediment to prevent his taking to wife such women among them as he thought fit; yet the commentators are of opinion that they are here forbidden to marry any of his wives.

[4] In the preserved table, or the Koran; or, as others suppose, in the Pentateuch.

[5] This passage was revealed on Mohammed's wives asking for more sumptuous clothes, and an additional allowance for their expenses; and he had no sooner received it than he gave them their option, either to continue with him or to be divorced, beginning with Ayesha, who chose God and his apostle, and the rest followed her example; upon which the prophet thanked them, and the following words were revealed, *viz.*, "It shall not be lawful for thee to take other women to wife hereafter," etc. From hence some have concluded that a wife who has her option given her, and chooses to stay with her husband, shall not be divorced, though others are of a contrary opinion.

soever of you shall commit a manifest wickedness, the punishment thereof shall be doubled unto her twofold; and this is easy with God: but whosoever of you shall be obedient unto God and his apostle, and shall do that which is right, we will give her her reward twice, and we have prepared for her an honorable provision in paradise. O wives of the prophet, ye are not as other women: if ye fear God, be not too complaisant in speech, lest he should covet, in whose heart is a disease of incontinence: but speak the speech which is convenient. And sit still in your houses; and set not out yourselves with the ostentation of the former time of ignorance: and observe the appointed times of prayer, and give alms; and obey God and his apostle; for God desireth only to remove from you the abomination of vanity, since ye are the household of the prophet, and to purify you by a perfect purification.

And remember that which is read in your houses, of the signs of God, and of the wisdom revealed in the Koran; for God is clear-sighted, and well acquainted with your actions. Verily the Moslems of either sex, and the true believers of either sex, and the devout men, and the devout women, and the men of veracity, and the women of veracity, and the patient men, and the patient women, and the humble men, and the humble women, and the alms-givers of either sex, and the men who fast, and the women who fast, and the chaste men, and the chaste women, and those of either sex who remember God frequently; for them hath God prepared forgiveness and a great reward. It is not fit for a true believer of either sex, when God and his apostle have decreed a thing, that they should have the liberty of choosing a different matter of their own: and whoever is disobedient unto God and his apostle surely erreth with a manifest error. And remember when thou saidst to him unto whom God had been gracious, and on whom thou also hadst conferred favors,[6] Keep thy wife to thy-

---

[6] Zeid was of the tribe of Calb, a branch of the Khodaites, descended from Hamyar, the son of Saba; and being taken in his childhood by a party of freebooters, was bought by Mohammed, or, as others say, by his wife Khadijah before she married him. Some years after, Haretha, hearing where his son was, took a journey to Mecca, and offered a considerable sum for his ransom; whereupon, Mohammed said, "Let Zeid

self, and fear God: and thou didst conceal that in thy mind which God had determined to discover,[7] and didst fear men; whereas it was more just that thou shouldst fear God. But when Zeid [8] had determined the matter concerning her, and had resolved to divorce her, we joined her in marriage unto thee; [9] lest a crime should be charged on the true believers, in marrying the wives of their adopted sons, when they have determined the matter concerning them: and the command of God is to be performed. No crime is to be charged on the prophet, as to what God hath allowed him, conformable to the ordinance of God with regard to those who preceded him (for the command of God is a determinate decree), who brought the messages of God, and feared him, and feared none besides God: and God is a sufficient accountant. Mohammed is not the father of any man among you; but the apostle of God, and the seal of the prophets: and God knoweth all things.

come hither; and if he chooses to go with you, take him without ransom: but if it be his choice to stay with me, why should I not keep him?" And Zeid being come, declared that he would stay with his master, who treated him as if he were his only son. Mohammed no sooner heard this, but he took Zeid by the hand, and led him to the black stone of the Kaaba, where he publicly adopted him for his son, and constituted him his heir, with which the father acquiesced, and returned home well satisfied. From this time Zeid was called the son of Mohammed, till the publication of Islam, after which the prophet gave him to wife Zeinab.

[7] Some years after his marriage, Mohammed, going to Zeid's house on some affair, and not finding him at home, accidentally cast his eyes on Zeinab, who was then in a dress which discovered her beauty to advantage, and was so smitten at the sight that he could not forbear crying out, "God be praised, who turneth the hearts of men as he pleaseth!" This Zeinab failed not to acquaint her husband with on his return home; whereupon, Zeid, after mature reflection, thought he could do no less than part with his wife in favor of his benefactor, and therefore resolved to divorce her, and acquainted Mohammed with his resolution; but he, apprehending the scandal it might raise, offered to dissuade him from it, and endeavored to stifle the flames which inwardly consumed him; but at length, his love for her being authorized by this revelation, he acquiesced, and after the term of her divorce was expired, married her in the latter end of the fifth year of the Hegira.

[8] It is observed that this is the only person, of all Mohammed's companions, whose name is mentioned in the Koran.

[9] Whence Zeinab used to vaunt herself above the prophet's other wives, saying that God had made the match between Mohammed and herself, whereas their matches were made by their relations.

O true believers, remember God with a frequent remembrance, and celebrate his praise morning and evening. It is he who is gracious unto you, and his angels intercede for you, that he may lead you forth from darkness into light; and he is merciful toward the true believers. Their salutation, on the day whereon they shall meet him, shall be, Peace! and he hath prepared for them an honorable recompense. O prophet, verily we have sent thee to be a witness, and a bearer of good tidings, and a denouncer of threats, and an inviter unto God, through his good pleasure, and a shining light. Bear good tidings therefore unto the true believers, that they shall receive great abundance from God. And obey not the unbelievers and hypocrites, and mind not their evil treatment: but trust in God; and God is a sufficient protector.

O true believers, when ye marry women who are believers, and afterward put them away before ye have touched them, there is no term prescribed you to fulfil toward them after their divorce; but make them a present, and dismiss them freely, with an honorable dismission. O prophet, we have allowed thee thy wives unto whom thou hast given their dower, and also the slaves which thy right hand possesseth, of the booty which God hath granted thee; and the daughters of thy uncle, and the daughters of thy aunts, both on thy father's side and on thy mother's side, who have fled with thee from Mecca, and any other believing woman, if she give herself unto the prophet; in case the prophet desireth to take her to wife. This is a peculiar privilege granted unto thee, above the rest of the true believers. We know what we have ordained them concerning their wives, and the slaves whom their right hands possess: lest it should be deemed a crime in thee to make use of the privilege granted thee; for God is gracious and merciful. Thou mayest postpone the turn of such of thy wives as thou shalt please, in being called to thy bed; and thou mayest take unto thee her whom thou shalt please, and her whom thou shalt desire of those whom thou shalt have before rejected: and it shall be no crime in thee.[10] This will be

[10] By this passage some further privileges were granted unto Mohammed; for, whereas other men are obliged to carry themselves equally

more easy, that they may be entirely content, and may not be grieved, but may be well pleased with what thou shalt give every of them: God knoweth whatever is in your hearts; and God is knowing and gracious. It shall not be lawful for thee to take other women to wife hereafter, nor to exchange any of thy wives for them, although their beauty please thee; except the slaves whom thy right hand shall possess: and God observeth all things.

O true believers, enter not the houses of the prophet, unless it be permitted you to eat meat with him, without waiting his convenient time: but when ye are invited, then enter. And when ye shall have eaten, disperse yourselves; and stay not to enter into familiar discourse: for this incommodeth the prophet. He is ashamed to bid you depart; but God is not ashamed of the truth. And when ye ask of the prophet's wives what ye may have occasion for, ask it of them from behind a curtain. This will be more pure for your hearts and their hearts. Neither is it fit for you to give any uneasiness to the apostle of God, or to marry his wives after him forever: for this would be a grievous thing in the sight of God. Whether ye divulge a thing, or conceal it, verily God knoweth all things. It shall be no crime in them, as to their fathers, or their sons, or their brothers, or their brothers' sons, or their sisters' sons, or their women, or the slaves which their right hands possess, if they speak to them unveiled: and fear ye God; for God is witness of all things. Verily God and his angels bless the prophet.

O true believers, do ye also bless him, and salute him with a respectful salutation. As to those who offend God and his apostle, God shall curse them in this world and in the next; and he hath prepared for them a shameful punishment. And they who shall injure the true believers of either sex, without

toward their wives, in case they had more than one, particularly as to the duties of the marriage-bed, to which each has a right to be called in her turn (which right was acknowledged in the most early ages), and can not take again a wife whom they have divorced the third time, till she has been married to another and divorced by him, the prophet was left absolutely at liberty to deal with them in these and other respects as he thought fit.

their deserving it, shall surely bear the guilt of calumny and a manifest injustice.

O prophet, speak unto thy wives, and thy daughters, and the wives of the true believers, that they cast their outer garments over them when they walk abroad; this will be more proper, that they may be known to be matrons of reputation, and may not be affronted by unseemly words or actions. God is gracious and merciful. Verily if the hypocrites, and those in whose hearts is an infirmity, and they who raise disturbances in Medina, do not desist; we will surely stir thee up against them, to chastise them: henceforth they shall not be suffered to dwell near thee therein, except for a little time, and being accursed; wherever they are found they shall be taken, and killed with a general slaughter, according to the sentence of God concerning those who have been before; and thou shalt not find any change in the sentence of God.

Men will ask thee concerning the approach of the last hour: answer, Verily the knowledge thereof is with God alone; and he will not inform thee: peradventure the hour is nigh at hand. Verily God hath cursed the infidels, and hath prepared for them a fierce fire, wherein they shall remain forever: they shall find no patron or defender. On the day whereon their faces shall be rolled in hell fire, they shall say, Oh that we had obeyed God, and had obeyed his apostle! And they shall say, O Lord, verily we have obeyed our lords and our great men; and they have seduced us from the right way. O Lord, give them the double of our punishment; and curse them with a heavy curse!

O true believers, be not as those who injured Moses; but God cleared him from the scandal which they had spoken concerning him; and he was of great consideration in God's sight.

O true believers, fear God, and speak words well directed; that God may correct your works for you, and may forgive you your sins: and whoever shall obey God and his apostle shall enjoy great felicity. We proposed the faith unto the heavens, and the earth, and the mountains: and they refused to undertake the same, and were afraid thereof; but man undertook it: verily he was unjust to himself, and foolish: that

God may punish the hypocritical men and the hypocritical women, and the idolaters, and the idolatresses; and that God may be turned unto the true believers, both men and women; for God is gracious and merciful.

CHAPTER XXXIV

ENTITLED, SABA; REVEALED AT MECCA

IN THE NAME OF THE MOST MERCIFUL GOD

Praise be to God, unto whom belongeth whatever is in the heavens and on earth: and unto him be praise in the world to come; for he is wise and intelligent. He knoweth whatsoever entereth into the earth, and whatsoever cometh out of the same, and whatsoever descendeth from heaven, and whatsoever ascendeth thereto: and he is merciful and ready to forgive. The unbelievers say, The hour of judgment will not come unto us. Answer, Yea, by my Lord, it will surely come unto you; it is he who knoweth the hidden secret: the weight of an ant, either in heaven or in earth, is not absent from him, nor anything lesser than this, or greater, but the same is written in the perspicuous book of his decrees; that he may recompense those who shall have believed and wrought righteousness: they shall receive pardon and an honorable provision. But they who endeavor to render our signs of none effect shall receive a punishment of painful torment. Those unto whom knowledge hath been given, see that the book which hath been revealed unto thee from thy Lord is the truth, and directeth into the glorious and laudable way. The unbelievers say to one another, Shall we show you a man who shall prophesy unto you, that when ye shall have been dispersed with a total dispersion, ye shall be raised a new creature? He hath forged a lie concerning God, or rather he is distracted. But they who believe not in the life to come shall fall into punishment and a wide error. Have they not therefore considered what is before them, and what is behind them, of the heaven and the earth? If we please, we will cause the earth to open and swallow them up, or will cause a piece of the heaven to fall upon them: verily herein is a sign unto every servant, who turneth unto God.

We heretofore bestowed on David excellence from us: and we said, O mountains, sing alternate praises with him; and we obliged the birds also to join therein. And we softened the iron for him, saying, Make thereof complete coats of mail, and rightly dispose the small plates which compose the same: and work ye righteousness, O family of David: for I see that which ye do. And we made the wind subject unto Solomon: it blew in the morning for a month, and in the evening for a month. And we made a fountain of molten brass to flow for him. And some of the genii were obliged to work in his presence, by the will of his Lord; and whoever of them turned aside from our command, we will cause him to taste the pain of hell fire. They made for him whatever he pleased, of palaces, and statues, and large dishes like fishponds, and caldrons standing firm on their trevets; and we said, Work righteousness, O family of David, with thanksgiving; for few of my servants are thankful. And when we had decreed that Solomon should die, nothing discovered his death unto them, except the creeping thing of the earth, which gnawed his staff. And when his body fell down, the genii plainly perceived that if they had known that which is secret, they had not continued in a vile punishment.

The descendants of Saba had heretofore a sign in their dwellings; namely, two gardens, on the right hand and on the left: and it was said unto them, Eat ye of the provision of your Lord, and give thanks unto him; ye have a good country and a gracious Lord. But they turned aside from what we had commanded them: wherefore we sent against them the inundation of al Arem, and we changed their two gardens for them into two gardens producing bitter fruit, and tamarisks, and some little fruit of the lote-tree. This we gave them in reward, because they were ungrateful: is any thus rewarded except the ungrateful? And we placed between them and the cities which we have blessed, cities situate near each other; and we made the journey easy between them, saying, Travel through the same by night and by day in security. But they said, O Lord, put a greater distance between our journeys: and they were unjust unto themselves; and we made them the subject of discourse, and dispersed them with a total dispersion. Verily herein are signs unto every patient, grateful person. And Eblis found his opinion of them to be true: and they followed him, except a party of the true believers: and he had no power over them, unless to tempt them, that we might know him who believed in the life to come, from him who doubted thereof. Thy Lord observeth all things.

Say unto the idolaters, Call upon those whom ye imagine to be gods, besides God, they are not masters of the weight of an ant in heaven or on earth, neither have they any share in the creation or government of the same; nor is any of them assistant to him therein. No intercession will be of service in his presence, except the intercession of him to whom he shall grant permission to intercede for others: and they shall wait in suspense until, when the terror shall be taken off from their hearts, they shall say to one another, What doth your Lord say? They shall answer, That which is just: and he is the high, the great God. Say, Who provideth food for you from heaven and earth? Answer, God: and either we, or ye, follow the true direction, or are in a manifest error. Say, Ye shall not be examined concerning what we shall have committed: neither shall we be examined concerning what ye shall have done. Say, Our Lord will assemble us together at the last day; then will he judge between us with truth; and he is the judge, the knowing. Say, show me those whom ye have joined as partners with him? Nay; rather he is the mighty, the wise God. We have not sent thee otherwise than unto mankind in general, a bearer of good tidings, and a denouncer of threats: but the greater part of men do not understand. And they say, When will this threat be fulfilled, if ye speak truth? Answer, A threat is denounced unto you of a day which ye shall not retard one hour, neither shall ye hasten. The unbelievers say, We will by no means believe in this Koran, nor in that which hath been revealed before it.

But if thou couldst see when the unjust doers shall be set before their Lord! They will iterate discourse with one

another: those who were esteemed weak shall say unto those
who behaved themselves arrogantly, Had it not been for you,
verily we had been true believers.   They who behaved themselves arrogantly shall say unto those who were esteemed weak,
Did we turn you aside from the true direction, after it had
come unto you?   On the contrary, ye acted wickedly of your
own free choice.   And they who were esteemed weak shall
say unto those who behave with arrogance, Nay, but the
crafty plot which ye devised by night and by day occasioned
our ruin, when ye commanded us that we should not believe
in God, and that we should set up other gods as equal unto
him.   And they shall conceal their repentance, after they
shall have seen the punishment prepared for them.   And we
will put yokes on the necks of those who shall have disbelieved: shall they be rewarded any otherwise than according to
what they shall have wrought?   We have sent no warner unto
any city, but the inhabitants thereof who lived in affluence
said, Verily we believe not that with which ye are sent.   And
those of Mecca also say, We abound in riches and children
more than ye, and we shall not be punished thereafter.   Answer, Verily my Lord will bestow provision in abundance unto
whom he pleaseth, and will be sparing unto whom he pleaseth:
but the greater part of men know not this.   Neither your
riches nor your children are the things which shall cause you
to draw nigh unto us with a near approach: only whoever
believeth, and worketh righteousness, they shall receive a
double reward for that which they have wrought; and they
shall dwell in security, in the upper apartments of paradise.
But they who shall endeavor to render our signs of none effect
shall be delivered up to punishment.   Say, Verily my Lord
will bestow provision in abundance unto whom he pleaseth of
his servants, and will be sparing unto whom he pleaseth: and
whatever thing ye shall give in alms, he will return it; and he
is the best provider of food.   On a certain day he shall gather
them all together: then shall he say unto the angels, Did these
worship you?   And the angels shall answer, God forbid! thou
art our friend, and not these: but they worshiped devils; the
greater part of them believed in them.   On this day the one

of you shall not be able either to profit or to hurt the other. And we will say unto those who have acted unjustly, Taste ye the pain of hell fire, which ye rejected as a falsehood.

When our evident signs are read unto them, they say of thee, O Mohammed, This is no other than a man, who seeketh to turn you aside from the gods which your fathers worshiped. And they say of the Koran, This is no other than a lie blasphemously forged. And the unbelievers say of the truth, when it is come unto them, This is no other than manifest sorcery: yet we have given them no books of scripture wherein to exercise themselves, nor have we sent unto them any warner before thee. They who were before them in like manner accused their prophets of imposture: but these have not arrived unto the tenth part of the riches and strength which we had bestowed on the former: and they accused my apostles of imposture; and how severe was my vengeance! Say, Verily I advise you unto one thing, namely, that ye stand before God by two and two, and singly; and then consider seriously, and you will find that there is no madness in your companion Mohammed: he is no other than a warner unto you, sent before a severe punishment. Say, I ask not of you any reward for my preaching; it is your own, either to give or not: my reward is to be expected from God alone; and he is witness over all things. Say, Verily my Lord sendeth down the truth to his prophets: he is the knower of secrets. Say, Truth is come, and falsehood is vanished, and shall not return any more. Say, If I err, verily I shall err only against my own soul: but if I be rightly directed, it will be by that which my Lord revealeth unto me; for he is ready to hear, and nigh unto those who call upon him. If thou couldst see, when the unbelievers shall tremble, and shall find no refuge, and shall be taken from a near place, and shall say, We believe in him! But how shall they receive the faith from a distant place: since they had before denied him, and reviled the mysteries of faith, from a distant place? And a bar shall be placed between them and that which they shall desire; as it hath been done with those who behaved like them heretofore: because they have been in a doubt which hath caused scandal.

CHAPTER XXXV.

ENTITLED, THE CREATOR: REVEALED AT MECCA

IN THE NAME OF THE MOST MERCIFUL GOD

Praise be unto God, the Creator of heaven and earth; who maketh the angels his messengers, furnished with two, and three, and four pair of wings:[1] God maketh what he pleaseth unto his creatures; for God is almighty. The mercy which God shall freely bestow on mankind, there is none who can withhold; and what he shall withhold, there is none who can bestow, besides him: and he is the mighty, the wise. O men, remember the favor of God toward you: is there any creator, besides God, who provideth food for you from heaven and earth? There is no God but he: how therefore are ye turned aside from acknowledging his unity? If they accuse thee of imposture, apostles before thee have also been accused of imposture; and unto God shall all things return.

O men, verily the promise of God is true: let not therefore the present life deceive you, neither let the deceiver deceive you concerning God: for Satan is an enemy unto you; wherefore hold him for an enemy: he only inviteth his confederates to be the inhabitants of hell. For those who believe not there is prepared a severe torment: but for those who shall believe and do that which is right is prepared mercy and a great reward. Shall he therefore for whom his evil work hath been prepared, and who imagineth it to be good, be as he who is rightly disposed and discerneth the truth? Verily God will cause to err whom he pleaseth, and will direct whom he pleaseth. Let not thy soul therefore be spent in sighs for their sakes, on account of their obstinacy; for God well knoweth that which they do.

It is God who sendeth the winds, and raiseth a cloud; and

[1] That is, some angels have a greater and some a lesser number of wings, according to their different orders, the words not being designed to express the particular number. Gabriel is said to have appeared to Mohammed, on the night he made his journey to heaven, with no less than six hundred wings.

THE MOHAMMEDANS' CENTRAL SPOT OF EARTH.

The rock enshrined within the Temple of Jerusalem, the scene of Abraham's sacrifice, sacred to Jews, Christians, and Mohammedans.

we drive the same unto a dead country, and thereby quicken the earth after it hath been dead: so shall the resurrection be. Whoever desireth excellence, unto God doth all excellence belong: unto him ascendeth the good speech; and the righteous work will he exalt. But as for them who devise wicked plots, they shall suffer a severe punishment; and the device of those men shall be rendered vain. God created you first of the dust, and afterward of seed: and he hath made you man and wife. No female conceiveth, or bringeth forth, but with his knowledge. Nor is anything added unto the age of him whose life is prolonged, neither is anything diminished from his age, but the same is written in the book of God's decrees. Verily this is easy with God. The two seas are not to be held in comparison: this is fresh and sweet, pleasant to drink; but that is salt and bitter: yet out of each of them ye eat fish, and take ornaments for you to wear. Thou seest the ships also plowing the waves thereof, that ye may seek to enrich yourselves by commerce, of the abundance of God: peradventure ye will be thankful. He causeth the night to succeed the day, and he causeth the day to succeed the night; and he obligeth the sun and the moon to perform their services: each of them runneth an appointed course. This is God, your Lord: his is the kingdom. But the idols which ye invoke besides him have not the power even over the skin of a date-stone: if ye invoke them, they will not hear your calling; and although they should hear, yet they would not answer you. On the day of resurrection they shall disclaim your having associated them with God: and none shall declare unto thee the truth, like one who is well acquainted therewith.

O men, ye have need of God; but God is self-sufficient, and to be praised. If he pleaseth, he can take you away, and produce a new creature in your stead: neither will this be difficult with God. A burdened soul shall not bear the burden of another: and if a heavy-burdened soul call on another to bear part of its burden, no part thereof shall be borne by the person who shall be called on, although he be ever so nearly related. Thou shalt admonish those who fear their Lord in secret, and are constant at prayer: and whoever cleanseth himself from the guilt of disobedience cleanseth himself to the advantage of his own soul; for all shall be assembled before God at the last day. The blind and the seeing shall not be held equal; neither darkness and light; nor the cool shade and the scorching wind: neither shall the living and the dead be held equal. God shall cause him to hear whom he pleaseth: but thou shalt not make those to hear who are in their graves. Thou art no other than a preacher: verily we have sent thee with truth, a bearer of good tidings, and a denouncer of threats. There hath been no nation, but a preacher hath in past times been conversant among them: if they charge thee with imposture, they who were before them likewise charged their apostles with imposture. Their apostles came unto them with evident miracles, and with divine writings, and with the enlightening book: afterward I chastised those who were unbelievers, and how severe was my vengeance! Dost thou not see that God sendeth down rain from heaven, and that we thereby produce fruits of various colors? In the mountain also there are some tracts white and red, of various colors; and other are of a deep black: and of men, and beasts, and cattle there are whose colors are in like manner various. Such only of his servants fear God as are endued with understanding: verily God is mighty and ready to forgive.

Verily they who read the book of God, and are constant at prayer, and give alms out of what we have bestowed on them, both in secret and openly, hope for a merchandise which shall not perish: that God may fully pay them their wages, and make them a superabundant addition of his liberality; for he is ready to forgive the faults of his servants, and to requite their endeavors. That which we have revealed unto thee of the book of the Koran, is the truth, confirming the scriptures which were revealed before it; for God knoweth and regardeth his servants.

And we have given the book of the Koran in heritage unto such of our servants as we have chosen: of them there is one who injureth his own soul; and there is another of them who keepeth the middle way; and there is another of them who outstrippeth others in good works, by the permission of God.

This is the great excellence. They shall be introduced into
gardens of perpetual abode; they shall be adorned therein
with bracelets of gold and pearls, and their clothing therein
shall be of silk: and they shall say, Praise be unto God, who
hath taken away sorrow from us! verily our Lord is ready
to forgive the sinners, and to reward the obedient; who hath
caused us to take up our rest in a dwelling of eternal stability, through his bounty, wherein no labor shall touch us,
neither shall any weariness affect us. But for the unbelievers is prepared the fire of hell: it shall not be decreed them to
die a second time; neither shall any part of the punishment
thereof be made lighter unto them. Thus shall every infidel
be rewarded. And they shall cry out aloud in hell, saying,
Lord, take us hence, and we will work righteousness, and not
what we have formerly wrought. But it shall be answered
them, Did we not grant you lives of length sufficient that
whoever would be warned might be warned therein; and did
not the preacher come unto you? taste, therefore, the pains
of hell. And the unjust shall have no protector.

Verily God knoweth the secrets both of heaven and earth,
for he knoweth the innermost part of the breasts of men. It
is he who hath made you to succeed in the earth. Whoever
shall disbelieve, on him be his unbelief: and their unbelief
shall only gain the unbelievers greater indignation in the sight
of their Lord; and their unbelief shall only increase the perdition of the unbelievers. Say, what think ye of your deities
which ye invoke besides God? Show me what part of the
earth they have created. Or had they any share in the creation of the heavens? Have we given unto the idolaters any
book of revelations, so that they may rely on any proof therefrom to authorize their practise? Nay: but the ungodly
make unto one another only deceitful promises.

Verily God sustaineth the heavens and the earth, lest they
fail: and if they should fail, none could support the same
besides him; he is gracious and merciful. The Koreish
swore by God, with a most solemn oath, that if a preacher had
come unto them, they would surely have been more willingly
directed than any nation. But now a preacher is come unto

them, it hath only increased in them their aversion from the truth, their arrogance in the earth, and their contriving of evil; but the contrivance of evil shall only encompass the authors thereof. Do they expect any other than the punishment awarded against the unbelievers of former times? For thou shalt not find any change in the ordinance of God; neither shalt thou find any variation in the ordinance of God. Have they not gone through the earth, and seen what hath been the end of those who were before them; although they were more mighty in strength than they? God is not to be frustrated by anything either in heaven or on earth; for he is wise and powerful. If God should punish men according to what they deserve, he would not leave on the back of the earth so much as a beast: but he respiteth them to a determined time; and when their time shall come, verily God will regard his servants.

CHAPTER XXXVI

ENTITLED, Y. S.; REVEALED AT MECCA

IN THE NAME OF THE MOST MERCIFUL GOD

Y. S.[1] I swear by the instructive Koran, that thou art one of the messengers of God, sent to show the right way. This is a revelation of the most mighty, the merciful God: that thou mayest warn a people whose fathers were not warned, and who live in negligence. Our sentence hath justly been pronounced against the greater part of them; wherefore they shall not believe. We have put yokes on their necks, which come up to their chins; and they are forced to hold up their heads: and we have set a bar before them, and a bar behind them; and we have covered them with darkness; wherefore they shall not see. It shall be equal unto them whether thou

[1] The meaning of these letters is unknown: some, however, from a tradition of Ebn Abbas, pretend they stand for *Ya insan*, *i.e.*, "O man." This chapter, it is said, had several other titles given it by Mohammed himself, and particularly that of "The heart of the Koran." The Mohammedans read it to dying persons in their last agony.

preach unto them, or do not preach unto them; they shall not believe. But thou shalt preach with effect unto him only who followeth the admonition of the Koran, and feareth the Merciful in secret. Wherefore bear good tidings unto him, of mercy, and an honorable reward.

Verily we will restore the dead to life, and will write down their works which they shall have sent before them, and their footsteps which they shall have left behind them; and everything do we set down in a plain register. Propound unto them as an example the inhabitants of the city of Antioch, when the apostles of Jesus came thereto: when we sent unto them two of the said apostles, but they charged them with imposture. Wherefore we strengthened them with a third. And they said, Verily we are sent unto you by God. The inhabitants answered, Ye are no other than men, as we are; neither hath the Merciful revealed anything unto you: ye only publish a lie. The apostles replied, Our Lord knoweth that we are really sent unto you: and our duty is only public preaching. Those of Antioch said, Verily we presage evil from you: if ye desist not from preaching we will surely stone you, and a painful punishment shall be inflicted on you by us. The apostles answered, Your evil presage is with yourselves: although ye be warned, will ye persist in your errors? Verily ye are a people who transgress exceedingly.

And a certain man came hastily from the farther parts of the city, and said, O my people, follow the messengers of God; follow him who demandeth not any reward of you: for these are rightly directed. What reason have I that I should not worship him who hath created me? for unto him shall ye return. Shall I take other gods besides him? If the merciful be pleased to afflict me, their intercession will not avail me at all, neither can they deliver me: then should I be in a manifest error. Verily I believe in your Lord; wherefore harken unto me. But they stoned him: and as he died, it was said unto him, Enter thou into paradise. And he said, O that my people knew how merciful God hath been unto me! for he hath highly honored me. And we sent not down against his people, after they had slain him, an army from heaven, nor the other instruments of destruction which we sent down on un-believers in former days: there was only one cry of Gabriel from heaven, and behold, they became utterly extinct. O the misery of men! No apostle cometh unto them, but they laugh him to scorn. Do they not consider how many gen-erations we have destroyed before them? Verily they shall not return unto them: but all of them in general shall be assembled before us.

One sign of the resurrection unto them is the dead earth: we quicken the same by the rain, and produce thereout vari-ous sorts of grain, of which they eat. And we make therein gardens of palm-trees, and vines; and we cause springs to gush forth in the same: that they may eat of the fruits thereof, and of the labor of their hands. Will they not therefore give thanks? Praise be unto him who hath created all the differ-ent kinds, both of vegetables, which the earth bringeth forth, and of their own species, by forming the two sexes, and also the various sorts of things which they know not. The night also is a sign unto them: we withdraw the day from the same, and behold, they are covered with darkness: and the sun hasteneth to his place of rest. This is the disposition of the mighty, the wise God. And for the moon have we appointed certain mansions, until she change and return to be like the old branch of a palm-tree. It is not expedient that the sun should overtake the moon in her course; neither doth the night outstrip the day: but each of these luminaries moveth in a peculiar orbit. It is a sign also unto them, that we carry their offspring in the ship filled with merchandise; and that we have made for them other conveniences like unto it, whereon they ride. If we please, we drown them, and there is none to help them; neither are they delivered, unless through our mercy, and that they may enjoy life for a season. When it is said unto them, Fear that which is before you, and that which is behind you, that ye may obtain mercy; they withdraw from thee: and thou dost not bring them one sign, of the signs of their Lord, but they turn aside from the same. And when it is said unto them, Give alms of that which God hath bestowed on you; the unbelievers say unto those who believe, by way of mockery, Shall we feed him whom God can feed, if he pleaseth? Verily we are in no other than a manifest error.

And they say, When will this promise of the resurrection be fulfilled, if ye speak truth? They only wait for one sounding of the trumpet, which shall overtake them while they are disputing together; and they shall not have time to make any disposition of their effects, neither shall they return to their family. And the trumpet shall be sounded again; and behold they shall come forth from their graves, and hasten unto their Lord. They shall say, Alas for us! who hath awakened us from our bed? This is what the Merciful promised us; and his apostles spoke the truth. It shall be but one sound of the trumpet, and behold, they shall be all assembled before us. On this day no soul shall be unjustly treated in the least; neither shall ye be rewarded, but according to what ye shall have wrought. On this day the inhabitants of paradise shall be wholly taken up with joy: they and their wives shall rest in shady groves, leaning on magnificent couches. There shall they have fruit, and they shall obtain whatever they shall desire. Peace shall be the word spoken unto the righteous, by a merciful Lord: but he shall say unto the wicked, Be ye separated this day, O ye wicked, from the righteous. Did I not command you, O sons of Adam, that ye should not worship Satan; because he was an open enemy unto you? And did I not say, Worship me; this is the right way? But now hath he seduced a great multitude of you: did ye not therefore understand? This is hell, with which ye were threatened: be ye cast into the same this day, to be burned; for that ye have been unbelievers. On this day we will seal up their mouths, that they shall not open them in their own defense; and their hands shall speak unto us, and their feet shall bear witness of that which they have committed. If we pleased we could put out their eyes, and they might run with emulation in the way they used to take; and how should they see their error? And if we pleased we could transform them into other shapes, in their places where they should be found; and they should not be able to depart: neither should they repent. Unto whomsoever we grant a long life, him do we cause to bow down his body through age. Will they not therefore understand?

We have not taught Mohammed the art of poetry; nor is it expedient for him to be a poet. This book is no other than an admonition from God, and a perspicuous Koran; that he may warn him who is living: and the sentence of condemnation will be justly executed on the believers. Do they not consider that we have created for them, among the things which our hands have wrought, cattle of several kinds, of which they are possessors; and that we have put the same in subjection under them? Some of them are for their riding; and on some of them do they feed: and they receive other advantages therefrom; and of their milk do they drink. Will they not, therefore, be thankful? They have taken other gods, besides God, in hopes that they may be assisted by them: but they are not able to give them any assistance: yet are they a party of troops ready to defend them. Let not their speech, therefore, grieve thee: we know that which they privately conceal, and that which they publicly discover. Doth not man know that we have created him of seed? yet behold, he is an open disputer against the resurrection; and he propoundeth unto us a comparison, and forgetteth his creation. He saith, Who shall restore bones to life, when they are rotten? Answer, He shall restore them to life, who produced them the first time: for he is skilled in every kind of creation: who giveth you fire out of the green tree, and behold, ye kindle your fuel from thence. Is not he who hath created the heavens and the earth able to create new creatures like unto them? Yea, certainly: for he is the wise Creator. His command, when he willeth a thing, is only that he saith unto it, Be; and it is. Wherefore praise be unto him, in whose hand is the kingdom of all things, and unto whom ye shall return at the last day.

CHAPTER XXXVII

ENTITLED, THOSE WHO RANK THEMSELVES IN ORDER;
REVEALED AT MECCA

IN THE NAME OF THE MOST MERCIFUL GOD

By the angels who rank themselves in order; and by those
who drive forward and dispel the clouds: and by those who
read the Koran for an admonition; verily your God is one:
the Lord of heaven and earth, and of whatever is between
them, and the Lord of the east.   We have adorned the lower
heaven with the ornament of the stars: and we have placed
therein a guard, against every rebellious devil; that they may
not listen to the discourse of the exalted princes (for they are
darted at from every side, to repel them, and a lasting torment is prepared for them) ; except him who catcheth a word
by stealth, and is pursued by a shining flame.   Ask the Meccans, therefore, whether they be stronger by nature, or the
angels whom we have created ?   We have surely created them
of stiff clay.   Thou wonderest at God's power and their obstinacy; but they mock at the arguments urged to convince them:
when they are warned, they do not take warning; and when
they see any sign, they scoff thereat, and say, This is no other
than manifest sorcery: after we shall be dead, and become
dust and bones, shall we really be raised to life, and our
forefathers also ?   Answer, Yea: and ye shall then be despicable.   There shall be but one blast of the trumpet, and they
shall see themselves raised: and they shall say, Alas for us!
this is the day of judgment; this is the day of distinction between the righteous and the wicked, which ye rejected as a
falsehood.   Gather together those who have acted unjustly,
and their comrades, and the idols which they worshiped besides God, and direct them in the way to hell: and set them
before God's tribunal; for they shall be called to account.
What aileth you that ye defend not one another ?   But on
this day they shall submit themselves to the judgment of
God: and they shall draw nigh unto one another, and shall
dispute among themselves.   And the seduced shall say unto

those who seduced them, Verily ye came unto us with presages of prosperity; and the seducers shall answer, Nay, rather ye were not true believers: for we had no power over you to compel you; but ye were people who voluntarily transgressed: wherefore the sentence of our Lord hath been justly pronounced against us, and we shall surely taste his vengeance. We seduced you; but we also erred ourselves. They shall both therefore be made partakers of the same punishment on that day. Thus will we deal with the wicked: because, when it is said unto them, There is no God besides the true God, they swell with arrogance, and say, Shall we abandon our gods for a distracted poet? Nay; he cometh with the truth, and beareth witness to the former apostles. Ye shall surely taste the painful torment of hell; and ye shall not be rewarded, but according to your works.

But as for the sincere servants of God, they shall have a certain provision in paradise, namely, delicious fruits: and they shall be honored: they shall be placed in gardens of pleasure, leaning on couches, opposite to one another: a cup shall be carried round unto them, filled from a limpid fountain, for the delight of those who drink: it shall not oppress the understanding, neither shall they be inebriated therewith. And near them shall lie the virgins of paradise, refraining their looks from beholding any besides their spouses, having large black eyes, and resembling the eggs of an ostrich covered with feathers from the dust. And they shall turn the one unto the other, and shall ask one another questions. And one of them shall say, Verily I had an intimate friend while I lived in the world, who said unto me, Art thou one of those who assertest the truth of the resurrection? After we shall be dead, and reduced to dust and bones, shall we surely be judged? Then he shall say to his companions, Will ye look down? And he shall look down, and shall see him in the midst of hell; and he shall say unto him, By God, it wanted little but thou hadst drawn me into ruin; and had it not been for the grace of my Lord, I had surely been one of those who had been delivered up to eternal torment. Shall we die any other than our first death; or do we suffer any punishment? Verily this is great felicity: for the obtaining a felicity like this let the laborers labor. Is this a better entertainment, or the tree of Al Zakkum?[1]

Verily we have designed the same for an occasion of dispute unto the unjust.[2] It is a tree which issueth from the bottom of hell: the fruit thereof resembleth the heads of devils;[3] and the damned shall eat of the same, and shall fill their bellies therewith; there shall be given them thereon a mixture of filthy and boiling water to drink: afterward shall they return into hell. They found their fathers going astray, and they trod hastily in their footsteps: for the greater part of the ancients erred before them. And we sent warners unto them heretofore: and see how miserable was the end of those who were warned; except the sincere servants of God. Noah called on us in former days, and we heard him graciously: and we delivered him and his family out of the great distress: and we caused his offspring to be those who survived to people the earth: and we left the following salutation to be bestowed on him by the latest posterity, namely, Peace be on Noah among all creatures! Thus do we reward the righteous; for he was one of our servants the true believers. Afterward we drowned the others.

Abraham also was of his religion: when he came unto his Lord with a perfect heart. When he said unto his father and his people, What do ye worship? Do ye choose false gods preferably to the true God? What therefore is your opinion of the Lord of all creatures? And he looked and observed the stars, and said, Verily I shall be sick, and shall not assist at your sacrifices: and they turned their backs and departed from him. And Abraham went privately to their gods, and said scoffingly unto them, Do ye not eat of the meat which is set before you? What aileth you that ye speak not? And he turned upon them, and struck them with his right

[1] There is a thorny tree so called, which grows in Tehama, and bears fruit like an almond, but extremely bitter; and therefore the same name is given to this infernal tree.

[2] The infidels not conceiving how a tree could grow in hell, where the stones themselves serve for fuel.

[3] Or of serpents ugly to behold; the original word signifies both.

hand, and demolished them. And the people came hastily unto him: and he said, Do ye worship the images which ye carve? whereas God hath created you, and also that which ye make. They said, Build a pile for him, and cast him into the glowing fire. And they devised a plot against him; but we made them the inferior, and delivered him. And Abraham said, Verily I am going unto my Lord, who will direct me. O Lord, grant me a righteous issue. Wherefore we acquainted him that he should have a son who should be a meek youth. And when he had attained to years of discretion, and could join in acts of religion with him; Abraham said unto him, O my son, verily I saw in a dream that I should offer thee in sacrifice: consider therefore what thou art of opinion I should do. He answered, O my father, do what thou art commanded: thou shalt find me, if God please, a patient person. And when they had submitted themselves to the divine will, and Abraham had laid his son prostrate on his face, we cried unto him, O Abraham, now hast thou verified the vision. Thus do we reward the righteous. Verily this was a manifest trial. And we ransomed him with a noble victim. And we left the following salutation to be bestowed on him by the latest posterity, namely, Peace be on Abraham! Thus do we reward the righteous: for he was one of our faithful servants.

And we rejoiced him with the promise of Isaac, a righteous prophet; and we blessed him and Isaac: and of their offspring were some righteous doers, and others who manifestly injured their own souls. We were also gracious unto Moses and Aaron, heretofore: and we delivered them and their people from a great distress. And we assisted them against the Egyptians; and they became the conquerors. And we gave them the perspicuous book of the law, and we directed them into the right way: and we left the following salutation to be bestowed on them by the latest posterity, namely, Peace be on Moses and Aaron! Thus do we reward the righteous; for they were two of our faithful servants. And Elias was also one of those who were sent by us. When he said unto his people, Do ye not fear God? Do ye invoke

Baal, and forsake the most excellent Creator? God is your Lord, and the Lord of your forefathers. But they accused him of imposture: wherefore they shall be delivered up to eternal punishment; except the sincere servants of God. And we left the following salutation to be bestowed on him by the latest posterity, namely, Peace be on Ilyasin! [4] Thus do we reward the righteous: for he was one of our faithful servants.

And Lot was also one of those who were sent by us. When we delivered him and his whole family, except an old woman, his wife, who perished among those that remained behind: afterward we destroyed the others. And ye, O people of Mecca, pass by the places where they once dwelt, as ye journey in the morning and by night: will ye not therefore understand? Jonas was also one of those who were sent by us. When he fled into the loaded ship; and those who were on board cast lots among themselves, and he was condemned: and the fish swallowed him; for he was worthy of reprehension. And if he had not been one of those who praised God, verily he had remained in the belly thereof until the day of resurrection. And we cast him on the naked shore, and he was sick: and we caused a plant of a gourd to grow up over him; and we sent him to a hundred thousand persons, or they were a greater number, and they believed: wherefore we granted them to enjoy this life for a season.

Inquire of the Meccans whether thy Lord hath daughters, and they sons? Have we created the angels of the female sex? and were they witnesses thereof? Do they not say of their own false invention, God hath begotten issue? and are they not really liars? Hath he chosen daughters preferably to sons? Ye have no reason to judge thus. Will ye not therefore be admonished? Or have ye a manifest proof

[4] The commentators do not well know what to make of this word. Some think it is the plural of Elias, or, as the Arabs write it, Ilyas, and that both that prophet and his followers, or those who resembled him, are meant thereby; others divide the word, and read *al Yasin*, *i.e.*, "the family of Yasin," who was the father of Elias according to an opinion mentioned above, and others imagine it signifies Mohammed, or the Koran, or some other book of scripture.

of what ye say? Produce now your book of revelations, if ye speak truth. And they make him to be of kin unto the genii; whereas the genii know that they who affirm such things shall be delivered up to eternal punishment (far be that from God which they affirm of him!) except the sincere servants of God. Moreover ye and that which ye worship shall not seduce any concerning God, except him who is destined to be burned in hell. There is none of us, but hath an appointed place: we range ourselves in order, attending the commands of God; and we celebrate the divine praise.

The infidels said, If we had been favored with a book of divine revelations, of those which were delivered to the ancients, we had surely been sincere servants of God: yet now the Koran is revealed, they believe not therein; but hereafter shall they know the consequence of their unbelief. Our word hath formerly been given unto our servants the apostles; that they should certainly be assisted against the infidels, and that our armies should surely be the conquerors. Turn aside therefore from them, for a season: and see the calamities which shall afflict them; for they shall see thy future success and prosperity. Do they therefore seek to hasten our vengeance? Verily when it shall descend into their courts an evil morning shall it be unto those who were warned in vain. Turn aside from them therefore for a season; and see: hereafter shall they see thy success and their punishment. Praise be unto thy Lord, the Lord who is far exalted above what they affirm of him! And peace be on his apostles!

CHAPTER XXXVIII

ENTITLED, S; REVEALED AT MECCA.

IN THE NAME OF THE MOST MERCIFUL GOD

S.[1] By the Koran full of admonition. Verily the unbe-

---

[1] The meaning of this letter is unknown; some guess it stands for *Sidk, i.e.,* " Truth"; or for *Sadaka, i.e.,* He (*viz.,* Mohammed) speaketh the truth," and others propose different conjectures, all equally uncertain.

lievers are addicted to pride and contention. How many generations have we destroyed before them; and they cried for mercy, but it was not a time to escape. They wonder that a warner from among themselves hath come unto them. And the unbelievers said, This man is a sorcerer and a liar: doth he affirm the gods to be but one God? Surely this is a wonderful thing. And the chief men among them departed, saying to one another, Go, and persevere in the worship of your gods: verily this is the thing which is designed. We have not heard anything like this in the last religion: this is no other than a false contrivance. Hath an admonition been sent unto him preferably to any other among us? Verily they are in a doubt concerning my admonition: but they have not yet tasted my vengeance. Are the treasuries of the mercy of thy Lord, the mighty, the munificent God, in their hands? Is the kingdom of the heavens and the earth, and of whatever is between them, in their possession? If it be so, let them ascend by steps unto heaven. But any army of the confederates shall even here be put to flight. The people of Noah, and the tribe of Ad, and Pharaoh the contriver of the stakes, and the tribe of Thamud, and the people of Lot, and the inhabitants of the wood near Madian, accused the prophets of imposture before them: these were the confederates against the messengers of God. All of them did no other than accuse their apostles of falsehood: wherefore my vengeance hath been justly executed upon them. And these wait only for one sounding of the trumpet; which there shall be no deferring. And they scoffingly say, O Lord, hasten our sentence unto us, before the day of account.

Do thou patiently bear that which they utter: and remind them of our servant David, endued with strength; for he was one who seriously turned himself unto God. We compelled the mountains to celebrate our praise with him, in the evening and at sunrise, and also the birds, which gathered themselves together unto him: all of them returned frequently unto him for this purpose. And we established his kingdom, and gave him wisdom and eloquence of speech. Hath the story of the two adversaries come to thy knowledge;

when they ascended over the wall into the upper apartment, when they went in unto David, and he was afraid of them? They said, Fear not: we are two adversaries who have a controversy to be decided. The one of us hath wronged the other: wherefore judge between us with truth, and be not unjust; and direct us into the even way. This my brother had ninety and nine sheep; and I had only one ewe: and he said, Give her me to keep; and he prevailed against me in the discourse which we had together. David answered, Verily he hath wronged thee, in demanding thine ewe as an addition to his own sheep: and many of them who are concerned together in business wrong one another, except those who believe and do that which is right; but how few are they! And David perceived that we had tried him by this parable, and he asked pardon of his Lord: and he fell down and bowed himself, and repented. Wherefore we forgave him this fault; and he shall be admitted to approach near unto us, and shall have an excellent place of abode in paradise. O David, verily we have appointed thee a sovereign prince in the earth: judge therefore between men with truth; and follow not thy own lust, lest it cause thee to err from the way of God: for those who err from the way of God shall suffer a severe punishment, because they have forgotten the day of account. We have not created the heavens and the earth, and whatever is between them, in vain. This is the opinion of the unbelievers: but woe unto those who believe not, because of the fire of hell. Shall we deal with those who believe and do good works, as with those who act corruptly in the earth? Shall we deal with the pious as with the wicked? A blessed book have we sent down unto thee, O Mohammed, that they may attentively meditate on the signs thereof, and that men of understanding may be warned.

And we gave unto David Solomon; how excellent a servant! for he frequently turned himself unto God. When the horses standing on three feet, and touching the ground with the edge of the fourth foot, and swift in the course, were set in parade before him in the evening, he said, Verily I have loved the love of earthly good above the remembrance of my Lord; and have spent the time in viewing these horses, until the sun is hidden by the veil of night: bring the horses back unto me. And when they were brought back, he began to cut off their legs and their necks. We also tried Solomon, and placed on his throne a counterfeit body:[2] afterward he turned unto God, and said, O Lord, forgive me, and give me a kingdom which may not be obtained by any after me; for thou art the giver of kingdoms. And we made the wind subject to him; it ran gently at his command, whithersoever he directed. And we also put the devils in subjection under him; and among them such as were every way skilled in building, and in diving for pearls: and others we delivered to him bound in chains; saying, This is our gift: therefore be bounteous, or be sparing unto whom thou shalt think fit, without rendering an account. And he shall approach near unto us, and shall have an excellent abode in paradise.

[2] The most received exposition of this passage is taken from the following Talmudic fable: Solomon, having taken Sidon, and slain the king of that city, brought away his daughter Jerada, who became his favorite; and because she ceased not to lament her father's loss, he ordered the devils to make an image of him for her consolation: which being done, and placed in her chamber, she and her maids worshiped it morning and evening, according to their custom. At length Solomon being informed of this idolatry, which was practised under his roof, by his vizir Asaf, he broke the image, and having chastised the woman, went out into the desert, where he wept and made supplications to God; who did not think fit, however, to let his negligence pass without some correction. It was Solomon's custom, while he eased or washed himself, to entrust his signet, on which his kingdom depended, with a concubine of his named Amina: one day, therefore, when she had the ring in her custody, a devil, named Sakhar, came to her in the shape of Solomon, and received the ring from her; by virtue of which he became possessed of the kingdom and sat on the throne in the shape which he had borrowed, making what alterations in the law he pleased. Solomon, in the meantime, being changed in his outward appearance, and known to none of his subjects, was obliged to wander about, and beg alms for his subsistence; till at length, after the space of forty days, which was the time the image had been worshiped in his house, the devil flew away, and threw the signet into the sea: the signet was immediately swallowed by a fish, which being taken and given to Solomon, he found the ring in its belly, and having by this means recovered the kingdom, took Sakhar, and tying a great stone to his neck, threw him into the lake of Tiberias.

And remember our servant Job; when he cried unto his Lord, saying, Verily Satan hath afflicted me with calamity and pain. And it was said unto him, Strike the earth with thy foot; which when he had done, a fountain sprang up, and it was said to him, This is for thee to wash in, to refresh thee, and to drink. And we restored unto him his family, and as many more with them, through our mercy; and for an admonition unto those who are endued with understanding. And we said unto him, Take a handful of rods in thy hand, and strike thy wife therewith; and break not thine oath. Verily we found him a patient person: how excellent a servant was he! for he was one who frequently turned himself unto us. Remember also our servants Abraham, and Isaac, and Jacob, who were men strenuous and prudent. Verily we purified them with a perfect purification, through the remembrance of the life to come; and they were, in our sight, elect and good men. And remember Ismael, and Elisha, and Dhu'lkefl: for all these were good men. This is an admonition.

Verily the pious shall have an excellent place to return unto, namely, gardens of perpetual abode, the gates whereof shall stand open unto them. As they lie down therein, they shall there ask for many sorts of fruits, and for drink; and near them shall sit the virgins of paradise, refraining their looks from beholding any besides their spouses, and of equal age with them. This is what ye are promised at the day of account. This is our provision; which shall not fail. This shall be the reward of the righteous. But for the transgressors is prepared an evil receptacle, namely, hell: they shall be cast into the same to be burned, and a wretched couch shall it be. This let them taste, to wit, scalding water, and corruption flowing from the bodies of the damned, and divers other things of the same kind. And it shall be said to the seducers, This troop which was guided by you, shall be thrown, together with you, headlong into hell: they shall not be bidden welcome; for they shall enter the fire to be burned. And the seduced shall say to their seducers, Verily ye shall not be bidden welcome: ye have brought it upon us; and a wretched abode is hell. They shall say, O Lord, doubly increase the torment of him who hath brought this punishment upon us, in the fire of hell. And the infidels shall say, Why do we not see the men whom we numbered among the wicked, and whom we received with scorn? Or do our eyes miss them? Verily this is a truth; to wit, the disputing of the inhabitants of hell fire.

Say, O Mohammed, unto the idolaters, Verily I am no other than a warner: and there is no god, except the one only God, the Almighty the Lord of heaven and earth, and of whatsoever is between them; the mighty, the forgiver of sins, Say, It is a weighty message, from which ye turn aside. I had no knowledge of the exalted princes, when they disputed concerning the creation of man (it hath been revealed unto me only as a proof that I am a public preacher): when thy Lord said unto the angels, Verily I am about to create man of clay: when I shall have formed him, therefore, and shall have breathed my spirit into him, do ye fall down and worship him. And all the angels worshiped him, in general; except Eblis, who was puffed up with pride, and became an unbeliever. God said unto him, O Eblis, what hindereth thee from worshiping that which I have created with my hands? Art thou elated with vain pride? Or art thou really one of exalted merit? He answered, I am more excellent than he; thou hast created me of fire and hast created him of clay. God said unto him, Get thee hence therefore, for thou shalt be driven away from mercy: and my curse shall be upon thee, until the day of judgment. He replied, O Lord, respite me, therefore, until the day of resurrection. God said, Verily thou shalt be one of those who are respited until the day of the determined time. Eblis said, By thy might do I swear, I will surely seduce them all, except thy servants who shall be peculiarly chosen from among them. God said, It is a just sentence: and I speak the truth: I will surely fill hell with thee, and with such of them as shall follow thee, altogether. Say unto the Meccans, I ask not of you any reward for this my preaching: neither am I one of those who assume a part which belongs not to them. The Koran is no other than an admo-

nition unto all creatures: and ye shall surely know what is
delivered therein to be true, after a season.

CHAPTER XXXIX

ENTITLED, THE TROOPS;[1] REVEALED AT MECCA

IN THE NAME OF THE MOST MERCIFUL GOD

The revelation of this book is from the mighty, the wise
God. Verily we have revealed this book unto thee with
truth: wherefore serve God, exhibiting the pure religion unto
him. Ought not the pure religion to be exhibited unto God?
But as to those who take other patrons besides him, saying,
We worship them only that they may bring us nearer unto
God; verily God will judge between them concerning that
wherein they disagree. Surely God will not direct him who
is a liar, or ungrateful. If God had been minded to have
had a son, he had surely chosen what he pleased out of that
which he hath created. But far be such a thing from him!
He is the sole, the almighty God. He hath created the
heavens and the earth with truth: he causeth the night to succeed the day, and he causeth the day to succeed the night, and
he obligeth the sun and the moon to perform their services;
each of them hasteneth to an appointed period. Is not he the
mighty, the forgiver of sins? He created you of one man,
and afterward out of him formed his wife: and he hath
bestowed on you four pair of cattle. He formeth you in the
wombs of your mothers, by several gradual formations, within
three veils of darkness. This is God, your Lord: his is the
kingdom: there is no God but he. Why therefore are ye
turned aside from the worship of him to idolatry?

If ye be ungrateful, verily God hath no need of you; yet he
liketh not ingratitude in his servants: but if ye be thankful,
he will be well pleased with you. A burdened soul shall not

[1] This title is taken from the latter end of the chapter, where it is
said the wicked shall be sent to hell, and the righteous admitted into
paradise by troops.

bear the burden of another: hereafter shall ye return unto your Lord, and he shall declare unto you that which ye have wrought, and will reward you accordingly; for he knoweth the innermost parts of your breasts. When harm befalleth a man, he calleth upon his Lord, and turneth unto him: yet afterward, when God hath bestowed on him favor from himself, he forgetteth that Being which he invoked before, and setteth up equals unto God, that he may seduce men from his way. Say unto such a man, Enjoy this life in thy infidelity for a little while: but hereafter shalt thou surely be one of the inhabitants of hell fire. Shall he who giveth himself up to prayer in the hours of the night, prostrate and standing, and who taketh heed as to the life to come, and hopeth for the mercy of his Lord, be dealt with as the wicked unbeliever? Say, Shall they who know their duty, and they who know it not, be held equal? Verily the men of understanding only will be warned. . . .

Verily we have revealed unto thee the book of the Koran, for the instruction of mankind, with truth. Whoso shall be directed thereby shall be directed to the advantage of his own soul; and whoso shall err shall only err against the same: and thou art not a guardian over them. God taketh unto himself the souls of men at the time of their death; and those which die not he also taketh in their sleep: and he withholdeth those on which he hath passed the decree of death, but sendeth back the others till a determined period. Verily herein are signs unto people who consider. Have the Koreish taken idols for their intercessors with God? Say, What, although they have not dominion over anything, neither do they understand? Say, Intercession is altogether in the disposal of God: his is the kingdom of heaven and earth; and hereafter shall ye return unto him. When the one sole God is mentioned, the hearts of those who believe not in the life to come shrink with horror: but when the false gods, which are worshiped besides him, are mentioned, behold, they are filled with joy.

Say, O God, the creator of heaven and earth, who knowest that which is secret and that which is manifest; thou shalt judge between thy servants concerning that wherein they dis-

agree. If those who act unjustly were masters of whatever is
in the earth, and as much more therewith, verily they would
give it to ransom themselves from the evil of the punishment,
on the day of resurrection: and there shall appear unto them,
from God, terrors which they never imagined; and there shall
appear unto them the evils of that which they shall have
gained; and that which they mocked at shall encompass them.
When harm befalleth man, he calleth upon us; yet afterward, when we have bestowed on him favor from us, he saith,
I have received it merely because of God's knowledge of my
deserts. On the contrary, it is a trial; but the greater part
of them know it not. Those who were before them said the
same: but that which they had gained profited them not; and
the evils which they had deserved fell upon them. And
whoever of these Meccans shall have acted unjustly, on them
likewise shall fall the evils which they shall have deserved;
neither shall they frustrate the divine vengeance. Do they
not know that God bestoweth provision abundantly on whom
he pleaseth, and is sparing unto whom he pleaseth? Verily
herein are signs unto people who believe.

Say, O my servants who have transgressed against your
own souls, despair not of the mercy of God: seeing that God
forgiveth all sins; for he is gracious and merciful. And be
turned unto your Lord, and resign yourselves unto him, before
the threatened punishment overtake you; for then ye shall not
be helped. And follow the most excellent instructions which
have been sent down unto you from your Lord, before the
punishment come suddenly upon you, and ye perceive not the
approach thereof; and a soul say, Alas! for that I have been
negligent in my duty to God: verily I have been one of the
scorners: or say, If God had directed me, verily I had been
one of the pious: or say, when it seeth the prepared punishment, If I could return once more into the world I would
become one of the righteous. But God shall answer, My
signs came unto thee heretofore, and thou didst charge them
with falsehood, and wast puffed up with pride; and thou
becamest one of the unbelievers. On the day of resurrection
thou shalt see the faces of those who have uttered lies concern-

ing God become black: is there not an abode prepared in hell for the arrogant? But God shall deliver those who shall fear him, and shall set them in their place of safety: evil shall not touch them, neither shall they be grieved. God is the creator of all things, and he is the governor of all things. His are the keys of heaven and earth: and they who believe not in the signs of God, they shall perish.

Say, Do ye therefore bid me to worship other than God, O ye fools? since it hath been spoken by revelation unto thee, and also unto the prophets who have been before thee, saying, Verily if thou join any partners with God, thy work will be altogether unprofitable, and thou shalt certainly be one of those who perish: wherefore rather fear God, and be one of those who give thanks. But they make not a due estimation of God: since the whole earth shall be but his handful, on the day of resurrection; and the heavens shall be rolled together in his right hand. Praise be unto him! and far be he exalted above the idols which they associate with him! The trumpet shall be sounded, and whoever are in heaven and whoever are on earth shall expire; except those whom God shall please to exempt from the common fate.[2] Afterward it shall be sounded again; and behold, they shall arise and look up. And the earth shall shine by the light of its Lord: and the book shall be laid open, and the prophets and the martyrs shall be brought as witnesses; and judgment shall be given between them with truth, and they shall not be treated unjustly. And every soul shall be fully rewarded, according to that which it shall have wrought; for he perfectly knoweth whatever they do. And the unbelievers shall be driven unto hell by troops, until, when they shall arrive at the same, the gates thereof shall be opened: and the keepers thereof shall say unto them, Did not apostles from among you come unto you, who rehearsed unto you the signs of your Lord, and warned you of the meeting of this your day? They shall answer, Yea:

[2] These, some say, will be the angels Gabriel, Michael, and Israfil, and the angel of death, who yet will afterward all die, at the command of God; it being the constant opinion of the Mohammedan doctors, that every soul, both of men and of animals, which live either on land or in

but the sentence of eternal punishment hath been justly pronounced on the unbelievers. It shall be said unto them, Enter ye the gates of hell, to dwell therein forever; and miserable shall be the abode of the proud!

But those who shall have feared their Lord shall be conducted by troops toward paradise, until they shall arrive at the same: and the gates thereof shall be ready set open; and the guards thereof shall say unto them, Peace be on you! ye have been good: wherefore enter ye into paradise, to remain therein forever. And they shall answer, Praise be unto God, who hath performed his promise unto us, and hath made us to inherit the earth, that we may dwell in paradise wherever we please! How excellent is the reward of those who work righteousness! And thou shalt see the angels going in procession round the throne, celebrating the praises of their Lord: and judgment shall be given between them with truth; and they shall say, Praise be unto God, the Lord of all creatures!

CHAPTER XL

ENTITLED, THE TRUE BELIEVER;[1] REVEALED AT MECCA

IN THE NAME OF THE MOST MERCIFUL GOD

H. M. The revelation of this book is from the mighty, the wise God; the forgiver of sin, and the accepter of repentance; severe in punishing; long-suffering. There is no God but he: before him shall be the general assembly at the last day. None disputeth against the signs of God, except the unbelievers: but let not their prosperous dealing in the land deceive thee with vain allurements. The people of Noah, and

the sea, and of the angels also, must necessarily taste of death: others suppose those who will be exempted are the angels who bear the throne of God, or the black-eyed damsels, and other inhabitants of paradise.

The space between these two blasts of the trumpet will be forty days, according to Yahya and others; there are some, however, who suppose it will be as many years.

[1] This title is taken from the passage wherein mention is made of one of Pharaoh's family who believed in Moses.

the confederated infidels which were after them, accused their respective prophets of imposture before these; and each nation hatched ill designs against their apostle, that they might get him into their power; and they disputed with vain reasoning, that they might thereby invalidate the truth: wherefore I chastised them; and how severe was my punishment! Thus hath the sentence of thy Lord justly passed on the unbelievers; that they shall be the inhabitants of hell fire.

The angels who bear the throne of God, and those who stand about it, celebrate the praise of their Lord, and believe in him; and they ask pardon for the true believers, saying, O Lord, thou encompassest all things by thy mercy and knowledge; wherefore forgive those who repent and follow thy path, and deliver them from the pains of hell: O Lord, lead them also into gardens of eternal abode, which thou hast promised unto them, and unto every one who shall do right, of their fathers, and their wives, and their children; for thou art the mighty, the wise God. And deliver them from evil; for whomsoever thou shalt deliver from evil on that day, on him wilt thou show mercy; and this will be great salvation.

But the infidels, at the day of judgment, shall hear a voice crying unto them, Verily the hatred of God toward you is more grievous than your hatred toward yourselves: since ye were called unto the faith, and would not believe. They shall say, O Lord, thou hast given us death twice, and thou hast twice given us life; and we confess our sins: is there therefore no way to get forth from this fire? And it shall be answered them, This hath befallen you, for that when one God was preached unto you, ye believed not; but if a plurality of gods had been associated with him, ye had believed; and judgment belongeth unto the high, the great God. It is he who showeth you his signs, and sendeth down food unto you from heaven: but none will be admonished, except he who turneth himself unto God. Call therefore upon God, exhibiting your religion pure unto him, although the infidels be averse thereto. He is the Being of exalted degree, the possessor of the throne; who sendeth down the spirit, at his command, on such of his servants as he pleaseth; that he may warn mankind of the day of meeting, the day whereon they shall come forth out of their graves, and nothing of what concerneth them shall be hidden from God. Unto whom will the kingdom belong, on that day? Unto the only, the almighty God. On that day shall every soul be rewarded according to its merits; there shall be no injustice done on that day. Verily God will be swift in taking an account. Wherefore warn them, O prophet, of the day which shall suddenly approach; when men's hearts shall come up to their throats, and strangle them. The ungodly shall have no friend or intercessor who shall be heard. God will know the deceitful eye, and that which their breasts conceal; and God will judge with truth: but the false gods which they invoke besides him shall not judge at all; for God is he who heareth and seeth. Have they not gone through the earth and seen what hath been the end of those who were before them? They were more mighty than these in strength, and left more considerable footsteps of their power in the earth: yet God chastised them for their sins, and there was none to protect them from God. This they suffered, because their apostles had come unto them with evident signs, and they disbelieved: wherefore God chastised them; for he is strong, and severe in punishing.

We heretofore sent Moses with our signs and manifest power, unto Pharaoh, and Haman, and Karun; and they said, He is a sorcerer and a liar. And when he came unto them with the truth from us, they said, Slay the sons of those who have believed with him, and save their daughters alive: but the stratagem of the infidels was no other than vain. And Pharaoh said, Let me alone, that I may kill Moses; and let him call upon his Lord: verily I fear lest he change your religion, or cause violence to appear in the earth. And Moses said unto his people, Verily I have recourse unto my Lord, and your Lord, to defend me against every proud person, who believeth not in the day of account. And a man who was a true believer, of the family of Pharaoh, and concealed his faith, said, Will ye put a man to death, because he saith,

God is my Lord; seeing he is come unto you with evident signs from your Lord? If he be a liar, on him will the punishment of his falsehood light; but if he speaketh the truth, some of those judgments with which he threateneth you will fall upon you: verily God directeth not him who is a transgressor or a liar. O my people, the kingdom is yours this day; and ye are conspicuous in the earth: but who shall defend us from the scourge of God, if it come unto us? Pharaoh said, I only propose to you what I think to be most expedient: and I guide you only into the right path. And he who had believed said, O my people, verily I fear for you a day like that of the confederates against the prophets in former times; a condition like that of the people of Noah, and the tribes of Ad and Thamud, and of those who have lived after them: for God willeth not that any injustice be done unto his servants. O my people, verily I fear for you the day whereon men shall call unto one another;[2] the day whereon ye shall be turned back from the tribunal, and driven to hell: then shall ye have none to protect you against God. And he whom God shall cause to err shall have no director. Joseph came unto you, before Moses, with evident signs; but ye ceased not to doubt of the religion which he preached unto you, until, when he died, ye said, God will by no means send another apostle after him. Thus doth God cause him to err, who is a transgressor and a skeptic. They who dispute against the signs of God, without any authority which hath come unto them, are in great abomination with God, and with those who believe. Thus doth God seal up every proud and stubborn heart. And Pharaoh said, O Haman, build me a tower, that I may reach the tracts, the tracts of heaven, and may view the God of Moses; for I verily think him to be a liar. And thus the evil of his work was prepared for Pharaoh, and he turned aside from the right path: and the stratagems of Pharaoh ended only in loss. And he who had believed said, O my people,

---

[2] *I.e.*, The day of judgment, when the inhabitants of paradise and of hell shall enter into mutual discourse: when the latter shall call for help, and the seducers and the seduced shall cast the blame upon each other.

follow me : I will guide you into the right way.   O my people, verily this present life is but a temporary enjoyment; but the life to come is the mansion of firm continuance.   Whoever worketh evil shall only be rewarded in equal proportion to the same : but whoever worketh good, whether male or female, and is a true believer, they shall enter paradise; they shall be provided for therein superabundantly.   And, O my people, as for me, I invite you to salvation; but ye invite me to hell fire : ye invite me to deny God, and to associate with him that whereof I have no knowledge; but I invite you to the most mighty, the forgiver of sins.   There is no doubt but that the false gods to which ye invite me deserve not to be invoked, either in this world or in the next; and that we must return unto God; and that the transgressors shall be the inhabitants of hell fire : and ye shall then remember what I now say unto you.   And I commit my affair unto God: for God regardeth his servants.   Wherefore God delivered him from the evils which they had devised; and a grievous punishment encompassed the people of Pharaoh.[3]   They shall be exposed to the fire of hell morning and evening:[4] and the day whereon the hour of judgment shall come, it shall be said unto them, Enter, O people of Pharaoh, into a most severe torment.

And think on the time when the infidels shall dispute together in hell fire; and the weak shall say unto those who behaved with arrogance, Verily we were your followers: will ye, therefore, relieve us from any part of this fire?   Those who behaved with arrogance shall answer, Verily we are all doomed to suffer therein: for God hath now judged between his servants.   And they who shall be in the fire shall say unto

[3] Some are of opinion that those who were sent by Pharaoh to seize the true believer, his kinsman, are the persons more particularly meant in this place: for they tell us that the said believer fled to a mountain, where they found him at prayers, guarded by the wild beasts, which ranged themselves in order about him, and that his pursuers thereupon returned in a great fright to their master, who put them to death for not performing his command.

[4] Some expound these words of the previous punishment they are doomed to suffer according to a tradition of Ebn Masud, which informs us that their souls are in the crops of black birds, which are exposed to hell fire every morning and evening until the day of judgment.

the keepers of hell, Call ye on your Lord, that he would ease us, for one day, from this punishment. They shall answer, Did not your apostles come unto you with evident proofs? They shall say, Yea. The keepers shall reply, Do ye therefore call on God: but the calling of the unbelievers on him shall be only in vain. We will surely assist our apostles, and those who believe, in this present life, and on the day whereon the witnesses shall stand forth: a day whereon the excuse of the unbelievers shall not avail them; but a curse shall attend them, and a wretched abode.

We heretofore gave unto Moses a direction: and we left as an inheritance unto the children of Israel the book of the law; a direction, and an admonition to men of understanding. Wherefore do thou, O prophet, bear the insults of the infidels with patience; for the promise of God is true: and ask pardon for thy fault; and celebrate the praise of thy Lord in the evening and in the morning. As to those who impugn the signs of God, without any convincing proof which hath been revealed unto them, there is nothing but pride in their breasts; but they shall not attain their desire: wherefore, fly for refuge unto God, for it is he who heareth and seeth. Verily the creation of heaven and earth is more considerable than the creation of man: but the greater part of men do not understand. The blind and the seeing shall not be held equal; nor they who believe and work righteousness, and the evil-doer: how few revolve these things in their mind! The last hour will surely come; there is no doubt thereof: but the greater part of men believe it not. Your Lord saith, Call upon me, and I will hear you: but they who proudly disdain my service shall enter with ignominy into hell.

It is God who hath appointed the night for you to take your rest therein, and the day to give you light: verily God is endued with beneficence toward mankind; but the greater part of men do not give thanks. This is God, your Lord; the creator of all things: there is no God besides him: how therefore are ye turned aside from his worship? Thus are they turned aside who oppose the signs of God. It is God who hath given you the earth for a stable floor, and the heaven for a ceiling: and who hath formed you, and made your forms beautiful; and feedeth you with good things. This is God, your Lord. Wherefore, blessed be God, the Lord of all creatures! He is the living God: there is no God but he. Wherefore call upon him, exhibiting unto him the pure religion. Praise be unto God, the Lord of all creatures! Say, Verily I am forbidden to worship the deities which ye invoke, besides God, after that evident proofs have come unto me from my Lord; and I am commanded to resign myself unto the Lord of all creatures. It is he who first created you of dust, and afterward of seed, and afterward of coagulated blood; and afterward brought you forth infants out of your mothers' wombs: then he permitteth you to attain your age of full strength, and afterward to grow old men (but some of you die before that age), and to arrive at the determined period of your life; that peradventure ye may understand. It is he who giveth life, and causeth to die: and when he decreeth a thing, he only saith unto it, Be, and it is.

Dost thou not observe those who dispute against the signs of God, how they are turned aside from the true faith? They who charge with falsehood the book of the Koran, and other scriptures and revealed doctrines which we sent our former apostle to preach, shall hereafter know their folly; when the collars shall be on their necks, and the chains by which they shall be dragged into hell: then shall they be burned in the fire. And it shall be said unto them, Where are the gods which ye associated, besides God? They shall answer, They have withdrawn themselves from us: yea, we called on nothing heretofore. Thus doth God lead the unbelievers into error. This hath befallen you, for that ye rejoice insolently on earth in that which was false; and for that ye were elated with immoderate joy. Enter ye the gates of hell, to remain therein forever: and wretched shall be the abode of the haughty!

Wherefore persevere with patience, O Mohammed; for the promise of God is true. Whether we cause thee to see any part of the punishment with which we have threatened them, or whether we cause thee to die before thou see it; before us

shall they be assembled at the last day.   We have sent a great
number of apostles before thee; the histories of some of whom
we have related unto thee, and the histories of others of them
we have not related unto thee: but no apostle had the power to
produce a sign, unless by the permission of God.   When the
command of God, therefore, shall come, judgment shall be
given with truth; and then shall they perish who endeavor
to render the signs of God of no effect.   It is God who hath
given you the cattle, that ye may ride on some of them, and
may eat of others of them (ye also receive other advantages
therefrom) ; and that on them ye may arrive at the business
proposed in your mind: and on them are ye carried by land,
and on ships by sea.   And he showeth you his signs; which,
therefore, of the signs of God will ye deny?   Do they not
pass through the earth, and see what hath been the end of
those who were before them?   They were more numerous
than these, and more mighty in strength, and left more considerable monuments of their power in the earth: yet that
which they had acquired profited them not.   And when their
apostles came unto them with evident proofs of their mission,
they rejoice in the knowledge which was with them: but that
which they mocked at encompassed them.   And when they
beheld our vengeance, they said, We believe in God alone, and
we renounce the idols which we associated with him: but their
faith availed them not, after they had beholden our vengeance.
This was the ordinance of God, which was formerly observed
in respect to his servants: and then did the unbelievers perish.

CHAPTER XLI

ENTITLED, ARE DISTINCTLY EXPLAINED; REVEALED AT MECCA

IN THE NAME OF THE MOST MERCIFUL GOD

H. M.   This is a revelation from the most Merciful: a
book the verses whereof are distinctly explained, an Arabic
Koran for the instruction of people who understand; bearing

good tidings, and denouncing threats: but the greater part of them turn aside, and harken not thereto. And they say, Our hearts are veiled from the doctrine to which thou invitest us; and there is a deafness in our ears, and a curtain between us and thee: wherefore act thou as thou shalt think fit; for we shall act according to our own sentiments. Say, Verily I am only a man like you. It is revealed unto me that your God is one God: wherefore direct your way straight unto him; and ask pardon of him for what is past. And woe be to the idolaters; who give not the appointed alms, and believe not in the life to come! But as to those who believe and work righteousness; they shall receive an everlasting reward.

Say, Do ye indeed disbelieve in him who created the earth in two days; and do ye set up equals unto him? He, is the Lord of all creatures. And he placed in the earth mountains firmly rooted, rising above the same: and he blessed it, and provided therein food of the creatures designed to be the inhabitants thereof, in four days; equally for those who ask. Then he set his mind to the creation of heaven; and it was smoke: and he said unto it, and to the earth, Come, either obediently, or against you will. They answered, We come, obedient to thy command. And he formed them into seven heavens, in two days; and revealed unto every heaven its office. And we adorned the lower heaven with lights, and placed therein a guard of angels. This is the disposition of the mighty, the wise God. If the Meccans withdraw from these instructions, say, I denounce unto you a sudden destruction, like the destruction of Ad and Thamud. When the apostle came unto them before them and behind them, saying, Worship God alone; they answered, If our Lord had been pleased to send messengers, he had surely sent angels: and we believe not the message with which ye are sent. As to the tribe of Ad, they behaved insolently in the earth, without reason, and said, Who is more mighty than we in strength? Did they not see that God, who had created them, was more mighty than they in strength? And they knowingly rejected our signs. Wherefore we sent against them a piercing wind, on days of ill luck, that we might make them taste the punishment of shame in this world: but the punishment of the life to come will be more shameful; and they shall not be protected therefrom. And as to Thamud, we directed them; but they loved blindness better than the true direction: wherefore the terrible noise of an ignominious punishment assailed them, for that which they had deserved; but we delivered those who believed and feared God. And warn them of the day, on which the enemies of God shall be gathered together unto hell fire, and shall march in distinct bands; until, when they shall arrive thereat, their ears, and their eyes, and their skins shall bear witness against them of that which they shall have wrought. And they shall say unto their skins, Wherefore do ye bear witness against us? They shall answer, God hath caused us to speak, who giveth speech unto all things: he created you the first time; and unto him are ye returned. Ye did not hide yourselves, while ye sinned, so that your ears, and your eyes, and your skins could not bear witness against you; but ye thought that God was ignorant of many things which ye did. This was your opinion, which ye imagined of your Lord: it hath ruined you; and ye are become lost people. Whether they bear their torment, hell fire shall be their abode; or whether they beg for favor, they shall not obtain favor. And we will give them the devils to be their companions; for they dressed up for them the false notions which they entertained of this present world, and of that which is to come; and the sentence justly fitteth them, which was formerly pronounced on the nations of genii and men who were before them; for they perished.

The unbelievers say, Harken not unto this Koran: but use vain discourse during the reading thereof; that ye may overcome the voice of the reader by your scoffs and laughter. Wherefore we will surely cause the unbelievers to taste a grievous punishment, and we will certainly reward them for the evils which they shall have wrought. This shall be the reward of the enemies of God, namely hell fire; therein is prepared for them an everlasting abode, as a reward for that they have wittingly rejected our signs. And the infidels shall say in hell, O Lord, show us the two who seduced us, of the genii and men,[1] and we will cast them under our feet, that they may become most base and despicable. As for those who say, Our Lord is God, and who behave uprightly; the angels shall descend unto them, and shall say, Fear not, neither be ye grieved; but rejoice in the hopes of paradise, which ye have been promised. We are your friends in this life, and in that which is to come: therein shall ye have that which your souls shall desire, and therein shall ye obtain whatever ye shall ask for; as a gift from a gracious and merciful God.

Who speaketh better than he who inviteth unto God, and worketh righteousness, and saith, I am a Moslem? Good and evil shall not be held equal. Turn away evil with that which is better; and behold the man between whom and thyself there was enmity, shall become, as it were, thy warmest friend: but none shall attain to this perfection, except they who are patient; nor shall any attain thereto, except he who is endued with a great happiness of temper. And if a malicious suggestion be offered unto thee from Satan, have recourse unto God; for it is he who heareth and knoweth. Among the signs of his power are the night, and the day, and the sun, and the moon. Worship not the sun, neither the moon: but worship God, who hath created them; if ye serve him. But if they proudly disdain his service; verily the angels, who are with thy Lord, praise him night and day, and are not wearied. And among his signs another is, that thou seest the land waste: but when we send down rain thereon, it is stirred and fermenteth. And he who quickeneth the earth will surely quicken the dead; for he is almighty. Verily those who impiously wrong our signs are not concealed from us. Is he, therefore, better, who shall be cast into hell fire, or he who shall appear secure on the day of resurrection? Work that which ye will: he certainly beholdeth whatever ye do.

Verily they who believe not in the admonition of the Koran, after it hath come unto them, shall one day be discovered. It is certainly a book of infinite value: vanity shall

[1] *I.e.*, Those of either species, who drew us into sin and ruin. Some suppose that the two more particularly intended here are Eblis and Cain, the two authors of infidelity and murder.

not approach it, either from before it or from behind it: it is a revelation from a wise God, whose praise is justly to be celebrated. No other is said unto thee by the infidels of Mecca, than what hath been formerly said unto the apostles before thee: verily thy Lord is inclined to forgiveness, and is also able to chastise severely. If we had revealed the Koran in a foreign language, they had surely said, Unless the signs thereof be distinctly explained, we will not receive the same: is the book written in a foreign tongue, and the person unto whom it is directed an Arabian? Answer, It is, unto those who believe, a sure guide, and a remedy for doubt and uncertainty: but unto those who believe not, it is a thickness of hearing in their ears, and it is a darkness which covereth them; these are as they who are called unto from a distant place. We heretofore gave the book of the law unto Moses; and a dispute arose concerning the same: and if a previous decree had not proceeded from thy Lord, to respite the opposers of that revelation, verily the matter had been decided between them, by the destruction of the infidels; for they were in a very great doubt as to the same. He who doth right doth it to the advantage of his own soul; and he who doth evil doth it against the same: for thy Lord is not unjust toward his servants.

Unto him is reserved the knowledge of the hour of judgment: and no fruit cometh forth from the knops which involve it; neither doth any female conceive in her womb, nor is she delivered of her burden, without his knowledge. On the day whereon he shall call them to him, saying, Where are my companions which ye ascribed unto me? they shall answer, We assure thee there is no witness of this matter among us: and the idols which they called on before shall withdraw themselves from them; and they shall perceive that there will be no way to escape. Man is not wearied with asking good; but if evil befall him, he despondeth and despaireth. And if we cause him to taste mercy from us, after affliction hath touched him, he surely saith, This is due to me on account of my deserts: I do not think the hour of judgment will ever come; and if I be brought before my Lord, I shall surely attain, with him, the most excellent condition. But we will then declare unto those who shall not have believed, that which they have wrought; and we will surely cause them to taste a most severe punishment. When we confer favors on man, he turneth aside, and departeth without returning thanks: but when evil toucheth him, he is frequently at prayer. Say, What think ye? if the Koran be from God, and ye believe not therein; who will lie under a greater error than he who dissenteth widely therefrom? Hereafter we will show them our signs in the regions of the earth, and in themselves, until it become manifest unto them that this book is the truth. Is it not sufficient for thee that thy Lord is witness of all things? Are they not in a doubt as to the meeting of their Lord at the resurrection? Doth not he encompass all things?

CHAPTER XLII

ENTITLED, CONSULTATION;[1] REVEALED AT MECCA.

IN THE NAME OF THE MOST MERCIFUL GOD

H. M. A. S. K. Thus doth the mighty, the wise God, reveal his will unto thee; and in like manner did he reveal it unto the prophets who were before thee. Unto him belongeth whatever is in heaven and in earth; and he is the high, the great God. It wanteth little but that the heavens be rent in sunder from above, at the awfulness of his majesty: the angels celebrate the praise of their Lord, and ask pardon for those who dwell in the earth. Is not God the forgiver of sins, the merciful? But as to those who take other gods for their patrons, besides him, God observeth their actions: for thou art not a steward over them. Thus have we revealed unto thee an Arabic Koran, that thou mayest warn the metropolis of Mecca, and the Arabs who dwell round about it; and mayest threaten them with the day of the general assembly, of which

[1] The title is taken from the verse wherein the believers are commended, among other things, for using deliberation in their affairs, and consulting together in order to act for the best. Some, instead of this word, prefix the five single letters with which the chapter begins.

there is no doubt: one part shall then be placed in paradise, and another part in hell. If God had pleased, he had made them all of one religion: but he leadeth whom he pleaseth into his mercy; and the unjust shall have no patron or helper. Do they take other patrons, besides him? whereas God is the only true patron: he quickeneth the dead; and he is almighty.

Whatever matter ye disagree about, the decision thereof appertaineth unto God. This is God, my Lord: in him do I trust, and unto him do I turn me; the Creator of heaven and earth: he hath given you wives of your own species, and cattle both male and female; by which means he multiplieth you: there is nothing like him; and it is he who heareth and seeth. His are the keys of heaven and earth: he bestoweth provision abundantly on whom he pleaseth, and he is sparing unto whom he pleaseth; for he knoweth all things. He hath ordained you the religion which he commanded Noah, and which we have revealed unto thee, O Mohammed, and which we commanded Abraham, and Moses, and Jesus: saying, Observe this religion, and be not divided therein. The worship of one God, to which thou invitest them, is grievous unto the unbelievers: God will elect thereto whom he pleaseth, and will direct unto the same him who shall repent. Those who lived in times past were not divided among themselves, until after that the knowledge of God's unity had come unto them; through their own perverseness: and unless a previous decree had passed from thy Lord, to bear with them till a determined time, verily the matter had been decided between them, by the destruction of the gainsayers. They who have inherited the scriptures after them are certainly in a perplexing doubt concerning the same. Wherefore invite them to receive the sure faith, and be urgent with them, as thou hast been commanded; and follow not their vain desires: and say, I believe in all the scriptures which God hath sent down; and I am commanded to establish justice among you: God is our Lord and your Lord: unto us will our works be imputed, and unto you will your works be imputed: let there be no wrangling between us and you; for God will assemble us all at the last day, and unto him shall we return.

As to those who dispute concerning God, after obedience hath been paid him by receiving his religion, their disputing shall be vain in the sight of their Lord; and wrath shall fall on them, and they shall suffer a grievous punishment. It is God who hath sent down the scripture with truth; and the balance of true judgment: and what shall inform thee whether the hour be nigh at hand? They who believe not therein wish it to be hastened by way of mockery: but they who believe dread the same, and know it to be the truth. Are not those who dispute concerning the last hour in a wide error? God is bounteous unto his servants: he provideth for whom he pleaseth; and he is the strong, the mighty. Whoso chooseth the tillage of the life to come, unto him will we give increase in his tillage; and whoso chooseth the tillage of this world, we will give him the fruit thereof; but he shall have no part in the life to come. Have the idolaters deities which ordain them a religion which God hath not allowed? But had it not been for the decree of respiting their punishment to the day of separating the infidels from the true believers, judgment had been already given between them: for the unjust shall surely suffer a painful torment. On that day thou shalt see the unjust in great terror, because of their demerits; and the penalty thereof shall fall upon them: but they who believe and do good works shall dwell in the delightful meadows of paradise; they shall obtain whatever they shall desire, with their Lord. This is the greatest acquisition. This is what God promiseth unto his servants who believe and do good works.

Say, I ask not of you, for this my preaching, any reward, except the love of my relations: and whoever shall have deserved well by one good action, unto him will we add the merit of another action thereto; for God is inclined to forgive, and ready to reward. Do they say, Mohammed hath blasphemously forged a lie concerning God? If God pleaseth, he will seal up thy heart: and God will absolutely abolish vanity, and will establish the truth in his words; for he knoweth the innermost parts of men's breasts. It is he who accepteth repentance from his servants, and forgiveth sins, and knoweth that which ye do. He will incline his ear unto those who

believe and work righteousness, and will add unto them above
what they shall ask or deserve, of his bounty: but the unbelievers shall suffer a severe punishment. If God should bestow abundance upon his servants, they would certainly behave insolently in the earth: but he sendeth down by measure
unto every one that which he pleaseth; for he well knoweth
and seeth the condition of his servants. It is he who sendeth down the rain, after men have despaired thereof, and
spreadeth abroad his mercy; and he is the patron justly to be
praised.

Among his signs is the creation of heaven and earth, and
of the living creatures with which he hath replenished them
both; and he is able to gather them together before his tribunal whenever he pleaseth. Whatever misfortune befalleth
you is sent you by God, for that which your hands have deserved; and yet he forgiveth many things: ye shall not frustrate the divine vengeance in the earth; neither shall ye have
any protector or helper against God. Among his signs also
are the ships running in the sea, like high mountains: if he
pleaseth he causeth the wind to cease, and they lie still on the
back of the water (verily herein are signs, unto every patient
and grateful person): or he destroyeth them by shipwreck,
because of that which their crews have merited; though he
pardoneth many things. And they who dispute against our
signs shall know that there will be no way for them to
escape our vengeance. Whatever things are given you, they
are the provision of this present life: but the reward which
is with God is better and more durable, for those who believe and put their trust in their Lord; and who avoid
heinous and filthy crimes, and when they are angry, forgive;
and who harken unto their Lord, and are constant at prayer,
and whose affairs are directed by consultation among themselves, and who give alms out of what we have bestowed on
them; and who, when an injury is done them, avenge themselves (and the retaliation of evil ought to be an evil pro-
portionate thereto): but he who forgiveth, and is reconciled
unto his enemy, shall receive his reward from God; for he
loveth not the unjust doers.

And whoso shall avenge himself, after he hath been injured; as to these, it is not lawful to punish them for it: but it is only lawful to punish those who wrong men, and act insolently in the earth, against justice; these shall suffer a grievous punishment. And whoso beareth injuries patiently, and forgiveth; verily this is a necessary work. Whom God shall cause to err, he shall afterward have no protector. And thou shalt see the ungodly, who shall say, when they behold the punishment prepared for them, Is there no way to return back into the world? And thou shalt see them exposed unto hell fire; dejected, because of the ignominy they shall undergo: they shall look at the fire sideways and by stealth; and the true believers shall say, Verily the losers are they who have lost their own souls, and their families, on the day of resurrection: shall not the ungodly continue in eternal torment? They shall have no protectors to defend them against God: and whom God shall cause to err, he shall find no way to the truth. Harken unto your Lord, before the day come, which God will not keep back: ye shall have no place of refuge on that day; neither shall ye be able to deny your sins. But if those to whom thou preachest turn aside from thy admonitions, verily we have not sent thee to be a guardian over them: thy duty is preaching only. When we cause man to taste mercy from us, he rejoiceth thereat: but if evil befall them, for that which their hands have formerly committed, verily man becometh ungrateful.

Unto God appertaineth the kingdom of heaven and earth: he createth that which he pleaseth; he giveth females unto whom he pleaseth, and he giveth males unto whom he pleaseth; or he giveth them males and females jointly: and he maketh whom he pleaseth to be childless; for he is wise and powerful. It is not fit for man that God should speak unto him otherwise than by private revelation, or from behind a veil, or by his sending of a messenger to reveal, by his permission, that which he pleaseth; for he is high and wise. Thus have we revealed unto thee a revelation, by our command. Thou didst not understand, before this, what the book of the Koran was, nor what the faith was: but we have ordained the same for a light; we will thereby direct such of our servants as we please: and thou shalt surely direct them into the right way, the way of God, unto whom belongeth whatever is in heaven and in earth. Shall not all things return unto God?

CHAPTER XLIII

ENTITLED, THE ORNAMENTS OF GOLD; REVEALED AT MECCA

IN THE NAME OF THE MOST MERCIFUL GOD

H. M. By the perspicuous book; verily we have ordained the same an Arabic Koran, that ye may understand: and it is certainly written in the original book, kept with us, being sublime and full of wisdom. Shall we therefore turn away from you the admonition, and deprive you thereof, because ye are a people who transgress? And how many prophets have we sent among those of old? and no prophet came unto them, but they laughed him to scorn: wherefore we destroyed nations who were more mighty than these in strength; and the example of those who were of old hath been already set before them. If thou ask them who created the heavens and the earth, they will certainly answer, The mighty, the wise God created them: who hath spread the earth as a bed for you, and hath made you paths therein, that ye may be directed: and who sendeth down rain from heaven by measure, whereby we quicken a dead country (so shall ye be brought forth from your graves): and who hath created all the various species of things, and hath given you ships and cattle, whereon ye are carried; that ye may sit firmly on the backs thereof, and may remember the favor of your Lord, when ye sit thereon and may say, Praise be unto him, who hath subjected these unto our service! for we could not have mastered them by our own power: and unto our Lord shall we surely return. Yet have they attributed unto him some of his servants as his offspring: verily man is openly ungrateful.

Hath God taken daughters out of those beings which he hath created; and hath he chosen sons for you? But when one of them hath the news brought of the birth of a child of that sex which they attribute unto the Merciful, as his similitude, his face becometh black, and he is oppressed with sorrow. Do they therefore attribute unto God female issue, which are brought up among ornaments, and are contentious without cause? And do they make the angels, who are the servants of the Merciful, females? Were they present at their creation? Their testimony shall be written down, and they shall be examined concerning the same, on the day of judgment. And they say, If the Merciful had pleased, we had not worshiped them. They have no knowledge herein: they only utter a vain lie. Have we given them a book of revelations before this; and do they keep the same in their custody? But they say, Verily we found our fathers practising a religion; and we are guided in their footsteps. Thus we sent no preacher, before thee, unto any city, but the inhabitants thereof who lived in affluence, said, Verily we found our fathers practising a religion: and we tread in their footsteps. And the preacher answered, What, although I bring you a more right religion than that which ye found your fathers to practise? And they replied, Verily we believe not that which ye are sent to preach. Wherefore we took vengeance on them: and behold what hath been the end of those who accused our apostles of imposture.

Remember when Abraham said unto his father, and his people, Verily I am clear of the gods which ye worship, except him who hath created me; for he will direct me aright. And he ordained this to be a constant doctrine among his posterity; that they should be turned from idolatry to the worship of the only true God. Verily I have permitted these Meccans and their fathers to live in prosperity, until the truth should come unto them, and a manifest apostle: but now the truth is come unto them, they say, This is a piece of forgery; and we believe not therein. And they say, Had this Koran been sent down unto some great man of either of the two cities, we would have received it. Do they distribute the mercy of thy Lord? We distribute their necessary provision among them, in this present life, and we raise some of them several degrees above the others, that the one of them may take the other to serve him: and the mercy of thy Lord is more valuable than the riches which they gather together. If it were not that mankind would have become one sect of infidels, verily we had given unto those who believe not in the Merciful, roofs of silver to their houses, and stairs of silver, by which they might ascend thereto, and doors of silver to their houses, and couches of silver for them to lean on; and ornaments of gold: for all this is the provision of the present life; but the next life with thy Lord shall be for those who fear him. Whoever shall withdraw from the admonition of the Merciful, we will chain a devil unto him; and he shall be his inseparable companion (and the devils shall turn them aside from the way of truth; yet they shall imagine themselves to be rightly directed): until, when he shall appear before us at the last day, he shall say unto the devil, Would to God that between me and thee there was the distance of the east from the west! Oh how wretched a companion art thou! But wishes shall not avail you on this day, since ye have been unjust; for ye shall be partakers of the same punishment. Canst thou, O prophet, make the deaf to hear, or canst thou direct the blind, and him who is in a manifest error? Whether we take thee away, we will surely take vengeance on them; or whether we cause thee to see the punishment with which we have threatened them, executed, we will certainly prevail over them. Wherefore hold fast the doctrine which hath been revealed unto thee; for thou art in a right way: and it is a memorial unto thee and thy people, and hereafter shall ye be examined concerning your observance thereof.

And ask our apostles whom we have sent before thee, whether we have appointed gods for them to worship, besides the Merciful. We formerly sent Moses with our signs unto Pharaoh and his princes, and he said, Verily I am the apostle of the Lord of all creatures. And when he came unto them with our signs, behold, they laughed him to scorn; although we showed them no sign, but it was greater than the other: and we inflicted a punishment on them, that peradventure they might be converted. And they said unto Moses, O magician, pray unto thy Lord for us, according to the covenant which he hath made with thee; for we will certainly be directed. But when we took the plague from off them, behold, they brake their promise. And Pharaoh made proclamation among his people, saying, O my people, is not the kingdom of Egypt mine, and these rivers which flow beneath me? Do ye not see? Am I not better than this Moses; who is a contemptible person, and can scarce express himself intelligibly? Have bracelets of gold, therefore, been put upon him; or do the angels attend him in orderly procession? And Pharaoh persuaded his people to light behavior; and they obeyed him: for they were a wicked people. And when they had provoked us to wrath, we took vengeance on them, and we drowned them all: and we made them a precedent and an example unto others. And when the son of Mary was proposed for an example; behold, thy people cried out through excess of joy thereat; and they said, Are our gods better, or he? They had proposed this instance unto thee no otherwise than for an occasion of dispute: yea, they are contentious men. Jesus is no other than a servant, whom we favored with the gift of prophecy; and we appointed him for an example unto the children of Israel (if we pleased, verily we could from yourselves produce angels, to succeed you in the earth): and he shall be a sign of the approach of the last hour; [1] wherefore doubt not thereof. And follow me: this is the right way. And let not Satan cause you to turn aside: for he is your open enemy. And when Jesus came with evident miracles, he said, Now am I come unto you with wisdom; and to explain unto you part of those things con-

[1] For some time before the resurrection Jesus is to descend on earth, according to the Mohammedans, near Damascus, or, as some say, near a rock in the holy land named Afik, with a lance in his hand, wherewith he is to kill Antichrist, whom he will encounter at Ludd, or Lydda, a small town not far from Joppa. They add that he will arrive at Jerusalem at the time of morning prayer, that he shall perform his devotions after the Mohammedan institution, and officiate instead of the Imam, who shall give place to him; that he will break down the cross, and destroy the churches of the Christians, of whom he will make a general slaughter, excepting only such as shall profess Islam, etc.

cerning which ye disagree: wherefore fear God, and obey me. Verily God is my Lord and your Lord; wherefore worship him: this is the right way. And the confederated sects among them fell to variance: but woe unto those who have acted unjustly, because of the punishment of a grievous day.

Do the unbelievers wait for any other than the hour of judgment; that it may come upon them suddenly, while they foresee it not? The intimate friends, on that day, shall be enemies unto one another; except the pious. O my servants, there shall no fear come on you this day, neither shall ye be grieved; who have believed in our signs, and have been Moslems: enter ye into paradise, ye and your wives, with great joy. Dishes of gold shall be carried round unto them, and cups without handles: and therein shall they enjoy whatever their souls shall desire, and whatever their eyes shall delight in: and ye shall remain therein forever. This is paradise, which ye have inherited as a reward for that which ye have wrought. Therein shall ye have fruits in abundance, of which ye shall eat. But the wicked shall remain forever in the torment of hell: it shall not be made lighter unto them; and they shall despair therein. We deal not unjustly with them, but they deal unjustly with their own souls. And they shall call aloud, saying, O Malec,[2] intercede for us that thy Lord may end us by annihilation. He shall answer, Verily ye shall remain here forever. We brought you the truth heretofore, but the greater part of you abhorred the truth.

Have the infidels fixed on a method to circumvent our apostle? Verily, we will fix on a method to circumvent them. Do they imagine that we hear not their secrets, and their private discourse? Yea; and our messengers who attend them write down the same. Say, If the Merciful had a son, verily I would be the first of those who should worship him. Far be the Lord of heaven and earth, the Lord of the throne, from that which they affirm of him! Wherefore

[2] This the Mohammedans suppose to be the name of the principal angel who has the charge of hell.

let them wade in their vanity, and divert themselves, until they arrive at their day with which they have been threatened. He who is God in heaven is God on earth also: and he is the wise, the knowing. And blessed be he unto whom appertaineth the kingdom of heaven and earth, and of whatever is between them; with whom is the knowledge of the last hour; and before whom ye shall be assembled. They whom they invoke besides him have not the privilege to intercede for others; except those who bear witness to the truth, and know the same. If thou ask them who hath created them, they will surely answer, God. How therefore are they turned away to the worship of others? God also heareth the saying of the prophet, O Lord, verily these are people who believe not: and he answered, Therefore turn aside from them; and say, Peace: hereafter shall they know their folly.

CHAPTER XLIV

ENTITLED, SMOKE; REVEALED AT MECCA

IN THE NAME OF THE MOST MERCIFUL GOD

H. M. By the perspicuous book of the Koran; verily we have sent down the same on a blessed night [1] (for we had engaged so to do), on the night wherein is distinctly sent down the decree of every determined thing, as a command from us. Verily we have ever used to send apostles with revelations, at proper intervals, as a mercy from thy Lord; for it is he who heareth and knoweth: the Lord of heaven and earth, and of whatever is between them; if ye are men of sure knowledge. There is no God but he: he giveth life, and he causeth to die; he is your Lord, and the Lord of your forefathers. Yet do they amuse themselves with doubt. But

---

[1] Generally supposed to be that between the twenty-third and twenty-fourth of Ramadan. Annually on this night, as the Mohammedans are taught, all the events of the ensuing year, with respect to life and death and the other affairs of this world, are disposed and settled. Some, however, suppose that these words refer only to that particular night on which the Koran, wherein are completely contained the divine determinations in respect to religion and morality, was sent down.

observe them on the day whereon the heaven shall produce a visible smoke, which shall cover mankind: [2] this will be a tormenting plague. They shall say, O Lord, take this plague from off us: verily we will become true believers. How should an admonition be of avail to them in this condition; when a manifest apostle came unto them, but they retired from him, saying, This man is instructed by others, or is a distracted person? We will take the plague from off you, a little: but we will certainly return to your infidelity. On the day whereon we shall fiercely assault them with great power, verily we will take vengeance on them. We made trial of the people of Pharaoh before them, and an honorable messenger came unto them, saying, Send unto me the servants of God; verily I am a faithful messenger unto you: and lift not yourselves up against God: for I come unto you with manifest power. And I fly for protection unto my Lord and your Lord, that ye stone me not. If ye do not believe me, at least depart from me. And when they accused him of imposture, he called upon his Lord, saying, These are a wicked people. And God said unto him, March forth with my servants by night; for ye will be pursued: and leave the sea divided, that the Egyptians may enter the same; for they are a host doomed to be drowned. How many gardens, and fountains, and fields of corn, and fair dwellings, and advantages which they enjoyed, did they leave behind them? Thus we dispossessed them thereof; and we gave the same for an inheritance unto another people. Neither heaven or earth wept for them; neither were they respited any longer. And we delivered the children of Israel from a shameful affliction; from Pharaoh; for he was haughty, and a transgressor: and we chose them, knowingly, above all peo-

[2] The commentators differ in their expositions of this passage. Some think it spoke of a smoke which seemed to fill the air during the famine which was inflicted on the Meccans in Mohammed's time, and was so thick that, though they could hear, yet they could not see one another. But, according to a tradition of Ali, the smoke here meant is that which is to be one of the previous signs of the day of judgment, and will fill the whole space from east to west, and last for forty days. This smoke, they say, will intoxicate the infidels, but will very little inconvenience the true believers.

ple; and we showed them several signs, wherein was an evident trial.

Verily these Meccans say, Assuredly our final end will be no other than our first natural death; neither shall we be raised again: bring now our forefathers back to life, if ye speak truth. Are they better, or the people of Tobba, and those who were before them? We destroyed them, because they wrought wickedness. We have not created the heavens and the earth, and whatever is between them, by way of sport: we have created them no otherwise than in truth; but the greater part of them do not understand. Verily the day of separation shall be the appointed term of them all; a day, whereon the master and the servant shall be of no advantage to one another, neither shall they be helped; excepting those on whom God shall have mercy: for he is the mighty, the merciful. Verily the fruit of the tree of al Zakkum shall be the food of the impious: as the dregs of oil shall it boil in the bellies of the damned, like the boiling of the hottest water. And it shall be said of the tormenters, Take him, and drag him into the midst of hell: and pour on his head the torture of boiling waters, saying, Taste this; for thou art that mighty and honorable person. Verily this is the punishment of which ye doubted. But the pious shall be lodged in a place of security; among gardens and fountains: they shall be clothed in fine silk and in satin; and they shall sit facing one another. Thus shall it be: and we will espouse them to fair damsels, having large black eyes. In that place shall they call for all kinds of fruits, in full security: they shall not taste death therein, after the first death; and God shall deliver from the pains of hell: through the gracious bounty of thy Lord. This will be great felicity. Moreover we have rendered the Koran easy for thee, by revealing it in thine own tongue: to the end that they may be admonished: wherefore do thou wait the event; for they wait to see some misfortune befall thee.

CHAPTER XLV

ENTITLED, THE KNEELING; REVEALED AT MECCA

IN THE NAME OF THE MOST MERCIFUL GOD

H. M. The revelation of this book is from the mighty, the wise God. Verily both in heaven and earth are signs of the divine power unto the true believers: and in the creation of yourselves, and of the beasts which are scattered over the face of the earth, are signs unto people of sound judgment; and also in the vicissitude of night and day, and the rain which God sendeth down from heaven, whereby he quickeneth the earth after it hath been dead: in the change of the winds also are signs, unto people of understanding. These are the signs of God; we rehearse them unto thee with truth. In what revelation therefore will they believe, after they have rejected God and his signs? Woe unto every lying and impious person; who heareth the signs of God which are read unto him, and afterward proudly persisteth in infidelity, as though he heard them not (denounce unto him a painful punishment): and who, when he cometh to the knowledge of any of our signs, receiveth the same with scorn. For these is prepared a shameful punishment: before them lieth hell: and whatever they shall have gained shall not avail them at all, neither shall the idols which they have taken for their patrons, besides God: and they shall suffer a grievous punishment. This is a true direction: and for those who disbelieve the signs of their Lord, is prepared the punishment of a painful torment. It is God who hath subjected the sea unto you, that the ships may sail therein, at his command; and that ye may seek advantage unto yourselves by commerce, of his bounty; and that ye may give thanks: and he obligeth whatever is in heaven and on earth to serve you; the whole being from him. Verily herein are signs, unto people who consider.

Speak unto the true believers, that they forgive those who hope not for the days of God, that he may reward people according to what they shall have wrought. Whoso doth that which is right doth it to the advantage of his own soul; and whoso doth evil doth it against the same: hereafter shall ye return unto your Lord. We gave unto the children of Israel the book of the law, and wisdom, and prophecy; and we fed them with good things, and preferred them above all nations; and we gave them plain ordinances concerning the business of religion; neither did they fall to variance, except after that knowledge had come unto them, through envy against themselves: but thy Lord will decide the controversy between them on the day of resurrection, concerning that wherein they disagree. Afterward we appointed thee, O Mohammed, to promulgate a law concerning the business of religion: wherefore follow the same, and follow not the desires of those who are ignorant. Verily they shall not avail thee against God at all: the unjust are the patrons of one another; but God is the patron of the pious.

This Koran delivereth evident precepts unto mankind; and is a direction and a mercy, unto people who judge aright. Do the workers of iniquity imagine that we will deal with them as with those who believe and do good works; so that their life and their death shall be equal? An ill judgment do they make. God hath created the heavens and the earth in truth; that he may recompense every soul according to that which it shall have wrought: and they shall not be treated unjustly. What thinkest thou? He who taketh his own lust for his God, and whom God causeth knowingly to err, and whose ears and whose heart he hath sealed up, and over whose eyes he hath cast a veil; who shall direct him, after God shall have forsaken him? Will ye not therefore be admonished? They say, There is no other life, except our present life: we die and we live; and nothing but time destroyeth us. But they have no knowledge in this matter; they only follow a vain opinion. And when our evident signs are rehearsed unto them, their argument which they offer against the same is no other than that they say, Bring to life our fathers who have been dead; if ye speak truth.

Say, God giveth you life; and afterward causeth you to die: hereafter will he assemble you together on the day of resur-

rection; there is no doubt thereof; but the greater part of
men do not understand. Unto God appertaineth the kingdom of heaven and earth; and the day whereon the hour shall
be fixed, on that day shall those who charge the Koran with
vanity perish. And thou shalt see every nation kneeling:
every nation shall be called unto its book of account; and it
shall be said unto them, This day shall ye be rewarded according to that which ye have wrought. This our book will
speak concerning you with truth; therein have we written
down whatever ye have done. As to those who shall have
believed and done good works, their Lord shall lead them into
his mercy: this shall be manifest felicity. But as to the
infidels, it shall be said unto them, Were not my signs rehearsed unto you? but ye proudly rejected them, and became
a wicked people? And when it was said unto you, Verily
the promise of God is true; and as to the hour of judgment,
there is no doubt thereof: ye answered, We know not what
the hour of judgment is: we hold an uncertain opinion only;
and we are not well assured of this matter. But on that day
the evils of that which they have wrought shall appear unto
them; and that which they mocked at shall encompass them:
and it shall be said unto them, This day will we forget you,
as ye did forget the meeting of this your day; and your abode
shall be hell fire; and ye shall have none to deliver you. This
shall ye suffer, because ye turned the signs of God to ridicule;
and the life of the world deceived you. On this day, therefore, they shall not be taken forth from thence, neither shall
they be asked any more to render themselves well pleasing
unto God. Wherefore praise be unto God, the Lord of the
heavens and the Lord of the earth; the Lord of all creatures:
and unto him be glory in heaven and earth; for he is the
mighty, the wise God!

CHAPTER XLVI

ENTITLED, AL AHKAF;[1] REVEALED AT MECCA

IN THE NAME OF THE MOST MERCIFUL GOD

H. M. The revelation of this book is from the mighty, the wise God. We have not created the heavens, and the earth, and whatever is between them, otherwise than in truth, and for a determined period: but the unbelievers turn away from the warning which is given them. Say, What think ye? Show me what part of the earth the idols which ye invoke, besides God, have created? Or had they any share in the creation of the heavens? Bring me a book of scripture revealed before this, or some footstep of ancient knowledge, to countenance your idolatrous practises; if ye are men of veracity. Who is in a wider error than he who invoketh, besides God, that which can not return him an answer, to the day of resurrection; and idols which regard not their calling on them: and which, when men shall be gathered together to judgment, will become their enemies, and will ungratefully deny their worship?

When our evident signs are rehearsed unto them, the unbelievers say of the truth, when it cometh unto them, This is a manifest piece of sorcery. Will they say, Mohammed hath forged it? Answer, If I have forged it, verily ye shall not obtain for me any favor from God: he well knoweth the injurious language which ye utter concerning it: he is a sufficient witness between me and you; and he is gracious and merciful. Say, I am not singular among the apostles; neither do I know what will be done with me or with you hereafter: I follow no other than what is revealed unto me; neither am I any more than a public warner. Say, What is your opinion? If this book be from God, and ye believe not therein; and a witness of the children of Israel bear witness to its consonancy with the law, and believeth therein;

---

[1] Al Ahkaf is the plural of Hekf, and signifies lands which lie in a crooked or winding manner; whence it became the name of a territory in the province of Hadramaut, where the Adites dwelt. It is mentioned about the middle of the chapter.

and ye proudly reject the same: are ye not unjust doers?
Verily God directeth not unjust people. But those who believe not, say of the true believers, If the doctrine of the
Koran had been good, they had not embraced the same before
us. And when they are not guided thereby, they say, This
is an antiquated lie. Whereas the book of Moses was revealed before the Koran, to be a guide and a mercy: and this
is a book confirming the same, delivered in the Arabic tongue;
to denounce threats unto those who act unjustly, and to bear
good tidings unto the righteous doers.

As to those who say, Our Lord is God; and who behave
uprightly: on them shall no fear come, neither shall they be
grieved. These shall be the inhabitants of paradise, they
shall remain therein forever: in recompense for that which
they have wrought. We have commanded man to show kindness to his parents: his mother beareth him in her womb with
pain, and bringeth him forth with pain: and the space of his
being carried in her womb, and of his weaning, is thirty
months; until, when he attaineth his age of strength, and
attaineth the age of forty years, he saith, O Lord, excite me,
by thy inspiration, that I may be grateful for thy favors,
wherewith thou hast favored me and my parents; and that I
may work righteousness, which may please thee: and be gracious unto me in my issue; for I am turned unto thee, and
am a Moslem. These are they from whom we accept the good
work which they have wrought, and whose evil works we
pass by; and they shall be among the inhabitants of paradise:
this is a true promise, which they are promised in this world.
He who saith unto his parents, Fie on you! do ye promise
me that I shall be taken forth from the grave, and restored
to life; when many generations have passed away before me,
and none of them has returned back? And his parents implore God's assistance, and say to their son, Alas for thee!
Believe: for the promise of God is true. But he answereth,
This is no other than silly fables of the ancients. These are
they whom the sentence passed on the nations which have
been before them, of genii and of men, justly fitteth: they
shall surely perish.

For every one is prepared a certain degree of happiness or misery, according to that which they shall have wrought; that God may recompense them for their works; and they shall not be treated unjustly. On a certain day, the unbelievers shall be exposed before the fire of hell; and it shall be said unto them, Ye received your good things in your lifetime, while ye were in the world; and ye enjoyed yourselves herein: wherefore this day ye shall be rewarded with the punishment of ignominy; for that ye behaved insolently in the earth, without justice, and for that ye transgressed. Remember the brother of Ad, when he preached unto his people in al Ahkaf (and there were preachers before him and after him), saying, Worship none but God: verily I fear for you the punishment of a great day. They answered, Art thou come unto us that thou mayest turn us aside from the worship of our gods? Bring on us now the punishment with which thou threatenest us, if thou art a man of veracity. He said, Verily the knowledge of the time when your punishment will be inflicted is with God; and I only declare unto you that which I am sent to preach; but I see ye are an ignorant people. And when they saw the preparation made for their punishment, namely, a cloud traversing the sky, and tending toward their valleys, they said, This is a traversing cloud, which bringeth us rain. Hud answered, Nay; it is what ye demanded to be hastened: a wind, wherein is a severe vengeance: it will destroy everything, at the command of its Lord. And in the morning nothing was to be seen, besides their empty dwellings. Thus do we reward wicked people.

We had established them in the like flourishing condition wherein we have established you, O men of Mecca; and we had given them ears, and eyes, and hearts: yet neither their ears, nor their eyes, nor their hearts profited them at all, when they rejected the signs of God; but the vengeance which they mocked at fell upon them. We heretofore destroyed the cities which were round about you; and we variously proposed our signs unto them, that they might repent. Did those protect them, whom they took for gods, besides God, and imagined to be honored with his familiarity? Nay; they withdraw from them: yet this was their false opinion which seduced them, and the blasphemy which they had devised.

Remember when we caused certain of the genii [2] to turn aside unto thee, that they might hear the Koran; and when they were present at the reading of the same, they said to one another, Give ear: and when it was ended, they returned back unto their people, preaching what they had heard. They said, Our people, verily we have heard a book read unto us, which hath been revealed since Moses, confirming the scriptures which was delivered before it; and directing unto the truth and the right way. Our people, obey God's preacher: and believe in him; that he may forgive you your sins, and may deliver you from a painful punishment. And whoever obeyeth not God's preacher shall by no means frustrate God's vengeance on earth: neither shall he have any protectors besides him. These will be in a manifest error. Do they not know that God, who hath created the heavens and the earth, and was not fatigued with the creation thereof, is able to raise the dead to life? Yea, verily: for he is almighty. On a certain day the unbelievers shall be exposed unto hell fire; and it shall be said unto them, Is not this really come to pass? They shall answer, Yea, by our Lord. God shall reply, Taste, therefore, the punishment of hell, for that ye have been unbelievers.

Do thou, O prophet, bear the insults of thy people with patience, as our apostles, who were endued with constancy, bare the injuries of their people: and require not their punishment to be hastened unto them. On the day whereon they shall see the punishment wherewith they have been threatened, it shall seem as though they had tarried in the world but an hour of a day. This is a fair warning. Shall any perish except the people who transgress?

[2] These genii, according to different opinions, were of Nisibin, or of Yaman, or of Ninive; and in number nine or seven. They heard Mohammed reading the Koran by night, or after the morning prayer, in the valley of al Nakhlah, during the time of his retreat to al Tayef, and believed on him.

CHAPTER XLVII

ENTITLED, MOHAMMED;[1] REVEALED AT MEDINA

IN THE NAME OF THE MOST MERCIFUL GOD

God will render of none effect the works of those who believe not, and who turn away men from the way of God: but as to those who believe, and work righteousness, and believe in the revelation which hath been sent down unto Mohammed (for it is the truth from their Lord), he will expiate their evil deeds from them, and will dispose their heart aright. This will he do, because those who believe not follow vanity, and because those who believe follow the truth from their Lord. Thus God propoundeth unto men their examples. When ye encounter the unbelievers, strike off their heads, until ye have made a great slaughter among them; and bind them in bonds: and either give them a free dismission afterward, or exact a ransom; until the war shall have laid down its arms. This shall ye do: Verily if God pleased, he could take vengeance on them, without your assistance; but he commandeth you to fight his battles, that he may prove the one of you by the other. And as to those who fight in defense of God's true religion, God will not suffer their works to perish: he will guide them, and will dispose their hearts aright; and he will lead them into paradise, of which he hath told them.

O true believers, if ye assist God, by fighting for his religion, he will assist you against your enemies; and will set your feet fast: but as for the infidels, let them perish; and their works shall God render vain. This shall befall them, because they have rejected with abhorrence that which God hath revealed: wherefore their works shall become of no avail. Do they not travel through the earth, and see what hath been the end of those who were before them? God utterly destroyed them: and the like catastrophe awaiteth the unbelievers. This shall come to pass, for that God is the patron of the true believers, and for that the infidels have no pro-

[1] Some entitle this chapter " War," which is therein commanded to be vigorously carried on against the enemies of the Mohammedan faith.

tector.   Verily God will introduce those who believe, and do good works, into gardens beneath which rivers flow: but the unbelievers indulge themselves in pleasures, and eat as beasts eat; and their abode shall be hell fire.   How many cities were more mighty in strength than thy city which hath expelled thee; yet have we destroyed them, and there was none to help them?   Shall he, therefore, who followeth the plain declaration of his Lord, be as he whose evil works have been dressed up for him by the devil; and who follow their own lusts?

The description of paradise, which is promised unto the pious: therein are rivers of incorruptible water; and rivers of milk, the taste whereof changeth not; and rivers of wine, pleasant unto those who drink; and rivers of clarified honey: and therein shall they have plenty of all kinds of fruits; and pardon from their Lord.   Shall the man for whom these things are prepared, be as he who must dwell forever in hell fire; and will have the boiling water given them to drink, which shall burst their bowels?   Of the unbelievers there are some who give ear unto thee, until, when they go out from thee, they say, by way of derision, unto those to whom knowledge hath been given, What hath he said now?   These are they whose hearts God hath sealed up, and who follow their own lusts: but as to those who are directed, God will grant them a more ample direction, and he will instruct them what to avoid.   Do the infidels wait for any other than the last hour, that it may come upon them suddenly?   Some signs thereof are already come: and when it shall actually overtake them, how can they then receive admonition?   Know, therefore, that there is no god but God: and ask pardon for thy sin, and for the true believers, both men and women.   God knoweth your busy employment in the world, and the place of your abode hereafter.   The true believers say, Hath not a Sura been revealed commanding war against the infidels? But when a Sura without any ambiguity is revealed, and war is mentioned therein, thou mayest see those in whose hearts is an infirmity look toward thee with the look of one whom death overshadoweth.   But obedience would be more eligible for them, and to speak that which is convenient.   And when the command is firmly established, if they give credit unto God, it will be better for them. Were ye ready, therefore, if ye had been put in authority, to commit outrages in the earth, and to violate your ties of blood? These are they whom God hath cursed, and hath rendered deaf, and whose eyes he hath blinded. Do they not therefore attentively meditate on the Koran? Are there locks upon their hearts? Verily they who turn their backs, after the true direction is made manifest unto them; Satan shall prepare their wickedness for them, and God shall bear with them for a time. This shall befall them, because they say privately unto those who detest what God hath revealed, We will obey you in part of the matter. But God knoweth their secrets. How therefore will it be with them, when the angels shall cause them to die, and shall strike their faces and their backs? This shall they suffer, because they follow that which provoketh God to wrath, and are averse to what is well pleasing unto him: and he will render their works vain. Do they in whose hearts is an infirmity, imagine that God will not bring their malice to light? If we pleased, we could surely show them unto thee, and thou shouldst know them by their marks; but thou shalt certainly know them by their perverse pronunciation of their words. God knoweth your actions: and we will try you, until we know those among you who fight valiantly, and who persevere with constancy; and we will try the reports of your behavior. Verily those who believe not, and turn away men from the way of God, and make opposition against the apostle, after the divine direction hath been manifested unto them, shall not hurt God at all; but he shall make their works to perish.

O true believers, obey God; and obey the apostle: and render not your works of no effect. Verily those who believe not, and who turn away men from the way of God, and then die, being unbelievers, God will by no means forgive. Faint not, therefore, neither invite your enemies to peace, while ye are the superior: for the God is with you, and will not defraud you of the merit of your works. Verily this present life is only a play and a vain amusement: but if ye believe, and fear

God, he will give you your rewards. He doth not require of you your whole substance: if he should require the whole of you. and earnestly press you, ye would become niggardly, and it would raise your hatred against his apostle. Behold, ye are those who are invited to expend part of your substance for the support of God's true religion; and there are some of you who are niggardly. But whoever shall be niggardly shall be niggardly toward his own soul: for God wanteth nothing, but ye are needy: and if ye turn back, he will substitute another people in your stead, who shall not be like unto you.

CHAPTER XLVIII

ENTITLED, THE VICTORY; REVEALED AT MEDINA

IN THE NAME OF THE MOST MERCIFUL GOD

Verily we have granted thee a manifest victory: [1] that God may forgive thee thy preceding and thy subsequent sin, and may complete his favor on thee, and direct thee in the right way; and that God may assist thee with a glorious assistance. It is he who sendeth down secure tranquillity into the hearts of the true believers, that they may increase in faith, beyond their former faith (the hosts of heaven and earth are God's; and God is knowing and wise): that he may lead the true believers of both sexes into gardens beneath which rivers flow, to dwell therein forever; and may expiate their evil deeds from them (this will be great felicity with God): and that he may punish the hypocritical men, and the hypocritical women, and the idolaters, and the idolatresses, who conceive an ill opinion of God. They shall experience a turn of evil fortune; and God shall be angry with them, and shall curse

[1] This victory, from which the chapter takes its title, according to the most received interpretation, was the taking of the city of Mecca. The passage is said to have been revealed on Mohammed's return from the expedition of al Hodeibiya, and contains a promise or prediction of this signal success, which happened not till two years after, the preterite tense being therein used, according to the prophetic style, for the future.

them, and hath prepared hell for them; an ill journey shall it be thither!

Unto God belong the hosts of heaven and earth; and God is mighty and wise. Verily we have sent thee to be a witness, and a bearer of good tidings, and a denouncer of threats; that ye may believe in God and his apostle; and may assist him, and revere him, and praise him morning and evening. Verily they who swear fealty unto thee swear fealty unto God: the hand of God is over their hands. Whoever shall violate his oath will violate the same to the hurt only of his own soul: but whoever shall perform that which he hath covenanted with God, he will surely give him a great reward. The Arabs of the desert who were left behind will say unto thee, Our substance and our families employed us, so that we went not forth with thee to war; wherefore ask pardon for us. They speak that with their tongues, which is not in their hearts. Answer, Who shall be able to obtain for you anything from God to the contrary, if he is pleased to afflict you, or is pleased to be gracious unto you? Yea verily, God is well acquainted with that which ye do. Truly ye imagined that the apostle and the true believers would never return to their families; and this was prepared in your hearts: but ye imagined an evil imagination; and ye are a corrupt people. Whoso believeth not in God and his apostle, verily we have prepared burning fire for the unbelievers.

Unto God belongeth the kingdom of heaven and earth: he forgiveth whom he pleaseth, and he punisheth whom he pleaseth; and God is inclined to forgive, and merciful. Those who were left behind will say, when ye go forth to take the spoil, Suffer us to follow you. They seek to change the word of God. Say, Ye shall by no means follow us: thus hath God said heretofore. They will reply, Nay; ye envy us a share of the booty. But they are men of small understanding. Say unto the Arabs of the desert who were left behind, Ye shall be called forth against a mighty and a warlike nation: ye shall fight against them, or they shall profess Islam. If ye obey, God will give you a glorious reward:

but if ye turn back, as ye turned back heretofore, he will chastise you with a grievous chastisement.

It shall be no crime in the blind, neither shall it be a crime in the lame, neither shall it be a crime in the sick, if they go not forth to war: and whoso shall obey God and his apostle, he shall lead him into the gardens beneath which rivers flow; but whoso shall turn back, he will chastise him with a grievous chastisement.

Now God was well pleased with the true believers, when they sware fidelity unto thee under the tree;[2] and he knew that which was in their hearts: wherefore he sent down on them tranquillity of mind, and rewarded them with a speedy victory, and many spoils which they took: for God is mighty and wise. God promised you many spoils which ye should take; but he gave you these by way of earnest; and he restrained the hands of men from you: and the same may be a sign unto the true believers; and that he may guide you into the right way. And he also promiseth you other spoils, which ye have not yet been able to take: but now hath God encompassed them for you; and God is almighty. If the unbelieving Meccans had fought against you, verily they had turned their backs, and they would not have found a patron or protector: according to the ordinance of God, which hath been put in execution heretofore against opposers of the prophets; for thou shalt not find any change in the ordinance of God. It was he who restrained their hands from you, and your hands from them, in the valley of Mecca; after that he had given you the victory over them: and God saw that which ye did. These are they who believed not, and hindered you from visiting the holy temple, and also hindered

[2] Mohammed, when at al Hodeibiya, sent Jawwas Ebn Omeyya the Khozaite, to acquaint the Meccans that he was come with a peaceable intention to visit the temple; but they, on some jealousy conceived, refusing to admit him, the prophet sent Othman Eban Affan, whom they imprisoned, and a report ran that he was slain; whereupon Mohammed called his men about him, and they took an oath to be faithful to him, even to death; during which ceremony he sat under a tree, supposed by some to have been an Egyptian thorn, and by others a kind of lote-tree.

the offering, being detained, that it should not arrive at the place where it ought to be sacrificed. Had it not been that ye might have trampled on divers true believers, both men and women, whom ye knew not, being promiscuously assembled with the infidels, and that a crime might therefore have lighted on you on their account, without your knowledge, he had not restrained your hands from them: but this was done, that God might lead whom he pleaseth into his mercy. If they had been distinguished from one another, we had surely chastised such of them as believed not with a severe chastisement.

When the unbelievers had put in their hearts an affected preciseness, the preciseness of ignorance, and God sent down his tranquillity on his apostle and on the true believers;[3] and firmly fixed in them the word of piety, and they were the most worthy of the same, and the most deserving thereof: for God knoweth all things. Now hath God in truth verified unto his apostle the vision, wherein he said, Ye shall surely enter the holy temple of Mecca, if God please, in full security; having your heads shaved, and your hair cut: ye shall not fear: for God knoweth that which ye know not; and he hath appointed you, besides this, a speedy victory. It is he who hath sent his apostle with the direction, and the religion of truth; that he may exalt the same above every religion: and God is a sufficient witness hereof. Mohammed is the apostle of God: and those who are with him are fierce against the unbelievers, but compassionate toward one another.

[3] This passage was occasioned by the stiffness of Sohail and his companions in wording the treaty concluded with Mohammed; for when the prophet ordered Ali to begin with the form, " In the name of the most merciful God," they objected to it, and insisted that he should begin with this: " In thy name, O God "; which Mohammed submitted to, and proceeded to dictate, " These are the conditions on which Mohammed, the apostle of God, has made peace with those of Mecca "; to this Sohail again objected, saying, " If we had acknowledged thee to be the apostle of God, we had not given thee any opposition "; whereupon Mohammed ordered Ali to write as Sohail desired, " These are the conditions which Mohammed, the son of Abdallah," etc. But the Moslems were so disgusted thereat, that they were on the point of breaking off the treaty, and had fallen on the Meccans, had not God appeased and calmed their minds, as it follows in the text.

Thou mayest see them bowing down, prostrate, seeking a recompense from God, and his good-will. Their signs are in their faces, being marks of frequent prostration. This is their description in the Pentateuch, and their description in the gospel: they are as seed which putteth forth its stalk, and strengthened it, and swelleth in the ear, and riseth upon its stem; giving delight unto the sower. Such are the Moslems described to be: that the infidels may swell with indignation at them. God hath promised unto such of them as believe and do good works pardon and a great reward.

CHAPTER XLIX

ENTITLED, THE INNER APARTMENTS; REVEALED AT MEDINA

IN THE NAME OF THE MOST MERCIFUL GOD

O true believers, anticipate not any matter in the sight of God and his apostle: and fear God; for God both heareth and knoweth. O true believers, raise not your voices above the voice of the prophet; neither speak loud unto him in discourse, as ye speak loud unto one another, lest your works become vain, and ye perceive it not. Verily they who lower their voices in the presence of the apostle of God are those whose hearts God hath disposed unto piety: they shall obtain pardon and a great reward. As to those who call unto thee from without the inner apartments; [1] the greater part of them do not understand the respect due to thee. If they wait with patience, until thou come forth unto them, it will certainly be better for them: but God is inclined to forgive, and merciful.

O true believers, if a wicked man come unto you with a tale, inquire strictly into the truth thereof; lest ye hurt people through ignorance, and afterward repent of what ye have done:[2] and know that the apostle of God is among you: if

[1] These, they say, were Oyeyna Ebn Osein, and al Akra Ebn Habes; who wanting to speak with Mohammed, when he was sleeping at noon in his women's apartment, had the rudeness to call out several times, "Mohammed, come forth to us."

[2] This passage was occasioned, it is said, by the following incident.

he should obey you in many things, ye would certainly be guilty of a crime, in leading him into a mistake. But God hath made the faith amiable unto you, and hath prepared the same in your hearts; and hath rendered infidelity, and iniquity, and disobedience hateful unto you. These are they who walk in the right way; through mercy from God, and grace: and God is knowing and wise.

If two parties of the believers contend with one another, do ye endeavor to compose the matter between them: and if the one of them offer an insult unto the other, fight against that party which offered the insult, until they return unto the judgment of God; and if they do return, make peace between them with equity: and act with justice; for God loveth those who act justly. Verily the true believers are brethren: wherefore reconcile your brethren; and fear God, that ye may obtain mercy.

O true believers, let not men laugh other men to scorn; who peradventure may be better than themselves; neither let women laugh other women to scorn; who may possibly be better than themselves. Neither defame one another; nor call one another by opprobrious appellations. An ill name it is to be charged with wickedness, after having embraced the faith: and whoso repenteth not, they will be the unjust doers.

O true believers, carefully avoid entertaining a suspicion of another: for some suspicions are a crime; and inquire not too curiously into other men's failings: neither let the one of you speak ill of another in his absence. Would any of you desire to eat the flesh of his dead brother? Surely ye would abhor it. And fear God; for God is easy to be reconciled, and merciful. O men, verily we have created you of a male and a female; and we have distributed you into nations and

Al Walid Ebn Okba being sent by Mohammed to collect the alms from the tribe of al Mostalek, when he saw them come out to meet him in great numbers, grew apprehensive they designed him some mischief, because of past enmity between him and them in the time of ignorance, and immediately turned back, and told the prophet they refused to pay their alms, and attempted to kill him; upon which Mohammed was thinking to reduce them by force: but on sending Khaled Ebn al Walid to them, he found his former messenger had wronged them, and that they continued in their obedience.

tribes, that ye might know one another. Verily the most honorable of you, in the sight of God, is the most pious of you: and God is wise and knowing.

The Arabs of the desert say, We believe. Answer, Ye do by no means believe; but say, We have embraced Islam: for the faith hath not yet entered into your hearts. If ye obey God and his apostle, he will not defraud you of any part of the merit of your works: for God is inclined to forgive, and merciful. Verily the true believers are those only who believe in God and his apostle, and afterward doubt not; and who employ their substance and their persons in the defense of God's true religion: these are they who speak sincerely.

Say, Will ye inform God concerning your religion? But God knoweth whatever is in heaven and in earth: for God is omniscient. They upbraid thee that they have embraced Islam. Answer, Upbraid me not with your having embraced Islam: rather God upbraideth you, that he hath directed you to the faith; if ye speak sincerely. Verily God knoweth the secrets of heaven and earth: and God beholdeth that which ye do.

CHAPTER L

ENTITLED, K; REVEALED AT MECCA

IN THE NAME OF THE MOST MERCIFUL GOD

K.[1] By the glorious Koran: verily they wonder that a preacher from among themselves is come unto them; and the unbelievers say, This is a wonderful thing: after we shall be dead, and become dust, shall we return to life? This is a return remote from thought. Now we know that the earth consumeth of them; and with us is a book which keepeth an

[1] Some imagine that this letter is designed to express the mountain Kaf, which several Eastern writers fancy encompasses the whole world. Others say it stands for *Kada al amr, i.e.,* "The matter is decreed," *viz.,* "the chastisement of the infidels."

account thereof. But they charge falsehood on the truth, after it hath come unto them: wherefore they are plunged in a confused business. Do they not look up to the heaven above them, and consider how we have raised it and adorned it; and that there are no flaws therein? We have also spread forth the earth, and thrown thereon mountains firmly rooted: and we cause every beautiful kind of vegetables to spring up therein; for a subject of meditation, and an admonition unto every man who turneth unto us. And we send down rain as a blessing from heaven, whereby we cause gardens to spring forth, and the grain of harvest, and tall palm-trees having branches laden with dates hanging one above another, as a provision for mankind; and we thereby quicken a dead country: so shall be the coming forth of the dead from their graves.

The people of Noah, and those who dwelt at Al Rass, and Thamud, and Ad, and Pharaoh accused the prophets of imposture before the Meccans; and also the brethren of Lot, and the inhabitants of the wood near Midian, and the people of Tobba: all these accused the apostles of imposture; wherefore the judgments which I threatened were justly inflicted on them. Is our power exhausted by the first creation? Yea; they are in a perplexity, because of a new creation which is foretold them, namely, the raising of the dead. We created man, and we know what his soul whispereth within him; and we are nearer unto him than his jugular vein. When the two angels deputed to take account of a man's behavior, take an account thereof; one sitting on the right hand, and the other on the left: he uttereth not a word, but there is with him a watcher, ready to note it.[2] And the agony of death shall come in truth: this, O man, is what thou soughtest to avoid. And the trumpet shall sound: this will be the day which hath been threatened. And every soul shall come; and there-

2 The Mohammedans have a tradition that the angel who notes a man's good actions has the command over him who notes his evil actions; and that when a man does a good action, the angel of the right hand writes it down ten times, and when he commits an ill action, the same angel says to the angel of the left hand, "Forbear setting it down for seven hours; peradventure he may pray, or may ask pardon."

with shall be a driver and a witness. And the former shall say unto the unbeliever, Thou wast negligent heretofore of this day: but we have removed thy veil from off thee; and thy sight is become piercing this day. And his companion shall say, This is what is ready with me to be attested. And God shall say, Cast into hell every unbeliever, and perverse person, and every one who forbade good, and every transgressor, and doubter of the faith, who set up another god with the true God; and cast him into a grievous torment. His companion shall say, O Lord, I did not seduce him; but he was in a wide error. God shall say, Wrangle not in my presence: since I threatened you beforehand with the torments which ye now see prepared for you. The sentence is not changed with me: neither do I treat my servants unjustly. On that day we will say unto hell, Art thou full? and it shall answer, Is there yet any addition? And paradise shall be brought near unto the pious; and it shall be said unto them, This is what ye have been promised; unto every one who turned himself unto God, and kept his commandments; who feared the Merciful in secret, and came unto him with a converted heart: enter the same in peace: this is the day of eternity. Therein shall they have whatever they shall desire; and there will be a superabundant addition of bliss with us.

How many generations have we destroyed before the Meccans, which were more mighty than they in strength? Pass, therefore, through the regions of the earth, and see whether there be any refuge from our vengeance. Verily herein is an admonition unto him who hath a heart to understand, or giveth ear, and is present with an attentive mind. We created the heavens and the earth, and whatever is between them, in six days; and no weariness affected us. Wherefore patiently suffer what they say; and celebrate the praise of thy Lord before sunrise, and before sunset, and praise him in some part of the night: and perform the additional parts of worship. And harken unto the day whereon the crier shall call men to judgment from a near place; the day whereon they shall hear the voice of the trumpet in truth: this will be the day of men's coming forth from their graves: we give life, and we cause to die; and unto us shall be the return of all creatures: the day whereon the earth shall suddenly cleave in sunder over them. This will be an assembly easy for us to assemble. We well know what the unbelievers say; and thou art not sent to compel them forcibly to the faith. Wherefore warn, by the Koran, him who feareth my threatening.

CHAPTER LI

ENTITLED, THE DISPERSING; REVEALED AT MECCA

IN THE NAME OF THE MOST MERCIFUL GOD

By the winds dispersing and scattering the dust; and by the clouds bearing a load of rain; by the ships running swiftly in the sea; and by the angels who distribute things necessary for the support of all creatures: verily that wherewith ye are threatened is certainly true; and the last judgment will surely come. By the heaven furnished with paths; ye widely differ in what ye say. He will be turned aside from the faith, who shall be turned aside by the divine decree. Cursed be the liars; who wade in deep waters of ignorance, neglecting their salvation. They ask, When will the day of judgment come? On that day shall they be burned in hell fire; and it shall be said unto them, Taste your punishment; this is what ye demanded to be hastened. But the pious shall dwell among gardens and fountains, receiving that which their Lord shall give them; because they were righteous doers before this day. They slept but a small part of the night; and early in the morning they asked pardon of God: and a due portion of their wealth was given unto him who asked, and unto him who was forbidden by shame to ask. There are signs of the divine power and goodness in the earth, unto men of sound understanding; and also in your own selves: will ye not therefore consider? Your sustenance is in the heaven; and also that which ye are promised. Wherefore by the Lord of heaven and earth I swear that his is certainly the truth; according to what yourselves speak.

Hath not the story of Abraham's honored guests come to thy knowledge? When they went in unto him, and said, Peace: he answered, Peace; saying within himself, These are unknown people. And he went privately unto his family, and brought a fatted calf. And he set it before them, and when he saw they touched it not, he said, Do ye not eat? And he began to entertain a fear of them. They said, Fear not: and they declared unto him the promise of a wise youth. And his wife drew near with exclamation, and she smote her face, and said, I am an old woman, and barren. The angels answered, Thus saith thy Lord: Verily he is the wise, the knowing. And Abraham said unto them, What is your errand, therefore, O messengers of God? They answered, Verily we are sent unto a wicked people: that we may send down upon them stones of baked clay, marked from thy Lord, for the destruction of transgressors. And we brought forth the true believers who were in the city: but we found not therein more than one family of Moslems. And we overthrew the same, and left a sign therein unto those who dread the severe chastisement of God. In Moses also was a sign: when we sent him unto Pharaoh with manifest power. But he turned back, with his princes, saying, This man is a sorcerer or a madman. Wherefore we took him and his forces, and cast them into the sea: and he was one worthy of reprehension. And in the tribe of Ad also was a sign: when we sent against them a destroying wind; it touched not aught, whereon it came, but it rendered the same as a thing rotten and reduced to dust. In Thamud likewise was a sign: when it was said unto them, Enjoy yourselves for a time. But they insolently transgressed the command of their Lord: wherefore a terrible noise from heaven assailed them, while they looked on; and they were not able to stand on their feet, neither did they save themselves from destruction. And the people of Noah did we destroy before these: for they were a people who enormously transgressed. We have built the heaven with might; and we have given it a large extent: and we have stretched forth the earth beneath; and how evenly have we spread the same! And of everything have we created two kinds, that peradventure ye may consider. Fly, therefore, unto God; verily I am a public warner unto you, from him. And set not up another god with the true God: verily I am a public warner unto you, from him.

In like manner there came no apostle unto their predecessors, but they said, This man is a magician or a madman. Have they bequeathed this behavior successively the one to the other? Yea, they are a people who enormously transgress. Wherefore withdraw from them; and thou shalt not be blameworthy in so doing. Yet continue to admonish: for admonition profiteth the true believers. I have not created genii and men for any other end than that they should serve me. I require not any sustenance from them; neither will I that they feed me. Verily God is he who provideth for all creatures; possessed of mighty power. Unto those who shall injure our apostle shall be given a portion like unto the portion of those who behaved like them in times past; and they shall not wish the same to be hastened. Woe, therefore, to the unbelievers!

CHAPTER LII

ENTITLED, THE MOUNTAIN; REVEALED AT MECCA

IN THE NAME OF THE MOST MERCIFUL GOD

By the mountain of Sinai; and by the book written in an expanded scroll, and by the visited house; [1] and by the elevated roof of heaven; and by the swelling ocean: verily the punishment of thy Lord will surely descend; there shall be none to withhold it. On that day the heaven shall be shaken, and shall reel; and the mountains shall walk and pass away. And on that day woe be unto those who accused God's apostles of imposture; who amused themselves in wading in vain disputes! On that day shall they be driven and thrust into the fire of hell; and it shall be said unto them, This is the fire

1 *I.e.*, the Kaaba, so much visited by pilgrims; or, as some rather think, the original model of that house in heaven, called al Dorah, which is visited and compassed by the angels, as the other is by men.

which ye denied as a fiction. Is this a magic illusion? Or do ye not see? Enter the same to be scorched: whether ye bear your torments patiently, or impatiently, it will be equal unto you: ye shall surely receive the reward of that which ye have wrought.

But the pious shall dwell amidst gardens and pleasures; delighting themselves in what their Lord shall have given them: and their Lord shall deliver them from the pains of hell. And it shall be said unto them, Eat and drink with easy digestion; because of that which ye have wrought: leaning on couches disposed in order: and we will espouse them unto virgins having large black eyes. And unto those who believe, and whose offspring follow them in the faith, we will join their offspring in paradise: and we will not diminish unto them aught of the merit of their works. (Every man is given in pledge for that which he shall have wrought.) And we will give them fruits in abundance, and flesh of the kinds which they shall desire. They shall present unto one another therein a cup of wine, wherein there shall be no vain discourse, nor any incitement unto wickedness. And youths appointed to attend them shall go round them: beautiful as pearls hidden in their shell. And they shall approach unto one another, and shall ask mutual questions. And they shall say, Verily we were heretofore amidst our family, in great dread with regard to our state after death; but God hath been gracious unto us, and hath delivered us from the pain of burning fire: for we called on him heretofore; and he is the beneficent, the merciful.

Wherefore do thou, O prophet, admonish thy people. Thou art not, by the grace of thy Lord, a soothsayer or a madman. Do they say, He is a poet: we wait, concerning him, some adverse turn of fortune? Say, Wait ye my ruin: verily I wait, with you, the time of your destruction. Do their mature understandings bid them say this; or are they people who perversely transgress? Do they say, He hath forged the Koran? Verily they believe not. Let them produce a discourse like unto it, if they speak truth. Were they created by nothing; or were they the creators of themselves?

Did they create the heavens and the earth? Verily they are not firmly persuaded that God hath created them. Are the stores of thy Lord in their hands? Are they the supreme dispensers of all things? Have they a ladder, whereby they may ascend to heaven, and hear the discourse of angels? Let one, therefore, who hath heard them, produce an evident proof thereof. Hath God daughters, and have ye sons? Dost thou ask them a reward for thy preaching? but they are laden with debts. Are the secrets of futurity with them; and do they transcribe the same from the table of God's decrees? Do they seek to lay a plot against thee? But the unbelievers are they who shall be circumvented. Have they any god, besides God? Far be God exalted above the idols which they associate with him! If they should see a fragment of the heaven falling down upon them, they would say, It is only a thick cloud. Wherefore leave them, until they arrive at their day wherein they shall swoon for fear: a day in which their subtle contrivances shall not avail them at all, neither shall they be protected. And those who act unjustly shall surely suffer another punishment besides this: but the greater part of them do not understand. And wait thou patiently the judgment of thy Lord concerning them; for thou art in our eye: and celebrate the praise of thy Lord, when thou risest up; and praise him in the night season, and when the stars begin to disappear.

CHAPTER LIII

ENTITLED, THE STAR; REVEALED AT MECCA

IN THE NAME OF THE MOST MERCIFUL GOD

By the star, when it setteth; your companion Mohammed erreth not, nor is he led astray: neither doth he speak of his own will. It is no other than a revelation, which hath been revealed unto him. One mighty in power, endued with understanding, taught it him: and he appeared [1] in the highest

---

[1] Namely, the angel Gabriel, who appeared in the eastern part of the sky. It is said that this angel appeared in his proper shape to none of

part of the horizon.   Afterward he approached the prophet, and drew near unto him; until he was at the distance of two bows' length from him, or yet nearer: and he revealed unto his servant that which he revealed.   The heart of Mohammed did not falsely represent that which he saw.   Will ye therefore dispute with him concerning that which he saw?   He also saw him another time, by the lote-tree beyond which there is no passing: [2] near it is the garden of eternal abode. When the lote-tree covered that which it covered,[3] his eyesight turned not aside, neither did it wander: and he really beheld some of the greatest signs of his Lord.[4]

What think ye of Allat, and al Uzza, and Manah, that other third goddess?[5]   Have ye male children, and God female? This, therefore, is an unjust partition.   They are no other than empty names, which ye and your fathers have named goddesses.   God hath not revealed concerning them anything to authorize their worship.   They follow no other than a vain opinion, and what their souls desire: yet hath the true direction come unto them from their Lord.   Shall man have whatever he wisheth for?   The life to come and the present life are God's: and how many angels soever there be in the heavens, their intercession shall be of no avail, until after God shall have granted permission unto whom he shall please and shall accept.   Verily they who believe not in the life to come give unto the angels a female appellation.   But they have no knowledge herein: they follow no other than a bare opinion; and a bare opinion attaineth not anything of truth. Wherefore withdraw from him who turneth away from our

the prophets, except Mohammed, and to him only twice: once when he received the first revelation of the Koran, and a second time when he took his night-journey to heaven; as it follows in the text.

[2] This tree, say the commentators, stands in the seventh heaven, on the right hand of the throne of God; and is the utmost bounds beyond which the angels themselves must not pass; or, as some rather imagine, beyond which no creature's knowledge can extend.

[3] The words seem to signify that what was under this tree exceeded all description and number.   Some suppose the whole host of angels worshiping beneath it are intended, and others, the birds which sit on its branches.

[4] Seeing the wonders both of the sensible and the intellectual world.

[5] Those were three idols of the ancient Arabs.

admonition, and seeketh only the present life. This is their highest pitch of knowledge. Verily thy Lord well knoweth him who erreth from his way; and he well knoweth him who is rightly directed.

Unto God belongeth whatever is in heaven and earth: that he may reward those who do evil, according to that which they shall have wrought; and may reward those who do well, with the most excellent reward. As to those who avoid great crimes and heinous sins, and are guilty only of lighter faults; verily thy Lord will be extensive in mercy toward them. He well knew you when he produced you out of the earth, and when ye were embryos in your mothers' wombs: wherefore justify not yourselves: he best knoweth the man who feareth him.

What thinkest thou of him who turneth aside from following the truth and giveth little, and covetously stoppeth his hands?[6] Is the knowledge of futurity with him, so that he seeth the same? Hath he not been informed of that which is contained in the books of Moses, and of Abraham who faithfully performed his engagements? To wit: that a burdened soul shall not bear the burden of another; and that nothing shall be imputed to a man for righteousness, except his own labor; and that his reward shall surely be made manifest hereafter, and that he shall be rewarded for the same with a most abundant reward; and that unto thy Lord will be the end of all things; and that he causeth to laugh, and causeth to weep; and that he putteth to death, and giveth life; and that he created the two sexes, the male and the female, of seed when it is emitted; and that unto him appertaineth another production, namely, the raising of the dead again to life hereafter; and that he enricheth, and causeth to acquire posses-

[6] This passage, it is said, was revealed on account of al Walid Ebn al Mogheira, who, following the prophet one day, was reviled by an idolater for leaving the religion of the Koreish, and giving occasion of scandal; to which he answered, that what he did was out of apprehension of the divine vengeance: whereupon the man offered, for a certain sum, to take the guilt of his apostasy on himself; and the bargain being made, al Walid returned to his idolatry, and paid the man part of what had been agreed on; but afterward, on further consideration, he thought it too much, and kept back the remainder.

sion; and that he is the Lord of the dog-star; and that he destroyed the ancient tribe of Ad and Thamud, and left not any them alive, and also the people of Noah, before them; for they were most unjust and wicked: and he overthrew the cities which were turned upside down; and that which covered them, covered them. Which, therefore, of thy Lord's benefits, O man, wilt thou call in question? This our apostle is a preacher like the preachers who preceded him. The approaching day of judgment draweth near: there is none who can reveal the exact time of the same, besides God. Do ye, therefore, wonder at this new revelation; and do ye laugh, and not weep, spending your time in idle diversions? But rather worship God, and serve him.

CHAPTER LIV

ENTITLED, THE MOON; REVEALED AT MECCA

IN THE NAME OF THE MOST MERCIFUL GOD

The hour of judgment approacheth; and the moon hath been split in sunder:[1] but if the unbelievers see a sign, they turn aside, saying, This is a powerful charm. And they accuse thee, O Mohammed, of imposture, and follow their own lusts: but everything will be immutably fixed. And now hath a message come unto them, wherein is a determent from obstinate infidelity; the same being consummate wisdom: but warners profit them not; wherefore do thou withdraw from them. The day whereon the summoner shall summon mankind to an ungrateful business, they shall come forth from their graves with downcast looks: numerous as

[1] This passage is expounded two different ways. Some imagine the words refer to a famous miracle supposed to have been performed by Mohammed; for it is said that, on the infidels demanding a sign of him, the moon appeared cloven in two, one part vanishing, and the other remaining; and Ebn Masúd affirmed that he saw Mount Hara interpose between the two sections. Others think the preter tense is here used in the prophetic style for the future, and that the passage should be rendered, "The moon shall be split in sunder"; for this, they say, is to happen at the resurrection.

locusts scattered far abroad; hastening with terror unto the summoner. The unbelievers shall say, This is a day of distress. The people of Noah accused that prophet of imposture, before thy people rejected thee: they accused our servant of imposture, saying, He is a madman; and he was rejected with reproach. He called, therefore, upon his Lord, saying, Verily, I am overpowered; wherefore avenge me. So we opened the gates of heaven, with water pouring down, and we caused the earth to break forth into springs; so that the water of heaven and earth met, according to the decree which had been established. And we bare him on a vessel composed of planks and nails; which moved forward under our eyes: as a recompense unto him who had been ungratefully rejected. And we left the said vessel for a sign: but is any one warned thereby? And how severe was my vengeance and my threatening!

Now have we made the Koran easy for admonition: but is any one admonished thereby? Ad charged their prophet with imposture: but how severe were my vengeance and my threatening! Verily we sent against them a roaring wind, on a day of continued ill luck; it carried men away, as though they had been roots of palm-trees forcibly torn up. And how severe were my vengeance and my threatening! Now have we made the Koran easy for admonition: but is any one admonished thereby? Thamud charged the admonitions of their prophet with falsehood, and said, Shall we follow a single man among us? verily we should then be guilty of error and preposterous madness: is the office of admonition committed unto him preferably to the rest of us? Nay; he is a liar and an insolent fellow. But God said to Saleh, To-morrow shall they know who is the liar and the insolent person: for we will surely send the she-camel for a trial of them; and do thou observe them, and bear their insults with patience: and prophesy unto them that the water shall be divided between them, and each portion shall be sat down to alternately. And they called their companion: and he took a sword, and slew her. But how severe were my vengeance and my threatening! For we sent against them one cry of the angel Gabriel, and they became like the dry sticks used by him who buildeth a fold for cattle. And now have we made the Koran easy for admonition: but is any one admonished thereby?

The people of Lot charged his preaching with falsehood: but we sent against them a wind driving a shower of stones, which destroyed them all except the family of Lot; whom we delivered early in the morning, through favor from us. Thus do we reward those who are thankful. And lot had warned them of our severity in chastising; but they doubted of that warning. And they demanded his guests of him, that they might abuse them: but we put out their eyes, saying, Taste my vengeance, and my threatening. And early in the morning a lasting punishment surprised them. Taste, therefore, my vengeance, and my threatening. Now have we made the Koran easy for admonition: but is any one admonished thereby?

The warning of Moses also came unto the people of Pharaoh; but they charged every one of our signs with imposture: wherefore we chastised them with a mighty and irresistible chastisement. Are your unbelievers, O Meccans, better than these? Is immunity from punishment promised unto you in the scriptures? Do they say, We are a body of men able to prevail against our enemies? The multitude shall surely be put to flight, and shall turn their back. But the hour of judgment is their threatened time of punishment: and that hour shall be more grievous and more bitter than their afflictions in this life. Verily the wicked wander in error, and shall be tormented hereafter in burning flames. On that day they shall be dragged into the fire on their faces; and it shall be said unto them, Taste ye the touch of hell. All things have we created bound by a fixed decree: and our command is no more than a single word, like the twinkling of an eye. We have formerly destroyed nations like unto you; but is any of your warned by their example? Everything which they do is recorded in the books kept by the guardian angels: and every action, both small and great, is written down in the preserved table. Moreover the pious shall dwell among gardens and rivers, in the assembly of truth.

CHAPTER LV

ENTITLED, THE MERCIFUL; REVEALED AT MECCA

IN THE NAME OF THE MOST MERCIFUL GOD

The Merciful hath taught his servant the Koran. He created man: he hath taught him distinct speech. The sun and the moon run their courses according to a certain rule: and the vegetables which creep on the ground, and the trees submit to his disposition. He also raised the heaven; and he appointed the balance, that ye should not transgress in respect to the balance: wherefore observe a just weight, and diminish not the balance. And the earth hath he prepared for living creatures: therein are various fruits, and palm-trees bearing sheaths of flowers; and grain having chaff, and leaves. Which, therefore, of your Lord's benefits will ye ungratefully deny?

He created man of dried clay like an earthen vessel: but he created the genii of fire clear from smoke. Which, therefore, of your Lord's benefits will ye ungratefully deny? He is the Lord of the east, and the Lord of the west. Which, therefore, of your Lord's benefits will ye ungratefully deny? He hath let loose the two seas, that they meet each other: between them is placed a bar which they can not pass. Which, therefore, of your Lord's benefits will ye ungratefully deny? From them are taken forth unions and lesser pearls. Which, therefore, of your Lord's benefits will ye ungratefully deny? His also are the ships, carrying their sails aloft in the sea, like mountains. Which, therefore, of your Lord's benefits will ye ungratefully deny?

Every creature which liveth on the earth is subject to decay: but the glorious and honorable countenance of thy Lord shall remain forever. Which, therefore, of your Lord's benefits will ye ungratefully deny? Unto him do all creatures which are in heaven and earth make petition: every day is he employed in some new work. Which, therefore, of your Lord's benefits will ye ungratefully deny? We will surely attend to judge you, O men and genii, at the last day.

Which, therefore, of your Lord's benefits will ye ungratefully deny? O ye collective body of genii and men, if ye be able to pass out of the confines of heaven and earth, pass forth: ye shall not pass forth but by absolute power. Which, therefore, of your Lord's benefits will ye ungratefully deny? A flame of fire without smoke, and a smoke without flame shall be sent down upon you; and ye shall not be able to defend yourselves therefrom. Which, therefore, of your Lord's benefits will ye ungratefully deny? And when the heaven shall be rent in sunder, and shall become red as a rose, and shall melt like ointment. (Which, therefore, of your Lord's benefits will ye ungratefully deny?)

On that day neither man nor genius shall be asked concerning his sin. Which, therefore, of your Lord's benefits will ye ungratefully deny? The wicked shall be known by their marks; and they shall be taken by the forelocks and the feet, and shall be cast into hell. Which, therefore, of your Lord's benefits will ye ungratefully deny? This is hell, which the wicked deny as a falsehood: they shall pass to and fro between the same and hot boiling water. Which, therefore, of your Lord's benefits will ye ungratefully deny?

But for him who dreadeth the tribunal of his Lord are prepared two gardens. (Which, therefore, of your Lord's benefits will ye ungratefully deny?) Planted with shady trees. Which, therefore, of your Lord's benefits will ye ungratefully deny? In each of them shall be two fountains flowing. Which, therefore, of your Lord's benefits will ye ungratefully deny? In each of them shall there be of every fruit two kinds. Which, therefore, of your Lord's benefits will ye ungratefully deny? They shall repose on couches, the linings whereof shall be of thick silk interwoven with gold: and the fruit of the two gardens shall be near at hand together. Which, therefore, of your Lord's benefits will ye ungratefully deny? Therein shall receive them beauteous damsels, refraining their eyes from beholding any besides their spouses, whom no man shall have deflowered before them, neither any genius. (Which, therefore, of your Lord's benefits will ye ungratefully deny?) Having complexions like rubies and pearls. Which, therefore, of your Lord's benefits will ye ungratefully deny?

Shall the reward of good works be any other than good? Which, therefore, of your Lord's benefits will ye ungratefully deny? And besides these there shall be two other gardens. (Which, therefore, of your Lord's benefits will ye ungratefully deny?) Of a dark green. Which, therefore, of your Lord's benefits will ye ungratefully deny? In each of them shall be two fountains pouring forth plenty of water. Which, therefore, of your Lord's benefits will ye ungratefully deny? In each of them shall be fruits, and palm-trees, and pomegranates. Which, therefore, of your Lord's benefits will ye ungratefully deny? Therein shall be agreeable and beauteous damsels. Which, therefore, of your Lord's benefits will ye ungratefully deny? Having fine black eyes; and kept in pavilions from public view. Which, therefore, of your Lord's benefits will ye ungratefully deny? Whom no man shall have deflowered, before their destined spouses, nor any genius. Which, therefore, of your Lord's benefits will ye ungratefully deny? Therein shall they delight themselves, lying on green cushions and beautiful carpets. Which, therefore, of your Lord's benefits will ye ungratefully deny? Blessed be the name of thy Lord, possessed of glory and honor!

CHAPTER LVI

ENTITLED, THE INEVITABLE; REVEALED AT MECCA

IN THE NAME OF THE MOST MERCIFUL GOD

When the inevitable day of judgment shall suddenly come, no soul shall charge the perdition of its coming with falsehood: it will abase some, and exalt others. When the earth shall be shaken with a violent shock; and the mountains shall be dashed in pieces, and shall become as dust scattered abroad; and ye shall be separated into three distinct classes: the companions of the right hand (how happy shall the companions of the right hand be!), and the companions of the left hand (how miserable shall the companions of the left hand be!), and those who have preceded others in the faith, shall precede them to paradise. These are they who shall approach near unto God: they shall dwell in gardens of delight. (There shall be many of the former religions; and few of the last.) Reposing on couches adorned with gold and precious stones; sitting opposite to one another thereon. Youths which shall continue in their bloom forever, shall go round about to attend them, with goblets, and beakers, and a cup of flowing wine: their heads shall not ache by drinking the same, neither shall their reason be disturbed: and with fruits of the sorts which they shall choose, and the flesh of birds of the kind which they shall desire. And there shall accompany them fair damsels having large black eyes; resembling pearls hidden in their shells: as a reward for that which they shall have wrought. They shall not hear therein any vain discourse, or any charge of sin; but only the salutation, Peace! Peace! And the companions of the right hand (how happy shall the companions of the right hand be!) shall have their abode among the lote-trees free from thorns, and trees of mauz loaded regularly with their produce from top to bottom; under an extended shade, near a flowing water, and amidst fruits in abundance, which shall not fail, nor shall be forbidden to be gathered: and they shall repose themselves on lofty beds. Verily we have created the damsels of paradise by a peculiar creation: and we have made them virgins, beloved by their husbands, of equal age with them; for the delight of the companions of the right hand. There shall be many of the former religions, and many of the latter.

And the companions of the left hand (how miserable shall the companions of the left hand be!) shall dwell amidst burning winds, and scalding water, under the shade of a black smoke, neither cool nor agreeable. For they enjoyed the pleasures of life before this, while on earth; and obstinately persisted in a heinous wickedness: and they said, After we shall have died, and become dust and bones, shall we surely be raised to life? Shall our forefathers also be raised with us? Say, Verily both the first and the last shall be surely gathered together to judgment, at the prefixed time of a known day. Then ye, O men, who have erred, and denied the resurrection as a falsehood, shall surely eat of the fruit of the tree of al Zakkum, and shall fill your bellies therewith: and ye shall drink thereon boiling water; and ye shall drink as a thirsty camel drinketh. This shall be their entertainment on the day of judgment.

We have created you: will ye not therefore believe that we can raise you from the dead? What think ye? The seed which ye emit, do ye create the same, or are we the creators thereof? We have decreed death unto you all: and we shall not be prevented. We are able to substitute others like unto you in your stead, and to produce you again in the condition or form which ye know not. Ye know the original production by creation; will ye not therefore consider that we are able to reproduce you by resuscitation? What think ye? The grain which ye sow, do ye cause the same to spring forth, or do we cause it to spring forth? If we pleased, verily we could render the same dry and fruitless, so that ye would not cease to wonder, saying, Verily we have contracted debts for seed and labor; but we are not permitted to reap the fruit thereof. What think ye? The water which ye drink, do ye send down the same from the clouds, or are we the senders thereof? If we pleased, we could render the same brackish. Will ye not therefore give thanks? What think ye? The fire which ye strike, do ye produce the tree whence ye obtain the same, or are we the producers thereof? We have ordained the same for an admonition, and an advantage unto those who travel through the deserts.

Wherefore praise the name of thy Lord, the great God. Moreover I swear by the setting of the stars (and it is surely a great oath, if ye know it); that this is the excellent Koran, the original whereof is written in the preserved book: none shall touch the same, except those who are clean. It is a revelation from the Lord of all creatures. Will ye, therefore, despise this new revelation? And do ye make this return for your food which ye receive from God, that ye deny yourselves to be obliged to him for the same? When the soul of a dying person cometh up to his throat, and ye at the same time are looking on (and we are nigher unto him than ye, but ye see not his true condition) : would ye not, if ye are not to be rewarded for your actions thereafter, cause the same to return into the body, if ye speak truth?

And whether he be of those who shall approach near unto God, his reward shall be rest, and mercy, and a garden of delights: or whether he be of the companions of the right hand, he shall be saluted with the salutation, Peace be unto thee! by the companions of the right hand his brethren: or whether he be of those who have rejected the true faith and gone astray, his entertainment shall consist of boiling water, and the burning of hell fire. Verily this is a certain truth. Wherefore praise the name of thy Lord, the great God.

CHAPTER LVII

ENTITLED, IRON; [1] REVEALED AT MECCA, OR AT MEDINA

IN THE NAME OF THE MOST MERCIFUL GOD

Whatever is in heaven and earth singeth praise unto God; and he is mighty and wise. His is the kingdom of heaven and earth; he giveth life, and he putteth to death; and he is almighty. He is the first and the last; the manifest and the hidden: and he knoweth all things. It is he who created the heavens and the earth in six days; and then ascended his throne. He knoweth that which entereth into the earth, and that which issueth out of the same; and that which descendeth from heaven, and that which ascendeth thereto: and he is with you wheresoever ye be: for God seeth that which ye do. His is the kingdom of heaven and earth; and unto God shall all things return. He causeth the night to succeed the day, and he causeth the day to succeed the night; and he knoweth the innermost part of men's breasts.

Believe in God and his apostle, and lay out in alms a part of the wealth whereof God hath made you inheritors: for

[1] The word occurs toward the end of the chapter.

unto such of you as believe, and bestow alms, shall be given a
great reward. And what aileth you, that ye believe not in
God, when the apostles inviteth you to believe in your Lord;
and he hath received your covenant concerning this matter, if
ye believe any proposition? It is he who hath sent down
unto his servant evident signs, that he may lead you out of
darkness into light; for God is compassionate and merciful
unto you. And what aileth you, that ye contribute not of
your substance for the defense of God's true religion? Since
unto God appertaineth the inheritance of heaven and earth.
Those among you who shall have contributed and fought in
defense of the faith, before the taking of Mecca, shall not be
held equal with those who shall contribute and fight for the
same afterward. These shall be superior in degree unto
those who shall contribute and fight for the propagation of
the faith after the above-mentioned success: but unto all hath
God promised a most excellent reward; and God well knoweth
that which ye do.

Who is he that will lend unto God an acceptable loan? for
he will double the same unto him, and he shall receive moreover an honorable reward. On a certain day, thou shalt see
the true believers of both sexes: their light shall run before
them, and on their right hands; and it shall be said unto
them, Good tidings unto you this day: gardens through which
rivers flow; ye shall remain therein forever. This will be
great felicity. On that day the hypocritical men and the
hypocritical women shall say unto those who believe, Stay for
us, that we may borrow some of your light. It shall be answered, Return back into the world, and seek light. And a
high wall shall be set betwixt them, wherein shall be a gate,
within which shall be mercy; and without it, over against the
same, the torment of hell. The hypocrites shall call out unto
the true believers, saying, Were we not with you? They
shall answer, Yea; but ye seduced your own souls by your
hypocrisy: and ye waited our ruin; and ye doubted concerning the faith; and your wishes deceived you, until the decree
of God came, and ye died; and the deceiver deceived you
concerning God. This day, therefore, a ransom shall not be

accepted of you, nor of those who have been unbelievers. Your abode shall be hell fire: this is what ye have deserved; and an unhappy journey shall it be thither.

Is not the time yet come unto those who believe, that their hearts should humbly submit to the admonition of God, and to that truth which hath been revealed; and that they be not as those unto whom the scripture was given heretofore, and to whom the time of forbearance was prolonged, but their hearts were hardened, and many of them were wicked doers? Know that God quickeneth the earth, after it hath been dead. Now have we distinctly declared our signs unto you, that ye may understand.

Verily as to the almsgivers, both men and women, and those who lend unto God an acceptable loan, he will double the same unto them; and they shall moreover receive an honorable reward. And they who believe in God and his apostles, these are the men of veracity, and the witnesses in the presence of their Lord: they shall have their reward and their light. But as to those who believe not, and accuse our signs of falsehood, they shall be the companions of hell.

Know that this present life is only a toy and a vain amusement: and worldly pomp, and the affectation of glory among you, and the multiplying of riches and children, are as the plants nourished by the rain, the springing up whereof delighteth the husbandmen; afterward they wither, so that thou seest the same turn yellow, and at length they become dry stubble. And in the life to come will be a severe punishment for those who covet worldly grandeur; and pardon from God, and favor for those who renounce it: for this present life is no other than a deceitful provision. Hasten with emulation to obtain pardon from your Lord, and paradise, to the extent whereof equaleth the extent of heaven and earth, prepared for those who believe in God and his apostles. This is the bounty of God; he will give the same unto whom he pleaseth; and God is endued with great bounty. No accident happeneth in the earth, nor in your persons, but the same was entered in the book of our decrees, before we created it: verily this is easy with God: and this is written lest ye immoderately grieve for the good which escapeth you, or rejoice for that which happeneth unto you; for God loveth no proud or vainglorious person, or those who are covetous. And whoso turneth aside from giving alms; verily God is self-sufficient, worthy to be praised.

We formerly sent our apostles with evident miracles and arguments; and we sent down with them the scriptures and the balance,[2] that men might observe justice: and we sent them down iron,[3] wherein is mighty strength for war, and various advantages unto mankind: that God may know who assisteth him and his apostles in secret; for God is strong and mighty. We formerly sent Noah and Abraham, and we established in their posterity the gift of prophecy, and the scripture: and of them some were directed, but many of them were evil-doers. Afterward we caused our apostles to succeed in their footsteps; and we caused Jesus the son of Mary to succeed them, and we gave him the gospel: and we put in the hearts of those who followed him compassion and mercy: but as to the monastic state, they instituted the same (we did not prescribe it to them) only out of a desire to please God; yet they observed not the same as it ought truly to be observed. And we gave unto such of them as believed, their reward: but many of them were wicked doers.

O ye who believe in the former prophets, fear God, and believe in his apostle Mohammed: he will give you two portions of his mercy, and he will ordain you a light wherein ye may walk, and he will forgive you; for God is ready to forgive and merciful: that those who have received the scriptures may know that they have not power over any of the favors of God, and that good is in the hand of God; he bestoweth the same on whom he pleaseth, for God is endued with great beneficence.

---

[2] *I.e.*, " A rule of justice." Some think that a balance was actually brought down from heaven by the angel Gabriel to Noah, the use of which he was ordered to introduce among his people.

[3] That is, we taught them how to dig the same from mines. Al Zamakhshari adds that Adam is said to have brought down with him from paradise five things made of iron, *viz.*, an anvil, a pair of tongs, two hammers, a greater and a lesser, and a needle.

CHAPTER LVIII

ENTITLED, SHE WHO DISPUTED; REVEALED AT MEDINA

IN THE NAME OF THE MOST MERCIFUL GOD

Now hath God heard the speech of her who disputed with
thee concerning her husband, and made her complaint unto
God; and God hath heard your mutual discourse; for God
both heareth and seeth. As to those among you who divorce
their wives by declaring that they will thereafter regard them
as their mothers; let them know that they are not their
mothers. They only are their mothers who brought them
forth; and they certainly utter an unjustifiable saying, and a
falsehood; but God is gracious and ready to forgive. Those
who divorce their wives by declaring that they will for the
future regard them as their mothers, and afterward would
repair what they have said, shall be obliged to free a captive,
before they touch one another. This is what ye are warned
to perform: and God is well apprised of that which ye do.
And whoso findeth not a captive to redeem shall observe a fast
of two consecutive months, before they touch one another.
And whoso shall not be able to fast that time shall feed three-
score poor men. This is ordained you, that ye may believe in
God and his apostle. These are the statutes of God: and for
the unbelievers is prepared a grievous torment.

Verily they who oppose God and his apostle shall be
brought low, as the unbelievers who preceded them were
brought low. And now have we sent down manifest signs:
and an ignominious punishment awaiteth the unbelievers.
On a certain day God shall raise them all to life, and shall
declare unto them that which they have wrought. God hath
taken an exact account thereof; but they have forgotten the
same: and God is witness over all things. Dost thou not
perceive that God knoweth whatever is in heaven and in
earth? There is no private discourse among three persons,
but he is the fourth of them; nor among five, but he is the
sixth of them; neither among a smaller number than this, nor
a larger, but he is with them, wheresoever they be: and he

will declare unto them that which they have done, on the day of resurrection; for God knoweth all things. Hast thou not observed those who have been forbidden to use clandestine discourse, but afterward return to what they have been forbidden, and discourse privily among themselves of wickedness, and enmity, and disobedience toward the apostle? And when they come unto thee, they salute thee with that form of salutation wherewith God doth not salute thee: and they say among themselves, by way of derision, would not God punish us for what we say, if this man were a prophet? Hell shall be their sufficient punishment: they shall go down into the same to be burned; and an unhappy journey shall it be!

O true believers, when ye discourse privily together, discourse not of wickedness, and enmity, and disobedience toward the apostle; but discourse of justice and piety: and fear God, before whom ye shall be assembled. Verily the clandestine discourse of the infidels proceedeth from Satan, that he may grieve the true believers: but there shall be none to hurt them in the least, unless by the permission of God; wherefore in God let the faithful trust. O true believers, when it is said unto you, Make room in the assembly; make room: God will grant you ample room in paradise. And when it is said unto you, Rise up; rise up: God will raise those of you who believe, and those to whom knowledge is given, to superior degrees of honor: and God is fully apprised of that which ye do.

O true believers, when ye go to speak with the apostle, give alms previously to your discoursing with him: this will be better for you and more pure. But if ye find not what to give, verily God will be gracious and merciful unto you. Do ye fear to give alms previously to your discoursing with the prophet, lest ye should impoverish yourselves? Therefore if ye do it not, and God is gracious unto you, by dispensing with the said precept for the future, be constant at prayer, and pay the legal alms; and obey God and his apostle in all other matters: for God well knoweth that which ye do. Hast thou not observed those who have taken for their friends a people against whom God is incensed? They are neither of you nor of them: and they swear to a lie knowingly. God hath prepared for them a grievous punishment; for it is evil which they do. They have taken their oaths for a cloak, and they have turned men aside from the way of God: wherefore a shameful punishment awaiteth them; neither their wealth nor their children shall avail them at all against God. These shall be the inhabitants of hell fire; they shall abide therein forever. On a certain day God shall raise them all: then will they swear unto him, as they swear now unto you, imagining that it will be of service to them. Are they not liars? Satan hath prevailed against them, and hath caused them to forget the remembrance of God. These are the party of the devil; and shall not the party of the devil be doomed to perdition?

Verily they who oppose God and his apostle shall be placed among the most vile. God hath written, Verily I will prevail, and my apostles: for God is strong and mighty. Thou shalt not find people who believe in God and the last day, to love him who opposeth God and his apostle; although they be their fathers, or their sons, or their brethren, or their nearest relations. In the hearts of these hath God written faith; and he hath strengthened them with his spirit: and he will lead them into gardens, beneath which rivers flow, to remain therein forever. God is well pleased in them, and they are well pleased in him. These are the party of God: and shall not the party of God prosper?

CHAPTER LIX

ENTITLED, THE EMIGRATION; REVEALED AT MEDINA

IN THE NAME OF THE MOST MERCIFUL GOD

Whatever is in heaven and earth celebrateth the praise of God: and he is the mighty, the wise. It was he who caused those who believed not, of the people who receive the scripture, to depart from their habitations at the first emigration. Ye did not think that they would go forth: and they thought that their fortresses would protect them against God. But the chastisement of God came upon them, from whence they did not expect; and he cast terror into their hearts. They pulled down their houses with their own hands, and the hands of the true believers. Wherefore take example from them, O ye who have eyes. And if God had not doomed them to banishment, he had surely punished them in this world; and in the world to come they shall suffer the torment of hell fire. This because they opposed God and his apostle: and whoso opposeth God, verily God will be severe in punishing him. What palm-trees ye cut down, or left standing on their roots, were so cut down or left by the will of God; and that he might disgrace the wicked doers.

And as to the spoils of these people which God hath granted wholly to his apostle, ye did not push forward any horses or camels against the same; but God giveth unto his apostles dominion over whom he pleaseth: for God is almighty. The spoils of the inhabitants of the towns which God hath granted to his apostle are due unto God and to the apostle, and him who is of kin to the apostle, and the orphans, and the poor, and the traveler; that they may not be forever divided in a circle among such of you as are rich. What the apostle shall give you, that accept; and what he shall forbid you, that abstain from: and fear God; for God is severe in chastising.

A part also belongeth to the poor Mohajerin, who have been dispossessed of their houses and their substance, seeking favor from God, and his good-will, and assisting God and his apostle. These are the men of veracity. And they who quietly possessed the town of Medina, and professed the faith without molestation, before them, love him who hath fled unto them, and find in their breasts no want of that which is given the Mohajerin, but prefer them before themselves, although there be indigence among them. And whoso is preserved from the covetousness of his own soul, those shall surely prosper. And they who have come after them say, O Lord, forgive us and our brethren who have preceded us in the faith, and put not into our hearts ill-will against those who have believed: O Lord, verily thou art compassionate and merciful.

Hast thou not observed them who play the hypocrites? They say unto their brethren who believe not, of those who have received the scriptures, Verily if ye expelled your habitations, we will surely go forth with you; and we will not pay obedience, in your respect, unto any one forever: and if ye be attacked, we will certainly assist you. But God is witness that they are liars. Verily if they be expelled, they will not go forth with them; and if they be attacked, they will not assist them; and if they do not assist them, they will surely turn their backs: and they shall not be protected. Verily ye are stronger than they, by reason of the terror cast into their breasts from God. This, because they are not people of prudence. They will not fight against you in a body, except in fenced towns, or from behind walls. Their strength in war among themselves is great: thou thinkest them to be united; but their hearts are divided. This, because they are people who do not understand. Like those who lately preceded them, they have tasted the evil consequence of their deed; and a painful torment is prepared for them hereafter. Thus have the hypocrites deceived the Jews: like the devil, when he saith unto a man, Be thou an infidel; and when he is become an infidel, he saith, Verily I am clear of thee; for I fear God, the Lord of all creatures. Wherefore the end of them both shall be that they shall dwell in hell fire, abiding therein forever: and this shall be the recompense of the unjust.

O true believers, fear God; and let a soul look what it sendeth before for the morrow: and fear God, for God is well acquainted with that which ye do. And be not as those who have forgotten God, and whom he hath caused to forget their own souls: these are the wicked doers. The inhabitants of hell fire and the inhabitants of paradise shall not be held equal. The inhabitants of paradise are they who shall enjoy felicity. If we had sent down this Koran on a mountain, thou wouldst certainly have seen the same humble itself, and cleave in sunder for fear of God. These similitudes do we propose unto men, that they may consider. He is God, besides whom there is no God; who knoweth that which is future and that which is present: he is the most Merciful;

he is God, besides whom there is no God: the King, the Holy,
the Giver of peace, the Faithful, the Guardian, the Powerful,
the Strong, the most High.   Far be God exalted above the
idols, which they associate with him!   He is God, the Creator, the Maker, the Former.   He hath most excellent names.
Whatever is in heaven and earth praiseth him: and he is the
Mighty, the Wise.

CHAPTER LX

ENTITLED, SHE WHO IS TRIED;[1] REVEALED AT MEDINA

IN THE NAME OF THE MOST MERCIFUL GOD

O true believers, take not my enemy and your enemy for
your friends,[2] showing kindness toward them; since they
believe not in the truth which hath come unto you, having
expelled the apostle and yourselves from your native city,
because ye believe in God, your Lord.   If ye go forth to fight
in defense of my religion, and out of a desire to please me,
and privately show friendship unto them; verily I well know
that which ye conceal, and that which ye discover: and whoever of you doth this hath already erred from the strait path.
If they get the better of you, they will be enemies unto you,
and they will stretch forth their hands and their tongues

[1] This chapter bears this title because it directs the women who desert
and come over from the infidels to the Moslems to be examined, and tried
whether they be sincere in their profession of the faith.

[2] This passage was revealed on account of Hateb Ebn Abi Balpaa, who
understanding that Mohammed had a design to surprise Mecca, wrote a
letter to the Koreish, giving them notice of the intended expedition,
and advised them to be on their guard: which letter he sent by Sarah,
a maid-servant belonging to the family of Hashem.   The messenger had
not been gone long, before Gabriel discovered the affair to the prophet,
who immediately sent after her; and having intercepted the letter,
asked Hateb how he came to be guilty of such an action?   To which
he replied that it was not out of infidelity, or a desire to return to
idolatry, but merely to induce the Koreish to treat his family, which
was still at Mecca, with some kindness; adding that he was well assured
his intelligence would be of no service at all to the Meccans, because he
was satisfied God would take vengeance on them.   Whereupon Mohammed received his excuse and pardoned him; but it was thought proper
to forbid any such practises for the future.

against you with evil: and they earnestly desire that ye should become unbelievers. Neither your kindred nor your children will avail you at all on the day of resurrection, which will separate you from one another: and God seeth that which ye do. Ye have an excellent pattern in Abraham, and those who were with him, when they said unto their people, Verily we are clear of you, and of the idols which ye worship, besides God: we have renounced you; and enmity and hatred is begun between us and you forever, until ye believe in God alone: except Abraham's saying unto his father, Verily I will beg pardon for thee; but I can not obtain aught of God in thy behalf.

O Lord, in thee do we trust, and unto thee are we turned; and before thee shall we be assembled hereafter. O Lord, suffer us not to be put to trial by the unbelievers: and forgive us, O Lord; for thou art mighty and wise. Verily ye have in them an excellent example, unto him who hopeth in God and the last day: and whoso turneth back; verily God is self-sufficient, and praiseworthy. Peradventure God will establish friendship between yourselves and such of them as ye now hold for enemies: for God is powerful; and God is inclined to forgive, and merciful. As to those who have not borne arms against you on account of religion, nor turned you out of your dwellings, God forbiddeth you not to deal kindly with them, and to behave justly toward them; for God loveth those who act justly. But as to those who have borne arms against you on account of religion, and have dispossessed you of your habitations, and have assisted in dispossessing you, God forbiddeth you to enter into friendship with them: and whosoever of you entereth into friendship with them, those are unjust doers.

O true believers, when believing women come unto you as refugees, try them: God well knoweth their faith. And if ye know them to be true believers, send them not back to the infidels; they are not lawful for the unbelievers to have in marriage; neither are the unbelievers lawful for them. But give their unbelieving husbands what they shall have expended for their dowers. Nor shall it be any crime in you if ye marry them, provided ye give them their dowries. And retain not the patronage of the unbelieving women: but demand back that which ye have expended for the dowry of such of your wives as go over to the unbelievers; and let them demand back that which they have expended for the dowry of those who come over to you. This is the judgment of God, which he establisheth among you: and God is knowing and wise. If any of your wives escape from you to the unbelievers, and ye have your turn by the coming over of any of the unbelievers' wives to you; give unto those believers whose wives shall have gone away, out of the dowries of the latter, so much as they shall have expended for the dowers of the former: and fear God, in whom ye believe. O prophet, when believing women come unto thee, and plight their faith unto thee, that they will not associate anything with God, nor steal, nor commit fornication, nor kill their children, nor come with a calumny which they have forged between their hands and their feet, nor be disobedient to thee in that which shall be reasonable: then do thou plight thy faith unto them, and ask pardon for them of God; for God is inclined to forgive, and merciful.

O true believers, enter not into friendship with a people against whom God is incensed: they despair of the life to come, as the infidels despair of the resurrection of those who dwell in the graves.

CHAPTER LXI

ENTITLED, BATTLE ARRAY; REVEALED AT MECCA

IN THE NAME OF THE MOST MERCIFUL GOD

Whatever is in heaven and in earth celebrateth the praise of God; for he is mighty and wise. O true believers, why do ye say that which ye do not? It is most odious in the sight of God, that ye say that which ye do not. Verily God loveth those who fight for his religion in battle array, as though they were a well compacted building. Remember when

Moses said unto his people, O my people, why do ye injure me; since ye know that I am the apostle of God sent unto you? And when they had deviated from the truth, God made their hearts to deviate from the right way; for God directeth not wicked people. And when Jesus the son of Mary said, O children of Israel, verily I am the apostle of God sent unto you, confirming the law which was delivered before me, and bringing good tidings of an apostle who shall come after me, and whose name shall be Ahmed.[1] And when he produced unto them evident miracles, they said, This is manifest sorcery. But who is more unjust than he who forgeth a lie against God, when he is invited unto Islam? And God directeth not the unjust people. They seek to extinguish God's light with their mouths: but God will perfect his light, though the infidels be averse thereto. It is he who hath sent his apostle with the direction, and the religion of truth, that he may exalt the same above every religion, although the idolaters be averse thereto.

O true believers, shall I show you a merchandise which will deliver you from a painful torment hereafter? Believe in God and his apostle; and defend God's true religion with your substance, and in your own persons. This will be better for you, if ye knew it. He will forgive you your sins, and will introduce you into gardens through which rivers flow, and agreeable habitations in gardens of perpetual abode. This will be great felicity. And ye shall obtain other things which ye desire, namely, assistance from God, and a speedy victory. And do thou bear good tidings to the true believers.

O true believers, be ye the assistants of God; as Jesus the son of Mary said to the apostles, Who will be my assistants with respect to God? The apostles answered, We will be the assistants of God. So a part of the children of Israel be-

[1] For Mohammed also bore the name of Ahmed; both names being derived from the same root, and nearly of the same signification. The Persian paraphrast, to support what is here alleged, quotes the following words of Christ, " I go to my father, and the Paraclete shall come "; the Mohammedan doctors unanimously teaching that by the Paraclete (or, as they choose to read it, the " Periclyte," or " Illustrious ") their prophet is intended, and no other.

lieved, and a part believed not: but we strengthened those who believed, above their enemy; wherefore they became victorious over them.

CHAPTER LXII

ENTITLED, THE ASSEMBLY; REVEALED AT MEDINA

IN THE NAME OF THE MOST MERCIFUL GOD

Whatever is in heaven and earth praiseth God; the King, the Holy, the Mighty, the Wise. It is he who hath raised up amidst the illiterate Arabians an apostle from among themselves, to rehease his signs unto them, and to purify them, and to teach them the scriptures and wisdom; whereas before they were certainly in a manifest error: and others of them have not yet attained unto them, by embracing the faith; though they also shall be converted in God's good time; for he is mighty and wise. This is the free grace of God: he bestoweth the same on whom he pleaseth: and God is endued with great beneficence.

The likeness of those who were charged with the observance of the law, and then observed it not, is as the likeness of an ass laden with books. How wretched is the likeness of the people who charge the signs of God with falsehood! and God directeth not the unjust people. Say, O ye who follow the Jewish religion, if ye say that ye are the friends of God above other men, wish for death, if ye speak truth. But they will never wish for it, because of that which their hands have sent before them: and God well knoweth the unjust. Say, Verily death, from which ye fly, will surely meet you: then shall ye be brought before him who knoweth as well what is concealed as what is discovered; and he will declare unto you that which ye have done.

O true believers, when ye are called to prayer on the day of the assembly,[1] hasten to the commemoration of God, and

---

[1] That is, Friday, which being more peculiarly set apart by Mohammed for the public worship of God, is therefore called *Yawm al jomá,* *i.e.,* the day of the assembly or congregation; whereas before it was

leave merchandizing. This will be better for you, if ye knew it. And when prayer is ended, then disperse yourselves through the land as ye list, and seek gain of the liberality of God:[2] and remember God frequently, that ye may prosper. But when they see any merchandizing or sport, they flock thereto, and leave thee standing up in thy pulpit.[3] Say, The reward which is with God is better than any sport or merchandise; and God is the best provider.

CHAPTER LXIII

ENTITLED, THE HYPOCRITES; REVEALED AT MEDINA

IN THE NAME OF THE MOST MERCIFUL GOD

When the hypocrites come unto thee, they say, We bear witness that thou art indeed the apostle of God. And God knoweth that thou art indeed his apostle: but God beareth witness that the hypocrites are certainly liars. They have taken their oaths for a protection, and they turn others aside from the way of God: it is surely evil which they do. This is testified of them, because they believed, and afterward became unbelievers: wherefore a seal is set on their hearts, and they shall not understand. When thou beholdest them, their persons please thee: and if they speak, thou hearest their discourse with delight. They resemble pieces of timber set up against a wall. They imagine every shout

called *al Aruba.* The first time this day was particularly observed, as some say, was on the prophet's arrival at Medina, into which city he made his first entry on a Friday. One reason given for the observation of Friday, preferably to any other day of the week, is because on that day God finished the creation.

[2] By returning to your commerce and worldly occupations, if ye think fit: for the Mohammedans do not hold themselves obliged to observe the day of their public assembly with the same strictness as the Christians and Jews do their respective Sabbaths; or particularly to abstain from work, after they have performed their devotions.

[3] It is related that one Friday, while Mohammed was preaching, a caravan of merchants happened to arrive with their drums beating, according to custom; which the congregation hearing, they all ran out of the mosque to see them, except twelve only.

to be against them. They are enemies; wherefore beware
of them. God curse them: how are they turned aside from
the truth! And when it is said unto them, Come, that the
apostle of God may ask pardon for you; they turn away
their heads, and thou seest them retire big with disdain. It
shall be equal unto them, whether thou ask pardon for them,
or do not ask pardon for them; God will by no means forgive
them: for God directeth not the prevaricating people. These
are the men who say to the inhabitants of Medina, Do not
bestow anything on the refugees who are with the apostle of
God, that they may be obliged to separate from him. Whereas unto God belong the stores of heaven and earth: but
the hypocrites do not understand. They say, Verily, if we
return to Medina, the worthier shall expel thence the meaner.
Whereas superior worth belongeth unto God, and his apostle,
and the true believers: but the hypocrites know it not.

O true believers, let not your riches or your children divert
you from the remembrance of God: for whosoever doth this,
they will surely be losers. And give alms out of that which
we have bestowed on you; before death come unto one of you,
and he say, O Lord, wilt thou not grant me respite for a
short term; that I may give alms, and become one of the
righteous? For God will by no means grant further respite
to a soul, when its determined time is come: and God is fully
apprised of that which ye do.

CHAPTER LXIV

ENTITLED, MUTUAL DECEIT; REVEALED AT MECCA

IN THE NAME OF THE MOST MERCIFUL GOD

Whatever is in heaven and earth celebrateth the praises of
God: his is the kingdom, and unto him is the praise due; for
he is almighty. It is he who hath created you; and one of
you is predestined to be an unbeliever, and another of you is
predestined to be a believer: and God beholdeth that which ye
do. He hath created the heavens and the earth with truth;

and he hath fashioned you, and given you beautiful forms: and unto him must ye all go. He knoweth whatever is in heaven and earth: and he knoweth that which ye conceal, and that which ye discover; for God knoweth the innermost part of men's breasts. Have ye not been acquainted with the story of those who disbelieved heretofore, and tasted the evil consequence of their behavior? And for them is prepared, in the life to come, a tormenting punishment. This shall they suffer, because their apostles came unto them with evident proofs of their mission, and they said, Shall men direct us? Wherefore they believed not, and turned their backs. But God standeth in need of no person: for God is self-sufficient, and worthy to be praised.

The unbelievers imagine that they shall not be raised again. Say, Yea, by my Lord, ye shall surely be raised again: then shall ye be told that which ye have wrought; and this is easy with God. Wherefore believe in God and his apostle, and the light which we have sent down: for God is well acquainted with that which ye do. On a certain day he shall assemble you, at the day of the general assembly: that will be the day of mutual deceit. And whoso shall believe in God, and shall do that which is right, from him will he expiate his evil deeds, and he will lead him into gardens beneath which rivers flow, to remain therein forever. This will be great felicity. But they who shall not believe, and shall accuse our signs of falsehood, those shall be the inhabitants of hell fire, wherein they shall remain forever; and a wretched journey shall it be thither! No misfortune happeneth but by the permission of God; and whoso believeth in God, he will direct his heart: and God knoweth all things. Wherefore obey God, and obey the apostle: but if ye turn back, verily the duty incumbent on our apostle is only public preaching. God! there is no God but he: wherefore in God let the faithful put their trust.

O true believers, verily of your wives and your children ye have an enemy: wherefore beware of them. But if ye pass over their offenses, and pardon and forgive them; God is likewise inclined to forgive, and merciful. Your wealth and your children are only a temptation; but with God is a great reward. Wherefore fear God, as much as ye are able; and hear, and obey: and give alms, for the good of your souls; for whoso is preserved from the covetousness of his own soul, they shall prosper. If ye lend unto God an acceptable loan, he will double the same unto you, and will forgive you: for God is grateful and long-suffering, knowing both what is hidden and what is divulged; the Mighty, the Wise.

CHAPTER LXV

ENTITLED, DIVORCE; REVEALED AT MEDINA

IN THE NAME OF THE MOST MERCIFUL GOD

O prophet, when ye divorce women, put them away at their appointed term; and compute the term exactly: and fear God, your Lord. Oblige them not to go out of their apartments, neither let them go out, until the term be expired, unless they be guilty of manifest uncleanness. These are the statutes of God: and whoever transgresseth the statutes of God assuredly injureth his own soul. Thou knowest not whether God will bring something new to pass, which may reconcile them, after this. And when they shall have fulfilled their term, either retain them with kindness, or part from them honorably; and take witnesses from among you, men of integrity; and give your testimony as in the presence of God.

This admonition is given unto him who believeth in God and the last day: and whoso feareth God, unto him will he grant a happy issue out of all his afflictions, and he will bestow on him an ample provision from whence he expecteth it not: and whoso trusteth in God, he will be his sufficient support; for God will surely attain his purpose. Now hath God appointed unto everything a determined period. As to such of your wives as shall despair having their courses, by reason of their age; if ye be in doubt thereof, let their term be three months: and let the same be the term of those who have not yet had their courses. But as to those who are pregnant, their term shall be until they be delivered of their burden. And whoso feareth God, unto him will he make his command easy. This is the command of God, which he hath sent down unto you. And whoso feareth God, he will expiate his evil deeds from him, and will increase his reward.

Suffer the women whom ye divorce to dwell in some part of the houses wherein ye dwell; according to the room and conveniences of the habitations which ye possess: and make them not uneasy, that ye may reduce them to straits. And if they be with child, expend on them what shall be needful, until they be delivered of their burden. And if they suckle their children for you, give them their hire; and consult among yourselves, according to what shall be just and reasonable. And if ye be put to a difficulty herein, and another woman shall suckle the child for him, let him who hath plenty expend proportionately, in the maintenance of the mother and the nurse, out of his plenty: and let him whose income is scanty expend in proportion out of that which God hath given him. God obligeth no man to more than he hath given him ability to perform: God will cause ease to succeed hardship.

How many cities have turned aside from the command of their Lord and his apostles? Wherefore we brought them to a severe account; and we chastised them with a grievous chastisement: and they tasted the evil consequence of their business; and the end of their business was perdition. God hath prepared for them a severe punishment; wherefore fear God, O ye who are endued with understanding.

True believers, now hath God sent down unto you an admonition, an apostle who may rehearse unto you the perspicuous signs of God; that he may bring forth those who believe and do good works, from darkness into light. And whoso believeth in God, and doth that which is right, him will he lead into gardens beneath which rivers flow, to remain therein forever: now hath God made an excellent provision for him. It is God who hath created seven heavens, and as many different stories of the earth: the divine command descendeth between them; that ye may know that God is omnipotent, and that God comprehendeth all things by his knowledge.

CHAPTER LXVI

ENTITLED, PROHIBITION; REVEALED AT MEDINA

IN THE NAME OF THE MOST MERCIFUL GOD

O prophet, why holdest thou that to be prohibited which God hath allowed thee, seeking to please thy wives; since God is inclined to forgive and merciful? God hath allowed you the dissolution of your oaths: and God is your master; and he is knowing and wise. When the prophet entrusted as a secret unto one of his wives a certain accident; and when she disclosed the same, and God made it known unto him; he acquainted her with part of what she had done, and forbore to upbraid her with the other part thereof. And when he had acquainted her therewith, she said, Who hath discovered this unto thee? He answered, The knowing, the sagacious God hath discovered it unto me.[1] If ye both be turned unto God (for your hearts have swerved) it is well: but if ye join against him, verily God is his patron; and Gabriel, and the good man among the faithful, and the angels also are his assistants. If he divorce you, his Lord can easily give him in exchange other wives better than you,

---

[1] When Mohammed found that his wife Hafsa knew of his having injured her, or Ayesha, by lying with his concubine Mary on the day due to one of them, he desired her to keep the affair secret, promising, at the same time, that he would not meddle with Mary any more; and foretold her, as a piece of news which might soothe her vanity, that Abu Becr and Omar should succeed him in the government of his people. Hafsa, however, could not conceal this from Ayesha, with whom she lived in strict friendship, but acquainted her with the whole matter: whereupon the prophet, perceiving that his secret had been discovered, upbraided Hafsa with her betraying him, telling her that God had revealed it to him; and not only divorced her, but separated him from all his other wives for a whole month, which time he spent in the apartment of Mary. In a short time, notwithstanding, he took Hafsa again, by the direction, as he gave out, of the angel Gabriel, who commended her for her frequent fasting and other exercises of devotion, assuring him likewise that she should be one of his wives in paradise.

women resigned unto God, true believers, devout, penitent, obedient, given to fasting, both such as have been known by other men, and virgins.

O true believers, save your souls, and those of your families, from the fire whose fuel is men and stones, over which are set angels fierce and terrible; who disobey not God in what he hath commanded them, but perform what they are commanded. O unbelievers, excuse not yourselves this day; ye shall surely be rewarded for what ye have done. O true believers, turn unto God with a sincere repentance: peradventure your Lord will do away from you your evil deeds, and will admit you into gardens, through which rivers flow; on the day whereon God will not put to shame the prophet, or those who believe with him: their light shall run before them and on their right hands, and they shall say, Lord, make our light perfect, and forgive us; for thou art almighty.

O prophet, attack the infidels with arms, and the hypocrites with arguments; and treat them with severity: their abode shall be hell, and an ill journey shall it be thither. God propoundeth as a similitude unto the unbelievers, the wife of Noah, and the wife of Lot: they were under two of our righteous servants, and they deceived them both; wherefore their husbands were of no advantage unto them at all, in the sight of God: and it shall be said unto them at the last day, Enter ye into hell fire, with those who enter therein. God also propoundeth as a similitude unto those who believe, the wife of Pharaoh;[2] when she said, Lord, build me a house with thee in paradise; and deliver me from Pharaoh and his doings, and deliver me from the unjust people: and Mary the daughter of Imran; who preserved her chastity, and into

[2] *Viz.*, Asia, the daughter of Mozahem. The commentators relate that, because she believed in Moses, her husband cruelly tormented her, fastening her hands and feet to four stakes, and laying a large mill-stone on her breast, her face at the same time being exposed to the scorching beams of the sun. These pains, however, were alleviated by the angels shading her with their wings, and the view of the mansion prepared for her in paradise, which was exhibited to her on her pronouncing the prayer in the text. At length God received her soul; or, as some say, she was taken up alive into paradise, where she eats and drinks.

whose womb we breathed of our spirit, and who believed in
the words of her Lord and his scriptures, and was a devout
and obedient person.[3]

CHAPTER LXVII

ENTITLED, THE KINGDOM; REVEALED AT MECCA

IN THE NAME OF THE MOST MERCIFUL GOD

Blessed be he in whose hand is the kingdom; for he is
almighty! Who hath created death and life, that he might
prove you, which of you is most righteous in his actions: and
he is mighty, and ready to forgive. Who hath created seven
heavens, one above another: thou canst not see in a creature
of the most Merciful any unfitness or disproportion. Lift
up thine eyes again to heaven, and look whether thou seest
any flaw: then take two other views; and thy sight shall
return unto thee dull and fatigued.

Moreover we have adorned the lowest heaven with lamps,
and have appointed them to be darted at the devils, for whom
we have prepared the torment of burning fire: and for those
who believe not in their Lord is also prepared the torment of
hell; an ill journey shall it be thither! When they shall be
thrown thereinto, they shall hear it bray like an ass; and it
shall boil, and almost burst for fury. So often as a company of them shall be thrown therein, the keepers thereof
shall ask them, saying, Did not a warner come unto you?
They shall answer, Yea, a warner came unto us: but we accused him of imposture, and said, God hath not revealed
anything; ye are in no other than a great error: and they
shall say, If ye had harkened, or had rightly considered, we
should not have been among the inhabitants of burning fire:

---

[3] On occasion of the honorable mention here made of these two extraordinary women, the commentators introduce a saying of their prophet,
" That among men there had been many perfect, but no more than four
of the other sex had attained perfection; to wit, Asia, the wife of Pharaoh; Mary, the mother of Christ; Khadîjah, the prophet's first wife;
and Fatima, the daughter of Mohammed."

and they shall confess their sins; but far be the inhabitants of burning fire from obtaining mercy!

Verily they who fear their Lord in secret shall receive pardon and a great reward. Either conceal your discourse, or make it public; he knoweth the innermost parts of your breasts: shall not he know all things who hath created them; since he is the sagacious, the knowing? It is he who hath leveled the earth for you: therefore walk through the regions thereof, and eat of his provision; unto him shall be the resurrection. Are ye secure that he who dwelleth in heaven will not cause the earth to swallow you up? and behold, it shall shake. Or are ye secure that he who dwelleth in heaven will not send against you an impetuous whirlwind, driving the sands to overwhelm you? then shall ye know how important my warning was. Those also who were before you disbelieved; and how grievous was my displeasure! Do they not behold the birds above them, extending and drawing back their wings? None sustaineth them, except the Merciful for he regardeth all things. Or who is he that will be as an army unto you, to defend you against the Merciful?

Verily the unbelievers are in no other than a mistake. Or who is he that will give you food, if he withholdeth his provision? yet they persist in perverseness, and flying from the truth. Is he, therefore, who goeth groveling upon his face, better directed than he who walketh upright in a straight way? Say, It is he who hath given you being, and endued you with hearing and sight, and understanding; yet how little gratitude have ye! Say, It is he who hath sown you in the earth, and unto him shall ye be gathered together. They say, When shall this menace be put to execution, if ye speak truth? Answer, The knowledge of this matter is with God alone: for I am only a public warner. But when they shall see the same nigh at hand, the countenance of the infidels shall grow sad: and it shall be said unto them, This is what ye have been demanding. Say, What think ye? Whether God destroy me and those who are with me, or have mercy on us; who will protect the unbelievers from a painful punishment? Say, He is the Merciful; in him do we believe, and in him do we put our trust. Ye shall hereafter know who is in a manifest error. Say, What think ye? If your water be in the morning swallowed up by the earth, who will give you clear and running water?

CHAPTER LXVIII

ENTITLED, THE PEN; REVEALED AT MECCA

IN THE NAME OF THE MOST MERCIFUL GOD

N. By the pen, and what they write,[1] thou, O Mohammed, through the grace of thy Lord, art not distracted. Verily there is prepared for thee an everlasting reward; for thou art of a noble disposition. Thou shalt see, and the infidels shall see, which of you are bereaved of your senses. Verily thy Lord well knoweth him who wandereth from his path; and he well knoweth those who are rightly directed: wherefore obey not those who charge thee with imposture. They desire that thou shouldst be easy with them, and they will be easy with thee. But obey not any who is a common swearer, a despicable fellow, a defamer, going about with slander, who forbiddeth that which is good, who is also a transgressor, a wicked person, cruel, and besides this, of spurious birth: although he be possessed of wealth and many children: when our signs are rehearsed unto him, he saith, They are fables of the ancients. We will stigmatize him on the nose.

Verily we have tried the Meccans, as we formerly tried the owners of the garden;[2] when they swore that they would

1 Some understand these words generally, and others of the pen with which God's decrees are written on the preserved table, and of the angels who register the same.

2 This garden was a plantation of palm-trees, about two parasangs from Sanaa, belonging to a certain charitable man, who, when he gathered his dates, used to give public notice to the poor, and to leave them such of the fruit as the knife missed, or was blown down by the wind, or fell beside the cloth spread under the tree to receive it: after his death, his sons, who were then become masters of the garden, apprehending they should come to want if they followed their father's example, agreed to gather the fruit early in the morning, when the poor could have no notice of the matter: but when they came to execute their pur-

gather the fruit thereof in the morning, and added not the exception, if it please God: wherefore a surrounding destruction from thy Lord encompassed it, while they slept; and in the morning it became like a garden whose fruits had been gathered. And they called the one to the other as they rose in the morning, saying, Go out early to your plantation, if ye intend to gather the fruit thereof: so they went on, whispering to one another, No poor man shall enter the garden upon you this day. And they went forth early, with a determined purpose. And when they saw the garden blasted and destroyed, they said, We have certainly mistaken our way: but when they found it to be their own garden, they cried, Verily we are not permitted to reap the fruit thereof. The worthier of them said, Did I not say unto you, Will ye not give praise unto God? They answered, Praise be unto our Lord! Verily we have been unjust doers. And they began to blame one another, and they said, Woe be unto us! verily we have been transgressors: peradventure our Lord will give us in exchange a better garden than this: and we earnestly beseech our Lord to pardon us. Thus is the chastisement of this life: but the chastisement of the next shall be more grievous; if they had known it, they would have taken heed.

Verily for the pious are prepared, with their Lord, gardens of delight. Shall we deal with the Moslems as with the wicked? What aileth you that ye judge thus? Have ye a book from heaven, wherein ye read that ye are therein promised that which ye shall choose? Or have ye received oaths which shall be binding upon us to the day of resurrection, that ye shall enjoy what ye imagine? Ask them, which of them will be the voucher of this. Or have they companions who will vouch for them? Let them produce their companions, therefore, if they speak truth. On a certain day the leg shall be made bare; and they shall be called upon to worship, but they shall not be able. Their looks shall be cast down: ignominy shall attend them: for that they were

pose, they found, to their great grief and surprise, that their plantation had been destroyed in the night.

invited to the worship of God, while they were in safety, but
would not hear.

Let me alone, therefore, with him who accuseth this new
revelation of imposture. We will lead them gradually to
destruction, by ways which they know not: and I will bear
with them for a long time; for my stratagem is effectual.
Dost thou ask them any reward for thy preaching? But
they are laden with debts. Are the secrets of futurity with
them; and do they transcribe the same from the table of God's
decree? Wherefore patiently wait the judgment of thy
Lord: and be not like him who was swallowed by the fish;
when he cried unto God, being inwardly vexed. Had not
grace from his Lord reached him, he had surely been cast
forth on the naked shore, covered with shame: but his Lord
chose him, and made him one of the righteous. It wanteth
little but that the unbelievers strike thee down with their
malicious looks, when they hear the admonition of the Koran;
and they say, He is certainly distracted: but it is no other than
an admonition unto all creatures.

CHAPTER LXIX

ENTITLED, THE INFALLIBLE; REVEALED AT MECCA

IN THE NAME OF THE MOST MERCIFUL GOD

The infallible! What is the infallible? And what shall
cause thee to understand what the infallible is? The tribes
of Thamud and Ad denied as a falsehood the day which shall
strike men's hearts with terror. But Thamud were destroyed by a terrible noise: and Ad were destroyed by a
roaring and furious wind; which God caused to assail them
for seven nights and eight days successively: thou mightest
have seen people, during the same, lying prostrate, as though
they had been the roots of hollow palm-trees; and couldst
thou have seen any of them remaining? Pharaoh also, and
those who were before him, and the cities which were overthrown, were guilty of sin; and they severally were disobe-

dient to the apostle of their Lord; wherefore he chastised them with an abundant chastisement. When the water of the deluge arose, we carried you in the ark which swam thereon; that we might make the same a memorial unto you, and the retaining ear might retain it.

And when one blast shall sound the trumpet, and the earth shall be moved from its place, and the mountains also, and shall be dashed in pieces at one stroke: on that day the inevitable hour of judgment shall suddenly come; and the heavens shall cleave in sunder, and shall fall in pieces, on that day: and the angels shall be on the sides thereof; and eight shall bear the throne of thy Lord above them, on that day. On that day ye shall be presented before the judgment-seat of God; and none of your secret actions shall be hidden. And he who shall have his book delivered into his right hand shall say, Take ye, read this my book; verily I thought that I should be brought to this my account: he shall lead a pleasing life, in a lofty garden, the fruits whereof shall be near to gather. Eat and drink with easy digestion; because of the good works which ye sent before you, in the days which are past. But he who shall have his book delivered into his left hand, shall say, Oh that I had not received this my book; and that I had not known what this my account was! Oh that death had made an end of me! My riches have not profited me; and my power is passed from me. And God shall say to the keepers of hell, Take him, and bind him, and cast him into hell to be burned; then put him into a chain of the length of seventy cubits: because he believed not in the great God; and was not solicitous to feed the poor: wherefore this day he shall have no friend here; nor any food, but the filthy corruption flowing from the bodies of the damned, which none shall eat but the sinners.

I swear by that which ye see, and that which ye see not, that this is the discourse of an honorable apostle, and not the discourse of a poet: how little do ye believe! Neither is it the discourse of a soothsayer: how little are ye admonished! It is a revelation from the Lord of all creatures. If Mohammed had forged any part of these discourses concerning

us, verily we had taken him by the right hand, and had cut
in sunder the vein of his heart; neither would we have withheld any of you from chastising him.   And verily this book
is an admonition unto the pious; and we well know that
there are some of you who charge the same with imposture:
but it shall surely be an occasion of grievous sighing unto
the infidels; for it is the truth of a certainty.   Wherefore
praise the name of thy Lord, the great God.

CHAPTER LXX

ENTITLED, THE STEPS; REVEALED AT MECCA

IN THE NAME OF THE MOST MERCIFUL GOD

One demanded and called for vengeance to fall on the unbelievers: there shall be none to avert the same from being
inflicted by God, the possessor of the steps; by which the
angels ascend unto him, and the spirit Gabriel also, in a day
whose space is fifty thousand years: wherefore bear the
insults of the Meccans with becoming patience; for they see
their punishment afar off, but we see it nigh at hand.   On
a certain day the heaven shall become like molten brass, and
the mountains like wool of various colors, scattered abroad
by the wind: and a friend shall not ask a friend concerning
his condition, although they see one another.   The wicked
shall wish to redeem himself from the punishment of that
day, by giving up his children, and his wife, and his brother,
and his kindred who showed kindness unto him, and all who
are in the earth; and that this might deliver him: by no
means: for hell fire, dragging them by their scalps, shall call
him who shall have turned his back, and fled from the faith,
and shall have amassed riches, and covetously hoarded them.
Verily man is created extremely impatient: when evil
toucheth him, he is full of complaint; but when good befalleth
him, he becometh niggardly: except those who are devoutly
given, and who persevere in their prayers; and those of whose
substance a due and certain portion is ready to be given unto
him who asketh, and him who is forbidden by shame to ask:

and those who sincerely believe the day of judgment, and who dread the punishment of their Lord (for there is none secure from the punishment of their Lord): and who abstain from the carnal knowledge of women other than their wives, or the slaves which their right hands possess (for as to them they shall be blameless; but whoever coveteth any woman besides these, they are transgressors): and those who faithfully keep what they are entrusted with, and their covenant; and who are upright in their testimonies, and who carefully observe the requisite rites in their prayers: these shall dwell amidst gardens, highly honored.

What aileth the unbelievers, that they run before thee in companies, on the right hand and on the left? Doth every man of them wish to enter into a garden of delight? By no means: verily we have created them of that which they know. I swear by the Lord of the east and of the west, that we are able to destroy them, and to substitute better than them in their room; neither are we to be prevented, if we shall please so to do. Wherefore suffer them to wade in vain disputes, and to amuse themselves with sport: until they meet their day with which they have been threatened; the day whereon they shall come forth hastily from their graves, as though they were troops hastening to their standard: their looks shall be downcast; ignominy shall attend them. This is the day with which they have been threatened.

CHAPTER LXXI

ENTITLED, NOAH; REVEALED AT MECCA

IN THE NAME OF THE MOST MERCIFUL GOD

Verily we sent Noah unto his people, saying, Warn thy people, before a grievous punishment overtake them. Noah said, O my people, verily I am a public warner unto you; wherefore, serve God and fear him, and obey me: he will forgive you part of your sins, and will grant you respite until a determined time: for God's determined time, when it cometh, shall not be deferred; if ye were men of understanding

ye would know this. He said, Lord, verily I have called
my people night and day; but my calling only increaseth
their aversion: and whensoever I call them to the true faith,
that thou mayest forgive them, they put their fingers in their
ears, and cover themselves with their garments, and persist
in their infidelity, and proudly disdain my counsel. Moreover I invited them openly, and I spake to them again in
public; and I also secretly admonished them in private: and
I said, Beg pardon of your Lord: for he is inclined to forgive; and he will cause the heaven to pour down rain plentifully upon you, and will give you increase of wealth and of
children; and he will provide you gardens, and furnish you
with rivers.

What aileth you, that ye hope not for benevolence in God;
since he hath created you variously? Do ye not see how
God hath created the seven heavens, one above another, and
hath placed the moon therein for a light, and hath appointed
the sun for a taper? God hath also produced and caused
you to spring forth from the earth: hereafter he will cause
you to return into the same; and he will again take you
thence, by bringing you forth from your graves. And God
hath spread the earth as a carpet for you, that ye may walk
therein through spacious paths. Noah said, Lord, verily
they are disobedient unto me, and they follow him whose
riches and children do no other than increase his perdition.
And they devised a dangerous plot against Noah: and the
chief men said to the others, Ye shall by no means leave
your gods; neither shall ye forsake Wadd, nor Sowa, nor
Yaghuth, and Yauk, and Nesr. And they seduced many (for
thou shalt only increase error in the wicked); because of their
sins they were drowned, and cast into the fire of hell; and
they found none to protect them against God. And Noah said,
Lord, leave not any families of the unbelievers on the earth:
for if thou leave them, they will seduce thy servants, and will
beget none but a wicked and unbelieving offspring. Lord, forgive me and my parents, and every one who shall enter my
house, being a true believer, and the true believers of both
sexes; and add unto the unjust doers nothing but destruction.

CHAPTER LXXII

ENTITLED, THE GENII; REVEALED AT MECCA

IN THE NAME OF THE MOST MERCIFUL GOD

Say, It hath been revealed unto me that a company of genii attentively heard me reading the Koran, and said, Verily we have heard an admirable discourse; which directeth unto the right institution: wherefore we believe therein, and we will by no means associate any other with our Lord. He (may the majesty of our Lord be exalted!) hath taken no wife, nor hath he begotten any issue. Yet the foolish among us hath spoken that which is extremely false of God; but we verily thought that neither man nor genius would by any means have uttered a lie concerning God. And there are certain men who fly for refuge unto certain of the genii:[1] but they increase their folly and transgression: and they also thought, as ye thought, that God would not raise any one to life.

And we formerly attempted to pry into what was transacting in heaven; but we found the same filled with a strong guard of angels, and with flaming darts: and we sat on some of the seats thereof to hear the discourse of its inhabitants; but whoever listeneth now findeth a flame laid in ambush for him, to guard the celestial confines. And we know not whether evil be hereby intended against those who are in the earth, or whether their Lord intendeth to direct them aright. There are some among us who are upright; and there are some among us who are otherwise: we are of different ways. And we verily thought that we could by no means frustrate God in the earth, neither could we escape him by flight: wherefore, when we had heard the direction contained in the Koran, we believed therein. And whoever believeth in his Lord need not fear any diminution of his reward, nor any

[1] For the Arabs, when they found themselves in a desert in the evening (the genii being supposed to haunt such places about that time), used to say, " I fly for refuge unto the Lord of this valley, that he may defend me from the foolish among his people."

injustice. There are some Moslems among us; and there are others of us who swerve from righteousness. And whoso embraceth Islam, they earnestly seek true direction; but those who swerve from righteousness shall be fuel for hell. If they tread in the way of truth, we will surely water them with abundant rain: that we may prove them thereby; but whoso turneth aside from the admonition of his Lord, him will he send into a severe torment.

Verily the places of worship are set apart unto God: wherefore invoke not any other therein together with God. When the servant of God stood up to invoke him, it wanted little but that the genii had pressed on him in crowds to hear him rehearse the Koran. Say, Verily I call upon my Lord only, and I associate no other god with him. Say, Verily I am not able, of myself, to procure you either hurt or a right institution. Say, Verily none can protect me against God; neither shall I find any refuge besides him. I can do no more than publish what hath been revealed unto me from God, and his messages. And whosoever shall be disobedient unto God and his apostle, for him is the fire of hell prepared; they shall remain therein forever. Until they see the vengeance with which they are threatened, they will not cease their opposition: but then shall they know who were the weaker in a protector, and the fewer in number. Say, I know not whether the punishment with which ye are threatened be nigh, or whether my Lord will appoint for it a distant term. He knoweth the secrets of futurity; and he doth not communicate his secrets unto any, except an apostle in whom he is well pleased: and he causeth a guard of angels to march before him and behind him, that he may know that they have executed the commissions of their Lord: he comprehendeth whatever is with them, and counteth all things by number.

CHAPTER LXXIII

ENTITLED, THE WRAPPED UP; REVEALED AT MECCA

IN THE NAME OF THE MOST MERCIFUL GOD

O thou wrapped up,[1] arise in prayer, and continue therein during the night, except a small part; that is to say, during one-half thereof: or do thou lessen the same a little, or add thereto. And repeat the Koran with a distinct and sonorous voice: for we will lay on thee a weighty word. Verily the rising by night is more efficacious for steadfast continuance in devotion, and more conducive to decent pronunciation: for in the daytime thou hast long employment. And commemorate the name of thy Lord: and separate thyself unto him, renouncing worldly vanities. He is the Lord of the east and of the west; there is no God but he. Wherefore take him for thy patron: and patiently suffer the contumelies which the infidels utter against thee; and depart from them with a decent departure. And let me alone with those who charge the Koran with falsehood, and who enjoy the blessings of this life; and bear with them for awhile: verily with us are heavy fetters, and a burning fire, and food ready to choke him who swalloweth it, and painful torment. On a certain day the earth shall be shaken, and the mountains also, and the mountains shall become a heap of sand poured forth.

Verily we have sent unto you an apostle, to bear witness against you; as we sent an apostle unto Pharaoh: but Pharaoh was disobedient unto the apostle; wherefore we chastised him with a heavy chastisement. How, therefore, will ye escape, if ye believe not, the day which shall make children become gray-headed through terror? The heaven shall be rent in sunder thereby: the promise thereof shall surely be performed. Verily this is an admonition; and whoever is

[1] When this revelation was brought to Mohammed, he was wrapped up in his garments, being affrighted at the appearance of Gabriel; or, as some say, he lay sleeping unconcernedly, or, according to others, praying, wrapped up in one part of a large mantle or rug, with the other part of which Ayesha had covered herself to sleep.

willing to be admonished will take the way unto his Lord. Thy Lord knoweth that thou continuest in prayer and meditation sometimes near a two-third part of the night, and sometimes one-half thereof, and at other times one-third part thereof: and a part of thy companions, who are with thee, do the same. But God measureth the night and the day; he knoweth that ye can not exactly compute the same: wherefore he turneth favorably unto you. Read, therefore, so much of the Koran as may be easy unto you. He knoweth that there will be some infirm among you; and others travel through the earth, that they may obtain a competency of the bounty of God; and others fight in the defense of God's faith. Read, therefore, so much of the same as may be easy. And observe the stated times of prayer, and pay the legal alms; and lend unto God an acceptable loan; for whatever good ye send before for your souls ye shall find the same with God. This will be better, and will merit a greater reward. And ask God forgiveness; for God is ready to forgive, and merciful.

CHAPTER LXXIV

ENTITLED, THE COVERED; REVEALED AT MECCA

IN THE NAME OF THE MOST MERCIFUL GOD

O thou covered,[1] arise and preach, and magnify thy Lord. And cleanse thy garments: and fly every abomination: and be not liberal in hopes to receive more in return: and patiently wait for thy Lord. When the trumpet shall sound, verily that day shall be a day of distress and uneasiness unto the unbelievers. Let me alone with him whom I have cre-

[1] It is related, from Mohammed's own mouth, that being on Mount Hara, and hearing himself called, he looked on each hand, and saw nobody; but looking upward, he saw the angel Gabriel on a throne, between heaven and earth; at which sight being much terrified, he returned to his wife Khadijah, and bade her cover him up; and that then the angel descended, and addressed him in the words of the text. From hence some think this chapter to have been the first which was revealed: but the more received opinion is that it was the 96th.

ated,[2] on whom I have bestowed abundant riches, and children dwelling in his presence, and for whom I have disposed affairs in a smooth and easy manner, and who desireth that I will yet add other blessings unto him. By no means: because he is an adversary to our signs.[3] I will afflict him with grievous calamities: for he hath devised and prepared contumelious expressions to ridicule the Koran. May he be cursed: how maliciously hath he prepared the same! And again, may he be cursed: how maliciously hath he prepared the same! Then he looked, and frowned, and put on an austere countenance: then he turned back, and was elated with pride; and he said, This is no other than a piece of magic, borrowed from others: these are only the words of a man. I will cast him to be burned in hell. And what shall make thee to understand what hell is? It leaveth not anything unconsumed, neither doth it suffer anything to escape: it scorcheth men's flesh: over the same are nineteen angels appointed. We have appointed none but angels to preside over hell fire: and we have expressed the number of them only for an occasion of discord to the unbelievers; that they to whom the scriptures have been given may be certain of the veracity of this book, and the true believers may increase in faith; and that those to whom the scriptures have been given, and the true believers, may not doubt hereafter; and that those in whose hearts there is an infirmity, and the unbelievers, may say, What mystery doth God intend by this number? Thus doth God cause to err whom he pleaseth; and he directeth whom he pleaseth.

None knoweth the armies of thy Lord, besides him: and this is no other than a memento unto mankind. Assuredly. By the moon, and the night when it retreateth, and the morning when it reddeneth, I swear that this is one of the most terrible calamities, giving warning unto men, as well unto him among you who desireth to go forward, as unto him who

[2] The person here meant is generally supposed to have been al Walid Ebn al Mogheira, a principal man among the Koreish.

[3] On the revelation of this passage it is said that Walid's prosperity began to decay, and continued daily so to do to the time of his death.

chooseth to remain behind. Every soul is given in pledge for that which it shall have wrought: except the companions of the right hand; who shall dwell in gardens, and shall ask one another questions concerning the wicked, and shall also ask the wicked themselves, saying, What hath brought you into hell? They shall answer, We were not of those who were constant at prayer, neither did we feed the poor; and we waded in vain disputes, with the fallacious reasoners; and we denied the day of judgment, until death overtook us: and the intercession of the interceders shall not avail them. What aileth them, therefore, that they turn aside from the admonition of the Koran, as though they were timorous asses flying from a lion? But every man among them desireth that he may have expanded scrolls delivered to him from God. By no means. They fear not the life to come. By no means: verily this is a sufficient warning. Whoso is willing to be warned, him shall it warn: but they shall not be warned, unless God shall please. He is worthy to be feared; and he is inclined to forgiveness.

CHAPTER LXXV

ENTITLED, THE RESURRECTION; REVEALED AT MECCA

IN THE NAME OF THE MOST MERCIFUL GOD

Verily I swear by the day of resurrection; and I swear by the soul which accuseth itself: doth man think that we will not gather his bones together? Yea: we are able to put together the smallest bones of his fingers. But man chooseth to be wicked, for the time which is before him. He asketh, When will the day of resurrection be? But when the sight shall be dazzled, and the moon shall be eclipsed, and the sun and the moon shall be in conjunction; on that day man shall say, Where is a place of refuge? By no means: there shall be no place to fly unto. With thy Lord shall be the sure mansion of rest on that day: on that day shall a man be told that which he hath done first and last. Yea, a man shall be

an evidence against himself: and though he offer his excuses,
they shall not be received. Move not thy tongue, O Mohammed, in repeating the revelations brought thee by Gabriel, before he shall have finished the same, that thou mayest
quickly commit them to memory: for the collecting the Koran
in thy mind, and the teaching thee the true reading thereof,
are incumbent on us. But when we shall have read the
same unto thee by the tongue of the angel, do thou follow
the reading thereof: and afterward it shall be our part to
explain it unto thee. By no means shalt thou be thus hasty
for the future. But ye love that which hasteneth away, and
neglect the life to come. Some countenances, on that day,
shall be bright, looking toward their Lord; and some countenances, on that day, shall be dismal: they shall think that a
crushing calamity shall be brought upon them. Assuredly.
When a man's soul shall come up to his throat, in his last
agony; and the standers-by shall say, Who bringeth a charm
to recover him? and shall think it to be his departure out of
this world; and one leg shall be joined with the other leg;
on that day unto thy Lord shall he be driven. For he believed not, neither did he pray; but he accused God's apostle
of imposture, and turned back from obeying him: then he
departed unto his family, walking with a haughty mien.
Wherefore, woe be unto thee; woe! And again, Woe be unto
thee; woe! Doth man think that he shall be left at full
liberty, without control? Was he not a drop of seed, which
was emitted? Afterwards he became a little coagulated
blood; and God formed him, and fashioned him with just proportion: and made of him two sexes, the male and the female.
Is not he who hath done this able to quicken the dead?

CHAPTER LXXVI

ENTITLED, MAN; REVEALED AT MECCA

IN THE NAME OF THE MOST MERCIFUL GOD

Did there not pass over man a long space of time; during which he was a thing not worthy of remembrance?[1] Verily we have created man of the mingled seed of both sexes, that we might prove him: and we have made him to hear and to see. We have surely directed him in the way; whether he be grateful or ungrateful. Verily we have prepared for the unbelievers chains, and collars, and burning fire. But the just shall drink of a cup of wine, mixed with the water of Cafur,[2] a fountain whereof the servants of God shall drink; they shall convey the same by channels whithersoever they please. These fulfil their vow, and dread the day, the evil whereof will disperse itself far abroad; and give food unto the poor, and the orphan, and the bondman, for his sake, saying, We feed you for God's sake only: we desire no recompense from you, nor any thanks: verily we dread, from our Lord, a dismal and calamitous day.[3] Wherefore God

[1] Some take these words to be spoken of Adam, whose body, according to the Mohammedan tradition, was at first a figure of clay, and was left forty years to dry before God breathed life into it; others understand them of man in general.

[2] Is the name of a fountain in paradise, so called from its resembling camphor (which the word signifies) in odor and whiteness. Some take the word for an appellative, and think the wine of paradise will be mixed with camphor, because of its agreeable coolness and smell.

[3] It is related that Hassan and Hosein, Mohammed's grandchildren, on a certain time being both sick, the prophet, among others, visited them, and they wished Ali to make some vow to God for the recovery of his sons: whereupon Ali, and Fatima, and Fidda, their maid-servant, vowed a fast of three days in case they did well; as it happened they did. This vow was performed with so great strictness that the first day, having no provisions in the house, Ali was obliged to borrow three measures of barley of one Simeon, a Jew, of Khaibar, one measure of which Fatima ground the same day, and baked five cakes of the meal, and they were set before them to break their fast with after sunset: but a poor man coming to them, they gave all their bread to him, and passed the night without tasting anything except water. The next day Fatima made another measure into bread, for the same purpose; but

shall deliver them from the evil of that day, and shall cast
on them brightness of countenance, and joy; and shall reward
them, for their patient persevering, with a garden, and silk
garments: therein shall they repose themselves on couches;
they shall see therein neither sun nor moon: and the shades
thereof shall be near spreading above them, and the fruits
thereof shall hang low, so as to be easily gathered. And
their attendants shall go round about unto them, with vessels
of silver, and goblets: the bottles shall be bottles of silver
shining like glass; they shall determine the measure thereof
by their wish. And therein shall they be given to drink of a
cup of wine, mixed with the water of Zenjebil, a fountain
in paradise named Salsabil: and youths, which shall continue forever in their bloom, shall go round to attend them;
when thou seest them, thou shalt think them to be scattered
pearls: and when thou lookest, there shalt thou behold delights, and a great kingdom. Upon them shall be garments
of fine green silk, and of brocades, and they shall be adorned
with bracelets of silver: and their Lord shall give them to
drink of a most pure liquor; and shall say unto them, Verily
this is your reward: and your endeavor is gratefully accepted.

Verily we have sent down unto thee the Koran, by a gradual revelation. Wherefore patiently wait the judgment of
the Lord; and obey not any wicked person or unbeliever
among them. And commemorate the name of thy Lord, in
the morning and in the evening: and during some part of the
night worship him, and praise him a long part of the night.
Verily these men love the transitory life, and leave behind
them the heavy day of judgment. We have created them,
and have strengthened their joints; and when we please, we
will substitute others like unto them, in their stead. Verily
this is an admonition: and whoso willeth, taketh the way
unto his Lord: but ye shall not will, unless God willeth; for

an orphan begging some food, they chose to let him have it, and passed
that night as the first; and the third day they likewise gave their whole
provision to a famished captive. Upon this occasion Gabriel descended
with the chapter before us, and told Mohammed that God congratulated
him on the virtues of his family.

God is knowing and wise. He leadeth whom he pleaseth into his mercy: but for the unjust hath he prepared a grievous punishment.

CHAPTER LXXVII

ENTITLED, THOSE WHICH ARE SENT; REVEALED AT MECCA

IN THE NAME OF THE MOST MERCIFUL GOD

By the angels which are sent by God, following one another in a continual series; and those which move swiftly, with a rapid motion; and by those which disperse his commands, by divulging them through the earth; and by those which separate truth from falsehood, by distinguishing the same; and by those which communicate the divine admonitions, to excuse, or to threaten: verily that which ye are promised is inevitable. When the stars, therefore, shall be out, and when the heaven shall be cloven in sunder, and when the mountains shall be winnowed, and when the apostles shall have a time assigned them to appear and bear testimony against their respective people; to what a day shall that appointment be deferred! to the day of separation: and what shall cause thee to understand what the day of separation is? On that day, woe be unto them who accused the prophets of imposture!

Have we not destroyed the obstinate unbelievers of old? We will also cause those of the latter times to follow them. Thus do we deal with the wicked. Woe be, on that day, unto them who accused the prophets of imposture! Have we not created you of a contemptible drop of seed, which we placed in a sure repository, until the fixed term of delivery? And we were able to do this: for we are most powerful. On that day, woe be unto those who accused the prophets of imposture! Have we not made the earth to contain the living and the dead, and placed therein stable and lofty mountains, and given you fresh water to drink? Woe be, on that day, unto those who accused the prophets of imposture! It shall be said unto them, Go ye to the punishment which ye denied as a falsehood: go ye into the shadow of the smoke of hell, which shall ascend in three columns, and shall not shade you from the heat, neither shall it be of service against the flame; but it shall cast forth sparks as big as towers, resembling yellow camels in color. Woe be, on that day, unto those who accused the prophets of imposture! This shall be a day whereon they shall not speak to any purpose; neither shall they be permitted to excuse themselves. Woe be, on that day, unto those who accused the prophets of imposture! This shall be the day of separation: we will assemble both you and your predecessors. Wherefore, if ye have any cunning stratagem, employ stratagems against me. Woe be, on that day, unto those who accused the prophets of imposture! But the pious shall dwell amidst shades and fountains, and fruits of the kinds which they shall desire: and it shall be said unto them, Eat and drink with easy digestion, in recompense for that which ye have wrought; for thus do we reward the righteous doers. Woe be, on that day, unto those who accused the prophets of imposture! Eat, O unbelievers, and enjoy the pleasures of this life, for a little while: verily ye are wicked men. Woe be, on that day, unto those who accused the prophets of imposture! And when it is said unto them, Bow down; they do not bow down. Woe be, on that day, unto those who accused the prophets of imposture! In what new revelation will they believe, after this?

CHAPTER LXXVIII

ENTITLED, THE NEWS; REVEALED AT MECCA

IN THE NAME OF THE MOST MERCIFUL GOD

Concerning what do the unbelievers ask questions of one another? Concerning the great news of the resurrection, about which they disagree. Assuredly they shall hereafter know the truth thereof. Again, Assuredly they shall hereafter know the truth thereof. Have we not made the earth for a bed, and the mountains for stakes to fix the same?

And have we not created you of two sexes; and appointed your sleep for rest; and made the night a garment to cover you; and destined the day to the gaining of your livelihood; and built over you seven solid heavens; and placed therein a burning lamp? And do we not send down from the clouds pressing forth rain, water pouring down in abundance, that we may thereby produce corn, and herbs, and gardens planted thick with trees?

Verily the day of separation is a fixed period: the day whereon the trumpet shall sound, and ye shall come in troops to judgment; and the heaven shall be opened, and shall be full of gates for the angels to pass through; and the mountains shall pass away, and become as a vapor; verily hell shall be a place of ambush, a receptacle for the transgressors, who shall remain therein for ages: they shall not taste any refreshment therein, or any drink, except boiling water, and filthy corruption: a fit recompense for their deeds! For they hoped that they should not be brought to an account, and they disbelieved our signs, accusing them of falsehood. But everything have we computed, and written down. Taste, therefore: we will not add unto you any other than torment.[1]

But for the pious is prepared a place of bliss: gardens planted with trees, and vineyards, and damsels with swelling breasts, of equal age with themselves, and a full cup. They shall hear no vain discourse there, nor any falsehood. This shall be their recompense from thy Lord; a gift fully sufficient: from the Lord of heaven and earth, and of whatever is between them; the Merciful. The inhabitants of heaven or of earth shall not dare to demand audience of him: the day whereon the spirit Gabriel and the other angels shall stand in order, they shall not speak in behalf of themselves or others, except he only to whom the Merciful shall grant permission, and who shall say that which is right. This is the infallible day. Whoso, therefore, willeth, let him return

[1] This, say the commentators, is the most severe and terrible sentence in the whole Koran, pronounced against the inhabitants of hell; they being hereby assured that every change in their torments will be for the worse.

unto his Lord. Verily we threaten you with a punishment
nigh at hand: the day whereon a man shall behold the good
or evil deeds which his hands have sent before him; and the
unbeliever shall say, Would to God I were dust!

CHAPTER LXXIX

ENTITLED, THOSE WHO TEAR FORTH; REVEALED AT MECCA

IN THE NAME OF THE MOST MERCIFUL GOD

By the angels who tear forth the souls of some with violence; and by those who draw forth the souls of others with
gentleness:[1] by those who glide swimmingly through the
air with the commands of God; and those who precede and
usher the righteous to paradise; and those who subordinately
govern the affairs of this world: on a certain day, the dis-
turbing blast of the trumpet shall disturb the universe; and
the subsequent blast shall follow it. On that day men's
hearts shall tremble: their looks shall be cast down. The
infidels say, Shall we surely be made to return whence we
came? After we shall have become rotten bones, shall we
be again raised to life? They say, This then will be a
return to loss. Verily it will be but one sounding of the
trumpet, and behold, they shall appear alive on the face of
the earth.

Hath not the story of Moses reached thee? When his
Lord called unto him in the holy valley Towa, saying, Go
unto Pharaoh; for he is insolently wicked: and say, Hast
thou a desire to become just and holy? and I will direct thee
unto thy Lord, that thou mayest fear to transgress. And
he showed him the very great sign of the rod turned into a
serpent: and he charged Moses with imposture, and rebelled
against God. Then he turned back hastily; and he assembled

[1] These are the angel of death and his assistants, who will take the
souls of the wicked in a rough and cruel manner from the inmost part of
their bodies, as a man drags up a thing from the bottom of the sea;
but will take the souls of the good in a gentle and easy manner from
their lips, as when a man draws a bucket of water at one pull,

the magicians, and cried aloud, saying, I am your supreme Lord. Wherefore God chastised him with the punishment of the life to come, and also of this present life. Verily herein is an example unto him who feareth to rebel. Are ye more difficult to create, or the heaven which God hath built? He hath raised the height thereof, and hath perfectly formed the same: and he hath made the night thereof dark, and hath produced the light thereof. After this he stretched out the earth, whence he caused to spring forth the water thereof, and the pasture thereof; and he established the mountains, for the use of yourselves and of your cattle.

When the prevailing, the great day shall come, on that day shall a man call to remembrance what he hath purposely done: and hell shall be exposed to the view of the spectator. And whoso shall have transgressed, and shall have chosen this present life; verily hell shall be his abode: but whoso shall have dreaded the appearing before his Lord, and shall have refrained his soul from lust; verily paradise shall be his abode. They will ask thee concerning the last hour, when will be the fixed time thereof. By what means canst thou give any information of the same? Unto thy Lord belongeth the knowledge of the period whereof: and thou art only a warner, who fearest the same. The day whereon they shall see the same, it shall seem to them as though they had not tarried in the world longer than an evening or a morning thereof.

CHAPTER LXXX

ENTITLED, HE FROWNED; REVEALED AT MECCA

IN THE NAME OF THE MOST MERCIFUL GOD

The prophet frowned, and turned aside, because the blind man came unto him:[1] and how dost thou know whether he shall peradventure be cleansed from his sins; or whether

[1] This passage was revealed on the following occasion. A certain blind man, named Abdallah Ebn Omm Mactum, came and interrupted Mo-

he shall be admonished, and the admonition shall profit him? The man who is wealthy thou receivest respectfully; whereas it is not to be charged on thee, that he is not cleansed: but him who cometh unto thee earnestly seeking his salvation, and who feareth God, dost thou neglect. By no means shouldst thou act thus. Verily the Koran is an admonition (and he who is willing retaineth the same); written in volumes honorable, exalted, and pure; by the hands of scribes honored and just. May man be cursed! What hath seduced him to infidelity? Of what thing doth God create him? Of a drop of seed doth he create him; and he formeth him with proportion; and then facilitateth his passage out of the womb: afterward he causeth him to die, and layeth him in the grave; hereafter, when it shall please him, he shall raise him to life. Assuredly. He hath not hitherto fully performed what God hath commanded him.

Let man consider his food; in what manner it is provided. We pour down water by showers; afterward we cleanse the earth in clefts, and we cause corn to spring forth therein, and grapes, and clover, and the olive, and the palm, and gardens planted thick with trees, and fruits, and grass, for the use of yourselves and of your cattle. When the stunning sound of the trumpet shall be heard; on that day shall a man fly from his brother, and his mother, and his father, and his wife, and his children. Every man of them, on that day, shall have business of his own sufficient to employ his thoughts. On that day the faces of some shall be bright, laughing, and joyful: and upon the faces of others, on that day, shall there be dust; darkness shall cover them. These are the unbelievers, the wicked.

hammed while he was engaged in earnest discourse with some of the principal Koreish, whose conversion he had hopes of; but the prophet taking no notice of him, the blind man, not knowing he was otherwise busied, raised his voice, and said: "O apostle of God, teach me some part of what God hath taught thee"; but Mohammed, vexed at this interruption, frowned and turned away from him; for which he is here reprehended. After this, whenever the prophet saw Ebn Omm Mactum, he showed him great respect, saying, "The man is welcome, on whose account my Lord hath reprimanded me"; and he made him twice governor of Medina.

CHAPTER LXXXI

ENTITLED, THE FOLDING UP; REVEALED AT MECCA

IN THE NAME OF THE MOST MERCIFUL GOD

When the sun shall be folded up; and when the stars shall fall; and when the mountains shall be made to pass away; and when the camels ten months gone with young shall be neglected; and when the wild beasts shall be gathered together; and when the seas shall boil; and when the souls shall be joined again to their bodies; and when the girl who hath been buried alive shall be asked for what crime she was put to death; [1] and when the books shall be laid open; and when the heaven shall be removed; and when hell shall burn fiercely; and when paradise shall be brought near: every soul shall know what it hath wrought.

Verily I swear by the stars which are retrograde, which move swiftly, and which hide themselves; and by the night, when it cometh on; and by the morning, when it appeareth; that these are the words of an honorable messenger, endued with strength, of established dignity in the sight of the possessor of the throne, obeyed by the angels under his authority, and faithful: and your companion Mohammed is not distracted. He had already seen him in the clear horizon: and he suspected not the secrets revealed unto him. Neither are these the words of an accursed devil. Whither, therefore, are ye going? This is no other than an admonition unto all creatures; unto him among you who shall be willing to walk uprightly: but ye shall not will, unless God willeth, the Lord of all creatures.

1 For it was customary among the ancient Arabs to bury their daughters alive as soon as they were born; for fear they should be impoverished by providing for them, or should suffer disgrace on their account.

CHAPTER LXXXII

ENTITLED, THE CLEAVING IN SUNDER; REVEALED AT MECCA

IN THE NAME OF THE MOST MERCIFUL GOD

When the heaven shall be cloven in sunder; and when the stars shall be scattered; and when the seas shall be suffered to join their waters; and when the graves shall be turned upside down: every soul shall know what it hath committed, and what it hath omitted. O man, what hath seduced thee against thy gracious Lord, who hath created thee, and put thee together, and rightly disposed thee? In what form he pleased hath he fashioned thee. Assuredly. But ye deny the last judgment as a falsehood. Verily there are appointed over you guardian angels, honorable in the sight of God, writing down your actions; who know that which ye do. The just shall surely be in a place of delight: but the wicked shall surely be in hell; they shall be cast therein to be burned, on the day of judgment, and they shall not be absent therefrom forever. What shall cause thee to understand what the day of judgment is? Again, What shall cause thee to understand what the day of judgment is? It is a day whereon one soul shall not be able to obtain anything in behalf of another soul: and the command on that day shall be God's.

CHAPTER LXXXIII

ENTITLED, THOSE WHO GIVE SHORT MEASURE OR WEIGHT; REVEALED AT MECCA

IN THE NAME OF THE MOST MERCIFUL GOD

Woe be unto those who give short measure or weight; who, when they receive by measure from other men, take the full; but when they measure unto them, or weigh unto them, defraud! Do not these think they shall be raised again at the great day; the day whereon mankind shall stand before the Lord of all creatures? By no means. Verily the register of the actions of the wicked is surely in Sejjin.[1] And what shall make thee to understand what Sejjin is? It is a book distinctly written. Woe be, on that day, unto those who accused the prophets of imposture; who denied the day of judgment as a falsehood! And none denieth the same as a falsehood, except every unjust and flagitious person: who, when our signs are rehearsed unto him, saith, They are fables of the ancients. By no means: but rather their lusts have cast a veil over their hearts. By no means. Verily they shall be shut out from their Lord on that day; and they shall be sent into hell to be burned: then shall it be said unto them, by the infernal guards, This is what ye denied as a falsehood. Assuredly. But the register of the actions of the righteous is in Illiyyun:[2] and what shall cause thee to understand what Illiyyun is? It is a book distinctly written: those who approach near unto God are witnesses thereto. Verily the righteous shall dwell among delights: seated on couches they shall behold objects of pleasure; thou shalt see in their faces the brightness of joy. They shall be given to drink of pure wine, sealed; the seal whereof shall be musk: and to this let those aspire, who aspire to happiness: and the water mixed therewith shall be of Tasnim,[3] a fountain whereof those shall drink who approach near unto the divine presence.

They who act wickedly laugh the true believers to scorn;

[1] Is the name of the general register, wherein the actions of all the wicked, both men and genii, are distinctly entered. *Sejjin* signifies " a prison "; and this book, as some think, derives its name from thence, because it will occasion those whose deeds are there recorded to be " imprisoned " in hell. *Sejjin,* or *Sajin,* is also the name of the dungeon beneath the seventh earth, the residence of Eblis and his host, where, it is supposed by some, that this book is kept, and where the souls of the wicked will be detained till the resurrection.

[2] The word is a plural, and signifies high places. Some say it is the general register wherein the actions of the righteous, whether angels, men, or genii, are distinctly recorded. Others will have it to be a place in the seventh heaven, under the throne of God, where this book is kept, and where the souls of the just, as many think, will remain till the last day.

[3] Is the name of a fountain in paradise, so called from its being conveyed to the highest apartments.

and when they pass by them, they wink at one another: and when they turn aside to their people, they turn aside making scurrilous jests: and when they see them, they say, Verily these are mistaken men. But they are not sent to be keepers over them. Wherefore one day the true believers, in their turn, shall laugh the infidels to scorn: lying on couches, they shall look down upon them in hell. Shall not the infidels be rewarded for that which they have done?

CHAPTER LXXXIV

ENTITLED, THE RENDING IN SUNDER; REVEALED AT MECCA

IN THE NAME OF THE MOST MERCIFUL GOD

When the heaven shall be rent in sunder, and shall obey its Lord, and shall be capable thereof; and when the earth shall be stretched out, and shall cast forth that which is therein, and shall remain empty, and shall obey its Lord, and shall be capable thereof: O man, verily laboring thou laborest to meet thy Lord, and thou shalt meet him. And he who shall have his book given into his right hand shall be called to an easy account, and shall turn unto his family with joy: but he who shall have his book given him behind his back shall invoke destruction to fall upon him, and he shall be sent into hell to be burned; because he rejoiceth insolently amidst his family on earth. Verily he thought that he should never return unto God: yea verily; but his Lord beheld him. Wherefore I swear by the redness of the sky after sunset, and by the night, and the animals which it driveth together, and by the moon when she is at the full; ye shall surely be transferred successively from state to state. What aileth them, therefore, that they believe not the resurrection; and that, when the Koran is read unto them, they worship not! Yea: the unbelievers accuse the same of imposture: but God well knoweth the malice which they keep hidden in their breasts. Wherefore denounce unto them a grievous punishment, except those who believe and do good works: for them is prepared a never-failing reward.

CHAPTER LXXXV

ENTITLED, THE CELESTIAL SIGNS; REVEALED AT MECCA

IN THE NAME OF THE MOST MERCIFUL GOD

By the heaven adorned with signs; by the promised day of judgment; by the witness, and the witnessed; cursed were the contrivers of the pit, of fire supplied with fuel; when they sat round the same, and were witnesses of what they did against the true believers: and they afflicted them for no other reason, but because they believed in the mighty, the glorious God, unto whom belongeth the kingdom of heaven and earth: and God is witness of all things. Verily for those who prosecute the true believers of either sex, and afterward repent not, is prepared the torment of hell; and they shall suffer the pain of burning. But for those who believe, and do that which is right, are destined gardens beneath which rivers flow: this shall be great felicity.

Verily the vengeance of thy Lord is severe. He createth, and he restoreth to life: he is inclined to forgive, and gracious: the possessor of the glorious throne; who effecteth that which he pleaseth. Hath not the story of the hosts of Pharaoh, and of Thamud, reached thee? Yet the unbelievers cease not to accuse the divine revelations of falsehood: but God encompasseth them behind, that they can not escape. Verily that which they reject is a glorious Koran; the original whereof is written in a table kept in heaven.

CHAPTER LXXXVI

ENTITLED, THE STAR WHICH APPEARETH BY NIGHT; REVEALED AT MECCA

IN THE NAME OF THE MOST MERCIFUL GOD

By the heaven, and that which appeareth by night: but what shall cause thee to understand what that which appeareth by night is? it is the star of piercing brightness: every soul hath a guardian set over it. Let a man consider, therefore, of what he is created. He is created of seed poured forth, issuing from the loins, and the breastbones. Verily God is able to restore him to life, the day whereon all secret thoughts and actions shall be examined into; and he shall have no power to defend himself, nor any protector. By the heaven which returneth the rain, and by the earth which openeth to let forth vegetables and springs: verily this is a discourse distinguishing good from evil; and it is not composed with lightness. Verily the infidels are laying a plot to frustrate my designs: but I will lay a plot for their ruin. Wherefore, O prophet, bear with the unbelievers: let them alone awhile.

CHAPTER LXXXVII

ENTITLED, THE MOST HIGH; REVEALED AT MECCA

IN THE NAME OF THE MOST MERCIFUL GOD

Praise the name of thy Lord, the most high; who hath created, and completely formed his creatures: and who determineth them to various ends, and directeth them to attain the same; and who produceth the pasture for cattle, and afterwards rendereth the same dry stubble of a dusky hue. We will enable thee to rehearse our revelations; and thou shalt not forget any part thereof, except what God shall please; for he knoweth that which is manifest, and that which is hidden. And we will facilitate unto thee the most easy way. Wherefore admonish thy people, if thy admonition shall be profitable unto them. Whoso feareth God, he will be admonished: but the most wretched unbeliever will turn away therefrom; who shall be cast to be broiled in the greater fire of hell, wherein he shall not die, neither shall he live. Now hath he attained felicity who is purified by faith, and who remembereth the name of his Lord, and prayeth. But ye prefer this present life: yet the life to come is better, and more durable. Verily this is written in the ancient books, the books of Abraham and Moses.

CHAPTER LXXXVIII

ENTITLED, THE OVERWHELMING; REVEALED AT MECCA

IN THE NAME OF THE MOST MERCIFUL GOD

Hath the news of the overwhelming day of judgment
reached thee? The countenances of some, on that day, shall
be cast down; laboring and toiling: they shall be cast into
scorching fire to be broiled: they shall be given to drink of a
boiling fountain: they shall have no food, but of dry thorns
and thistles; which shall not fatten, neither shall they satisfy
hunger. But the countenances of others, on that day, shall
be joyful; well pleased with their past endeavor: they shall
be placed in a lofty garden, wherein thou shalt hear no vain
discourse: therein shall be a running fountain: therein shall
be raised beds, and goblets placed before them, and cushions
laid in order, and carpets ready spread. Do they not consider the camels, how they are created; and the heaven, how
it is raised; and the mountains, how they are fixed; and the
earth, how it is extended? Wherefore warn thy people; for
thou art a warner only: thou art not empowered to act with
authority over them. But whoever shall turn back, and disbelieve, God shall punish him with the greater punishment
of the life to come. Verily unto us shall they return: then
shall it be our part to bring them to account.

CHAPTER LXXXIX

ENTITLED, THE DAYBREAK; REVEALED AT MECCA

IN THE NAME OF THE MOST MERCIFUL GOD

By the daybreak, and ten nights; [1] by that which is double,
and that which is single; [2] and by the night when it cometh

[1] That is, the ten nights of Dhu'lhajja, or the 10th of that month,
or the nights of the 10th of Moharram; which are days peculiarly sacred
among the Mohammedans.

[2] These words are variously interpreted. Some understand thereby
all things in general; some, all created beings (which are said to have
been created by pairs, or of two kinds), and the Creator, who is single;

on: is there not in this an oath formed with understanding? Hast thou not considered how thy Lord dealt with Ad, the people of Irem, adorned with lofty buildings, the like whereof hath not been erected in the land; and with Thamud, who hewed the rocks in the valley into houses; and with Pharaoh, the contriver of the stakes: who had behaved insolently in the earth, and multiplied corruption therein? Wherefore thy Lord poured on them various kinds of chastisement: for thy Lord is surely in a watch-tower, whence he observeth the actions of men. Moreover man, when his Lord trieth him by prosperity, and honoreth him, and is bounteous unto him, saith, My Lord honoreth me: but when he proveth him by afflictions, and withholdeth his provisions from him, he saith, My Lord despiseth me. By no means: but ye honor not the orphan, neither do ye excite one another to feed the poor; and ye devour the inheritance of the weak, with undistinguishing greediness; and ye love riches, and much affection. By no means should ye do thus. When the earth shall be minutely ground to dust; and thy Lord shall come, and the angels rank by rank; and hell, on that day, shall be brought nigh: on that day shall man call to remembrance his evil deeds; but how shall remembrance avail him? He shall say, Would to God that I had heretofore done good works in my lifetime! On that day none shall punish with his punishment; nor shall any bind with his bonds. O thou soul which art at rest, return unto thy Lord, well pleased with thy reward, and well pleasing unto God: enter my paradise.

CHAPTER XC

ENTITLED, THE TERRITORY; REVEALED AT MECCA

IN THE NAME OF THE MOST MERCIFUL GOD

I swear by this territory (and thou, O prophet, residest in this territory), and by the begetter, and that which he hath begotten; verily we have created man in misery. Doth he

and some, of the day of slaying the victims (the 10th of Dhu'lhajja), and of the day of Arafat, which is the day before, etc.

think that none shall prevail over him? He saith, I have wasted plenty of riches. Doth he think that none seeth him? Have we not made him two eyes, and a tongue, and two lips; and shown him the two highways of good and evil? Yet he attempteth not the cliff. What shall make thee to understand what the cliff is? It is to free the captive; or to feed, in the day of famine, the orphan who is of kin, or the poor man who lieth on the ground. Whoso doth this, and is one of those who believe, and recommend perseverence unto each other, and recommend mercy unto each other; these shall be the companions of the right hand. But they who shall disbelieve our signs shall be the companions of the left hand: above them shall be arched fire.

CHAPTER XCI

ENTITLED, THE SUN; REVEALED AT MECCA

IN THE NAME OF THE MOST MERCIFUL GOD

By the sun, and its rising brightness; by the moon, when she followeth him; by the day, when it showeth his splendor; by the night, when it covereth him with darkness; by the heaven, and him who built it; by the earth, and him who spread it forth; by the soul, and him who completely formed it, and inspired into the same its faculty of distinguishing, and power of choosing, wickedness and piety: now is he who hath purified the same happy; but he who hath corrupted the same is miserable. Thamud accused their prophet Saleh of imposture, through the excess of their wickedness: when the wretch among them was sent to slay the camel; and the apostle of God said unto them, Let alone the camel of God; and hinder not her drinking. But they charged him with imposture; and they slew her. Wherefore their Lord destroyed them, for their crime, and made their punishment equal unto them all: and he feareth not the issue thereof.

CHAPTER XCII

ENTITLED, THE NIGHT; REVEALED AT MECCA

IN THE NAME OF THE MOST MERCIFUL GOD

By the night, when it covereth all things with darkness; by the day, when it shineth forth; by him who hath created the male and the female: verily your endeavor is different. Now whoso is obedient, and feareth God, and professeth the truth of that faith which is most excellent; unto him will we facilitate the way to happiness: but whoso shall be covetous, and shall be wholly taken up with this world, and shall deny the truth of that which is most excellent; unto him will we facilitate the way to misery; and his riches shall not profit him, when he shall fall headlong into hell. Verily unto us appertaineth the direction of mankind: and ours is the life to come and the present life. Wherefore I threaten you with fire which burneth fiercely, which none shall enter to be burned except the most wretched; who shall have disbelieved, and turned back. But he who strictly bewareth idolatry and rebellion shall be removed far from the same; who giveth his substance in alms, and by whom no benefit is bestowed on any, that it may be recompensed, but who bestoweth the same for the sake of his Lord, the most High: and hereafter he shall be well satisfied with his reward.

CHAPTER XCIII

ENTITLED, THE BRIGHTNESS; REVEALED AT MECCA

IN THE NAME OF THE MOST MERCIFUL GOD

By the brightness of the morning; and by the night, when it groweth dark: thy Lord hath not forsaken thee, neither doth he hate thee.[1] Verily the life to come shall be better for

[1] It is related that no revelation having been vouchsafed to Mohammed for several days, in answer to some questions put to him by the Koreish, because he had confidently promised to resolve them the next day, without adding the exception, "if it please God," or because he had repulsed

thee than this present life: and thy Lord shall give thee a reward wherewith thou shalt be well pleased. Did he not find thee an orphan, and hath he not taken care of thee? And did he not find thee wandering in error, and hath he not guided thee into the truth? And did he not find thee needy, and hath he not enriched thee? Wherefore oppress not the orphan; neither repulse the beggar: but declare the goodness of thy Lord.

CHAPTER XCIV

ENTITLED, HAVE WE NOT OPENED; REVEALED AT MECCA

IN THE NAME OF THE MOST MERCIFUL GOD

Have we not opened thy breast; and eased thee of thy burden, which galled thy back; and raised thy reputation for thee? Verily a difficulty shall be attended with ease. Verily a difficulty shall be attended with ease. When thou shalt have ended thy preaching, labor to serve God in return for his favors; and make thy supplication unto thy Lord.

CHAPTER XCV

ENTITLED, THE FIG; WHERE IT WAS REVEALED IS DISPUTED

IN THE NAME OF THE MOST MERCIFUL GOD

By the fig, and the olive; and by Mount Sinai, and this territory of security: verily we created man of a most excellent fabric; afterward we rendered him the vilest of the vile: except those who believe and work righteousness; for they shall receive an endless reward. What therefore shall cause thee to deny the day of judgment after this? Is not God the most wise judge?

an importunate beggar, or else because a dead puppy lay under his seat; his enemies said that God had left him; whereupon this chapter was sent down for his consolation.

CHAPTER XCVI

ENTITLED, CONGEALED BLOOD; REVEALED AT MECCA [1]

IN THE NAME OF THE MOST MERCIFUL GOD

Read, in the name of thy Lord, who hath created all things; who hath created man of congealed blood. Read, by thy most beneficent Lord; [2] who taught the use of the pen; who teacheth man that which he knoweth not. Assuredly. Verily man becometh insolent, because he seeth himself abound in riches.[3] Verily unto thy Lord shall be the return of all. What thinkest thou as to him who forbiddeth our servant, when he prayeth?[4] What thinkest thou; if he follow the right direction; or command piety? What thinkest thou; if he accuse the divine revelations of falsehood, and turn his back? Doth he not know that God seeth? Assuredly. Verily, if he forbear not, we will drag him by the forelock, the lying, sinful forelock. And let him call his council to his assistance: we also will call the infernal guards to cast him into hell. Assuredly. Obey him not: but continue to adore God; and draw nigh unto him.

[1] The first five verses of this chapter, ending with the words, "Who teacheth man that which he knoweth not," are generally allowed to be the first passage of the Koran which was revealed, though some give this honor to the seventy-fourth chapter, and others to the first, the next, they say, being the sixty-eighth.

[2] These words, containing a repetition of the command, are supposed to be a reply to Mohammed, who, in answer to the former words spoken by the angel, had declared that he could not read, being perfectly illiterate; and intimate a promise that God, who had inspired man with the art of writing, would graciously remedy this defect in him.

[3] The commentators agree the remaining part of the chapter to have been revealed against Abu Jahl, Mohammed's great adversary.

[4] For Abu Jahl threatened that if he caught Mohammed in the act of adoration, he would set his foot on his neck; but when he came and saw him in that posture, he suddenly turned back as in a fright, and, being asked what was the matter, said there was a ditch of fire between himself and Mohammed, and a terrible appearance of troops, to defend him.

CHAPTER XCVII

ENTITLED, AL KADR; WHERE IT WAS REVEALED IS DISPUTED

IN THE NAME OF THE MOST MERCIFUL GOD

Verily we sent down the Koran in the night of al Kadr.[1] And what shall make thee understand how excellent the night or al Kadr is? The night of al Kadr is better than a thousand months. Therein do the angels descend, and the spirit Gabriel also, by the permission of their Lord, with his decrees concerning every matter. It is peace, until the rising of the morn.

CHAPTER XCVIII

ENTITLED, THE EVIDENCE; WHERE IT WAS REVEALED IS DISPUTED

IN THE NAME OF THE MOST MERCIFUL GOD

The unbelievers among those to whom the scriptures were given, and among the idolaters, did not stagger, until the clear evidence had come unto them: an apostle from God, rehearsing unto them pure books of revelations; wherein are contained right discourses. Neither were they unto whom the scriptures were given divided among themselves, until after the clear evidence had come unto them. And they were commanded no other in the scriptures than to worship

[1] The word *al Kadr* signifies " power," and " honor " or " dignity," and also the " divine decree "; and the night is so named either from its excellence above all other nights in the year, or because, as the Mohammedans believe, the " divine decrees " for the ensuing year are annually on this night fixed and settled, or taken from the " preserved table " by God's throne, and given to the angels to be executed. On this night Mohammed received his first revelations; when the Koran, say the commentators, was sent down, entire and in one volume, to the lowest heaven, from whence Gabriel revealed it to Mohammed by parcels, as occasion required. The Moslem doctors are not agreed where to fix the night of *al Kadr;* the greater part are of opinion that it is one of the ten last nights of Ramadan, and, as is commonly believed, the seventh of those nights, reckoning backward; by which means it will fall between the 23d and 24th days of that month.

God, exhibiting unto him the pure religion, and being orthodox; and to be constant at prayer, and to give alms: and this is the right religion. Verily those who believe not, among those who have received the scriptures, and among the idolaters, shall be cast into the fire of hell, to remain therein forever. These are the worst of creatures. But they who believe, and do good works; these are the best of creatures: their reward with their Lord shall be gardens of perpetual abode, through which rivers flow; they shall remain therein forever. God will be well pleased in them; and they shall be well pleased in him. This is prepared for him who shall fear his Lord.

CHAPTER XCIX

ENTITLED, THE EARTHQUAKE; WHERE IT WAS REVEALED IS DISPUTED

IN THE NAME OF THE MOST MERCIFUL GOD

When the earth shall be shaken by an earthquake; and the earth shall cast forth her burdens; and a man shall say, What aileth her? On that day the earth shall declare her tidings, for that thy Lord will inspire her. On that day men shall go forward in distinct classes, that they may behold their works. And whoever shall have wrought good of the weight of an ant, shall behold the same. And whoever shall have wrought evil of the weight of an ant, shall behold the same.

CHAPTER C

ENTITLED, THE WAR-HORSES WHICH RUN SWIFTLY; WHERE IT WAS REVEALED IS DISPUTED

IN THE NAME OF THE MOST MERCIFUL GOD

By the war-horses which run swiftly to the battle, with a panting noise; and by those which strike fire, by dashing their hoofs against the stones; and by those which make a sudden incursion on the enemy early in the morning, and therein raise the dust, and therein pass through the midst of the adverse troops: verily man is ungrateful unto his Lord; and he is witness thereof: and he is immoderate in the love of worldly good. Doth he not know, therefore, when that which is in the graves shall be taken forth and that which is in men's breasts shall be brought to light, that their Lord will, on that day, be fully informed concerning them?

CHAPTER CI

ENTITLED, THE STRIKING; REVEALED AT MECCA

IN THE NAME OF THE MOST MERCIFUL GOD

The striking! What is the striking? And what shall make thee to understand how terrible the striking will be? On that day men shall be like moths scattered abroad, and the mountains shall become like carded wool of various colors driven by the wind. Moreover he whose balance shall be heavy with good works shall lead a pleasing life: but as to him whose balance shall be light, his dwelling shall be the pit of hell. What shall make thee to understand how frightful the pit of hell is? It is a burning fire.

CHAPTER CII

ENTITLED, THE EMULOUS DESIRE OF MULTIPLYING; WHERE IT WAS REVEALED IS DISPUTED

IN THE NAME OF THE MOST MERCIFUL GOD

The emulous desire of multiplying riches and children employeth you, until ye visit the graves. By no means should ye thus employ your time: hereafter shall ye know your folly. Again, By no means: hereafter shall ye know your folly. By no means: if ye knew the consequence hereof with certainty of knowledge, ye would not act thus. Verily ye shall see hell: again, ye shall surely see it with the eye of certainty. Then shall ye be examined, on that day, concerning the pleasures with which ye have amused yourselves in this life.

CHAPTER CIII

ENTITLED, THE AFTERNOON; REVEALED AT MECCA

IN THE NAME OF THE MOST MERCIFUL GOD

By the afternoon; verily man employeth himself in that which will prove of loss: except those who believe, and do that which is right; and who mutually recommend the truth, and mutually recommend perseverance unto each other.

CHAPTER CIV

ENTITLED, THE SLANDERER; REVEALED AT MECCA

IN THE NAME OF THE MOST MERCIFUL GOD

Woe unto every slanderer and backbiter: who heapeth up riches, and prepareth the same for the time to come! He thinketh that his riches will render him immortal. By no means. He shall surely be cast into al Hotama. And what shall cause thee to understand what al Hotama is? It is the kindled fire of God; which shall mount above the hearts of those who shall be cast therein. Verily it shall be as an arched vault above them, on columns of vast extent.

CHAPTER CV

ENTITLED, THE ELEPHANT; REVEALED AT MECCA

IN THE NAME OF THE MOST MERCIFUL GOD

Hast thou not seen how thy Lord dealt with the masters of the elephant?[1] Did he not make their treacherous design an occasion of drawing them into error; and send against them

[1] This chapter relates to the following tale, which is famous among the Arabs. Abraha Ebn al Sabah, King or Viceroy of Yaman, who was an Ethiopian, and of the Christian religion, having built a magnificent church at Sanaa, with a design to draw the Arabs to go in pilgrimage thither, instead of visiting the temple of Mecca, vowed the destruction

flocks of birds, which cast down upon them stones of baked clay; and render them like the leaves of corn eaten by cattle?

CHAPTER CVI

ENTITLED, KOREISH; REVEALED AT MECCA

IN THE NAME OF THE MOST MERCIFUL GOD

For the uniting of the tribe of Koreish; their uniting in sending forth the caravan of merchants and purveyors [1] in winter and summer: let them serve the Lord of this house; who supplieth them with food against hunger, and hath rendered them secure from fear.

of the Kaaba, and accordingly set out against Mecca at the head of a considerable army, wherein were several elephants, which he had obtained of the King of Ethiopia, their numbers being, as some say, thirteen, though others mention but one. The Meccans, at the approach of so considerable a host, retired to the neighboring mountains, being unable to defend their city or temple: but God himself undertook the protection of both. For when Abraha drew near to Mecca, and would have entered it, the elephant on which he rode, which was a very large one, and named Mahmud, refused to advance any nigher to the town, but knelt down whenever they endeavored to force him that way, though he would rise and march briskly enough if they turned him toward any other quarter: and while matters were in this posture, on a sudden a large flock of birds, like swallows, came flying from the sea coast, every one of which carried three stones, one in each foot, and one in its bill; and these stones they threw down upon the heads of Abraha's men, certainly killing every one they struck. Then God sent a flood, which swept the dead bodies, and some of those who had not been struck by the stones, into the sea: the rest fled toward Yaman, but perished by the way; none of them reaching Sanaa, except only Abraha himself, who died soon after his arrival there, being struck with a sort of plague or putrefaction, so that his body opened, and his limbs rotted off by piecemeal. It is said that one of Abraha's army, named Abu Yacsum, escaped over the Red Sea into Ethiopia, and going directly to the King, told him the tragical story; and upon that prince's asking him what sort of birds they were that had occasioned such a destruction, the man pointed to one of them, which had followed him all the way, and was at that time hovering directly over his head, when immediately the bird let fall the stone, and struck him dead at the King's feet. This remarkable defeat of Abraha happened the year Mohammed was born.

[1] It was Hashem, the great-grandfather of Mohammed, who first appointed the two yearly caravans here mentioned; one of which set out in the winter for Yaman, and the other in summer for Syria.

CHAPTER CVII

ENTITLED, NECESSARIES; WHERE IT WAS REVEALED IS DISPUTED

IN THE NAME OF THE MOST MERCIFUL GOD

What thinkest thou of him who denieth the future judgment as a falsehood? It is he who pusheth away the orphan; and stirreth not up others to feed the poor. Woe be unto those who pray, and who are negligent at their prayer; who play the hypocrites, and deny necessaries to the needy.

CHAPTER CVIII

ENTITLED, AL CAWTHAR; REVEALED AT MECCA

IN THE NAME OF THE MOST MERCIFUL GOD

Verily we have given thee al Cawthar.[1] Wherefore pray unto thy Lord; and slay the victims. Verily he who hateth thee shall be childless.

CHAPTER CIX

ENTITLED, THE UNBELIEVERS; REVEALED AT MECCA

IN THE NAME OF THE MOST MERCIFUL GOD

Say: O unbelievers,[1a] I will not worship that which ye wor-

[1] This word signifies "abundance," especially of "good," and thence "the gift of wisdom and prophecy," the Koran, the "office of intercessor," etc. Or it may imply "abundance of children, followers," and the like. It is generally, however, expounded of a river in paradise of that name, whence the water is derived into Mohammed's pond, of which the blessed are to drink before their admission into that place. According to a tradition of the prophet's, this river, wherein his Lord promised him abundant good, is sweeter than honey, whiter than milk, cooler than snow, and smoother than cream; its banks are of chrysolites, and the vessels to drink thereout of silver; and those who drink of it shall never thirst.

[1a] It is said that certain of the Koreish once proposed to Mohammed that if he would worship their gods for a year, they would worship his God for the same space of time; upon which this chapter was revealed.

ship; nor will ye worship that which I worship. Neither do I worship that which ye worship; neither do ye worship that which I worship. Ye have your religion, and I my religion.

CHAPTER CX

ENTITLED, ASSISTANCE; REVEALED AT MECCA

IN THE NAME OF THE MOST MERCIFUL GOD

When the assistance of God shall come, and the victory; and thou shalt see the people enter into the religion of God by troops: celebrate the praise of thy Lord, and ask pardon of him;[1] for he is inclined to forgive.

CHAPTER CXI

ENTITLED, ABU LAHEB; REVEALED AT MECCA

IN THE NAME OF THE MOST MERCIFUL GOD

The hands of Abu Laheb shall perish, [1a] and he shall perish. His riches shall not profit him, neither that which he hath gained. He shall go down to be burned into flaming fire; and his wife also, bearing wood, having on her neck a cord of twisted fibers of a palm-tree.

[1] Most of the commentators agree this chapter to have been revealed before the taking of Mecca, and suppose it gave Mohammed warning of his death; for they say that when he read it al Abbas wept, and being asked by the prophet what was the reason of his weeping, answered, "Because it biddeth thee to prepare for death"; to which Mohammed replied, "It is as thou sayest." And hence, adds Jallalo'ddin, after the revelation of this chapter the prophet was more frequent in praising and asking pardon of God, because he thereby knew that his end approached; for Mecca was taken in the eighth year of the Hegira, and he died in the beginning of the tenth.

[1a] Abu Laheb was the surname of Abd'al Uzza, one of the sons of Abd'-almotalleb, and uncle to Mohammed. He was a most bitter enemy to his nephew, and opposed the establishment of his new religion to the utmost of his power. When that prophet, in obedience to the command he had received to "admonish his near relations," had called them together, and told them he "was a warner sent unto them before a grievous chastisement," Abu Laheb cried out, "Mayest thou perish! Hast thou called us together for this?" and took up a stone to cast at him. Whereupon this passage was revealed.

CHAPTER CXII

ENTITLED, THE DECLARATION OF GOD'S UNITY; [1] WHERE IT WAS REVEALED IS DISPUTED

IN THE NAME OF THE MOST MERCIFUL GOD

Say, God is one God; the eternal God: he begetteth not, neither is he begotten: and there is not any one like unto him.

CHAPTER CXIII

ENTITLED, THE DAYBREAK; WHERE IT WAS REVEALED IS DISPUTED

IN THE NAME OF THE MOST MERCIFUL GOD

Say, I fly for refuge unto the Lord of the daybreak, that he may deliver me from the mischief of those things which he hath created; and from the mischief of the night, when it cometh on; and from the mischief of women blowing on knots; [1a] and from the mischief of the envious, when he envieth.

[1] This chapter is held in particular veneration by the Mohammedans, and declared, by a tradition of their prophet, to be equal in value to a third part of the whole Koran. It is said to have been revealed in answer to the Koreish, who asked Mohammed concerning the distinguishing attributes of the God he invited them to worship.

[1a] That is, of witches, who used to tie knots in a cord, and to blow on them, uttering at the same time certain magical words over them, in order to work on or debilitate the person they had a mind to injure. The commentators relate that Lobeid, a Jew, with the assistance of his daughters, bewitched Mohammed, by tying eleven knots on a cord, which they hid in a well; whereupon Mohammed falling ill, God revealed this chapter and the following, and Gabriel acquainted him with the use he was to make of them, and of the place where the cord was hidden: according to whose directions the prophet sent Ali to fetch the cord, and the same being brought, he repeated the two chapters over it, and at every verse (for they consist of eleven) a knot was loosed, till on finishing the last words, he was entirely freed from the charm.

CHAPTER CXIV

ENTITLED, MEN; WHERE IT WAS REVEALED IS DISPUTED

IN THE NAME OF THE MOST MERCIFUL GOD

Say, I fly for refuge unto the Lord of men, the king of men, the God of men, that he may deliver me from the mischief of the whisperer who slyly withdraweth,[1] who whispereth evil suggestions into the breasts of men; from genii and men.

---

[1] *I.e.,* "The devil"; who withdraweth when a man mentioneth God, or hath recourse to his protection.

END OF THE KORAN

BIBLIOGRAPHY

For the general subject of early Arabic literature the reader is recommended to the following books:

R. A. NICHOLSON, "A Literary History of the Arabs" (Scribners, New York, 1907).

F. F. ARBUTHNOT, "Arabic Authors" (London, 1890).

For Pre-Mohammedan poetry, both the texts and a discussion of them, read

LADY ANNE BLUNT and W. S. BLUNT, "The Seven Golden Odes of Pagan Arabia" (London, 1903).

SIR WILLIAM JONES, "The Mo'allakat or Seven Arabian Poems" (new ed., Calcutta, 1877).

F. E. JOHNSON, "The Seven Poems Suspended in the Temple at Mecca" (Bombay, 1893).

CHARLES J. LYALL, "Ancient Arabian Poetry."

CHARLES J. LYALL, "The Diwans of 'Abid ibn al-Abras and 'Amir ibn at-Tufail" (London, 1913).

W. A. CLOUSTON, "Arabian Poetry for English Readers" (Edinburgh).

For the Koran itself there are three standard works:

E. H. PALMER, "The Quran" (in the Sacred Books edited by Max Müller, Oxford, 1880).

J. M. RODWELL, "The Koran."

GEORGE SALE, "The Koran."

For briefer reviews of the Koran, read

E. W. LANE, "Selections from the Kuran" (London, 1843).

S. LANE-POOLE, "Speeches and Table-Talk of the Prophet Mohammed" (London, 1882).

For Mohammed himself, the best English authorities are the following:

WILLIAM MUIR, "Life of Mohammed" (four volumes, latest edition, Edinburgh, 1912.)

D. S. MARGOLIOUTH, "Mohammed and the Rise of Islam" (London 1905).

CPSIA information can be obtained at www.ICGtesting.com
Printed in the USA
LVOW030143230112

264983LV00001B/10/A